MASTERING

# BRITISH POLITICS

## MACMILLAN MASTER SERIES

Banking
Basic Management
Biology
British Politics
Business Communication
Chemistry
COBOL Programming
Commerce
Computer Programming
Computers
Data Processing
Economics
Electronics
English Grammar
English Language
English Literature
French
French II
German
Hairdressing
Italian
Keyboarding
Marketing
Mathematics
Modern British History
Modern World History
Nutrition
Office Practice
Pascal Programming
Physics
Principles of Accounts
Social Welfare
Sociology
Spanish
Statistics
Study Skills
Typewriting Skills
Word Processing

# MASTERING BRITISH POLITICS

F. N. FORMAN

First published 1985

Published by
MACMILLAN EDUCATION LTD
Houndmills, Basingstoke, Hampshire RG21 2XS and London
Companies and representatives
throughout the world

Printed in Great Britain by
Camelot Press Ltd, Southampton

British Library Cataloguing in Publication Data
Forman, F. N.
Mastering British politics.—(Macmillan Master series)
1. Great Britain—Politics and government—1979-
I. Title II. Series
320.941 JN231
ISBN 0-333-36650-6 (hc)
ISBN 0-333-36651-4 (pb)
ISBN 0-333-36652-2 (pb export)

To the memory
of my father

# ACKNOWLEDGEMENTS

The author and publishers wish to thank the following who have kindly given permission for the use of copyright material:-

Cambridge University Press for figures from *The Machinery of Justice in England* by R. M. Jackson.

The Controller of Her Majesty's Stationery Office for an extract from *The Government's Expenditure Plans 1984–5 and 1986–7* (Cmnd 9143).

F. W. S. Craig for a table from *Britain Votes 3* published by Parliamentary Research Services.

The BBC and Mr Speaker for the front cover photograph showing the House of Commons Debating Chamber.

# CONTENTS


*Preface* xii
*List of Tables and Diagrams* xiii

**I THE POLITICAL AND ELECTORAL CONTEXT** 1

**1 British political culture**
1.1 Key characteristics 3
1.2 Other significant features 7
1.3 Conclusion 9

**2 The living constitution**
2.1 Key characteristics 11
2.2 Views of the constitution 14
2.3 The scope for change 17
2.4 Conclusion 20

**3 The electoral system**
3.1 The system today 22
3.2 Criteria of assessment 26
3.3 Conclusion 29

**4 Voting behaviour**
4.1 Groups in the electorate 32
4.2 Main influences on voting 37
4.3 Future uncertainties 42
4.4 Conclusion 46

**II SOURCES OF POWER, PRESSURE AND OPINION** 49

**5 The political parties**
5.1 Ideological principles 51
5.2 Political functions 57
5.3 National organisation 59
5.4 Constituency activities 68
5.5 Conclusion 73

**6 Pressure groups**
6.1 Main functions 77
6.2 Organisation and power 80
6.3 Involvement in politics 85
6.4 Conclusion 90

**7 The media**
7.1 The current situation 93
7.2 The influence of the press 99
7.3 The power of broadcasting 103
7.4 Conclusion 108

# CONTENTS


**8 Public opinion**
- 8.1 The composition of opinion 111
- 8.2 The formation of opinion 114
- 8.3 The effects of opinion 116
- 8.4 Conclusion 120

**III PARLIAMENT** 123

**9 The Monarchy**
- 9.1 Powers and functions 125
- 9.2 The Monarchy and the public 133
- 9.3 Conclusion 136

**10 The House of Lords**
- 10.1 Composition of the Lords 140
- 10.2 Powers and functions 142
- 10.3 Proposals for change 149
- 10.4 Conclusion 150

**11 The House of Commons**
- 11.1 Composition of the Commons 153
- 11.2 Principal powers 157
- 11.3 Main functions 159
- 11.4 Prospects for reform 164
- 11.5 Conclusion 167

**IV CENTRAL GOVERNMENT** 171

**12 Prime Minister and Cabinet**
- 12.1 The machinery of Cabinet government 174
- 12.2 The power of the Prime Minister 181
- 12.3 The role of the Cabinet 186
- 12.4 Conclusion 191

**13 Policy- and decision-making**
- 13.1 Stages in the process 195
- 13.2 Key aspects 203
- 13.3 Possible improvements 208
- 13.4 Conclusion 210

**14 Ministers and Departments**
- 14.1 The work of central Government 214
- 14.2 The role of Ministers 218
- 14.3 The problems of central Government 223
- 14.4 Conclusion 225

**15 The Civil Service**
- 15.1 Composition and functions 228
- 15.2 Key aspects 233
- 15.3 Methods of control 238
- 15.4 Possible future developments 241
- 15.5 Conclusion 246

V OTHER PUBLIC INSTITUTIONS 249

16 The public sector
16.1 Public corporations 252
16.2 Methods of control 256
16.3 Fringe bodies 259
16.4 Other public bodies 261
16.5 Future prospects 264
16.6 Conclusion 266

17 Local government
17.1 Structure and composition 269
17.2 Powers and functions 273
17.3 Relations with central Government 276
17.4 Methods of central control 278
17.5 Future possibilities 284
17.6 Conclusion 288

18 The law and the judiciary
18.1 Criminal justice 292
18.2 Civil justice 295
18.3 Judicial appeal 299
18.4 Citizens and the state 302
18.5 Administrative law 307
18.6 Conclusion 314

VI DEMOCRACY IN BRITAIN 319

19 British politics compared
19.1 Political culture 321
19.2 Electoral systems 323
19.3 Patterns of government 324
19.4 Role of the bureaucracy 325
19.5 Role of Parliament 327
19.6 Legal systems 328
19.7 Conclusion 330

20 British Parliamentary democracy
20.1 The conditions of democracy 333
20.2 Essential characteristics 335
20.3 Other significant features 337
20.4 Some unresolved issues 340
20.5 Conclusion 342

*Index of subjects* 344
*Index of authors and politicians* 356

# PREFACE

This book is a general introduction to British politics. It is an attempt to convey clear information about every significant aspect of the subject and to facilitate an adequate understanding of the British political system as a whole. However, within the compass of a brief introductory text it is not possible to provide a detailed description or analysis of all the topics covered. Readers who wish to delve more deeply into any particular aspect of the subject should turn to the suggestions for further reading at the end of each chapter.

Part I deals with the political and electoral context within which the process of British politics takes place. Chapter 1 considers British political culture which is defined as the historical, cultural and attitudinal setting within which British political institutions have to operate. Chapter 2 considers the living constitution by describing the key characteristics and analysing some of the main interpretations of constitutional developments in Britain. Chapter 3 describes the electoral system and assesses its strengths and weaknesses in the eyes of academics and politicians alike. Chapter 4 deals with voting behaviour by identifying the most significant groups in the electorate, the main influences on voting and some notable uncertainties about the future.

Part II considers the sources of power, pressure and opinion within the British political system. Chapter 5 deals principally with the two major political parties by considering their ideological principles, political functions, national organisation and constituency activities. It also takes account of the other parties and the prospects for political change now that there are more than two viable contenders for power at national level. Chapter 6 deals with the main functions, organisation and power of pressure groups and analyses the nature of their involvement in the policy- and decision-making process. Chapter 7 looks at the role of the media and assesses the nature and extent of their influence within the political system. Chapter 8 considers public opinion by seeking to clarify its composition, the process by which it is formed and its effects upon the rest of British politics.

Part III describes the activity and significance of the three institutions which constitute Parliament in Britain. Chapter 9 considers the Monarchy by examining not only its powers and functions but also its relationship with the British public. Chapter 10 on the House of Lords describes the composition, powers and functions of that ancient institution and goes on to review briefly the various proposals for its reform. Chapter 11 on the

House of Commons also begins by describing its composition, powers and functions before going on to review briefly the prospects for its reform.

Part IV deals with the main components of central Government in Britain. Chapter 12 describes the machinery of Cabinet government and goes on to consider the power of the Prime Minister and the role of the Cabinet. Chapter 13 looks at the policy- and decision-making process by identifying the main stages and analysing some of the key aspects and possible improvements. Chapter 14 describes the work of central Government Departments, considers the role of Ministers and reviews some of the key problems which arise in Whitehall. Chapter 15 deals with the civil service, describing its composition and functions and considering the various methods of controlling the bureaucracy, as well as some possible future developments.

Part V is concerned with the other public institutions in the British political system. Chapter 16 deals with the public sector, notably the problems posed by the public corporations and the continuing argument about how best to control them. The chapter also deals with fringe bodies (often known as Quasi-Autonomous Non-Governmental Organisations or QUANGOs) and other public bodies, such as the Water Authorities and the Health Authorities. Chapter 17 describes the structure and composition, powers and functions of local government before going on to consider its relations with central Government and the various methods of central control. It also discusses some of the ways in which the balance between central power and local autonomy might be changed in the future. Chapter 18 on the law and the judiciary deals briefly with criminal justice, civil justice and judicial appeal before examining the politically more significant issues of civil rights and administrative law.

Part VI considers some more philosophical questions about the nature and limits of democracy in Britain. Chapter 19 compares certain key aspects of British politics with those of the United States, France and West Germany. Chapter 20 concludes the book with a few broader observations about the essence of British Parliamentary democracy.

Many people have helped in the preparation of this book. I would particularly like to thank the following for having given valuable time to read and comment upon various parts: Clifford Boulton, Kenneth Bradshaw, Keith Britto, Dr David Butler, Rt Hon. James Callaghan MP, John Cole, Professor Ivor Crewe, Bryan Davies, Charles Douglas-Home, Frank Field MP, Robin Grove-White, John Hanvey, Rt Hon. Edward Heath MP, Hon. Douglas Hogg MP, Lord Hunt of Tanworth, Peter Kellner, David Lipsey, Dr Edmund Marshall, Peter McGregor, Dr David Menhennet, Dr Janet Morgan, Dr Roger Morgan, Chris Patten MP, William Plowden, Rt Hon. Enoch Powell MP, John Roper, John Sainty, Jack Straw MP, Alan Taylor and David Walter. I should also like to thank Dermot Englefield, Geoffrey

Lock and John Palmer in the Library of the House of Commons. Indeed, all the staff of that excellent institution have been unfailingly courteous and helpful in providing me with background material and advice.

Colleagues in the House of Commons and friends everywhere are asked to forgive the unintentionally pretentious title of the book. This was made necessary by the standard format of the Macmillan Masters series in which it is being published. Any insights achieved owe a great deal to the help and advice which I have received from those already mentioned and many others with whom I have discussed aspects of British politics over the years. Any errors of fact or opinion are, of course, entirely my own responsibility.

*London, November 1983* F. N. Forman

# TABLES AND DIAGRAMS


| | | |
|---|---|---|
| 1.1 | Map of the British Isles | 5 |
| 2.1 | Classic liberal view of the constitution | 15 |
| 2.2 | Governmental view of the constitution | 16 |
| 2.3 | Empirical view of the constitution | 18 |
| 3.1 | Voting by party, June 1983 | 25 |
| 4.1 | Profiles of some typical voters | 37 |
| 5.1 | Conservative party organisation | 60 |
| 5.2 | Labour party organisation | 63 |
| 5.3 | Liberal party organisation | 67 |
| 5.4 | Social Democratic party organisation | 69 |
| 6.1 | Pressure group involvement in politics | 86 |
| 7.1 | Main national newspapers | 95 |
| 7.2 | Structure of television and radio | 97 |
| 8.1 | The flow of public opinion | 112 |
| 9.1 | Functions of the Monarchy | 133 |
| 10.1 | Functions of the House of Lords | 144 |
| 11.1 | Functions of the House of Commons | 164 |
| 12.1 | The structure of Cabinet committees | 177 |
| 13.1 | The policy- and decision-making process | 195 |
| 14.1 | The structure of central Government | 215 |
| 15.1 | Civil service numbers to 1.4.1988 | 230 |
| 16.1 | The composition of the public sector | 251 |
| 17.1 | The structure of local government in the United Kingdom | 270 |
| 17.2 | The distribution of local authority powers and functions | 274 |
| 18.1 | The system of Courts exercising criminal jurisdiction | 293 |
| 18.2 | The system of Courts exercising civil jurisdiction | 297 |

# PART I

# THE POLITICAL AND ELECTORAL CONTEXT

# CHAPTER 1

# BRITISH POLITICAL CULTURE

Any book on British politics has to begin with a chapter on British political culture, since this is the context within which our politics takes place. The term 'political culture' is taken to mean the historical, cultural and attitudinal setting in which our political institutions have to function.[1] It is not easy to generalise about political culture, but it is possible to identify some key characteristics which influence both the procedure and the output of politics in Britain.

## 1.1 KEY CHARACTERISTICS

The key characteristics of British political culture can be stated quite simply, but they need to be qualified and refined if they are to be useful to students of British politics. It has often been stated that politics in this country is influenced by the notable continuity of our national history, the underlying cohesion of our society and the extent of political consensus on fundamental issues. It has also been observed that there is usually considerable moderation in the policies pursued by central Government and a remarkable degree of public detachment from the process of politics, except of course at election times. General statements of this kind are frequently made and sometimes in a rather complacent tone. Yet we would be unwise to accept them at face value and we would do well to examine the extent to which they accord with the evidence available to us.

### Historical continuity

There has been notable continuity in our national history and this country is one of the oldest nation-states in Europe. Such continuity is symbolised by some of our national institutions, such as the Monarchy and Parliament, which date back at least to medieval times. Although there have also been some notable discontinuities in our national history, such as the Civil War and the Interregnum in the mid-seventeenth century, this country has not been invaded successfully against the popular will since 1066 and the only successful revolution since the Civil War was the peaceful *coup* of 1688 when James II fled the throne and William and Mary were invited by Parliament to take his place.

Furthermore, this continuity applies to all parts of the United Kingdom. In the case of Wales, the Welsh have been living in the same kingdom as the English since the fourteenth century English conquests which were later ratified in law by Act of Parliament in 1536. In the case of Scotland, the constitutional bond between the Scots and the English was sealed by the Act of Union in 1707, although the Hanoverian succession to the unified kingdom was not really secure until the defeat of the Young Pretender in 1745. In the case of Ireland, the troubled relationship between the Irish and the English can be traced back at least to the Anglo-Norman invasion of Ireland in 1169-71, although the Act of Union in 1800, which marked the constitutional unification of the two countries in one kingdom, was later upset by the partition of Ireland in 1921 and the creation of the Irish Republic in 1949. The result of this chequered history is that we now live in what is known officially as the United Kingdom of Great Britain and Northern Ireland, although it will be convenient for us to use the more colloquial term 'Britain' throughout this book. Figure 1.1 is a map of the British Isles clearly showing the boundaries of England, Wales, Scotland and Northern Ireland.

**Cultural cohesion**

There is considerable cultural cohesion in this country which is reinforced by the fact that four-fifths of the total population of 56 million are English and about four-fifths live in urban or suburban areas. This means that in many respects the great majority of the British people live similar lives. They purchase many similar goods, they use broadly standard public services, they earn their living in a number of standard ways and they share broadly similar aspirations for themselves and their families.

Of course, there are some significant variations which derive from a range of economic and social, geographical and ethnic factors. The more traditional industrial structure in the north of the country is significantly different from the more modern technological structure in the more prosperous south of the country. While in the nation as a whole coloured people make up no more than one-twentieth of the entire population, there are some parts of our large cities - for example, London, Bradford or Leicester - where coloured people account for more than one-fifth of the population. In all parts of the country British society still divides on class lines, although it is also true that over the past thirty years or so the sharper edges of the traditional class distinctions have been blurred by

Fig 1.1 *Map of the British Isles*

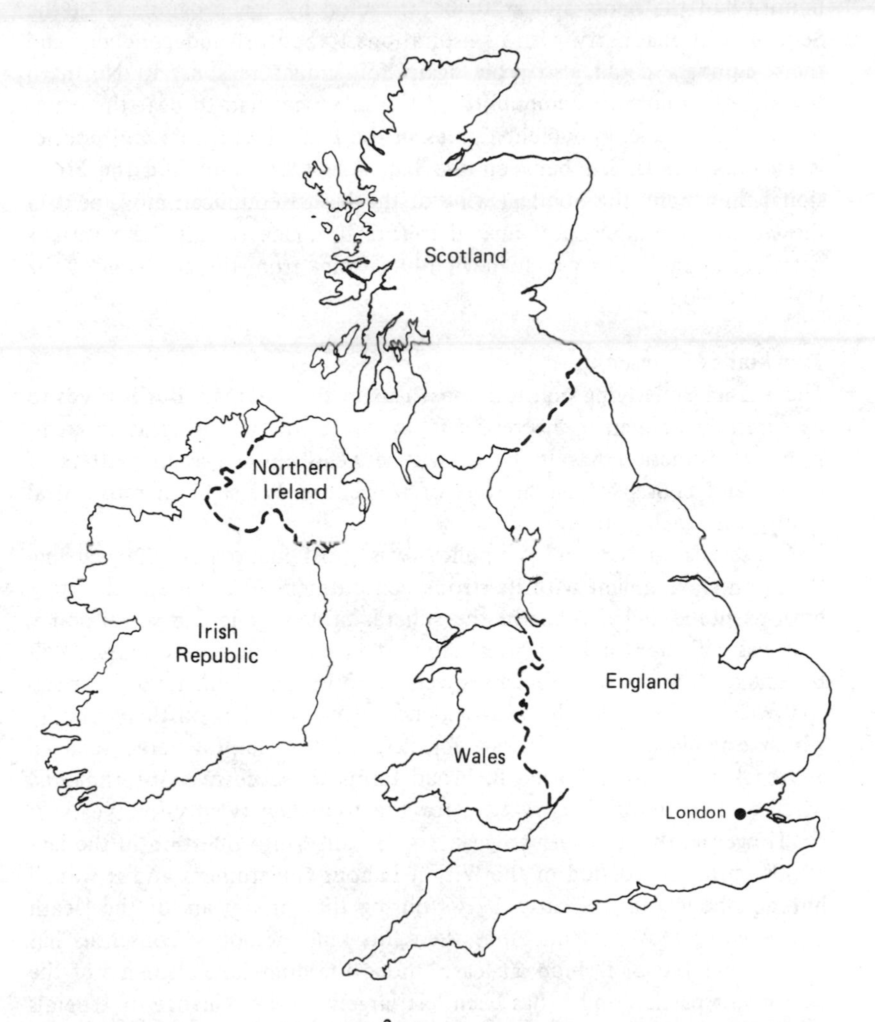


the convergence of life-styles.[2] Indeed, as many people in all classes become more imitative in their social habits and economic aspirations - a development which has been encouraged by mass advertising and the influence of the national media - the tendency towards social uniformity may even increase.

In future much will depend upon the extent to which the fulfilment of common economic and social aspirations is thwarted by a lack of opportunities for many people in many parts of the country. A minority of the Welsh are attracted by the political programme of Plaid Cymru, the Welsh Nationalist party, and their numbers could grow in future if that part of the country appeared to languish under London rule. A somewhat larger minority of the Scots appear to be attracted by the programme of the Scottish National party with its aspirations to Scottish independence and their numbers could also grow again for similar reasons. In Northern Ireland, the minority community of Catholics has had to bear the brunt of the highest unemployment figures in the United Kingdom and politics is becoming polarised between the hard-line Protestants and the Provisional Sinn Fein, the political wing of the Irish Republican movement in the north. Due allowance must therefore be made for all these various nationalist tendencies which inevitably detract from the cohesion of the United Kingdom.[3]

**Two kinds of consensus**

There is an underlying political consensus in this country, but it needs to be carefully defined if the reader is not to get the wrong ideas about it. A clear distinction has to be drawn between consensus on matters of policy and consensus on matters of procedure. We shall therefore deal briefly with each in turn.

Consensus on matters of policy was most marked in the wartime Coalition Government with its strong commitment to a united war effort both at home and abroad. In the spheres of economic and social policy this was reflected in the general support given to the goals of the 1942 Beveridge Report which foreshadowed the principal elements in the post-war Welfare State and the 1944 Keynesian White Paper on the economy which established the post-war objective of full employment. Such an approach was duly followed in broad terms by successive Governments, whether Labour or Conservative, for the following twenty-five years or so. However, this consensus began to be called into question in the late 1960s during the period of the Wilson Labour Government and it was all but abandoned in the early 1970s during the early years of the Heath Conservative Government. Since then this kind of policy consensus has been rather out of fashion, at least among the dominant elements of the two major parties, and it has been left largely to the Alliance of Liberals and Social Democrats to try to keep the idea alive. Nevertheless it should be added that there are some politicians and political commentators who argue that a new policy consensus is now being formed in Britain in the 1980s and that this is in the process of replacing the policy consensus of earlier years. It is too soon to be sure about this, but there is certainly some evidence for this point of view in the adjustments now being made by politicians in all parties to some of the basic assumptions of the present Conservative Government.

Consensus on matters of procedure, on the other hand, seems to have survived intact for a much longer period. Ever since the successive extensions of the franchise in the nineteenth and early twentieth centuries, this kind of consensus has been signified by the widespread agreement upon the desirability of using Parliamentary channels for the implementation of political change, although certain powerful pressure groups have occasionally challenged that view. It has included general recognition of the view that General Election results should be regarded as decisive, provided that the electoral system produces a clear Parliamentary majority for the victorious party. It has also included broad acceptance of the impracticality and unwisdom of making major constitutional changes unless it is clear that they are backed by overwhelming all-party support. However, all these examples of procedural consensus need to be seen against the background of the constitutional arguments which have been pursued at least since the mid-1970s on such matters as proportional representation, devolution to Scotland, Wales and Northern Ireland, on the future of the House of Lords, the use of referenda and the desirability or otherwise of moving towards a new constitutional settlement. The result is that there is now somewhat less consensus than there used to be on the rules of the game in British politics.

## 1.2 OTHER SIGNIFICANT FEATURES

### Moderation of Governments

It has been argued that another significant feature of British political culture is the moderation and restraint demonstrated by all Governments.[4] Whereas all modern British Governments with working majorities in the House of Commons have had almost unlimited power of legislation and decision, they have usually exercised that power in a relatively moderate and restrained manner. While such an assertion is bound to seem more credible to the supporters rather than the opponents of any Government, there are some compelling reasons why it has usually been borne out in practice, notwithstanding the noticeably more ideological tone and actions of recent Governments.

Such moderation and restraint on the part of Governments stems from the clear recognition by most politicians that the vast majority of the British people always prefer comfortable co-operation to unsettling conflict and are more than likely to cast their votes at election time under the influence of that preference. An even more fundamental reason for moderation and restraint is that the political realities of the modern world impose such cautious behaviour upon Governments, whether the politicians in office like it or not. In the complex conditions of an interdependent world all Governments soon discover that they can wield little constructive power, except on the surface or in the margin of events. Both at home and abroad there are too many other participants in the political process with the power to prevent them from achieving much more than that. It is in this sense of impaired capacity for taking truly independent and effective action that modern Governments simply have to be moderate and restrained in what they do.

**Public detachment from politics**

It has also been said of British political culture that the people of this country are relatively detached from the process of politics, that they put a high value upon the maintenance of political stability and that they are not usually keen to face up to the need for radical change.[5] This view accords with the continuing strong support for some of our most traditional institutions, for example, the Monarchy or the police. It is also reflected in the widespread public preference for the quiet life which finds expression in the various social institutions from pubs to pigeon-fancying clubs which absorb so much of the spare time and energy of many British people. In such circumstances the idea of active and continuous participation in the process of politics appeals to no more than a very small minority of the population.

However, it should not be assumed that this relatively benign neglect of the political process by the majority of the British people means that they are particularly sanguine about the role or the capacity of Governments. Indeed, there is at least anecdotal evidence to suggest that one of the consequences of our disappointing national performance over many years has been the increasingly widespread realisation on the part of many people that it is not very sensible to hold high expectations of central Government or other public agencies. On the other hand, this growing scepticism and even mistrust of Governments does not prevent the poorer and more vulnerable sections of society from looking to the Government and other public agencies for material help and redress of grievances.

Although many people appear to recognise that in economic terms this country has not done as well as it might have done over many years, few people appear keen to take the appropriate action to put things right. No doubt this is partly because most people realise that the price of the necessary economic and social adjustments is likely to include the implementation of some quite radical changes in social attitudes and working practices. However, it is mainly because our steady tumble down the international league tables (from second in the world in terms of GNP per head in 1939 to thirteenth in 1966 and twenty-third in 1980) does not seem to have worried many British people.

As Paul Barker has written, there has been 'an undoubted retreat into the shell of self (or perhaps self plus family)'.[6] Concern with relative advantage or deprivation within the confines of peer groups has been much more evident than general public concern with the relatively poor performance of this country in competition with other comparable nations. Many people seem to be interested simply in getting by and most pay little attention to the national economy or national politics. The struggle for material satisfaction, and in some cases even survival, is so all-consuming for most people that relatively few have either the time or the inclination to become directly involved in the political process. In these circumstances the idea of a conscious political culture has little meaning for any but a few politicians and political observers.

## 1.3 CONCLUSION

When we consider British political culture, the main need is to distinguish between the cluster of familiar myths and stereotypes which still appear in some accounts and the changing social realities which must qualify such simple notions. If we wish to be up-to-date in our ideas, we need to realise that many of the traditional values and assumptions of British political culture may be called into question by contemporary developments in our society. For example, the cumulative influence of relative national decline has moved many of our social conflicts into the realm of 'zero sum' politics – that is, one group's gain is another group's loss. This has led in its turn to the erosion of many of the traditional forms of social restraint and self-discipline and to a much more Darwinian struggle (that is, survival of the fittest) between the various sectional interests in society.

In such circumstances there can be no certainty that the general public will continue to show its customary respect for the rules of the game in British politics. After all, in the summer of 1981 there were serious outbreaks of social unrest and rioting in some British cities and such public disorder could not be dismissed as simply another form of extra-Parliamentary protest. Indeed, it is quite likely that there will be more manifestations of direct political action, such as the public demonstrations against the deployment of American cruise missiles at Greenham Common in 1983, and that the traditional commitment to political change via Parliamentary channels will become more attenuated. On the other hand, the continuation of high levels of unemployment in many parts of the country may have the effect of cowing large sections of the population into a mood of apathy and resignation. In either case the key characteristics of British political culture could change significantly, although it is difficult to be sure about when and how this might happen.

## SUGGESTED QUESTIONS

1. What are the key characteristics of British political culture?

2. Is the nature of British society conducive to the practice of democratic politics?

## NOTES

1. See D. Kavanagh: 'Political culture in Great Britain, the decline of the civic culture' in G. Almond and S. Verba (eds) *The Civic Culture Revisited* (Boston: Little Brown, 1980) pp. 136–62.
2. For example, 78 per cent of white-collar and 46 per cent of blue-collar trade union members were owner-occupiers according to a MORI poll in *The Sunday Times*, 31 August 1980. Equally, information in *Social Trends* no. 12 (1982) revealed that 92 per cent of all households owned a washing machine, 97 per cent a refrigerator and 75 per cent a colour television, a telephone and a car. At work 80 per cent of all manual workers had a basic holiday entitlement of at least four weeks paid leave a year, 84 per cent of all full-time employees were covered by sick pay schemes and 66 per cent were in jobs with private pension plans.
3. Another measure of nationalist support in Scotland and Wales was provided by the 1979 Referenda results which showed that only 33 per cent of the Scottish electorate and only 12 per cent of the Welsh electorate were prepared to support the devolution proposals of the Callaghan Government. See also A. H. Birch, *Political Integration and Disintegration in the British Isles* (London: Allen & Unwin, 1977) pp. 98–133, for further discussion of Scottish and Welsh nationalism.
4. See R. M. Punnett, *British Government and Politics*, 4th edn (London: Heinemann, 1980) p. 193.
5. See A. H. Birch: *The British System of Government*, 6th edn (London: Allen & Unwin, 1983) pp. 14–17.
6. *New Society*, 29 November 1979.

## FURTHER READING

Almond, G. A. and Verba, S. (eds) *The Civic Culture Revisited* (Boston: Little Brown, 1980).
Birch, A. H., *Political Integration and Disintegration in the British Isles* (London: Allen & Unwin, 1977).
Blondel, J., *Voters, Parties and Leaders* (Harmondsworth: Penguin, 1974).
Butler, D. E. and Sloman, A., *British Political Facts, 1900–79*, 5th edn (London: Macmillan, 1980).
Butler, D. E. and Stokes, D., *Political Change in Britain*, 2nd edn (London: Macmillan, 1977).
Dahrendorf, R., *On Britain* (London: BBC, 1982).
Finer, S.E., *Comparative Government* (Harmondsworth: Penguin, 1974).
Marwick, A., *British Society since 1945* (Harmondsworth: Penguin, 1982).
Noble, T., *Modern Britain, Structure and Change* (London: Batsford, 1975).
Rose, R., (ed.) *Studies in British Politics*, 3rd edn (London: Macmillan, 1976).

# CHAPTER 2

# THE LIVING CONSTITUTION

A constitution is usually defined as a body of fundamental principles, rules and conventions according to which a state or other organisation is governed. According to such a definition, Britain has a constitution. Yet, as we shall see, it is notably different from the constitutions of most other democratic countries.

## 2.1 KEY CHARACTERISTICS

Although the key characteristics of the British constitution can be stated quite simply, they contain some powerful paradoxes and internal contradictions. This is mainly because it is a living constitution which is changing and developing all the time. At one time some characteristics may be particularly significant, at another time others and so on. This makes it a fascinating subject to study, but one which is hard to describe in a definitive or lasting way.

### No codification

The British constitution is unusual in that it is uncodified and has not been assembled at any time into one consolidated document. This makes it very different from the American constitution or those of many Commonwealth countries which derived their constitutional arrangements from Britain. Indeed, of all the democratic countries only Israel, Australia and New Zealand are comparable to Britain in having no single consolidated document codifying the ways in which their political institutions are supposed to operate and setting out the basic rights and duties of their citizens.

Yet in the absence of a basic constitutional text, it should not be assumed that we have no constitutional documents from which guidance can be derived when we need to elucidate the laws and conventions which govern British politics. Magna Carta, signed by King John in 1215, is perhaps our best known constitutional document. However, there have been many other examples of equal or greater constitutional significance since that time.

The Bill of Rights in 1689 put the stamp of Parliamentary approval on the succession of William and Mary to the throne deserted by James II and extended the powers of Parliament at the expense of the Crown. The Act of Settlement in 1701 was described in its preamble as 'an Act for the further limitation of the Crown and the better securing of the rights and liberties of the subject'. The Act of Union with Scotland in 1707 declared in Article 3 that 'the United Kingdom of Great Britain be represented by one and the same Parliament to be styled the Parliament of Great Britain'. The Act of Union with Ireland in 1800 brought about the formation of the United Kingdom of Great Britain and Ireland, an event which has affected the course of history ever since.

The Reform Act in 1832 was the first of a series of statutes over the period from then until modern times which were designed to extend the franchise at Parliamentary elections. The Ballot Act in 1872 introduced secret ballots for all elections to Parliament and all contested municipal elections. The Local Government Act in 1888 established elected County Councils for the new administrative Counties. The Parliament Act in 1911 regulated the relations between the two Houses of Parliament and confirmed the legislative supremacy of the Commons. The Redistribution of Seats Act in 1944 established independent Parliamentary Boundary Commissions to demarcate the constituencies. The Representation of the People Act in 1969 lowered the voting age to eighteen.

Except for Magna Carta, all the examples given are drawn from statute law, in other words Acts of Parliament. Yet there are many other important documents which clarify our constitution and set out the civil rights and duties which we now take for granted.

There are the judicial proceedings which have served to clarify and confirm the rights and duties of British citizens over the centuries. For example, in Bushell's case of 1670 Lord Chief Justice Vaughan established the independence of juries. In Sommersett's case of 1772 Lord Mansfield recognised the freedom of a former slave from the American colonies on the grounds of residence in England and argued that slavery was 'so odious that nothing can be suffered to support it but positive law'. In Beatty *v*. Gillbanks of 1882 Justice Field established the principle that a man may not be convicted for a lawful act, even if he knows that it may cause another to commit an unlawful act.

Other documentary sources for our uncodified constitution include Erskine May, the classic and constantly updated guide to the procedures and privileges of Parliament, and certain learned works written by constitutional theorists, such as Blackstone and Bagehot.[1]

**Considerable flexibility**

Another key characteristic of the British constitution is its considerable flexibility. This derives partly from the absence of neat, constitutional formulae consolidated in a single authoritative document, as is the case in the constitution of the Fifth Republic in France. However, it is essentially because no Parliament can bind its successors and one Parliament can with impunity undo the legislation of its predecessors that it is idle to seek formal methods of constitutional limitation in Britain.

It soon becomes apparent to students of British history that the flexibility of our constitution stems essentially from the way in which the theoretically absolute and unlimited power of Parliament has been severely modified and limited in practice by political tradition and precedent, the influence of constitutional conventions and the well-established commitment to the rule of law. All these intuitive and practical constraints upon the theoretical supremacy of Parliament are surpassed in significance by the political supremacy of the electorate at periodic General Elections. Yet the former constraints remain vital moderating influences which help to preserve a kind of constitutional balance without recourse to any formal separation of powers, as is the case in the constitution of the United States.

**Importance of conventions**

Another key characteristic of the British constitution is the importance of conventions, in other words established custom and practice. The conventions which have been so powerful in their influence upon constitutional developments in Britain are the product of organic growth over the centuries. They include, for example, the convention that the Monarch should send first for the Leader of the largest single Parliamentary party after the result of a General Election or the demise of a Prime Minister in office and the convention that Ministers are responsible and can be held to account in Parliament for what happens (or fails to happen) in their Departments.

This helps to explain why certain principles not declared in law, such as the Royal prerogative or Ministerial responsibility, have developed so fully over the years. It also suggests why there are such formidable obstacles to the achievement of major constitutional reform. We discover a paradoxical quality in our constitutional arrangements which can best be understood only after close study of how our political institutions have evolved over the centuries rather than by reference to any basic constitutional texts. This is why we must refer to our living constitution which has been part of the more general development of British politics and society over the centuries.

## 2.2 VIEWS OF THE CONSTITUTION

### Classic liberal view

Of the various interpretations of the British constitution which have been put forward over the years, perhaps the best known is the classic liberal view which is associated with the nineteenth-century writings of Bagehot and Dicey.[2] This view holds that the House of Commons is the supreme political institution with the power to make and unmake Governments, pass any laws and resolve the great political issues of the day. It accords only subsidiary constitutional significance to the Monarchy and the House of Lords. It takes little account of the political parties, pressure groups, the civil service, the media or public opinion. As R. H. S. Crossman pointed out, such a view could only have been valid before any significant extension of the franchise, before the establishment of the national party organisations and before the development of the modern civil service.[3]

The classic liberal view applied only during the brief era, 1832-67, when the House of Commons really did reign supreme. By about 1885 the main principles propounded by Bagehot and Dicey were already being eroded or counterbalanced by new political realities which became steadily more apparent during the last quarter of the nineteenth century. For example, the legislative supremacy of Parliament was gradually counteracted by the growing political power of the electorate as the franchise was extended in successive Reform Bills. The rule of law, which Dicey had identified as the fundamental principle of the constitution, was not necessarily the paramount consideration for all participants in the political process, at any rate for disadvantaged sections of the community which tended to appeal to superior notions of natural justice. The importance of conventions meant little to all who were outside the charmed circle of Parliamentary politics.

In modern times students of the British constitution need to make sense of a much more complex and bureaucratic form of democracy in which Parliamentary supremacy is only one important principle among many. The classic liberal view, although still regarded with respect and firmly established among the received ideas of British politics, is no longer particularly instructive as a guide to contemporary politics. It has been rendered somewhat obsolete by the enormously increased scope of modern Government and by the growing power of pressure groups, party organisations and public opinion. The élitist Parliamentary ideas of the mid-nineteenth century have had to give way to the claims of a more pluralist democracy in the late twentieth century. The classic liberal view is shown diagrammatically in Figure 2.1.

Fig 2.1 *Classic liberal view of the constitution*

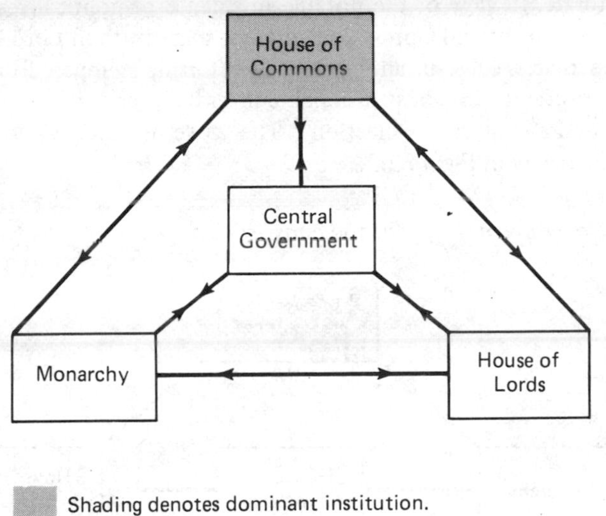


**Governmental view**

Another well-known interpretation of the British constitution may be called the governmental view. This holds that the former power of the Crown has been passed not to Parliament but to the Prime Minister and Cabinet, subject only to criticism in Parliament and periodic rejection or confirmation by the mass electorate at General Elections. It is a view usually associated with the writings of L. S. Amery and Herbert Morrison.[4] It maintains that the Government has a clear responsibility to govern and that the essential form of political accountability is the responsibility of the Government to the electorate. Accordingly, the role of back-bench MPs and pressure groups is to act essentially as filters or megaphones between the Government and the electorate. L. S. Amery was succinct when he wrote 'the combination of responsible leadership by Government with responsible criticism in Parliament is the essence of our constitution'.[5]

Although this view, too, has to be qualified if we are to form an accurate impression of how the British constitution really works, it has more validity today than the classic liberal view which is now characterised by sentimentality towards a vanished era of truly Parliamentary government. In the legislative sphere at any rate modern British Governments have virtually unlimited power, provided they have an overall working majority in the House of Commons and as long as they are careful to keep their Parliamentary supporters united behind them. Under the terms of the 1911 Parliament Act a Government can retain this power for a maximum period of five years before it is obliged to seek a fresh endorsement from the electorate. In view of the notable imbalance of political resources between Government and Opposition, there is some truth in Lord Hailsham's allegation that we live in an 'elective dictatorship' tempered only by the minimal restraints of constitutional conventions and the ruling party's normal desire to win re-election.[6] The governmental view is shown diagrammatically in Figure 2.2.

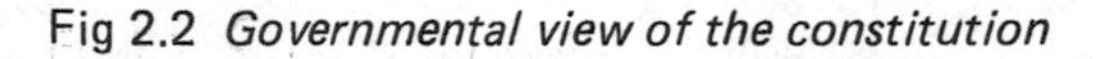

Fig 2.2 *Governmental view of the constitution*

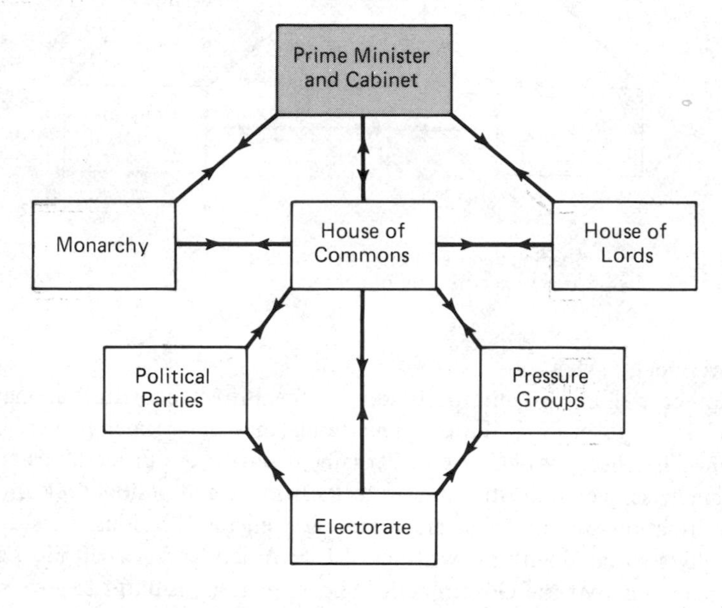


Shading denotes dominant institution.
Arrows denote lines of contact.

**Empirical view**

More accurate still in modern British conditions is the empirical view of the constitution which emphasises both the weakness of Parliament in relation to the Government of the day and the weakness of the Government in relation to pressure groups and public opinion. It emphasises the way in which an extension of constitutional power can lead to a decline of effective power, no matter what the ideology or policy of the party in office. Undoubtedly, some have been disappointed or frustrated by this state of affairs. Yet comfort can be obtained from Ian Gilmour's shrewd observation that 'the essence of the British political system is that it is more important to travel peacefully than to arrive'.[7]

Indeed, a dispassionate reading of British constitutional history leads to the important conclusion that the most abiding political problem has been the gaining and retaining of public consent for the actions of Government. Stage by stage from the thirteenth century to the present time, Governments in Britain, whether Monarchical or Parliamentary, have had to cede and share power with the other great interests in the land. Effective government has been possible only with the consent, or at least the tacit acquiescence, of those most directly affected by it. Against this background it makes sense to regard successive British Governments as stable rather than strong and to avoid confusing the concentration of responsibility with the concentration of power. Today administrative convenience and public opinion are just two examples of notable forces which condition the exercise of governmental power, although there are many other factors which limit the freedom of manoeuvre available to any Government.

Thus the contemporary British constitution is based upon two key paradoxes. The first is the limited power of Parliament which reflects the fact that whereas Parliament is legislatively supreme, it is politically capable usually of criticising but not fully controlling the Government of the day. The second is the limited power of Government which reflects the fact that whereas a Government can normally get its legislation through Parliament, there is little point in doing so if the implementation is unduly limited by the negative force of the civil service, powerful interest groups or public opinion. Thus a complicated network of informal checks and balances ensures that the living constitution continues to develop organically, but makes it ill-suited for rapid adjustment to new challenges or effective response to those who do not recognise the rules of the game. For a diagrammatic representation of this view see Figure 2.3.

## 2.3 THE SCOPE FOR CHANGE

In recent years constitutional changes have occurred piecemeal, even haphazardly in response to the needs of public policy or the dictates of political necessity. No coherent pattern seems to have emerged and there has been no real attempt to co-ordinate the various initiatives which have been taken.

### The advent of referenda

Probably the most notable development has been the introduction of referenda in a few attempts to settle major constitutional disputes.[8] The referendum is still a most unusual device to be used in a political system which has been dominated for so long by the assumptions and practices of Parliamentary democracy. It combines uneasily with our traditional

Fig 2.3 *Empirical view of the constitution*

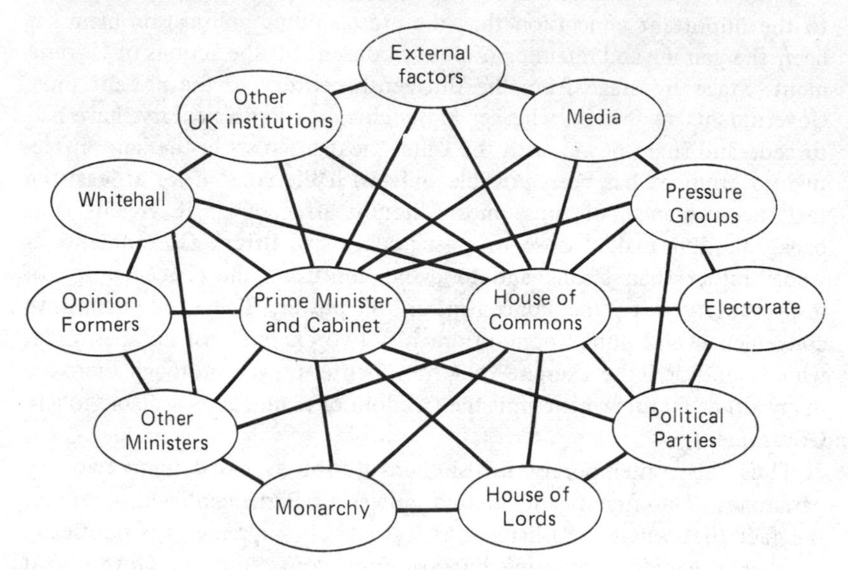


N.B. No dominant institution.
Everything influences and is influenced by everything else.

constitutional arrangements, although its apparently satisfactory use on two important occasions in the 1970s testifies to the flexibility of the British constitution.

In 1975 British membership of the European Community, for which Parliament had legislated in 1972, was put to a national referendum by the then Labour Government, mainly because the two major parties were still deeply divided on the issue and because it was thought that this would settle the matter once and for all. Indeed, the Wilson Government was so seriously split on the issue that it was necessary to suspend the normal convention of collective responsibility for the duration of the referendum campaign, so that senior Cabinet Ministers could freely argue against each other in public, something which had not happened since the open agreement to differ in the National Government in 1931 on the issue of tariff reform.

In 1979 the proposals of the Callaghan Government for devolution to Scotland and Wales had to be put to separate referenda in each of those parts of the United Kingdom, because there seemed to be no other way of trumping persistent and effective Parliamentary opposition to the legislation. As it happened, the House of Commons passed an amendment to the legislation which insisted that unless at least 40 per cent of those entitled to vote in each relevant part of the country supported the Government's devolution policy, the provisions of the legislation could not be put into effect. In the event this proved to be a sufficient obstacle to the implementation of the legislation, since in neither Scotland nor Wales did as many as 40 per cent vote 'Yes'.

These two special cases have been seen by some people as valid precedents for the use of referenda on other occasions, especially when the position taken by the majority in the House of Commons is at odds with the majority view of public opinion, for example, on the emotive issue of capital punishment. The pressure for the use of a referendum in such a case reflects public impatience with the fastidious views of many individual MPs in all parties. It is also testimony to the diminished status and prestige of Parliament in the eyes of the public. This can be attributed to a number of factors, among which are the decline of political deference and the tendency for most recent Governments to enter office promising too much and leave office having delivered too little. The calls for referenda are therefore largely the result of public cynicism or impatience with the traditional operation of representative democracy in this country.

**Other pressures for reform**

These and other constitutional developments may have been misinterpreted or even misrepresented in some cases. However, they have encouraged searching reconsideration of many of our basic constitutional assumptions and strengthened demands for procedural, electoral and constitutional reform.

The Alliance of Liberals and Social Democrats has campaigned for electoral reform and specifically the introduction of proportional representation. In this cause they have been joined by minority elements in each of the major parties. Notable legal figures, including Lord Hailsham and Lord Scarman, have argued the case for a new constitutional settlement based upon a new Bill of Rights and a codified constitution which would be interpreted and protected by a Supreme Court. The Labour party may well be committed once again to the abolition of the House of Lords, while a fair number of prominent Conservatives favour reform of the second Chamber in order to put it on a more secure and powerful basis. Those in all parties who are still opposed to British membership of the European Community have argued that Parliament at Westminster must reclaim complete legislative sovereignty by amending or repealing the 1972 European Communities Act. The advocates of Parliamentary reform have argued for further procedural changes at Westminster which would strengthen the role of Select Committees and make more effective the rather antiquated procedures of financial control. The Conservative Government of 1979-83 legislated to restrict the already limited autonomy of local government and the present Conservative Government has introduced legislation to curb high-spending local authorities and to abolish the Greater London Council and the other Metropolitan Councils. The Left wing of the Labour party is dedicated to the idea that Labour MPs should be held accountable to their party activists and to party Conference decisions rather than to the wishes of the wider electorate in the constituencies and the country at large.

All these developments are examples of the scope and significance of recent pressures for reform of the British political system. They suggest that far-reaching changes could be made if there were to be sufficiently powerful and widespread support for these or any other ideas.

## 2.4 CONCLUSION

Nevil Johnson has argued that 'the gap between the theory and the reality of British political institutions and procedures has assumed serious dimensions' and that 'the root of the political difficulty is to be found in a refusal to recognise that much of the traditional language of the British constitution . . . has lost its vitality'.[9] It is a tenable point of view, but the wide range of often radical reform proposals which has just been cited would suggest that there is still a great deal of vitality in the debate about constitutional issues in this country.

Constitutional change is nearly always on the agenda of British politics. The fact that so many of the would-be reformers are seeking institutional solutions to political problems which are often attitudinal in origin should not obscure the strength of their desire for change, even if it might be wise to doubt the appropriateness or value of some of the changes proposed. At least it should remind us that change is constant, if not always predictable or desirable, in our living constitution.

## SUGGESTED QUESTIONS

1. What are the key features of the British constitution?
2. Which view of the British constitution accords best with contemporary political realities?
3. How great is the scope for change in British constitutional arrangements?

## NOTES

1. William Blackstone, who was Professor of Common Law at Oxford University, published his famous *Commentaries on the Laws of England*

between 1765 and 1769. In them he presented a clear and systematic description of the state of English law in the mid-eighteenth century. Walter Bagehot was equally famous in his day for his work, *The English Constitution*, which was published in 1867 and which set out the principles of British Parliamentary government at that time.

2. See W. Bagehot, *The English Constitution* (London: Fontana, 1978) and A. V. Dicey: *The Law of the Constitution* (London: Macmillan, 1959).
3. Introduction to W. Bagehot, *The English Constitution*, p. 35.
4. See L. S. Amery: *Thoughts on the Constitution* (London: OUP, 1947) and H. Morrison, *Government and Parliament* (London: OUP, 1959).
5. L.S. Amery, *Thoughts on the Constitution*, p. 32.
6. See Q. Hailsham: *The Dilemma of Democracy* (London: Collins, 1978) for exposition of this argument.
7. I. Gilmour: *The Body Politic* (London: Hutchinson, 1969) p. 14.
8. Referendum is defined in the Concise Oxford Dictionary (6th edn) as 'the referring of political questions to the electorate for direct decision by general vote'. For a fuller discussion of this subject see D. E. Butler and A. Ranney (eds) *Referendums, a comparative study of practice and theory* (Washington, D.C: American Enterprise Institute, 1978) and V. Bogdanor, *The People and the Party System* (London: CUP, 1981) pp. 11–93.
9. N. Johnson: *In Search of the Constitution* (London: Methuen, 1980) p. 26.

## FURTHER READING


Amery, L. S., *Thoughts on the Constitution* (Oxford: Oxford University Press, 1947).

Bagehot, W., *The English Constitution* (London: Fontana, 1978).

Birch, A. H., *Representative and Responsible Government* (London: Allen & Unwin, 1964).

Bogdanor, V., *The People and the Party System* (Cambridge: Cambridge University Press, 1981).

Bromhead, P. A., *Britain's Developing Constitution* (London: Allen & Unwin, 1974).

Butler, D. E. and Ranney, A. (eds) *Referendums, a Comparative Study of Practice and Theory* (Washington, DC: American Enterprise Institute, 1978).

Dicey, A. V., *The Law of the Constitution* (London: Macmillan, 1959).

Finer, S. E. (ed.) *Five Constitutions* (Harmondsworth: Penguin, 1979).

Gilmour, I., *The Body Politic* (London: Hutchinson, 1969).

Hailsham, Q., *The Dilemma of Democracy* (London: Collins, 1978).

Johnson, N., *In Search of the Constitution* (London: Methuen, 1980).

Marshall, G. and Moodie, G. C., *Some Problems of the Constitution*, 5th edn (London: Hutchinson, 1971).

Morrison, H., *Government and Parliament* (Oxford: Oxford University Press, 1959).

Norton, P., *The British Constitution in Flux* (Oxford: Martin Robertson, 1982).

CHAPTER 3

# THE ELECTORAL SYSTEM

The electoral system in Britain is the product of centuries of development. It began to be put on a democratic basis at the time of the 1832 Reform Act. Subsequent Acts in 1867, 1884, 1918, 1928, 1948 and 1969 completed the process. The result is that today we have a system of universal adult suffrage in which everyone aged 18 and over has the right to vote, with the exception of convicted felons, certified lunatics and peers of the realm.

## 3.1 THE SYSTEM TODAY

At the 1983 General Election 2579 candidates stood for election to Parliament and 42 703 019 people were eligible to vote. The 650 constituencies varied considerably in population and geographical area, but the average electorate in each constituency was about 67 000. For example, the Western Isles with the smallest electorate of only about 23 000 was one of the largest in geographical area, whereas the Isle of Wight with the largest electorate of about 94 000 was geographically confined to quite a small area. The discrepancies of population and geographical area derive mainly from the fact that the population has expanded in some parts of the country - for example, East Anglia and the South-West of England - and contracted in other parts - for example the inner city areas of London, Birmingham and Glasgow. The independent Boundary Commissions attempt every ten to fifteen years to rectify the most glaring anomalies, but they can never quite keep pace with the movements of population during the intervening periods.

### Electoral mechanisms

On election day voters go to the polls to cast their votes in secret by putting an 'X' against one name on the ballot paper. Any other mark produces a spoiled vote which is usually judged invalid later on during the count. The marked ballot papers are folded and deposited by the voters in locked ballot boxes where they remain until the polling stations close at 10.00p.m. The ballot boxes are then transported to a central point in the constituency (often a Town Hall) where the counting of the votes takes place under the supervision of the Acting Returning Officer (normally the Chief Executive of the local authority concerned). The results are declared at varying times depending upon the nature and size of the constituency, but usually not less than about three hours after the closing of the polls and sometimes not until the following day.

Since 1948 it has also been permissible to cast postal votes if the voters concerned apply to be put on their constituency postal registers at least two weeks before polling day. Those who qualify for postal votes include people prevented by the nature of their jobs from voting in person (for example, merchant seamen or long-distance lorry-drivers), people who are too sick or handicapped to vote in person and those who have moved out of the constituency but are still on the electoral register where they used to live. People away on holiday on polling day do not qualify for postal votes, but it has been announced by the present Conservative Government that this aspect of electoral law is to be changed in order to extend to holiday-makers the right to vote by post. Hitherto postal votes have accounted for about 2 per cent of the votes cast, so in very marginal constituencies they can make a difference to the electoral results.

Any British citizen, who is resident in this country and who will be at least 21 years old when the new Parliament meets, is legally entitled to stand for election to the Commons. The only provisos are that he must get ten qualified voters in the constituency to sign his nomination papers and that he must deposit a sum of £150 with the Returning Officer which is refunded to him after the election if he gets more than 12½ per cent of the votes cast.[1] There is no requirement that candidates should reside in the constituency for which they seek election and only a few limited categories of people are automatically disqualified from standing for Parliament.[2] Since 1970 candidates have been allowed to put on the ballot papers not only their names (in alphabetical order) but also a description of their party or political position in not more than six words, for example, 'Conservative', 'Labour Party Candidate', 'Liberal-Alliance Candidate', 'Independent against the Common Market', etc.

Each candidate is restricted by law to a maximum expenditure during the three to five weeks campaign of £2700 plus 3.1p for every voter in rural constituencies and 2.3p for every voter in urban constituencies. This allows a maximum expenditure of about £4700 in rural seats and about £4400 in urban seats, although most candidates report expenses about half or less of the legal maxima. Each candidate has to have a designated Agent who is legally responsible for seeing that all aspects of election law are observed. The Agent also serves in most cases as the local campaign manager for his candidate, although this is not part of his legal duties.

**First-past-the-post**

The British electoral system is popularly described as 'first-past-the-post'. This means that in each constituency the candidate with the largest number of votes wins the seat. Usually this has the effect of turning the largest single minority of votes cast in the national electorate into a clear majority of seats in Parliament for the largest single party. In this way the system has benefited the two leading parties and discriminated against the political fortunes of all other parties, unless their votes are geographically concentrated in a particular part of the country.

This pattern of discrimination has been discernible for years in the British electoral system. At the twelve General Elections since the Second World War no party has ever won more than half the votes cast, although individual candidates often achieve this in safe seats. Yet the winning party has seldom won fewer than half the seats in the House of Commons, except notably in February 1974 when the Labour party won power with fewer popular votes than the Conservative party, but votes which produced a larger number of seats in the House of Commons. This occurred because the votes for the Labour party happened to be more effectively concentrated in a number of marginal constituencies, thus giving it the edge over the Conservative party in Parliament.

In normal circumstances the two leading parties have benefited from this multiplier effect which can produce a sizeable majority of Parliamentary seats on the basis of a minority of the popular votes cast.[3] For example, the Labour party enjoyed a positive differential (that is, between the percentage of seats won and votes cast) of 14 per cent in 1945 and 11 per cent in October 1974, while the Conservative party enjoyed a similar differential of 8 per cent in 1959 and 9 per cent in 1979. On the other hand, the Liberal party has been the most notable victim of the system during the period since 1945. From 1945 to 1979 the Liberal share of the popular vote ranged from 2 per cent in 1951 to 19 per cent in February 1974. Yet the system prevented the Liberals from winning more than 2 per cent of the seats in the Commons even in their most successful effort in February 1974. In the 1983 General Election this multiplier effect worked even more dramatically against the interest of the Alliance of Liberals and Social Democrats which won 25 per cent of the votes cast, but only 3 per cent of the seats in the House of Commons. Plainly the number of seats won is in no way proportional to the number of votes cast. Yet the system has never been arithmetically fair to all parties and its merits lie elsewhere, for example, in the tendency for most General

Elections to produce effective Parliamentary majorities for single party Governments. Figure 3.1 demonstrates the multiplier effect.

Fig 3.1 *Voting by party, June 1983*

| | *Number of votes* | *Votes as % of electorate (a)* | *Votes as % of votes cast (b)* | *Seats won as % total* |
|---|---|---|---|---|
| Conservative | 13 012 316 | 30.8 | 42.4 | 61.1 |
| Labour | 8 456 934 | 20.0 | 27.6 | 32.2 |
| Liberal/SDP Alliance | 7 780 949 | 18.4 | 25.4 | 3.5 |
| Scottish National | 331 975 | 0.8 | 1.1 | 0.3 |
| Plaid Cymru | 125 309 | 0.3 | 0.4 | 0.3 |
| Ulster Unionist | 259 952 | 0.6 | 0.8 | 1.7 |
| Democratic Unionist | 152 749 | 0.4 | 0.5 | 0.5 |
| SDLP | 137 012 | 0.3 | 0.4 | 0.2 |
| Sinn Fein | 102 701 | 0.2 | 0.3 | 0.2 |
| Popular Unionist | 22 861 | 0.1 | 0.1 | 0.2 |
| Others | 288 379 | 0.7 | 0.9 | - |
| TOTAL | 30 671 137 | 72.7 | 100.0 | 100.0 |

(a) Estimated electorate at 9 June 1983: 42 192 999
(b) Excluding ballot papers spoilt or rejected.

Source: F. W. S. Craig, *Britain Votes*, pp. 96-8

**Proportional representation**

These characteristics of the British electoral system have led many people, especially supporters of the Alliance, to argue strongly for the introduction of proportional representation.[4] There are a number of variants of the basic idea. However, the proposal which has found most favour with the Liberal and Social Democrat parties is for proportional representation on the basis of a single transferable vote in large multi-member constituencies. This would allow the electorate to vote in each constituency for individual candidates in order of preference. To get elected a candidate would need a certain quota of votes and his votes surplus to the quota would then be redistributed among the other candidates according to the second preferences of the voters until the requisite number of candidates (for example, five) had qualified for election on this basis. This system was recommended by a Speaker's Conference in 1917, was used in some of the multi-member University seats between 1918 and 1948 and advocated by the Kilbrandon Commission in 1973 as part of its proposals for devolved Assemblies in Scotland and Wales. It is now used for Parliamentary elections in the Irish Republic and local government elections in Northern Ireland.

The other variant of proportional representation which has received support is based upon the additional member principle. In this system the majority of MPs are directly elected from single-member constituencies in the normal way, but they are supplemented by additional members drawn from party lists (either national or regional) who are elected in proportion to the number of votes cast for each of the parties at the election concerned. This system is used for federal elections in West Germany where it has ensured Parliamentary representation for those minor parties which otherwise would not have had enough concentrated voting strength to get any candidates elected to the *Bundestag* on the basis of first-past-the-post. However, in West Germany it is modified by the so-called 5 per cent rule which prevents fringe parties with less than 5 per cent of the popular vote from qualifying for any Parliamentary representation.

There are some MPs in both major parties who favour a change to proportional representation in one form or another. However, the great majority of MPs in both major parties clearly share a strong vested interest in the present electoral system and are therefore opposed to any change. Thus electoral reform is unlikely to occur, unless it is forced upon one or other of the major parties by the imperatives of political bargaining in a future 'hung Parliament' in which no single party has an overall majority in the House of Commons.

## 3.2 CRITERIA OF ASSESSMENT

In a celebrated text W. J. M. Mackenzie suggested four criteria by which an electoral system could be assessed. These were the quality of those elected, the effectiveness of the legislature, the fairness of the electoral results and the degree of public confidence inspired.[5] It may therefore be convenient to consider the British electoral system in the light of these four, admittedly rather ideal criteria.

### The quality of the MPs

Members of Parliament in Britain are not strictly representative of the general public in that they are usually better educated and more middle class than the electorate as a whole. Taking the House of Commons which was elected in June 1983, 96 per cent of the Conservative MPs and 57 per cent of the Labour MPs came from middle-class or professional occupations. Of all the MPs 79 per cent had had higher or further education and 36 per cent had been to university at Oxford or Cambridge. Of the

Conservative MPs 60 per cent had been educated at private schools, as had 16 per cent of the Labour MPs. The remaining forty-four MPs from the minor parties came overwhelmingly from middle-class or professional occupations (98 per cent of the total), but less than one quarter of them (23 per cent of the total) had been educated at private schools and less than one fifth of them (18 per cent of the total) had been to university at Oxford or Cambridge.

Of course, these characteristics are not necessarily signs of quality and the standard of MPs could always be higher. Yet the quality is not really a function of the electoral system. It derives much more from the part-time nature of Parliamentary work, the frustrations of life on the back-benches, the unwillingness of many employers to encourage their employees to stand for Parliament and the relatively low esteem in which politicians are held by the vast majority of the British people. All these factors may discourage many able people from standing for Parliament or even from entering active politics in the first place (which is usually a necessary prelude to seeking a Parliamentary candidature). Furthermore, in our front-bench constitution no more than about ninety MPs are paid members of any Government and no more than about another ninety are involved in the tasks of front-bench Opposition. Thus the vast majority of MPs in the House of Commons at any time are obliged to spend most of their time upon other forms of political activity, such as welfare work in their constituencies. This can be useful to their constituents and help them to get re-elected, but it does not necessarily attract the most talented people into Parliament.

**Effectiveness of the legislature**

It is hard to see why any shortcomings in the legislature should necessarily be attributed to the working of the electoral system. Quite the contrary, since one of the familiar charges against our system is that it makes it all too easy for one or other of the parties to win an overall majority in the Commons which can then be used to push through its legislation often against ineffective Parliamentary opposition and sometimes in defiance of the expressed wishes of the general public.

According to this argument, Parliament is actually too effective at churning out ill-considered and partisan legislation and too ineffective at controlling the actions of the Government of the day. If this is so, it is essentially because all MPs not in the Government have little involvement and no responsibility in the formative stages of policy- and decision-making and because Government back-benchers in particular are usually inhibited by party loyalty from pursuing continuous public criticism of their own Ministers. Parliamentary control is therefore left very largely in the hands of the Opposition which is usually unable to do much more than kick up a fuss about controversial Government decisions or seek to delay the contentious elements in the Government's legislative programme.

**Fairness of the results**

It is here that we enter the area of greatest public controversy. In Britain our electoral system enables the electorate to choose a Government every four or five years. It does not produce a House of Commons which is an exact reflection of the votes cast for each party. Essentially, it is a system which enables the largest single minority of voters in the national electorate to bring about the return of a single-party Government with an overall majority in the Commons. There is, in fact, a threshold of between 35 per cent and 40 per cent of the votes cast above which (especially in marginal seats with three or more candidates) a party has a good chance of capturing seats, but below which it is likely to be defeated.

This situation arises because most General Elections in Britain tend to be contests between at least three parties in which the second- and third-ranking parties frequently split the losing vote, thus ensuring that neither has a real chance of defeating the winning party. Obviously, there is always the possibility of tactical voting by the supporters of one or other of the losing parties. Yet on the whole this has not made much difference (except very occasionally at by-elections), since none of the parties can be sure of delivering enough of its supporters to guarantee such an outcome.

In the General Election of February 1974 the third party (in this case the Liberals) got more than 6 million votes, but won only fourteen seats in the House of Commons. Conversely, the party which won the election (in this case Labour) did so with fewer popular votes than the party which came second in Parliament (in this case the Conservatives), since Labour votes were distributed more effectively than Conservative votes in the marginal seats. In the 1983 General Election the discrepancy between votes and seats was even more striking in the case of the Alliance parties which together got more than 7 million popular votes, but won only twenty-three seats in the House of Commons.

Of course, the results could change significantly if the potential supporters of third parties, those who abstain from voting and those who are deterred from supporting their real first preference for fear of casting wasted votes, were all to vote in accordance with their real wishes. In that case there would be a real possibility of third parties coming first in many parts of the country. The most sensible conclusion is that the British electoral system is likely to remain unfair to third parties, but it is by no means clear that a given party will always come third. In this scheme of things fairness is not the prime consideration. The overriding purpose is to elect a single party to Government with a sufficient Parliamentary majority to ensure its authority to govern throughout the period of a normal four or five year Parliament.

**Public confidence inspired**

It is difficult to produce reliable measures of public confidence in something as abstract as an electoral system. However, one way of assessing it is to note the degree of popular support for electoral reform as measured in opinion polls. This has been consistently strong among Liberal and Social Democrat voters, but it has also proved attractive to representative samples of the electorate as a whole.[6]

Another way of assessing public confidence in the electoral system is to log the performance of the two major parties at successive General Elections. The proportion of the electorate voting for the Conservative and Labour parties fell consistently from 79 per cent in 1951 to 56 per cent in October 1974. It rose briefly to 62 per cent in 1979, but fell back to 51 per cent in 1983.[7] The Conservatives won the 1983 General Election with the support of only 31 per cent of the total electorate and Labour theoretically came third with 20 per cent behind the 27 per cent of the electorate who did not bother to vote at all. In so far as any valid or lasting conclusion can be drawn from this evidence, it can hardly be that the British public has given a massive vote of confidence to an electoral system which is so obviously tailored to the interests of the two major parties.

## 3.3 CONCLUSION

The British electoral system has come a long way since Queen Victoria confided to her diary that 'it seems to me a defect in our much famed constitution to have to part with an admirable Government . . . merely on account of the number of votes'.[8] Nowadays a General Election is usually seen as a public verdict upon the record of the party in Government and the competing attractions of the various Opposition parties. Yet the mass electorate is politically sovereign only on condition that it exercises its sovereignty when invited to do so by the Prime Minister of the day and within the limits of political choice offered by the electoral system.

Modern British politics is essentially about the struggle for power between the political parties. Of course, there has always been some ideology in the political rhetoric and the party Manifestos. Yet for most of those who reach the top of the political tree the ideological content has usually been little more than a necessary part of the political ritual, the tribute which party leaders have had to pay to their followers especially when in Opposition. It remains to be seen whether this tendency will continue or whether the ideologues will secure greater influence in the various parties.

In short, the conduct of elections and the Parliamentary results which ensue are seldom more important than the actual behaviour of the parties either when elected into Government or when released from the responsibilities of public office. While free elections on the basis of universal adult suffrage are an indispensable foundation of our political system, it is the quality of party politics between elections and the conduct of every Government in office which is more important to the future of our democracy. Contemporary political realities are so limiting in their effects that it is usually wrong to expect any politicians to achieve major changes through the ballot box.

## SUGGESTED QUESTIONS

1. Describe the working of the British electoral system.
2. To what extent does the British electoral system satisfy W. J. M. Mackenzie's four criteria?
3. Analyse the arguments for and against a change to proportional representation in Britain.

## NOTES

1. Following a report of the House of Commons Select Committee on Home Affairs in April 1983, Ministers in the present Government have indicated that they intend to raise the deposit to £1000 and lower the threshold below which it is forfeited to 5 per cent of the votes cast. They also propose to extend the right to vote to British citizens living abroad, subject to certain qualifications.
2. Those disqualified from standing for Parliament are certified lunatics, deaf mutes, English and Scottish peers, people serving in the civil service, the armed services and the police, and ordained clergymen in the Church of England, the Church of Ireland, the Church of Scotland and the Roman Catholic Church. Since the Bobby Sands case in 1981 convicted offenders detained for more than one year have also been disqualified for the duration of their sentences under the provisions of the 1981 Representation of the People Act.
3. The evidence for the multiplier effect in British politics is derived from successive Nuffield Election Studies since 1950.
4. See V. Bogdanor, *The People and the Party System*; (London: CUP, 1981) pp. 97–258, for a fuller discussion of proportional representation.
5. See W. J. M. Mackenzie, *Free Elections* (London: Allen & Unwin, 1958) pp. 69–71.
6. For example, see the poll by Opinion Research and Communication published in *The Times*, 17 January 1980, which showed that 72 per cent of those questioned thought it would be a good idea to have an electoral system based upon the principle of proportionality. This was typical of opinion-poll findings on the subject over many years.

7. Note that the statistics on turn-out depend very much upon the accuracy of the Electoral Register. On average it is little more than 90 per cent accurate and very much less so in inner city areas where the population has a large transient element. The high turn-out in 1950 and 1951 reflected at least in part the exceptional accuracy of the Electoral Register in those years. (Information supplied by Dr David Butler in correspondence with the author).
8. Quoted in E. Longford, *Victoria R. I.* (London: Weidenfeld & Nicolson, 1964) p. 518.

## FURTHER READING

Bogdanor, V., *The People and the Party System* (Cambridge: Cambridge University Press, 1981).

Bromhead, P. A., *Britain's Developing Constitution* (London: Allen & Unwin, 1974).

Butler, D. E., *The Electoral System in Britain since 1918*, 2nd edn, (Oxford: Oxford University Press, 1963).

Finer, S. E. (ed.) *Adversary Politics and Electoral Reform* (London: Anthony Wigram, 1975).

Lakeman, E., *How Democracies Vote*, 4th edn (London: Faber, 1974).

Leonard, R. L., *Elections in Britain* (London: Von Nostrand, 1968).

Mackenzie, W. J. M., *Free Elections* (London: Allen and Unwin, 1958).

Mackintosh, J. P. (ed.) *People and Parliament* (Farnborough: Saxon House, 1978).

McLean, I., *Elections*, 2nd edn (London: Longman, 1980).

Penniman, H. R. (ed.) *Britain at the Polls, 1979* (Washington, DC: American Enterprise Institute, 1981).

Pulzer, P., *Political Representation and Elections in Britain*, 3rd edn (London: Allen & Unwin, 1975).

# CHAPTER 4

# VOTING BEHAVIOUR

Voting behaviour in Britain since the war has been characterised mainly by the tendency of the electorate at General Elections to divide between two major parties. This pattern has clear antecedents in British political history. In the late eighteenth and early nineteenth centuries there was the struggle between the Whigs and the Tories. In the late nineteenth and early twentieth centuries there was the struggle between the Liberals and the Conservatives. During the first few decades of this century it was uncertain whether or not Labour would displace the Liberals as the main opponent of the Conservatives. However, since the end of the Second World War the effective choice at General Elections has been between the Conservative and Labour parties. Of course, the formation in 1981 of the Alliance between the Liberal and Social Democratic parties and its impressive performance in terms of popular votes at the 1983 General Election may presage yet another major change in the map of British politics. At present it is too soon to tell what will be the outcome of the triangular struggle for power in Britain in the 1980s.

## 4.1 GROUPS IN THE ELECTORATE

### Party loyalists

At General Elections since the war the Conservative and Labour parties have each usually been able to count upon the loyal support of at least 7.5 million voters, most of whom have voted consistently for one or other of the two major parties at every General Election. Since 1964 there have also been at least 600 000 voters who have voted consistently for the Liberal party at General Elections, although prior to that the number of Liberal loyalists had been considerably smaller during the thirteen years of Conservative rule from 1951 to 1964.

In Scotland and Wales there have been smaller sections of the electorate which have voted for the nationalist parties, namely the Scottish National party and Plaid Cymru. It is hard to ascertain how many of these voters were 'loyalists', since both parties have always attracted substantial and varying protest votes and their electoral fortunes at General Elections have fluctuated accordingly. However, at the 1983 General Election they collected together about 457 000 votes. In Northern Ireland there have been about 700 000 voters of whom the large majority have voted for an assortment of Protestant and Unionist candidates, while the minority has voted traditionally for the largely Catholic Social Democratic and Labour party (SDLP) and more recently to some extent for Provisional Sinn Fein, the political wing of the Irish Republican movement in the north.

**Floaters and abstainers**

The vital group of floating voters has varied in number and composition at each General Election since the war. This volatile section of the electorate, which by definition is never made up of the same people from one General Election to the next, seems to have grown in numbers over the years. Over the period 1959–79 about half the electorate changed its voting behaviour at least once, including moves to and from abstention.[1] More recently, over one third of those who voted Labour in 1979 deserted the party in 1983, as did nearly one quarter of those who voted Conservative, thus effectively determining the outcome of the 1983 election. Such voters therefore provide the key to electoral victory or defeat for the parties at every General Election.

In particular, the floating voters determine the electoral fortunes of the minor parties, since without desertions from both major parties it would be difficult for them to collect many additional votes. Of course, there is always the possibility that a third party can become one of the major parties in the House of Commons, provided that it manages to break through the key threshold of about 35 per cent to 40 per cent of the votes cast, above which it is likely to win a substantial number of seats in Parliament, but below which it is likely to languish in frustrating Parliamentary weakness. After all it was in just such a manner that the Labour party gradually displaced the Liberals during the first half of this century and a similar achievement could now be in prospect for the Alliance.

Turning to those who do not vote for whatever reason, we discover that such people have accounted for between 16 per cent and 28 per cent of the total electorate at General Elections since the war.[2] Since voting is voluntary in Britain, such non-voters can have a decisive influence upon the electoral outcome. For example, it has been estimated that differential non-voting had a vital influence upon the results of the 1951 and the two 1974 General Elections.

**Social class as a basis for voting**

The most significant divisions in the British electorate are still based upon class factors of one kind or another. Yet the correlation of social class with voting behaviour is by no means conclusive, as this section will show.

The Conservative vote at General Elections since the war has traditionally been made up of perhaps two thirds of the total middle-class vote and about one third of the total working-class vote according to the broadest socio-economic definitions. The Labour vote has traditionally been made up of perhaps one quarter of the total middle-class vote and more than one half of the total working-class vote according to the same broad definitions. The Liberal (and recently the Alliance) vote has tended to be even more classless and there has been little class bias in the votes of the other parties.

There are, however, a growing number of people in Britain whose voting behaviour cannot really be explained or predicted on traditional class lines. In this category the most notable example has always been that of working-class Conservatives.[3] Typically, more than one third of all Conservative votes at General Elections have come from working-class men and their families. This means, for example, that at the 1983 General Election there were at least 4 million working-class people who voted Conservative. Because of the shape of the social pyramid in Britain, it is evident that the Conservative party could never get elected to office if it did not attract a sufficient proportion of the working-class votes. Equally, it is clear that the Labour party would never lose an election if it could be sure of retaining the support of all working-class voters. Thus the outcome of every British General Election hinges in large part upon the relative strength or weakness of each party's appeal to the working class.

In general, class-based voting has weakened steadily in Britain over the years, especially within the working class. In 1959 Labour's share of the votes of manual workers and their familes was 40 per cent larger than its share of the votes of white-collar workers and their families. By 1983 the gap had narrowed to 21 per cent. For some time the Labour party has been losing working-class votes to the Conservatives. Indeed, at the 1983 General Election there was a swing from Labour to the Conservatives of 2.5 per cent among skilled manual workers and 4 per cent among semi-skilled and unskilled manual workers. However, at the 1983 General Election it was the Alliance which was the main beneficiary of working-class desertions from Labour, since it collected three times as many such votes as the Conservatives. Whereas at the 1959 General Election 62 per cent of all manual workers and their families voted Labour, by 1983 Labour support from this quarter had fallen to 38 per cent. Such a transformation of working-class voting behaviour has rightly been described by Ivor Crewe as 'the most significant post-war change in the social basis of British politics'.[4]

The decline of class-based voting in Britain can be attributed most to the steady desertion of the Labour party by manual workers and their families and especially the new working class, typically those working in the private sector and living as owner-occupiers in the south of England. A Gallup survey conducted at the time of the 1983 General Election showed that Labour trailed the Conservatives by 22 per cent among working-class owner-occupiers and by 16 per cent among working-class voters living in the south of England.[5] Among all private sector manual workers Labour led the Conservatives by only 1 per cent. On the other hand, Labour retained strong support among Council tenants (a 33 per cent lead over the Alliance), public sector workers (a 17 per cent lead over the Conservatives) and working-class voters living in the north of England and Scotland (a 10 per cent lead over the Conservatives). Thus it seems that today Disraeli's 'two nations' are no longer to be found only in different classes, but also within the working class itself.

**Sex and age as bases for voting**

Two further criteria for categorising the electorate are sex and age.[6] With regard to sex differences in voting behaviour, Labour has traditionally had a clear lead among male voters at General Elections since the war, scoring a notable 19 per cent advantage over the Conservatives in both 1945 and 1966. On the other hand, the Conservatives have traditionally had a clear lead among female voters, scoring an almost equally impressive 12 per cent and 13 per cent advantage over Labour in 1951 and 1955 respectively. In the 1979 General Election the Conservatives managed to maintain their strength among female voters with an impressive 9 per cent lead over Labour and since it was such a good result for the Conservatives, they also scored a 5 per cent lead over Labour among male voters. However, at the 1983 General Election for the first time for many years the Conservatives drew more of their support from men than from women. This was mainly because the Alliance increased its share of the female vote to 28 per cent, compared with the 14 per cent achieved by the Liberals in 1979. It is too soon to tell whether this represents the beginning of a new trend in favour of the Alliance or simply a transient protest against the Conservatives among female voters.

With regard to age-related differences in voting behaviour, Labour has traditionally done particularly well among voters under the age of 30, scoring a 28 per cent lead over the Conservatives in 1945, a 17 per cent lead in 1966 and a 16 per cent lead in October 1974. On the other hand, the Conservatives have traditionally done rather well among those in late middle age (50-64), scoring an 18 per cent lead over Labour in 1951, a 14 per cent lead in 1955 and a 13 per cent lead in 1959. The fortunes of the two major parties in the other age groups (30-49 and 65 plus) have been more evenly balanced. Whereas Labour did well among the 30-49 age group in 1945 and 1966 with leads over the Conservatives of 16 per cent and 13 per cent respectively, the Conservatives did well among those of 65 plus in 1955, 1970 and February 1974 with leads over Labour of 9 per cent, 9 per cent and 14 per cent respectively. In 1979 Labour was able to retain a small lead of 1 per cent over the Conservatives among the 18-24 age group of voters, notwithstanding the fact that it trailed the Conservatives by 7 per cent among voters of all ages and by 10 per cent in the age groups 35-54, and 55 plus.

At the 1983 General Election Conservative voting support increased steadily with age, but on a gentler gradient than before. The largest Conservative lead was 20 per cent over Labour in the 35-44 age group, while the smallest was 11 per cent over the Alliance in the 18-22 age group. The Conservatives retained their lead over Labour among those aged 65 plus, although there was a small notional swing to Labour (0.5 per cent) among that group which could perhaps be attributed to the continued voting solidarity of the 'cohort' which had come of age politically in 1945 when Labour had its greatest victory at the polls. The Conservatives did surprisingly well among first-time voters by taking 41 per cent of those who voted in that age group, compared with 30 per cent for the Alliance and 29 per cent for Labour. However, this could have been influenced by the fact that 47 per cent of the unemployed in that age group did not bother to vote at all, which must have reduced the potential Labour and Alliance votes from that source.

**Geographical and sociological variations**

There are, of course, other variations in voting behaviour in Britain, notably those which derive from various geographical and sociological factors. At the 1979 General Election there were considerable local and regional variations in voting behaviour. The Midlands and the south of England voted strongly for the Conservatives, especially in the new towns and the more prosperous working-class suburbs. On the other hand, South Wales, the north of England and much of Scotland remained largely loyal to the Labour party.[7] At the 1983 General Election the Conservatives had a 16 per cent lead over Labour among working-class voters in the south of England, while Labour had a 10 per cent lead over the Conservatives among the same socio-economic group in the north of England and Scotland. The result of the Labour collapse in the south of England is that the party now holds no seats south of a line from London to Bristol and, excluding Greater London, only three seats (Ipswich, Thurrock and Bristol South) south of a line from the Severn Estuary to the Wash. On the other hand, the Conservatives now hold no seats in Glasgow or Liverpool and only one seat in Manchester.

As for sociological differences in voting behaviour, perhaps the most remarkable are those associated with housing tenure. At the 1983 General Election Labour led the Alliance by 33 per cent and the Conservatives by 38 per cent among voters who were Council tenants, while the Conservatives had a 19 per cent lead over the Alliance among owner-occupiers in the new working class and a 22 per cent lead over Labour in the same category. Among trade-unionist voters the Conservatives improved their position and at 32 per cent support came second to Labour (39 per cent) in that category. At the same time the defection of trade-unionist voters was responsible for the biggest drop in any single sociological category of the Labour vote (down by 14 per cent to 39 per cent), while the Alliance increased its support among trade-unionist voters by 12 per cent in line with the average increase in its support in all socio-economic categories. Only among those of the unemployed who bothered to vote did Labour do reasonably well by gaining a 15 per cent lead over the Conservatives. Yet only the Alliance actually increased its support in that category from 15 per cent to 26 per cent.

In short, the British electorate no longer divides neatly into two large class-based voting groups, even assuming that such a model of voting behaviour ever really fitted all the facts. The voters have become more volatile, more heterogeneous and less inclined to adhere to their expected voting allegiances. In such circumstances the degree of variation in voting behaviour seems likely to increase rather than diminish over the years ahead. Profiles of some typical voters are shown in tabular form in Figure 4.1.

Fig 4.1 *Profiles of some typical voters*

* *Conservative loyalist*: Man or woman of more than 50, middle class, owner-occupier, living in the south of England and working in the private sector.

* *Labour loyalist*: Man of less than 30, working class, Council tenant, living in the north of England, Scotland or Wales, working in the public sector and a member of a trade union.

* *Alliance voter*: Man or woman of less than 50, middle or working class, owner-occupier or Council tenant, living in any part of Britain and working in a white collar job in the private sector.

## 4.2 MAIN INFLUENCES ON VOTING

Traditionally, it has been argued that there are three main influences on voting behaviour in Britain, namely political inheritance, self-interest and the record of the party in office.[8] However, it is now clear that there are other important influences which cannot be ignored, such as policy and sentiment, image and technique. We must therefore include these too in our review of the subject.

**Political inheritance**

The influence of political inheritance means the political loyalties and attitudes which voters derive from their parents and families. On the basis of surveys conducted in the 1960s Butler and Stokes showed a high correlation (typically over 75 per cent) between the voting behaviour of one generation and the next within family households.[9] This is not surprising in view of the well-established fact that the opinions of young people on all issues, whether political or non-political, tend to accord with those of their parents in the majority of cases.

Even at the 1983 General Election, when the Labour party suffered its heaviest defeat for about fifty years, 38 per cent of the voters continued to regard themselves as essentially Labour supporters.[10] This suggests a considerable inertia of party political loyalty which in many cases can only be derived from family inheritance and socialisation. For better or worse the influence of families and other tight-knit social communities remains rather strong.

**Self-interest**

The influence of self-interest derives very largely from the personal experience, favourable or unfavourable, consistent or contradictory, of millions of individual voters. For example, there is a fortunate minority of people in Britain today who are born into well-off families, benefit from a good education and encounter relatively few problems in leading happy and successful lives. In the majority of cases such people tend to vote Conservative. Equally, there is a large section of the population (typically several million) for whom life is a constant struggle against adverse material conditions from the time they are born to the time they die. Their lives are characterised by financial insecurity, dependence upon the state and its agencies, and limited material expectations. In the majority of cases such people tend to vote Labour, if they bother to vote at all.

Certainly the 62 per cent of the professional and managerial class which supported the Conservative party at the 1983 General Election are likely to have done so principally for reasons of self-interest, even though such people usually describe their reasons for voting Conservative in terms of the national interest. The rest of that socio-economic group, who probably voted for Labour or the Alliance, are more likely to have done so for ideological or altruistic reasons. On the other hand, it is interesting to note that although 33 per cent of a representative sample at the time of the election considered that their self-interest lay in voting Labour, only 20 per cent of the total electorate actually did so.[11] This suggests that self-interest cannot always be a dominant influence upon voting behaviour and that other factors, such as ideology and altruism, apathy and disillusion, often play an important part as well.

**Government record**

The record of the party in office might seem to be an influence on voting behaviour too obvious to be worth stating, if it were not for the fact that it emphasises the importance of the relatively new tendency for many voters to vote pragmatically. This is a way of describing what happens when millions of floating voters strike a bargain with the politicians whereby they reward the party in office with re-election or punish it with electoral defeat according to their assessment of its period in Government.

This is a view of voting behaviour which is widely held by practising politicians in Britain. It also coincides with the well-established axiom that parties in Government tend to lose elections rather than parties in Opposition to win them. However, it is also clear from the 1983 General Election that an official Opposition party which was divided, whose policies and leadership had lost credibility in the eyes of many voters, could also have a significant effect upon the final result. Truly it was the Labour party which lost that election more than the Conservative party which won it.

**Policy and sentiment**

In recent years policy and sentiment have also been important influences upon voting behaviour in Britain. With regard to policy based voting, Bo Särlvik and Ivor Crewe have shown that more than two-thirds of the votes cast for the three national parties at the 1979 General Election could have been predicted correctly on the basis of the views held by the voters on certain policy issues and that the correlation was over 90 per cent for Conservative and Labour voters.[12] They have argued that this was a reflection of the fact that over the period 1964-79 there had been a dramatic decline in the degree of popular support for three key Labour policies - that is, further nationalisation, the reinforcement of trade union power and higher tax-financed spending upon the Welfare State. These policies, which had commanded majority support in 1964, at any rate among those voters who identified with the Labour party, commanded less than 25 per cent support among Labour voters in 1979.

Policy-based voting is also a reflection of the continuing alignment between Conservative policies and the views of many voters (especially Conservatives) on many of the salient political issues. This should remind us that all voters are less inclined than they used to be to vote in accordance with traditional class or family loyalties and more inclined to vote in the light of their own policy preferences. Indeed, Särlvik and Crewe have shown that voters' opinions on the policies and performances of the various parties are twice as likely to explain their voting behaviour as all the economic and social characteristics of the electorate taken together.[13] The Gallup survey conducted for the BBC at the time of the 1983 election also showed that when the voters preferred the policies of one party and the leader of another, they decided in favour of the former by 83 per cent to 17 per cent, thus giving a clear advantage to the Conservatives over the Alliance.[14] Furthermore, when voters were faced with a choice between one party with 'the best policies' and another with 'the best for people like me', they decided in favour of the former by 72 per cent to 28 per cent, this time benefiting the Conservatives over Labour.

With regard to capricious sentiment as an influence upon voting behaviour, Hilde Himmelweit and others have shown that 'although in practice both consistency (i.e. party loyalty) and ideological thinking (i.e. policy considerations) influence the decision (to vote), each election is like a new shopping expedition in a situation where new as well as familiar goods are on offer'.[15] This means that evidence from recent General Elections can be interpreted and explained by using a consumer model of voting behaviour. In this a great deal depends upon how voters feel during the limited period of the campaign and whether during that time the public is persuaded to vote in a positive or negative spirit.

At the 1983 General Election, for example, the Conservative party won a landslide majority in Parliament largely by default. This was because there was a sharp increase in negative voting, with 59 per cent of all voters and 63 per cent of Alliance supporters giving negative reasons for their votes. Indeed, of the voters who did not make up their minds until the course of the campaign, 73 per cent voted negatively, including a notable 78 per cent of Conservative voters who said they were voting against Michael Foot and the Labour Left. In short, it could be said that the Labour vote was predominantly a protest against the record of the 1979-83 Conservative Government, the Conservative vote was predominantly a protest against the Left-wing policies and leadership of the Labour party, and the Alliance vote was predominantly a protest against both major parties. In all three cases sentiment was a powerful common denominator.

**Image and technique**

Party images and campaign techniques are other significant influences on voting behaviour in the age of the modern mass media. Party images are formed by the party leaders themselves - for example 'the resolute Mrs Thatcher' or 'that nice Mr Steel' - and by the record of the parties both in Government and in Opposition. Naturally, the party leaders and their advisers work hard to preserve or improve their images, since all their public appearances, especially on radio and television, affect the ratings of their parties in the opinion polls and the voting behaviour of the electorate at General Elections.

Party images are also formed incrementally, even subliminally, over a longer period by what the various parties do or fail to do when in Government and by how they behave when in Opposition. For example, the 1979–83 Conservative Government undoubtedly benefited at the 1983 election from Mrs Thatcher's resolute public image and her personal identification with the success of the British armed forces in recapturing the Falklands in 1982.

Equally, at the 1983 General Election the Labour party suffered from its poor image in the eyes of the public which was the product of several years of weak leadership, party in-fighting and ideological struggles. In neither case was there much that the parties could do about their images, since they derived from factors which were not really susceptible to deliberate interference or control. Such images become part of the data of politics and even the party professionals find it hard to alter them. Usually the best that each party can do is to emphasise repeatedly the unattractive aspects of its main opponent's image and the attractive aspects of its own.

Campaign techniques can also have an important influence upon voting behaviour, especially since many of the floating voters do not make up their minds until the final few days of the campaign. The parties therefore make every effort during the campaign period to get as much media coverage as possible and to present their leaders in the most favourable light. In the case of the major parties, such efforts may or may not succeed, depending upon the leading figures with which the party professionals have to work. However, in the case of the minor parties, which in normal times do not get so much media attention, effective campaign techniques can be disproportionately successful in drawing public attention both to their leaders and to their policies.

**Summary**

There are a variety of influences upon voting behaviour in Britain. The traditional influences – that is, political inheritance, self-interest and the record of the party in office, are still of fundamental importance. However, the more ephemeral influences which have made themselves felt in recent years, for instance, policy and sentiment, image and technique, have assumed an increasing importance as the voters have shown more volatility in their voting behaviour and as General Election campaigns seem to have become more presidential in style and content. Indeed, nowadays the parties sometimes attempt to manufacture news and events during a campaign simply in order to create certain political effects. An example of this practice during the 1983 General Election campaign was the tendency for the Alliance parties to release early news of favourable opinion poll results, so that their leaders could then comment positively upon them and thus contribute to an artificially created 'band-wagon' effect designed to induce the doubters to support the Alliance. The use of such techniques emphasises the manipulative aspect of modern party politics, especially during General Election campaigns. Yet in spite of such developments it is still the ordinary voters who decide the outcome on polling day.

## 4.3 FUTURE UNCERTAINTIES

In the future there are some key uncertainties which are likely to have a significant influence upon the outcome of General Elections in Britain. Will the voters be more or less concerned with issues of policy? Will a substantial part of the working class continue to vote Conservative and a substantial part of the middle class continue to vote Labour? Will men and women have markedly different political leanings? Will the electorate become more or less volatile in its voting behaviour? Will the Alliance parties succeed in breaking the mould of post-war British politics? Will public participation in elections grow or decline and to what extent will people show signs of political alienation? No matter what the difficulties, it is worth speculating about these important questions.

### Policy based voting

There was a time in the late 1950s and early 1960s when some observers were proclaiming the end of ideology in Britain and other advanced Western societies. In more recent times it has seemed that ideological considerations are once again a significant influence on voting behaviour, as they were, for example, in the 1930s.

In the 1980s it now seems a reasonable assumption that the positions taken by the different parties on the major issues of policy will have a significant and perhaps increasing effect upon voting behaviour. This is partly because of the continued weakening of the previously firm associations between objective class and voting behaviour. However, it is also a result of the increasing sophistication, even fastidiousness, of many floating voters who now regard their decisions at General Elections as little more than another form of consumer choice. As long as there appears to be a new or improved political product on offer, a significant number of voters will measure its claims not only against their own policy preferences but also their feelings towards the other parties. In such a political beauty contest with all the related media interest and the stimulus from opinion polls the voters' perceptions of political issues and party policies are likely to have a significant effect upon the final results. At the very least it would be unwise to underestimate the influence of policy-based voting at a time when more and more voters seem to be breaking away from their traditional class allegiances.

**Working-class Conservatives**

It is reasonable to assume that as long as the Conservative party continues to pursue national rather than sectional policies, it will continue to get the support of a significant number of working class voters. In particular, this will depend upon the image of the party in the eyes of the so-called 'authoritarian' working class, that is, those voters who are attracted by whichever party takes the toughest line on issues such as law and order, immigration and trade union reform.

Unless the Conservative party were to forfeit all its claims to competence in office or launch an ill-advised attack upon the very foundations of the Welfare State, it seems likely that the inherent conservatism of a large part of the British working class will ensure a substantial Conservative vote from that quarter for many years to come. However, although the patriotic effects of the 1982 Falklands conflict strengthened the Conservative appeal to this section of the electorate at the 1983 General Election, it now seems less certain that these effects will last in changed political circumstances.

**Middle-class Labour voters**

It is worth noting that over the last decade or so, even when the Labour party has done badly at General Elections, its middle-class voting support has held up rather well. There is no complete explanation for this and no certainty that it will continue to be the case in future. It may partly be explained by Labour's strong support among white-collar voters in the public sector, for example, teachers and health service workers. In future it may also be supposed that as the electorate in general and middle-class voters in particular become more sophisticated and demanding in their political outlook, there may be an increasing tendency for at least some of them to cast their votes in accordance with abstract principles or notions of rational idealism. If this were to be the case, the Labour party ought to be well placed to retain and even increase its support from such quarters.

Of course, another explanation for this phenomenon is simply that as the electorate as a whole becomes more middle class, so Labour voters are bound to become more middle class as well as they move up the social hierarchy with everyone else. This means that many Labour voters clearly remain politically loyal to their family and social origins, even though their current circumstances and material life-style are more consistent with Conservative voting behaviour.

### Sex differences in voting

In so far as women usually live longer than men and Conservative voting behaviour is usually more prevalent later in life, it is likely that women will continue to have a tendency to vote Conservative. Yet the evidence on this issue no longer points to only one conclusion.

On the one hand, the limitations of conventional family life (that is, two parents and two children with the wife staying at home when the children are young) suggest that many women are likely to remain fairly insulated from the pro-Labour voting pressures which usually characterise at least the highly unionised sectors of employment. Furthermore, when married women go out to work, many of them take part-time employment in the service sector in order that their jobs should be compatible with their family responsibilities. Once again this does not make it very likely that they will develop habits of Labour voting as a consequence of their work.

On the other hand, at the 1983 General Election the Conservative party got more votes from men than women, a result which flew in the face of the traditional assumption that the party does better with the female electorate. There are a number of plausible explanations for this particular occurrence. One is that some women may not have liked Mrs Thatcher's forceful personal style. Another is that on several key issues of the campaign - for example, unemployment, nuclear weapons and the future of the Welfare State - many women may have found the Conservative party either unconvincing or unattractive or both. Yet another is that women of all ages, but especially middle-class women under 40, may have been attracted by the personalities and style of the Alliance leaders. It remains to be seen whether similar factors will operate at future elections and if so, what the voting results will be. All that can be said at this stage is that the Conservative party cannot afford to take women voters for granted.

### Electoral volatility

There is no way of knowing for certain whether or not the British electorate will become more volatile in future. However, there have been signs of considerable volatility in the recent past and it seems likely that the trend will continue.

At the 1983 General Election there was further evidence of electoral volatility, since all parties suffered from significant desertions by the voters (quite apart from any net gains which they may have made in certain voting groups). The Labour party lost 37 per cent of the vote which it had obtained in 1979, with 22 per cent going to the Alliance, 7 per cent to the Conservatives and 8 per cent staying at home. The Conservative party lost 23 per cent of the vote which it had obtained in 1979, with 13 per cent going to the Alliance, 4 per cent to Labour and 6 per cent staying at home.

The Alliance lost 20 per cent of the vote which the Liberal party had obtained in 1979, with 14 per cent going to the Conservatives, 9 per cent to Labour and 5 per cent staying at home. Indeed, it can be argued that it was the Alliance which suffered most from the effects of electoral volatility. Nearly three fifths of potential Alliance voters explained their eventual decision to vote differently in terms of their realisation of the dangers of casting wasted votes for the Alliance which could have had the effect of facilitating victory for whichever major party they were most keen to prevent from winning.[16] In such circumstances it seems that the Alliance actually lost more votes than it won from those in the electorate who indulged in tactical voting.

In future the impact of electoral volatility will depend upon the net effect of a number of different factors. It is likely that increased volatility will be encouraged by the relative weakening of traditional associations between class and party, the growing tendency for voters to cast their votes pragmatically, the advent of capricious 'consumer' voting, the unsettling influence of the media and opinion polls, and the corrosive effects of repeatedly disappointed public expectations. On the other hand, volatility could decrease if there were to be a general recognition of the futility of casting wasted votes for third parties or attempting to vote pragmatically at a time when no politicians in office are likely to be able to deliver enough economic growth to satisfy the expectations of all the voters. The outcome is therefore uncertain. All that can be said at this stage is that when Labour is in office increased volatility is likely to favour the Conservatives, whereas when the Conservatives are in office it is more likely to benefit the Alliance of Liberals and Social Democrats (although even that is not certain).

Thus the great unresolved question of voting behaviour in Britain is whether the traditional bias in the electoral system will continue to work against all third parties or whether the social basis of traditional voting behaviour will become so shaky that all the normal assumptions will be called into question. Only time and future General Elections will settle the outcome of this 'all-British game of Russian roulette'.[17]

### Participation or alienation

If political participation is measured simply in terms of the voting turn-out at General Elections since the war, we can see that it has fluctuated between a high point of 84 per cent in 1950 and a low point of 72 per cent in 1970 with an average of 76 per cent over the entire period. In 1970 and 1983 for seasonal reasons (both elections were held in June when many people were on holiday) and in October 1974 for reasons directly connected with public alienation from the political process (two General Elections in one year) the number of those not voting rivalled or exceeded the number of those who voted for the party which came second. Given that the two-party struggle has been the essence of British voting behaviour since the war, these facts could be interpreted as signs of real alienation from the political process.

Of course, it is also reasonable to argue that such signs of disenchantment with the two major parties are not necessarily signs of dissatisfaction with the electoral system or alienation from the entire political process. Yet there can be no escape from the fact that the struggle for power between the two major parties has been the predominant characteristic of the British political system since the war, so perhaps the conclusion is justified.

It remains to be seen whether the secular trend away from the two major parties will continue. If it does, such a significant change in voting behaviour will affect more than the transient balance of power at Westminster. It could well alter the character and conventions of the entire political system.

## 4.4 CONCLUSION

In conclusion we can say that the major influences upon voting behaviour in Britain are political inheritance, self-interest and the record of the party in office. However, these all tend to be subjective influences in that they usually depend upon the personal conclusions which voters draw from their own experience and observations of the political scene. From an objective point of view it seems clear that social class, economic occupation, housing tenure and geographical location are among the most important influences on how people cast their votes at General Elections. Furthermore, the voters do not vote in a vacuum. They go to the polls (or decide not to bother) after several weeks or even months of verbal bombardment by the politicians and the media as well as attention from the opinion pollsters. All these various forces help to shape the views of the voters much of whose voting behaviour has become volatile and even capricious in consequence.

It is probably still right to agree with Jean Blondel that 'the simple division between working and middle class . . . contributes to the clearest cleavage in British political attitudes and voting behaviour'.[18] Yet such a statement no longer tells us all we need to know if we try to predict future voting behaviour in Britain. That will depend upon the development of the British economy over the years. It will depend upon the record of the party or parties in Government. It will depend upon the popularity and credibility of the parties in Opposition. Above all, it will depend upon the special characteristics of the British electoral system with its bias against all third parties (except those which are socially or geographically concentrated). Whatever happens in future, the definitive answers can only be given by the politically sovereign electorate at periodic General Elections.

## SUGGESTED QUESTIONS

1. What are the main divisions in the British electorate?
2. Which are the most significant influences on voting behaviour in Britain?
3. Is social class likely to be a decisive factor in determining the outcome of future General Elections in Britain?

## NOTES

1. B. Särlvik and I. Crewe, *Decade of Dealignment* (London: CUP, 1983) p. 66.
2. Since about 6 per cent of the names on the Electoral Register are redundant (i.e. dead, double-counted, emigrated, etc) the true non-voting rate is lower than these figures suggest.
3. For a more detailed account of this subject see R. T. McKenzie and A. Silver, *Angels in Marble* (London: Heinemann, 1968) and J. H. Goldthorpe, *Social Mobility and Class Structure in Modern Britain* (Oxford: Clarendon Press, 1980).
4. The *Guardian*, 13 June 1983.
5. Ibid.
6. The evidence on differences in voting behaviour by sex and age has been tabulated in successive Nuffield Election Studies since 1950. The figures given here are derived from those studies.
7. For a detailed breakdown of regional variations in voting behaviour see *The Times Guide to the House of Commons, May 1979*; and *The Times Guide to the House of Commons, June 1983*; both published by Times Books, London.
8. For example, see A. H. Birch, *The British System of Government*, 6th edn (London: Allen & Unwin, 1983) pp. 78–82.
9. See D. E. Butler and D. Stokes, *Political Change in Britain*, 2nd edn (London: Macmillan, 1974) pp. 48–66.
10. The *Guardian*, 14 June 1983.
11. Ibid.
12. See B. Särlvik and I. Crewe, *Decade of Dealignment*, pp. 247–344.
13. Ibid, p. 113.
14. The *Guardian*, 14 June 1983.
15. H. T. Himmelweit *et al., How Voters Decide* (London: Academic Press, 1981), p. 14.
16. The *Guardian*, 14 June 1983.
17. *The Times*, 10 February 1981.
18. J. Blondel, *Voters, Parties and Leaders* (Harmondsworth: Penguin, 1974) p. 86.

## FURTHER READING

Alford, R., *Party and Society* (London: Murray, 1964).
Blondel, J., *Voters, Parties and Leaders* (Harmondsworth; Penguin, 1974).
Butler, D. E. and Stokes, D., *Political Change in Britain*, 2nd edn (London: Macmillan, 1974).
Cook, C. and Ramsden, J., *By-elections in British Politics* (London: Macmillan, 1973).
Goldthorpe, J. H., *Social Mobility and Class Structure in Modern Britain* (Oxford: Clarendon Press, 1980).
Himmelweit, H. T. *et al.*, *How Voters Decide* (London: Academic Press, 1981).
McKenzie, R. T. and Silver, A., *Angels in Marble* (London: Heinemann, 1968).
McLean, I., *Elections*, 2nd edn (London: Longman, 1980).
Miller, W. L., *The End of British Politics*? (Oxford: Clarendon Press, 1981).
Penniman, H. R. (ed.) *Britain at the Polls, 1979* (Washington, DC: American Enterprise Institute, 1981).
Robertson, D., *Class and the British Electorate* (Oxford: Martin Robertson, 1983).
Särlvik, B. and Crewe, I., *Decade of Dealignment* (Cambridge: Cambridge University Press, 1983).

# PART II
# SOURCES OF POWER, PRESSURE AND OPINION

CHAPTER 5

# THE POLITICAL PARTIES

In this chapter we shall focus principally upon the Conservative and Labour parties, since they have been the dominant forces and among the defining characteristics of the British political system at any rate since the Second World War. This means that British politics is party politics which takes place in what is fundamentally a two-party system. It remains to be seen whether the establishment of the Social Democratic party in 1981 and its formation of an electoral Alliance with the Liberal party will produce significant and enduring changes in this situation.

In the eighteenth century Edmund Burke defined party as 'a body of men united for promoting by their just endeavours the national interest upon some particular principle in which they are all agreed'.[1] In 1864 Benjamin Disraeli defined party quite simply as 'organised opinion'.[2] Each of these definitions captures an essential aspect of the matter, but neither is complete in modern conditions.

In contemporary circumstances we may define a political party as an organised and relatively disciplined group of people who freely combine together to advance a set of political attitudes and beliefs with a view to translating them via victory at elections into Government decisions or Parliamentary legislation. In other words, all parties try to capture, or at least to influence, the power of Government.

## 5.1 IDEOLOGICAL PRINCIPLES

Since the Second World War it has been the Conservative and Labour parties which have dominated British politics. They have brought to British political thought two distinct ideological traditions within which their respective political principles have been advanced in the light of the circumstances prevailing at the time.

**The Conservative party**

The Conservative tradition stresses the importance of strong government in the sense that Conservatives believe that a Government should act with determination and self-confidence based upon the democratic legitimacy provided by its Parliamentary majority in the House of Commons. Conservatives have usually been suspicious of political ideology of an imperative or all-embracing kind, although Conservatism has been seen by some of its opponents as an ideology of class rule.[3] In the opinion of Samuel Beer the ideas of independent authority for the Executive, class rule by those deemed best equipped to govern, pragmatic decisions of a non-ideological character and strong determined government have been discernible in Conservative political thought for a long time.[4] In the opinion of Ian Gilmour the Conservative approach to politics has been more a function of temperament and experience than ideology or intellect. In his words, 'Conservatives take life as they find it, while always seeking to ameliorate its harshness'.[5]

Occasionally in the course of its long history the Conservative party has been swept along on the wave of some particular ideology, but such periods have not usually lasted or brought enduring political success. Joseph Chamberlain, a refugee from the Liberal party, did not get very far with his campaign for tariff reform during the early years of this century. Edward Heath was obliged to reverse the radical free market policies with which he had entered office in 1970 once it became clear that the unintended consequences in terms of rising unemployment and threats to public order were too serious to be tolerated without adjustments of policy. Historically speaking, the general conclusion seems clear: a conscious political ideology does not really belong in the Conservative tradition.

In present circumstances the contemporary Conservative party stands for a return to sound money (sometimes called 'monetarism'), the revival of the private sector, the diminution of the public sector, the curbing of trade union power and privileges, the encouragement of individual initiative through lower levels of direct taxation, greater freedom of individual choice especially in health and education, a more selective approach towards social security, a tougher emphasis upon the maintenance of law and order, the strengthening of our defence forces and continued British membership of the European Community. The party has also made a point, even a fetish, of preserving party unity (or at least the appearance of unity), since it is well aware of the advantage over the Labour party which this provides. However, this has not prevented the conduct of a continuing, coded argument between what the press has called the 'Wets' and the 'Dries', the former associating themselves principally with the Disraelian tradition of 'One Nation' and the latter with the nineteenth century doctrine of liberal individualism. It remains to be seen which of these two strands in the Conservative outlook will prove the most permanent.

Since Margaret Thatcher became leader of the party in 1975, the emphasis in Conservative rhetoric has been put on the paramount importance of individual attitudes and behaviour in response either to material incentives or to legislative penalties. During this period party spokesmen have been at pains to emphasise the comparatively limited role of the state and other public agencies, and to stress individual or group responsibilities for the fate of families, firms and, indeed, the entire nation. There has been much talk of the need for realism and the desirability of reducing the burden of the public sector upon the rest of the economy. There has been a limited attempt to restore both rewards for success and penalties for failure. Above all, there has been a sustained attempt to persuade people to lower their material expectations to more realistic levels.

**The Labour party**

The Labour tradition has been based upon a commitment to the ideology of Socialism ever since the party constitution was adopted in 1918. Yet from the beginning the importance of ideology was balanced to some extent by the more pragmatic outlook of the Fabians and the Christian Socialists. It was also tempered by trade union scepticism towards some Socialist principles. Nevertheless, as Samuel Beer has observed, 'if the implication of sudden and violent change is extracted . . . it is correct to say that the meaning of Socialism to the Labour party was a commitment to ultimate social revolution'.[6] To the Labour party this has always meant more than a commitment to the public ownership of the means of production, distribution and exchange, as laid down in Clause IV of the party constitution. It has also meant a commitment to a form of moral collectivism which has drawn upon the reserves of fellowship and fraternity traditionally associated with the trade unions. In this scheme of things the party has always regarded itself as part of the wider Labour movement. Labour MPs are therefore supposed to act more as the Parliamentary instrument of the movement than as independent representatives of their constituents, although the independence of the Parliamentary party is also acknowledged in the party constitution.

The Socialist tradition continues in the modern Labour party. For example, the October 1974 Manifesto contained a clear commitment to 'an irreversible shift in the balance of wealth and power' in favour of working people. The fact that the Labour party, when in office, has not always acted in a truly Socialist way has merely engendered disillusion and recrimination among its more zealous members. As a result many activists in the constituency Labour parties have given strong support to the campaign of Tony Benn and others on the Left of the party in favour of constitutional changes within the Labour movement designed to make Labour MPs more accountable to their constituency parties and to diminish the cautious influence of the Parliamentary leadership upon Labour policy.[7]

In view of the dynamics of policy developments it is difficult to give a definitive description of what the Labur party now stands for (in 1983), since the struggle for the future of the party continues and it is impossible to predict the final outcome. In general, however, the party favours the extension of public ownership and national planning, the use of the tax system for the redistribution of income and wealth, higher spending upon universal social services, greater financial support for the existing nationalised industries, a more relaxed attitude towards increased public spending and borrowing, controls on prices, dividends and capital movements, greater emphasis upon equality of provision in education and health, a higher priority to tackling unemployment than controlling inflation, the reduction of arms spending and new initiatives for unilateral nuclear disarmament and further renegotiation, if not withdrawal, from the European Community.

Since the party's defeat at the 1979 General Election, there appears to have been a signficant shift further to the Left. This has been particularly noticeable on some sensitive and important issues, such as pay policy and defence spending, but it has also been evident across the board. For example, mainstream Labour attitudes on public ownership, education policy and civil rights in relation to the police are now more radical than they were when the party was last in Government. Furthermore, it seems almost certain that the party will commit itself to repeal all the trade union legislation introduced by the Thatcher Government and may also take the opportunity when next in office to extend the power of the trade unions beyond the point reached in 1979.

In the past neither major party, when in Government, has allowed a completely free rein to its ideological tendencies. In office, each party has been restrained by the harness of political realities and the need to respond to the non-ideological views of the general public. However, developments in both major parties since the early 1970s have cast doubt upon the comfortable assumption that the non-ideological pragmatists will always win the arguments. Even a cursory examination of the major party Manifestos since about 1970 (with the notable exception of the Conservative Manifesto in October 1974) reveals that each party, when in Opposition, has come forward with proposals of far greater ideological content than used to be the case for the first twenty-five years or so after the Second World War. It seems that as each major party has been disappointed by its achievements in office, its more zealous members have tended to lay the blame increasingly at the door of their more pragmatic colleagues. Thus some Labour politicians have continued to argue that future salvation for the party is to be found in more Socialism, while some Conservatives have continued to argue the case for a return to what are held to be fundamental Conservative principles.

**The Alliance parties**
The ideological principles of the other parties have been less important in post-war British politics. For some time the Liberal party has sought to occupy the central ground of British politics by consciously distancing itself from what it portrays as the dogma and polarised ideology of each major party. More recently, it has been joined on that ground by the Social Democratic party which was formed in 1981. Together these two parties have had a strong interest in defining their common position in clear contrast to each of the two major parties. This means that they stand for a political middle way which differentiates them most sharply from the right wing of the Conservative party and the left wing of the Labour party, but not necessarily from the moderate wings of either major party.[8]

Thus the Alliance parties favour the continuation of the mixed economy and see distinctive roles for both the public and private sectors. Their approach to industrial relations puts the emphasis upon greater employee participation and flirts with the encouragement of co-operative models. Both parties recognise the need for some sort of incomes policy on a permanent basis, although there are differences between them as to how it should be enforced or implemented.

Both parties favour continued British membership of the European Community and adequate defence spending in support of Britain's NATO commitments. Although both are opposed to the purchase of the Trident missile system, they seem to disagree somewhat about the precise form in which Britain should seek to maintain an independent strategic nuclear capability. Both parties strongly advocate the introduction of proportional representation for elections to Parliament at Westminster, although there seems to be some dispute among the Social Democrats about the best version to use. Above all, both parties stand for a less divisive, less ideological and more decentralised approach to the main problems of British politics.

**The Nationalist parties**
Plaid Cymru, the Welsh Nationalist party, has an ideology which is based mainly upon its determination to preserve the Welsh language and culture as the foundation of a separate Welsh identity within the United Kingdom. However, the party has both a radical and a moderate wing, with the former being attracted to certain forms of direct action in protest against the English dominance of Wales (for example, on the issues of Welsh water for English cities or English second homes in Wales) and the latter seeming more content to use the traditional Parliamentary channels to advance the Welsh Nationalist cause.

The Scottish National party has been motivated principally by the quest for complete Scottish independence and has therefore been able to encompass a broad ideological spectrum of opinion on nearly all other issues. However, in more recent times the party has tended to split between those who see its destiny as an alternative left-of-centre opposition to the Conservative Goverment in London and those who remain wedded to the more romantic and less precise vision of an independent Scotland within the European Community.

**The fringe parties**

There are many fringe parties in British politics and some of the smallest wax and wane with bewildering frequency. On the extreme Right, the National Front is based upon a white racialist ideology which is heavily tinged with xenophobia and impatience with the democratic methods of Parliamentary politics. On the extreme Left, the Communist party of Great Britain is one of the most unreconstructed and Stalinist parties in the whole of Western Europe, since it strongly opposes any firm Western response to the Soviet military threat and any revisionist or liberalising tendencies in Eastern Europe. Also on the extreme Left are the Socialist Workers' party and the Workers' Revolutionary party which are distinguishable from the Communist party mainly by their attachment to the idea of workers' control in industry and commerce and their persistent criticism of the Soviet Union. In a different category altogether there is the Ecology party which stands for an ecological approach to all political issues. This is somewhat comparable to the 'Green' parties on the Continent and it is possible that it will make a growing impact upon British politics over the years to come.

**Northern Ireland parties**

In Northern Ireland the majority Protestant community is represented at Westminster by various factions of the Unionist party. All of them stand, to a greater or lesser extent, for continued Protestant supremacy and the maintenance of Northern Ireland as an integral part of the United Kingdom. The minority Catholic community is represented mainly by the Social Democratic and Labour party (SDLP) which campaigns to improve the economic and social conditions of its people and favours closer links between Northern Ireland and the Irish Republic as a step towards eventual unity in Ireland. However, in recent years the SDLP seems to have lost ground in the Catholic community to the more radical Provisional Sinn Fein, the political wing of the Irish Republican movement in the north, which campaigns openly for British withdrawal from Northern Ireland and the early establishment of a united Ireland, if necessary by force.

There are signs that the politics of Northern Ireland are becoming even more polarised between the hard men in the Unionist and Nationalist camps. Many of the former seem to have adopted an increasingly garrison mentality, especially since they felt that the constitutional position of Northern Ireland had been placed in doubt by the 1982 initiative of the Thatcher Government in launching a scheme of 'rolling devolution' based upon the establishment of a new Northern Ireland Assembly.[9] Many of the latter seem to have become more radical and uncompromising in their nationalist demands, notably since the ill-fated H-Block hunger strikes in 1981 when Bobby Sands and a number of other Republican prisoners starved themselves to death in a fruitless quest for the restoration of 'political status' for IRA prisoners.

## 5.2 POLITICAL FUNCTIONS

The political parties in Britain perform a range of political functions. Essentially, these can be reduced to one primary function and a number of subsidiary functions, all of which contribute to the satisfactory working of the British political system.

### Primary function

The primary function of the main political parties in Britain, as Robert McKenzie made clear, is 'to sustain competing teams of potential leaders in the House of Commons in order that the electorate as a whole may choose between them'.[10] Indeed, any attempt by the parties to play a more prominent role in their own right cuts across the chain of responsibility from Cabinet to Parliament to electorate which is fundamental to the British system of Parliamentary democracy. In our political system constitutional power resides essentially in the Cabinet supported by a working majority in the Commons. In these circumstances the supreme function of the parties is bound to be the gaining and the retaining of such power. Any other conception of their paramount task would be inaccurate and improper according to the conventional wisdom.

### Subsidiary functions

All the parties perform similar subsidiary functions which vary in importance depending upon the particular circumstances. Firstly, they encourage public interest and participation in the process of politics. In other words, they provide permanent structures within which individuals and groups can act if they wish to play a part in politics at local or national level.

Secondly, they reflect, moderate and direct into constitutional channels the views and interests of a wide range of sectional groups. Of course, pressure groups have a powerful independent existence in their own right within the political system. Yet the existence of the parties enables and encourages all sectional groups to act in a constitutional manner and leads them to pay more attention to Parliament than might otherwise be the case.

Thirdly, they provide legitimate frameworks for the ventilation, discussion and criticism of political issues. This function is more prominent in the Labour, Liberal and Social Democratic parties than it is in the Conservative party, because all the former believe in the virtues of considerable grass roots influence upon the process of party policy-making, while the latter has traditionally allowed only a very limited role for party activists in this sphere. Indeed, in the Labour party any motion at the annual Conference which secures a two-thirds majority of the total votes automatically becomes party policy, unless and until it is amended or replaced at a subsequent Conference.

Lastly, and by no means least important, the political parties exist to build up membership, raise money, select candidates and organise political campaigns at both local and national levels. In the Labour party the greater part of the money and (nominally at least) the vast majority of the membership comes from the affiliated trade unions. In individual constituencies the local branches of trade unions contribute much of the income for the constituency parties (but on average less than 50 per cent) and nationally 80 per cent of the party's income comes from the trade unions which affiliate to the party varying proportions of their memberships. In the Conservative party the greater part of the money comes from donations made by industry and commerce, although at local level in the consituencies the Conservatives (like Labour) usually manage to raise considerable sums of money through the efforts of their voluntary workers. The Liberals and Social Democrats seek to raise money both nationally and locally in broadly similar ways.

However, in modern conditions all parties are finding it increasingly difficult to keep going financially at a time when the costs of political activity are rising and the membership of political parties is dwindling in a disturbing way. Since the publication of the Houghton Report in 1976, there has been the additional possibility for the parties to receive financial support from public funds in proportion to the votes which they secure at General Elections.[11] In theory, this could go a long way towards alleviating the financial problems of the parties, as it has done on the Continent. In practice, it has proved impossible so far to get the necessary all-party agreement to anything more than token financial support for the Leader of the Opposition and a few senior Opposition spokesmen. This is mainly because the Conservative party is ideologically opposed to state aid, does not wish to discourage the fund-raising efforts of its voluntary workers and seeks to retain the comparative advantage which it derives from the present arrangements.

## 5.3 NATIONAL ORGANISATION

In matters of national party organisation there is a notable contrast between the Conservative party, which was created from the centre and the top down, and the Labour party which was created from the periphery and the bottom up. The Conservative organisation was originally intended to act as the handmaid of the Parliamentary party, whereas the Labour organisation has always been the servant of the National Executive Committee and ultimately the annual party Conference. Such contrasting origins and traditions have left contrasting marks upon the way in which each of the major parties is organised today.

### The Conservative party

The Conservative party organisation is under the control of the party Chairman who is appointed by and responsible to the Leader of the party. The party Chairman is normally a trusted colleague of the party Leader from the Commons or the Lords and very often has a place in the Cabinet. It is unusual for the Chairman to be publicly at odds with the Leader of the party. If that happens, it is the Chairman who has to go.

The whole of Conservative Central Office exists to carry out the wishes of the Leader of the party and to meet the various organisational needs of the party at every level. It is also the head office and central co-ordinator of the party organisation in the different parts of the country and thus provides support and advice for the constituency Associations. It includes the Conservative Research Department which acts as a sort of political 'think-tank' for the party as a whole and a kind of alternative civil service for the Parliamentary leadership when the party is in Opposition.

The party Conference is organised by the National Union of Conservative Associations, but with the guidance of the party Chairman and key officials at Central Office. The Conference provides an annual occasion not so much for policy-making as for activists from constituencies all over the country (at least 5000 people in all) to come together for a mixture of social and political purposes, including habitual adulation of the party Leader on the final day.

Between annual Conferences (held every autumn) the National Union continues to function on behalf of the party in the country and helps to maintain cohesion and morale in the constituency Associations. The governing body of the National Union is called the Central Council. However, since this consists of about 4000 people and meets only once a year in the spring, it is really a slightly smaller-scale party Conference.

Fig 5.1 *Conservative party organisation*

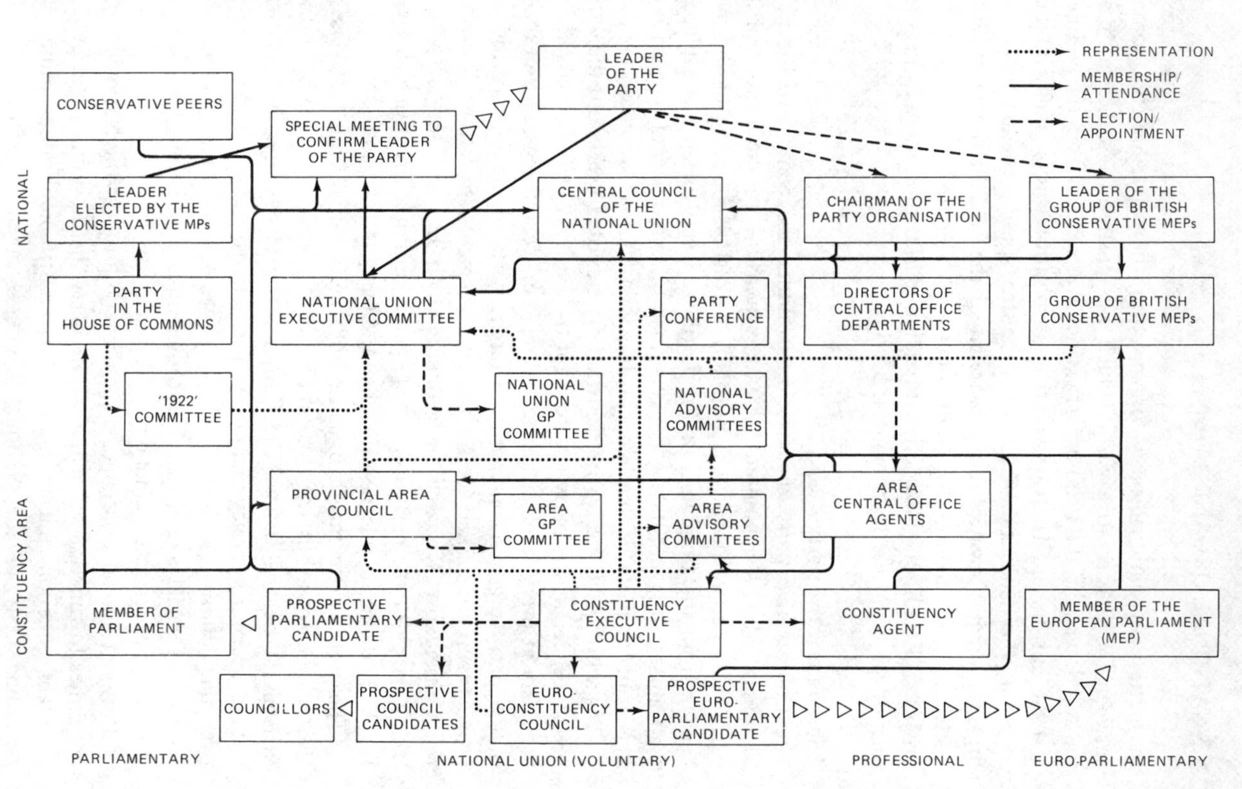

Consequently it has an Executive Committee of about 200 people representative of all sections of the party which meets five times a year. This in turn elects a General Purposes Committee of about sixty people who make most of the day-to-day decisions of the National Union, including those related to the agenda and arrangements of the annual party Conference.

Within the framework of the National Union there are seven advisory committees at national level which are often reflected at area and constituency levels as well. These include the Conservative Women's National Committee, the National Local Government Advisory Committee, the Conservative Trade Union Advisory Committee, the Young Conservative National Advisory Committee, the Conservative Political Centre National Advisory Committee and so on. However, none of these bodies is much more than a sounding-board for a particular section of party opinion. Nearly all those in prominent positions in the various National Union hierarchies have to be elected by those below them, although a very few are co-opted on the basis of their special knowledge or personal contacts. Such organisations provide useful frameworks for political discussion within the party (especially the Conservative Political Centre whose prime purpose this is), although there is usually no question of deflecting the party leadership from a particular course of action upon which it is determined to embark.

In the House of Commons the party is organised within a framework capped by the 1922 Committee, which was named after a famous meeting of Conservative back-benchers held at the Carlton Club in that year. The Committee is led by its Chairman, who is a senior and influential back-bencher elected annually by his back-bench colleagues. It has an influential Executive Committee made up of other senior back-benchers also elected annually by their colleagues. Under its auspices there is a considerable sub-structure of party back-bench committees each covering an area of policy – for example, finance, industry, agriculture, employment, education, defence, foreign affairs, etc – and each with a slate of Officers elected annually by their colleagues.

When the party is in Government, such committees can have an influence on policy via the subtle process of the politics of anticipated reaction, that is, when Ministers adjust their intended actions in the light of expected or actual responses from the relevant back-bench committees. When the party is in Opposition, such committees are probably even more influential, since the various Shadow Ministers are appointed Chairmen of the relevant committees and those who are elected as committee Officers can have considerable influence upon the process of party policy-making. In recent years there has also been a so-called Business Committee made up of the Officers of the 1922 Committee and the Officers of the other back-bench committees. This has served as a broader institutional link between the Shadow Cabinet and the various subject committees when the party is in Opposition.

As for the position of the party Leader, before 1965 the Leader was said to 'emerge' from a process of informal soundings and consultations within all sections of the party, but principally in the Commons. However, since 1965 the choice of party Leader has resulted from a process of election by all members of the Parliamentary party in the Commons, who are expected to consult together and take account of the views of the party in the country as well. Such elections take place every year in the autumn. Yet as long as the Leader maintains the confidence of the Parliamentary party, the contest is merely an annual formality with only one nomination.

**The Labour party**

The Labour party organisation is under the control of the General Secretary, who is the senior paid official responsible to the National Executive Committee which is accountable in its turn to the annual party Conference. In view of the dual hierarchy in the party, the Leader of the party and his senior Parliamentary colleagues can be at odds over matters of policy and procedure with prominent members of the National Executive Committee who are often back-bench MPs of a more radical disposition elected to the NEC by the constituency Labour parties.

The staff at Labour party headquarters, including the Research Department, are responsible to the General Secretary. They perform a range of support functions similar to those performed by Conservative Central Office, but the main focus of their activity is upon serving the party in the country rather than the party in Parliament. The party Chairman, who can normally hold the office for one year only, is usually the member of the NEC with the longest, continuous membership of that body, in other words, the post is allocated on the basis of 'Buggins' turn'. He is responsible to the party as a whole rather than to the Leader of the party.

The Labour party Conference has always been a much more powerful gathering than its Conservative counterpart. Its claim to a real political role is based upon the fact that it is constitutionally the policy-making body of the party, while the party in Parliament is little more than the Parliamentary wing of the entire Labour movement.[12] The Conference is presided over by the Chairman of the party who is assisted by a Conference Arrangements Committee composed of representatives of all the main sections of the Labour movement. Out of a total notional party membership of about 7.2 million, a few of the largest affiliated trade unions wield enormous block votes at Conference. For example, the Transport and General Workers Union has about 1.2 million votes and the Amalgamated Union of Engineering Workers has about 840 000 votes.

Fig 5.2 *Labour party organisation*

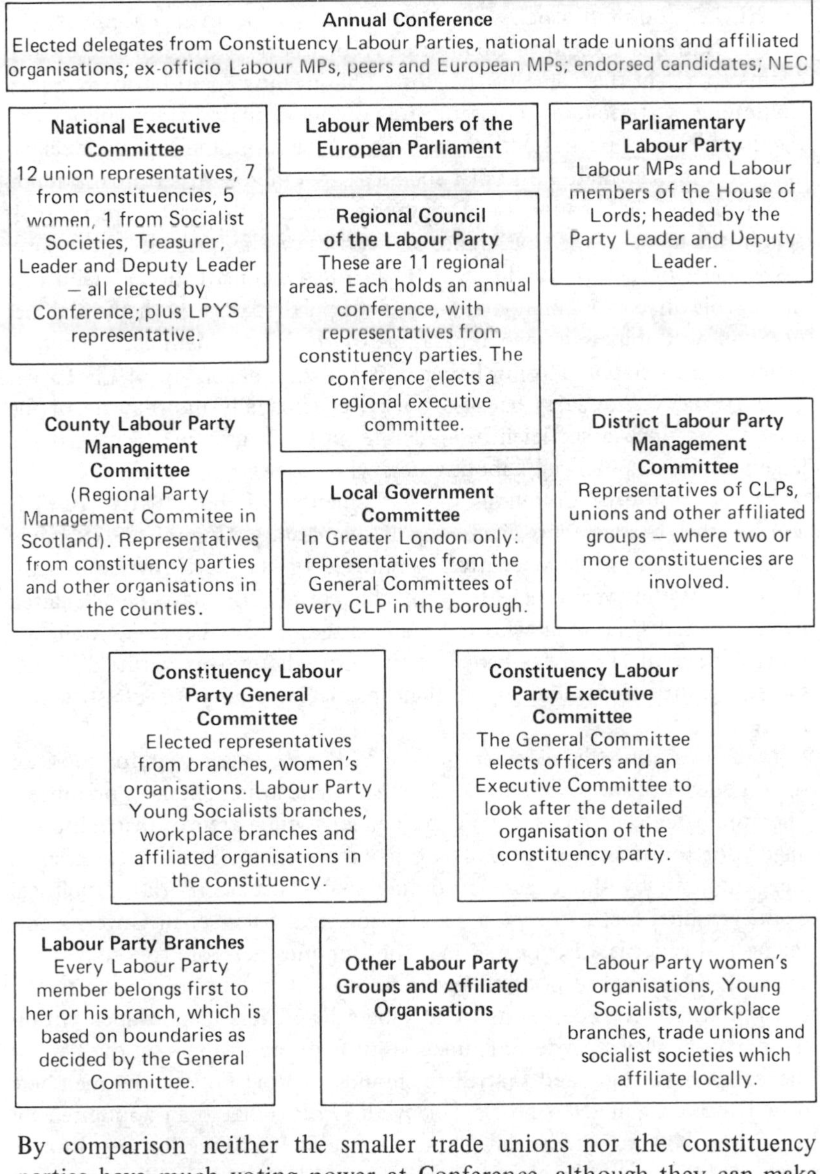


By comparison neither the smaller trade unions nor the constituency parties have much voting power at Conference, although they can make up for it to some extent with extra militancy. The Conference is composed of mandated delegations which are expected to vote in accordance with the decisions previously taken by the organisations which they represent. Members of Parliament can attend, but can vote only in the elections of Leader and Deputy Leader or if they are also delegates from other constituent bodies, such as affiliated trade unions. Unless they are members of the NEC they do not usually play a prominent part in the proceedings.

The National Executive Committee (NEC) is the powerful body which claims to act in the name of the entire Labour movement between annual Conferences. It includes representatives of the affiliated trade unions and the constituency parties and of the Women's Section, the Young Socialists and the other affiliated Socialist societies, together with automatic representation for the Leader, the Deputy Leader and the party Treasurer. It acts in the name of the Conference and carries on the business of the party from one Conference to the next. It also has a constitutional claim to a major role in party policy-making and to participation with the Cabinet or Shadow Cabinet in the preparation of the party Manifesto. There is therefore an inherent tension between it and the leadership of the Parliamentary party, not least because the latter is usually more aware of the need to produce a sufficiently moderate party programme to attract the large number of potential Labour voters who are not party zealots.

In the House of Commons the Parliamentary Labour Party (PLP) is led by the Leader who chairs the Parliamentary Committee (Shadow Cabinet) which is the executive committee of the party in Parliament. Since 1970 the weekly meetings of the entire PLP have been chaired by an elected Chairman who is usually a senior back-bencher. As in the Conservative party, back-benchers involve themselves with different subject groups depending upon their particular policy or constituency interests.

In Opposition, the members of the PLP vote every year for those of their colleagues who aspire to places on the Parliamentary Committee. The top fifteen are elected and the Leader is then free to distribute the major portfolios among them. The other more junior Shadow spokesmen are appointed by the Leader according to the usual criteria of political clout, personal merit or regional and ideological balance. In Government, the party Leader is, of course, Prime Minister and therefore free to allocate the real Ministerial responsibilities as he sees fit, subject of course to the usual political considerations of ideological and regional balance within the party. However, in recent times Tony Benn and others on the Left of the party have suggested that there should be provision for the members of a Labour Cabinet to be elected by the PLP rather than appointed by the Prime Minister of the day.[13] As a move in this direction provision is now made for all the elected members of the outgoing Parliamentary Committee to become members of the Cabinet automatically when the party moves from Opposition into Government.

From 1922 to 1980 the Leader of the party was elected exclusively by the PLP. However, after the 1979 General Election the Left of the party was successful in its long-standing campaign to take this power out of the exclusive hands of Labour MPs and following the agreement at Bishops Stortford in 1981 it was entrusted to an electoral college in which the three main sections of the movement are represented. Under these arrangements the affiliated trade unions have 40 per cent of the franchise, the PLP has 30 per cent and the constituency parties have 30 per cent. Candidates for the leadership must be MPs and their nominations must be supported by at least 5 per cent of their Parliamentary colleagues. Michael Foot was the last Leader of the party to be elected under the old arrangements in 1980 and Neil Kinnock the first to be elected under the new arrangements in 1983.

**Major party contrasts**

The organisation of each of the major parties reflects the contrast between the traditionally hierarchic principles of the Conservative party and the traditionally democratic aspirations of the Labour party. In the former case, this means that party decisions are normally taken expeditiously and implemented without undue difficulty. In the latter case, it means that the origins of party decisions are often blurred and the implementation sometimes challenged by those involved. In short, the Conservative party tends to be more amenable to firm leadership from the top, whereas the Labour party tends to be temperamentally and organisationally averse to it.

The problem for Labour is that it is very difficult adequately to control a party which serves a movement which aspires to be both ideological and democratic, although the ideology of democratic Socialism holds that there is no conflict between these two characteristics. The problems of the Conservatives have been more subtle, but just as real on occasions. In spite of their autocratic style and tradition, the management of the party has not been trouble-free. For example, exposure to the traditionally deferential party Conference can be an unpleasant and tricky ordeal for even the most experienced politicians when the representatives are baying for blood on some of the more atavistic issues, such as de-colonisation in the 1950s or law and order in the 1980s.

In the Conservative party effective power is wielded mainly by the Leader and to a lesser extent by the other senior Parliamentary figures. The extra-Parliamentary figures in the hierarchy of the National Union are frequently soothed with knighthoods rather than consulted on matters of policy and on the whole the voluntary side of the party knows its place in the scheme of things. Yet even a powerful Conservative leader cannot afford to ignore party opinion, since the activists can put pressure upon back-benchers who then feel obliged to lobby Ministers or shadow spokesmen. It has also been noticeable over the years that Conservative leaders seem to have been more vulnerable than their Labour counterparts to political 'assassination' when they fail to win elections or are directly involved in other political calamities for their party.

In the Labour party power has always been more diffused, since it has been shared at least since the adoption of the party constitution in 1918 between the PLP on the one hand and the trade unions and constituency parties operating through the party Conference on the other. This uneasy alliance has been balanced sometimes in favour of the NEC and sometimes in favour of the PLP. More recently, greater efforts have been made by the constituency parties to seize a larger share of power, to some extent encouraged by Tony Benn who sought to make them his own power-base within the Labour movement and to strengthen the NEC against the PLP. Power has tended to reside with the Parliamentary leadership more when Labour has been in Government and less when the party has been in Opposition. A great deal has depended upon the inclinations and ambitions of the leading figures in the movement at different times. Yet if a Labour leader is determined to assert his authority, he can still do so, provided he has the backing of the most powerful trade unions.

**The Liberal party**

The organisation of the Liberal party is essentially federal in that there are separate component parts for England, Wales, Scotland and Northern Ireland. The Liberal Assembly is composed of representatives from the constituencies, the Parliamentary party and the national organisation. It elects the Council which is a smaller body charged with handling the issues which arise between annual Assemblies. A standing committee of the Council provides liaison between the Parliamentary party and the constituencies. The party has a National Executive Committee on which are represented all the various sections of the party. This has certain powers of co-ordination, but not much more than that.

The process of party policy-making remains ultimately in the hands of the Leader of the party and his principal colleagues in Parliament. However, Liberal activists do generate a considerable number of policy proposals and produce a wide range of position papers which have to be taken into account by the leadership. National fund-raising, which has often been a problem for the Liberals, is the responsibility of a special Finance and Administration Board, although successive Leaders of the party have had to take a close interest in such matters as well. Since 1976 the party Leader has been elected by a special Convention of constituency representatives and others, with the former obliged to vote in accordance with the previously balloted views of the rank and file.

Fig 5.3 *Liberal party organisation*

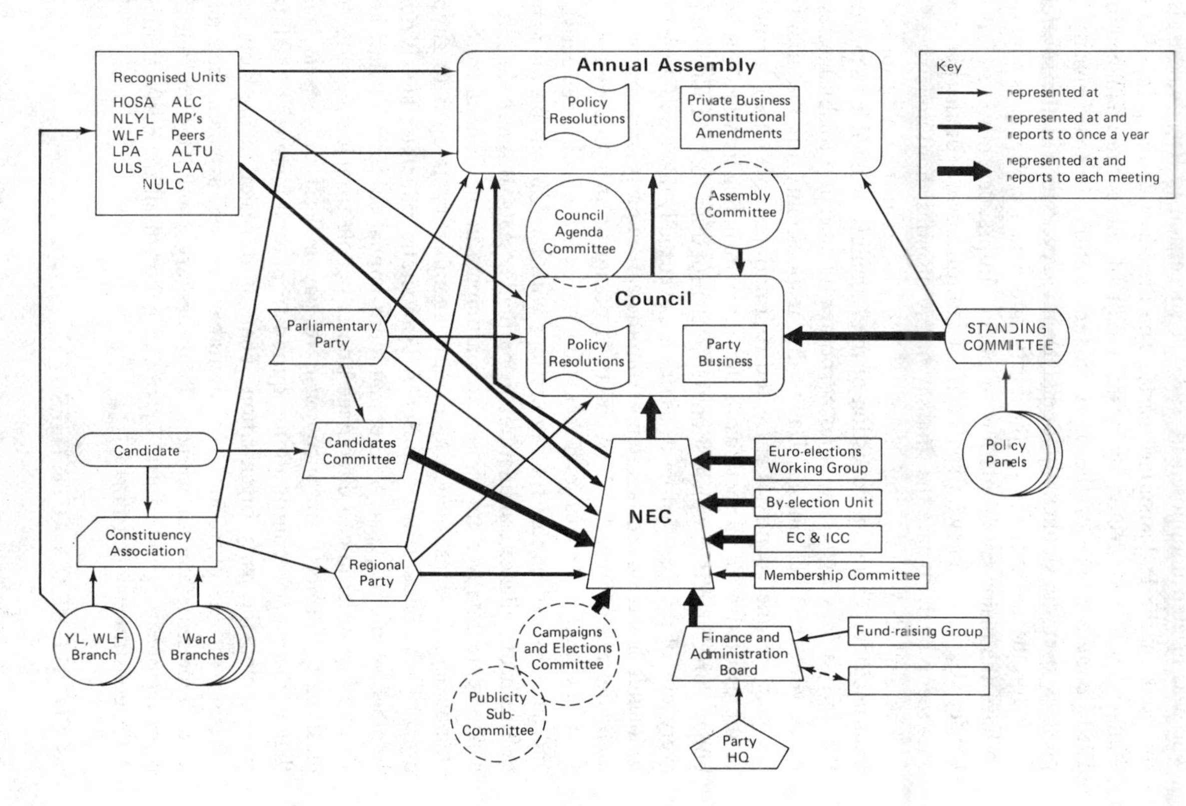

**The Social Democratic party**

The organisation of the Social Democratic party takes the form of two inter-connected political pyramids. The Leader of the party, David Owen, who was elected unopposed in 1983 in succession to Roy Jenkins, is at the apex of the Parliamentary party. The President of the party, Shirley Williams, who was elected by postal ballot of the entire membership in 1981, is at the apex of the party in the country. In that capacity she presides over the Council for Social Democracy, which is the sovereign body for the membership of the party and which in theory is supposed to have the major say on matters of policy. In practice, however, it is the Leader, David Owen, who speaks most authoritatively for the party and who seems likely to have the final say in any disputes about policy.

The annual Assembly of the party has powers of consultation rather than decision. There is no question of the Assembly being able to mandate the party's MPs and there is no corporate membership for businesses or block vote for trade unions. Day-to-day responsibility for the affairs of the party in the country is entrusted to a national committee composed of representatives of all sections of the party, including its MPs. This has a policy sub-committee which submits draft proposals for consideration at every level of the party before decisions are eventually taken about whether to include or exclude certain items from the agreed party programme.

Below the national level the party is organised at both area and constituency levels. The area level seeks to co-ordinate constituency activities and has been responsible for negotiations with the Liberals on the apportionment of Alliance candidatures in particular seats. It is also the level at which representatives are chosen to participate in the Council for Social Democracy. At constituency level party membership is open to anyone over 16 who is committed to Social Democratic principles and is not a member of another party. The minimum annual subscription has been set at £4 in order not to discourage poorer people from joining, although most party members are encouraged to pay at least £11 a year, since that is the average contribution required from each member to maintain and develop the party organisation. There is provision in the party constitution for the expulsion of undesirables, as well as guaranteed minimum representation for women. Parliamentary candidates are selected from regionally approved lists by postal ballot of all the party members in the constituency concerned.

## 5.4 CONSTITUENCY ACTIVITIES

It is when we consider the constituency activities of the parties that we notice more similarities than contrasts, in spite of the wide variety of people who are involved. For example, both major parties try to main-

Fig 5.4 *Social Democratic party organisation*

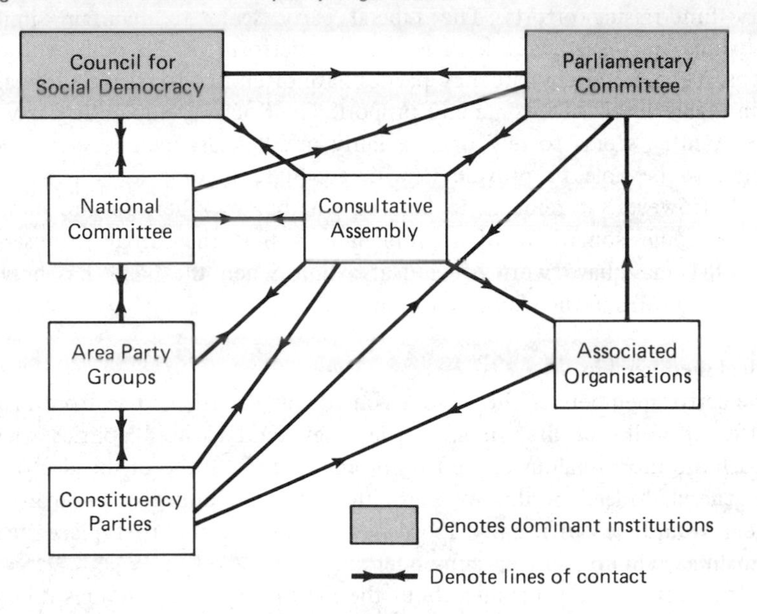


tain political activities in all the constituencies, except those in Northern Ireland. The Liberals and Social Democrats have not been so ambitious and have tended to concentrate their efforts in those constituencies where they already have strong local support or where the electoral prospects of the Alliance look quite good. Constituency organisations range in size from a few hundred members in some cases to more than 10 000 in the strongest areas of the major parties. In all cases they exist to serve the campaign and fund-raising purposes of the various parties and to enable them to contest both Parliamentary and local Council elections.

**Financial matters**

Unlike local party organisations in the United States, the various constituency parties in Britain try to remain solvent and operational throughout the periods between General Elections. They are assisted in doing this by the need to contest local elections at regular intervals and occasionally Parliamentary by-elections as well. Yet they really rely for their continued existence upon individual and corporate subscribers, and the voluntary efforts and local fund-raising activities of party workers.

In the Labour party, the constituency organisations receive considerable financial support from local trade union branches and in some cases individual MPs are sponsored and supported by particular trade unions. In the Conservative party, a considerable portion of the income at constituency level comes from local business and commercial interests, although the bulk of the money is raised from individual subscriptions and voluntary fund-raising efforts. The Liberal party seeks to maintain similar activities at constituency level in order to perform similar political functions. Yet Liberal constituency parties have often had to struggle to maintain viable levels of income and support. The Social Democratic party in the country seems to rely upon a fairly middle-class membership which ought to be able to provide it with adequate income at constituency level. However, it remains to be seen whether membership and money will become something of a problem now that the initial enthusiasm of 1981 may have worn off and at a time when the party has only a handful of MPs in the House of Commons.

**Local membership**

The active members of the various constituency parties come from many different walks of life. In all parties they tend to hold political views which are more zealous and uncompromising than those of the electorate in general. Indeed, if this were not the case, it is unlikely that many of them would be sufficiently motivated to join in the first place or to remain as paid-up members subsequently.

It is difficult to generalise about the local membership of constituency parties, since such a wide variety of people become involved at one time or another. Suffice it to say that the active members of Conservative constituency Associations often include middle-aged and elderly women, retired people, farmers, small businessmen and local traders. On the other hand, the active members of constituency Labour parties often include men rather than women, members of public sector trade unions, people involved in various cause groups and a number of more traditional supporters for whom involvement in Labour politics almost runs in the family. The active members of the Liberal and other parties tend to be drawn from a wider cross-section of the population and include many people who are not usually so closely identified with obvious class or economic interests. In the case of the Social Democrats, it appears that the constituency activists have been drawn to a considerable extent from the middle class and from the ranks of those who have not previously been active in party politics.

In the final analysis no generalisations about party membership are really satisfactory. All that can be said with any certainty is that the trends over many years have been characterised by a steady erosion of active support for each of the two major parties and by significantly changing social composition in each case. With regard to the former aspect, no one knows exactly how many paid-up members there are in either of the major parties. However, it has been estimated that the Conservative figure nationally may be about 1.5 million and the Labour figure about 300 000 (not including the block membership of those in affiliated trade unions which would raise the figure to a nominal 7 million or more). To get some idea of the decline in major party membership, these figures can be compared with the figures for 1953 when the national membership of the Conservative party was estimated to be about 2.8 million and that of the Labour party to be about 1 million on the same basis. As for the latter aspect of changing social composition, it is noticeable that over the last decade or so the Conservative party has become more classless at constituency level and less dominated by traditional middle-class people, while the Labour party in the constituencies has come to include more of what has been described as 'the professional Left', in other words younger, middle-class people drawn principally from public sector organisations and white-collar trade unions. It remains to be seen whether these social changes will leave permanent marks upon the character of the major parties.

**Political power**

In so far as members of constituency parties exercise effective political power, they do so mainly through their right to select and re-select Parliamentary and local government candidates. Labour activists probably have greater power than this, since they now have a 30 per cent share in the electoral college which chooses the party leader. It would also be true to say that in all the political parties, save the Conservative party, there is constitutional provision for ordinary party members to have real influence over party policy-making. However, in the Social Democractic party it is not clear whether things will work out like this in due course.

In the Conservative party the key constituency bodies are the Executive Councils of perhaps thirty to eighty members, composed partly of Association Officers (that is, Chairman, Vice-Chairmen, Treasurer, etc) but mostly of representatives from the various wards in the constituency. In the Labour party the key constituency bodies are the General Management Committees which are composed in the same sort of way, but which are usually somewhat smaller. In such gatherings local party activists can have direct and significant influence upon the political process, especially in the Labour party with its procedures for sending resolutions to the annual party Conference where they can become agreed party policy. In view of the fact that roughly two-thirds of all the seats in the Commons have been considered 'safe' in the post-war period for one or other of the two major parties, the power to select candidates has usually amounted to the ability to determine the choice of MPs in many parts of the country. This has been the real foundation of political power at constituency level and it has had to be taken very seriously by MPs and candidates, especially in the Labour party with its procedures for mandatory re-selection.

**Candidate selection**

In each of the major parties the candidates for Parliament chosen by the 'selectorates' have tended to be rather different both from the groups which select them and from the electorate as a whole. There has been a tendency over the years for social convergence between the Parliamentary candidates of the two major parties. This has often meant the selection of middle-aged, middle-class men with families in preference to women, blue-collar workers or people from the ethnic minorities.

However, it has become increasingly necessary to qualify this overall description. In the Conservative party there is nowadays a wider variety of candidates for Parliament. Although the privileged origins of some Conservative aspirants remain very noticeable, there has also been a growing number of self-made men and a few women who have managed to fight their way into Parliament. In the Labour party the changes have gone even further in recent years. Nowadays more Labour candidates are being selected from the ranks of the 'talking classes' in white-collar and public-sector occupations to the exclusion of many of the more traditional types from the old-fashioned working class. This has coincided with a marked shift towards more radical attitudes in constituency Labour parties which now put a greater emphasis upon the selection of candidates who are eager to carry out the wishes of the party activists.

The position is rather different in the Liberal and Social Democratic parties. The Liberal party has traditionally attracted men and women of broadly liberal outlook who wish to see the liberal point of view reflected in public policy. It has not, however, laid great insistence upon strict adherence to party orthodoxy, although in recent years the activists seem to have become conspicuously more zealous as has happened in the other parties. The Social Democratic party inevitably began by attracting into its ranks many who had little or no direct experience of party politics. Consequently many of its Parliamentary candidates do not belong to any of the familiar political stereotypes, even though its original founders – the so-called Gang of Four – were all former Labour Cabinet Ministers.

While the nature and strength of a candidate's commitment to his party's ideology seems to have become more important in determining his progress in nearly all parties, it is no longer usually the case that the wealth or family connections of an aspiring candidate has much bearing upon his chances of success at constituency level. Since the late 1940s all parties have set low limits on the personal donations which candidates or MPs may make to their constituency parties, so it is no longer possible to purchase a nomination as it used to be in the Conservative party before the war. However, some candidates still have a better chance of success than others, especially at by-elections and in competition for the safest seats.

In the Labour party, candidates seeking selection have to be nominated by at least one branch of the constituency party, a process which can often be strongly influenced by the affiliated trade union with the largest representation in the locality. At national level there are two lists of Parliamentary candidates which are kept at party headquarters in London following endorsement of the names by the NEC. List *A* is made up of trade-union-sponsored candidates and List *B* of the rest. On the whole those on List *A* have more success in securing candidatures, although it is noticeable that less than half (47 per cent) of those elected to Parliament in June 1983 were trade-union sponsored, which suggests that they may not do quite so well in the competition for safe Labour seats. Moreover, many candidates who emerge as 'favourite sons' of their constituency parties do not appear on either of the national lists, but nevertheless usually have to be endorsed by the NEC if they are selected.[14]

In the Conservative party, there is also a list of approved Parliamentary candidates which is kept centrally at party headquarters in London. In order to get on this list aspirants have to go through a complicated process of written submissions and personal interviews, as well as a subsequent assessment process. In some cases these stages can prove more difficult than the later appearances before constituency selection committees. Furthermore, each constituency Association has the unfettered right to select anyone it likes, even if the person concerned is not on the centrally-approved list of Parliamentary candidates at the time.

Initially, the Liberals and Social Democrats faced special problems in their candidate selections, since they had to agree upon who should be the standard-bearers for the Alliance in each of at least 600 constituencies in different parts of the country. At by-elections during the 1979–83 Parliament they tended to proceed on a basis of strict alternation between the two parties. Even so there were still some bitter squabbles in a few constituencies where the Liberals had been established as a local force for many years. Indeed, it looks as though similar difficulties could arise in future if the leadership of each party does not make strenuous efforts to sort out differences at local level.

## 5.5 CONCLUSION

While the two major parties differ quite considerably in their history, ideology and constituency membership, they are more similar in many other respects than some accounts have suggested. When in Opposition, each major party has tended to use a distinctive political language and to develop a distinctive political style in order to differentiate itself from the party in Government and often from its own record when previously in office. When in Government, each major party has traditionally behaved in a broadly responsible and moderate way and until recently each has pursued policies which belong within the framework of the post-war consensus. This has happened because both major parties have discovered (and sometimes had to rediscover) that public office is more likely to be gained from a platform of political moderation and more likely to be retained on the basis of a creditable record of economic and social achievement.

However, since the early 1970s there have been a number of significant developments in each of the major parties which have led them both to depart quite markedly from their previous adherence to the post-war consensus. The Labour party began to change significantly when in Opposition from 1970–4, as Tony Benn and others on the Left of the party began to denigrate the 1964–70 Labour Government for its failure to be sufficiently Socialist. The Conservative party began to change when in Opposition from 1974-9 as Sir Keith Joseph and Margaret Thatcher began to re-define the purposes and priorities of modern Conservatism in contradistinction to the policies pursued during the second half of the 1970–4 Conservative Government. As a consequence of these movements of opinion the ideological gap between the two major parties has become wider and the Alliance of Liberals and Social Democrats has sought to occupy the middle ground between the two.

In such circumstances there is likely to be considerable argument over the coming years about whether or not the two-party system in its present polarised form is beneficial to Britain. Certainly this is the major issue upon which the Alliance of Liberals and Social Democrats is likely to concentrate in its continuing efforts 'to break the mould of British politics'. On the other hand, it can be argued that it is the Labour and Conservative radicals who have really broken the mould by altering the ideological framework of the political battle in Britain.

Only the passage of time and the verdict of the voters will decide the outcome of this triangular struggle for power. Much will depend upon whether the so-called 'new realism' of the British people has changed some of the basic tenets and assumptions of British politics. Much will depend upon whether this change of attitudes proves to be temporary or permanent. Much will depend upon events and influences quite outside the control of politicians in all parties. Indeed, a durable or definitive picture may not be discernible for many years to come. Meanwhile we might do well to remember that in politics, as in life, the journey sometimes matters more than the destination.

## SUGGESTED QUESTIONS

1. For what principles does each of the British political parties stand in contemporary circumstances?

2. What are the main functions of the political parties in Britain?
3. Where does real power lie in either the Conservative party or the Labour party?

## NOTES

1. E. Burke, *Thoughts on the Cause of the Present Discontents* (London: Dodsley, 1770).
2. *The Times*, 26 November 1864.
3. See R. Eccleshall, 'English Conservatism as Ideology' in *Political Studies*, March 1977.
4. S. Beer, *Modern British Politics* (London: Faber, 1969), p. 247.
5. I. Gilmour, *Inside Right* (London: Quartet, 1978) p. 158.
6. S. Beer, *Modern British Politics*, p. 135.
7. The two main changes which have been pushed through by the Labour Left since 1979 are mandatory re-selection of sitting MPs and election of the Leader and Deputy Leader by an electoral college of the trade unions (40 per cent), the PLP (30 per cent) and the constituency parties (30 per cent). The further attempt to alter the 1918 constitutional arrangement whereby the Parlimentary leadership and the NEC jointly prepare the Manifesto and to vest sole authority for this in the NEC was rejected by the party at the Wembley Conference in 1980.
8. See the Statement of Principles published jointly by the Liberal and Social Democratic parties in *The Times*, 17 June 1981.
9. The elections to the Northern Ireland Assembly took place on 21 October 1982 and resulted in twenty-six seats for the Official Unionists, twenty-one for the Democratic Unionists, fourteen for the SDLP, ten for the Alliance party and five for Provisional Sinn Fein. Since then the SDLP and the Provisional Sinn Fein have refused to take their seats and following a terrorist attack on a Protestant congregation at a Pentecostal church in Armagh in November 1983, the Official Unionists voted to withdraw from the Assembly in protest.
10. R. T. McKenzie, *British Political Parties*, 2nd edn (London: Heinemann, 1963) p. 645.
11. See the Report of the Committee on Financial Aid to Political Parties, Cmnd 6601 (London: HMSO, 1976).
12. For further discussion of this subject see L. Minkin, *The Labour Party Conference* (Manchester: Manchester University Press, 1980).
13. See T. Benn: 'The case for a constitutional Premiership' in *Parliamentary Affairs*, Winter 1980.
14. Under the Labour party constitution it is also possible for the NEC to reject candidates selected by the constituency parties. For example, this happened in 1981 in Bermondsey in the case of Peter Tatchell, a Left-winger who was selected by the constituency party to succeed Bob Mellish, the retiring Labour MP. This led to a second selection process the following year when Peter Tatchell was again selected by the constituency party and on this occasion the NEC decided to acquiesce in their choice.

## FURTHER READING

Ball, A. R., *British Political Parties* (London: Macmillan, 1981).
Beer, S. H., *Modern British Politics* (London: Faber, 1969).
Benn, A., *Arguments for Socialism* (Harmondsworth: Penguin, 1980).
Blondel, J., *Voters, Parties and Leaders* (Harmondsworth: Penguin, 1974).
Drucker, H. M. (ed.) *Multi-Party Britain* (London: Macmillan, 1979).
Finer, S. E., *The Changing British Party System* (Washington, DC: American Enterprise Institute, 1980).
Gilmour, I., *Inside Right* (London: Quartet, 1978).
McKenzie, R. T., *British Political Parties*, 2nd edn (London: Heinemann, 1963).
Miller, W. L., *The End of British Politics?* (Oxford: Clarendon Press, 1981).
Rose, R., *The Problem of Party Government* (London: Macmillan, 1974).
Rose, R., *Do Parties Make a Difference?* (London: Macmillan, 1980).
Williams, S., *Politics is for People* (Harmondsworth: Penguin, 1981).

# CHAPTER 6

# PRESSURE GROUPS

In the British context pressure groups have been defined in a number of different ways. W. J. M. Mackenzie defined them as 'organised groups possessing both formal structure and real common interests in so far as they influence the decisions of public bodies'.[1] Moodie and Studdert-Kennedy defined them as 'any organised group which attempts to influence Government decisions without seeking itself to exercise the formal powers of Government'.[2] Samuel Finer defined them as 'organisations . . . trying to influence the policy of public bodies in their own chosen direction, though never themselves prepared to undertake the direct government of the country'.[3]

The expression 'pressure group' is a comprehensive term which subsumes both sectional interest groups and more widely-based cause groups. The former are usually well-established groups defending a vested interest through close and continuous contacts with Whitehall and Westminster. The latter tend to be more ephemeral organisations which rely for success principally upon securing sufficient media coverage sympathetic to their cause.

The term presupposes that all pressure groups are promotional in the sense that they seek to promote their various objectives in the most effective possible ways. It also implies that they are irresponsible in the sense that they are not democratically accountable to the general public. It is the political parties which have to accept that democratic responsibility and which are vulnerable to the verdict of the electorate at every General Election.

## 6.1 MAIN FUNCTIONS

In looking at the main functions of pressure groups it is necessary to distinguish clearly between interest and cause groups. The former tend to be more defensive in their functions and to be more closely involved with the institutions of central Government. The latter tend to rely to a greater extent upon the use of media publicity and to fight their battles as institutional outsiders. In practice, of course, there is considerable overlap between the two types and some pressure groups find a place in both categories.

**Interest groups**

In the contemporary British context interest groups have a number of main functions. Firstly, they act as intermediaries between Government and the public. This is a role which has become more important as the scope and complexity of politics has increased and as it has become more difficult for the political parties on their own to perform all the representative functions. This means that they act as spokesmen and negotiators on behalf of clearly-defined sectional interests, for example, the National Farmers Union on behalf of farmers or the British Medical Association on behalf of doctors. It also means that they help all Governments to develop and implement their policies by entering into detailed consultations on proposals for administrative action or draft legislation and subsequently by delivering a measure of public consent to the output of the policy- and decision-making process, for example, the influence of Shelter upon housing legislation, the Child Poverty Action Group upon measures to help families with children, or the Magistrates Association upon the development of the criminal law.

Secondly, they act as opponents and critics of all Governments on behalf of the interests which they claim to represent, such as the National Federation of the Self-Employed on behalf of independent businessmen or the Building Societies Association on behalf of all who save with them or borrow from them. In this respect some people might argue that they are duplicating or even usurping the rightful role of the political parties. Yet that is really too stuffy a view of our modern pluralist democracy. As Robert McKenzie pointed out 'the voters undertake to do far more than select their elected representatives; they also insist on their right to advise, cajole and warn them regarding the policies which they should adopt and they do this for the most part through the pressure group system.'[4]

Thirdly, they act as extensions or agents of Government. This is a role which has grown in importance whenever the tendency towards corporatism has grown in our society.[5] For example, the British Medical Association has a number of expert and advisory functions under the auspices of the 1946 National Health Service Act. The National Farmers Union has a number of similar functions under the auspices of the 1947 and 1957 Agriculture Acts. The Law Society is responsible for administering the system of state-financed legal aid. However, perhaps the most familiar example of corporatism, especially under Labour Governments, has been the prominent role played by the Confederation of British Industry (CBI) and the Trades Union Congress (TUC) both as economic interest groups and as virtually obligatory partners with Government in nearly all matters to do with the management of the economy, for instance, the special employment and training measures administered by the Manpower Services Commission or the regulations made by the Health and Safety Executive under the auspices of the 1974 Health and Safety at Work Act.

Fourthly, they may act occasionally as substitutes for or outright opponents of Government itself. This is a very rare occurrence in Britain and it is not a role which even the most powerful groups are keen to play. If it happens, it has usually been preceded either by a breakdown of Government authority in certain areas or by the deliberate implementation of some form of syndicalism.[6] To some extent the former conditions applied in certain circumstances during the extensive trade union disruption which took place in the public services during the winter of 1979. The latter conditions applied on a local scale during the time of the Meriden Co-operative in the late 1970s when the workers themselves decided to take over and run their own motor-cycle factory in the Midlands.

**Cause groups**

The main function of any cause group is to publicise its cause in the best available ways in order to promote its particular point of view or to defend its particular interest. For example, the Campaign for Nuclear Disarmament (CND) has been very active in recent years in its efforts to secure media coverage and publicity for its cause of unilateral nuclear disarmament in Britain as an example to the rest of the world. It has sought to do this by organising public meetings, mass demonstrations and other carefully planned media events, as well as by producing a wide range of campaign literature and propaganda material. Equally, some environmental groups, such as Friends of the Earth and Greenpeace, have used similar techniques in their successful campaigns, for example, for the introduction of returnable bottles or the preservation of rare animal species.

In nearly all cases the most familiar and successful technique of cause groups involves the staging of media events to attract initial publicity and then further steps to capitalise upon the public attention thus gained by advancing persuasive arguments in suitable supporting material. The publicity techniques may involve an unlikely combination of endorsement by show-business personalities and follow-up with detailed and well-researched arguments. Sometimes those concerned even go so far as to undertake difficult or dangerous adventures in order to capture media attention for their cause, for example, the Greenpeace campaigns to save whales and seals by sailing small boats into the hunting areas in order to disrupt the whale hunts or the seal culls to which they objected. The media coverage achieved for campaigns of this kind is not an end in itself, but rather a means of getting such issues onto the political agenda and of putting pressure on the politicians to take appropriate action. Some other cause groups are essentially defensive, for instance, the Wing Airport Resistance Association which helped to prevent the siting of a third London airport at Cublington in Buckinghamshire or the M23 Action Group which helped to persuade the Government to drop its plans to extend that particular motorway through residential Wallington in south London.

## 6.2 ORGANISATION AND POWER

Pressure groups in Britain are organised in almost as many ways as there are different groups. The pattern of organisation which evolves and the degree of power which can be exerted depends upon a number of different factors. It is therefore worth considering the various aspects in turn.

### Nature and scope of membership

When the interests of the membership are immediate and material, a group will usually reflect them and concentrate most of its resources upon defending them by whatever means are most effective. For example, the National Union of Mineworkers (NUM) has proved its ability over the years to exploit both the strength of its organisation and the concentration of its interest as a way of gaining substantial material rewards for its members. The result has been that the miners have managed to stay consistently at or near the top of the league table of industrial earnings and all Governments have treated them with wary respect.

On the other hand, when the interests of the membership are diffuse and disaggregated, a group will usually find it difficult to secure substantial material advantages for its members. For example, the Consumers Association, which has a paid-up membership equivalent to a mere 3 per cent of all families in the country, has proved rather ineffective as a defensive or promotional organisation.

The power of a group therefore depends to a considerable extent upon both the coverage and the cohesion of its membership. If a group has a clear identity and purpose and if it manages to attract into its membership a high proportion of those eligible to join, it has good coverage and is likely to be effective in defence of its members' interests. For example, this has been borne out by the British Medical Association (BMA) and the National Union of Mineworkers (NUM) over the years, since over 80 per cent of all doctors are members of the BMA and over 90 per cent of all miners are members of the NUM. Such impressive coverage has contributed greatly to the power of both groups over many years.

On the other hand, if a group seeks to represent a wide range of different interests, it has little cohesion and is likely to be rather ineffective in defence of its members' interests, unless there are other powerful factors working in a positive direction. For example, neither the Trade Union Congress (TUC), which seeks to represent more than 100 affiliated trade unions and about 10 million individual trade unionists, nor the Confederation of British Industry (CBI), which seeks to do the same for more than 5000 subscribing companies and about 300 employers' associations, can be really effective on behalf of its members, since the need to be inclusive weakens the cohesion and hence the effectiveness of each organisation. The TUC has the added problem that the membership of trade unions has declined by about 2 million overall during the recent economic recession, while the CBI has the added difficulty of trying to represent employers both large and small, and in both the public and private sectors. For these reasons neither organisation is as powerful or effective as it might have been in different circumstances.

**Loyalty of the rank and file**

The degree of loyalty shown by the rank and file towards their leaders and spokesmen is another aspect of the power or weakness of any group. Certainly such loyalty cannot be taken for granted in an age of declining deference. However, in most circumstances the leaders of a pressure group have more scope for initiative if they are in the job for life and not subject to periodic recall or re-election, an advantage enjoyed by the President of the National Union of Mineworkers (NUM) and the General Secretary of the General and Municipal Workers Union (GMWU). It is also the case that the leadership enjoys more latitude if the material interests of the rank and file are not directly threatened by any initiatives proposed. For example, leadership advocacy of an embargo on the sale of equipment to South Africa will be tolerated and may even be supported as long as the members of the group concerned have no material interest which would be threatened by such a move.

On the other hand, when the activities of pressure group leaders seem likely to prejudice the material interests of the ordinary members, the rank and file are quite likely to reject the lead which is given. For example, Clive Jenkins, who is General Secretary of the Association of Scientific, Technical and Managerial Staffs (ASTMS), has been allowed to indulge in Left-wing political posturing on virtually any issue except the idea of nationalising the banks and insurance companies, since that would pose a direct threat to the jobs of many of his members. Equally, Arthur Scargill, who is President of the National Union of Mineworkers (NUM), was opposed by a majority of his own members when he was precipitate in seeking their endorsement for a political campaign of industrial action against the 1979–83 Conservative Government, since at that time most ordinary miners were more interested in the continuity of their pay and the security of their employment.[7]

**Political leverage**

The power of pressure groups also depends upon the degree of political leverage which they can exert. If a group is in a position to exert significant leverage, it can be truly formidable. Such leverage often takes the form of an ability to deny to the rest of society the provision of goods or services which the community cannot easily do without and which others are not able to supply. For example, power-station workers or air-traffic controllers can be in such a position, as can computer operators in the civil service or safety workers in the water authorities. Currency speculators and company treasurers can also wield a degree of financial power and influence which amounts to a kind of political leverage.

Such leverage on its own may not necessarily be sufficient for the attainment of a pressure group's aims without the support of other attributes of group power, such as civil service contacts, the ability to attract favourable publicity and financial or electoral power. Yet it can achieve a great deal in our complex modern society in which some groups can sometimes be in a position to hold the rest of the community to ransom. Only very rarely does it consist in the ability to create completely new balances of power in society which allow one particular group or interest to coerce everyone else. On such occasions the Government of the day may have to use the full powers of the modern state – for instance, military units or special security squads – in order to counter one brand of ruthlessness with another. No system of government can afford to tolerate, still less allow itself to be defeated, by groups using the sort of leverage through violence which is the stock-in-trade of some ruthless groups in the world today.

**Civil service contacts**

The strength and frequency of contacts with the civil service is another aspect of the power and influence of groups. As J. J. Richardson and A. G. Jordan have pointed out, 'it is the relationships involved in committees, the policy community of Departments and groups, the practices of co-option and the consensual state which account better for policy outcomes than examinations of party stances, manifestos or Parliamentary influence.'[8]

On the whole established groups prefer to have a continuous, quiet influence upon the process of government rather than an intermittent and noisy relationship based upon the use of media publicity and the staging of public demonstrations. Widely-publicised campaigns are something of a last resort for groups which normally succeed in keeping in close touch with the civil service and the rest of the policy-making community. They use their reliable and frequent contacts with Whitehall and the expertise of their own professional staff to influence Ministerial decisions and the detailed content of legislation.

In many cases they secure official representation on advisory committees established within the orbits of particular Departments and in this way support and monitor the detailed implementation of public policy. This gives them extra status and recognition in Whitehall, rights of access to Ministers when the need arises and opportunities for consultation and influence not available to others outside the charmed circle of approved consultative arrangements in central Government. For example, the National Farmers Union (NFU) has been deeply involved in the development and application of British agricultural policy ever since the 1947 Agriculture Act gave it statutory consultative rights. Equally, the Confederation of British Industry (CBI) and the Trade Union Congress (TUC) have both managed to establish the convention that they should be widely and frequently consulted by central Government on all matters of direct interest to them.

Obviously, the nature and extent of such consultation has varied from time to time and from Government to Government, depending upon the priorities and prejudices of the Ministers concerned. However, at least since the establishment of the National Economic Development Council (NEDDY in popular parlance) in 1962, it has been generally accepted practice that what are called 'the two sides of industry' should be consulted by Government on a frequent and extensive basis. Many of these consultations have been formalised within the NEDDY framework and have taken place within a large number of sector working parties. Other contacts take place directly between central Government Departments and the officials of the CBI and TUC respectively. Such habitual consultation has been an important element of the policy and decision-making process, although it seems to be temporarily out of favour with the present Conservative Government.

**Publicity value**

The publicity value of the causes espoused by different pressure groups is another factor which influences the success or failure of such organisations. For example, the favourable publicity secured by Age Concern in its campaign in the 1970s to get a better financial deal for pensioners was clearly beneficial to that particular cause. Equally, the publicity habitually secured by the Child Poverty Action Group for poor families or by Shelter for the homeless has proved beneficial to those particular sections of society.

On the other hand, the publicity secured by the Campaign for Nuclear Disarmament (CND) in the late 1950s and early 1960s had little effect upon public policy at the time other than to harden the resolve of the then Conservative Government to oppose such a policy. In general, the publicity gained by such groups for their causes depends upon the spirit of the times as much as their technical skill in using the media to their own advantage. Thus the public demonstrations and other media events organised by CND and other 'peace groups' in the early 1980s seem to have had more effect than the Aldermarston marches of the 1950s, perhaps because the general public is now more alarmed by the dangers of nuclear war. Yet it still remains to be seen whether any such campaigns by pressure groups will alter Government policy to any significant extent.

**Financial power**

The mere possession of wealth and financial power cannot buy success in pressure-group politics, although it obviously helps to pay the bills and routine expenses. An examination of the available evidence suggests that there is no reason to suppose that even the most lavishly funded campaigns will achieve their objectives simply because they can out-spend their opponents. This may be because of the impartiality and probity of the British civil service or because of the way in which the British party system shelters politicians from the full force of group pressures. Whatever the reasons, it is difficult to point clearly to occasions when money on its own has bought success for pressure groups.

For example, there is no conclusive evidence that the expensive 'Mr Cube' campaign of Tate & Lyle and others against the proposed nationalisation of the sugar refining industry in the late 1940s had any decisive influence upon the subsequent decision of the Labour Government not to proceed with such a policy after the 1950 General Election. Similarly, there is no conclusive evidence that the 'Keep Britain In' campaign of the European Movement in the early 1970s had any decisive effect upon the way in which the British people voted in the 1975 Referendum on EEC membership. However, it does seem that the coalition of political authority represented by the leading personalities of the pro-European campaign did have some positive impact upon the result, since their public reputations then compared favourably with those of the leading personalities on the other side of the argument.

**Voting power**

As for the power of groups to deliver votes at elections, British history has shown that the pull of party consistently triumphs over the pull of groups.

Ever since the emergence of recognisably modern political parties during the last quarter of the nineteenth century, the nature of our electoral system and the strong influence of party discipline has left all groups with a poor chance of striking any effective political bargains with individual Members of Parliament or Parliamentary candidates. Yet this is not to say that it is impossible for certain influential groups to exercise some influence upon the parties, especially parties in Opposition when they are unshielded by civil service advice.

Unlike in the United States, individual politicians in Britain do not have to construct precarious coalitions of electoral support by seeking to appeal directly to every powerful interest or cause group in their constituencies. If their party has been in office, they merely need to concentrate upon presenting the record of their party in the most favourable light. If their party has been in opposition, they merely need to demonstrate how bad things have been under the stewardship of their opponents and how they could do better in future. Yet this is not to say that even in the hey-day of two-party dominance it was ever sensible for a prudent politician to ignore the pressure of any group which was notably active in his constituency.

Of course, there remains the special case of trade union influence upon the Labour party.[9] This stems from the fact that the creation of the Labour party at the turn of the century was largely the work of the trade unions and ever since that time trade union influence within the wider Labour movement has been always significant and occasionally decisive. Yet no matter how close and crucial this relationship may have been over the years, it is unwise to generalise from it when assessing the role of all other pressure groups in the British political system.

## 6.3 INVOLVEMENT IN POLITICS

Since the British political system is pluralistic, liberal and democratic, it affords many opportunities for the involvement of pressure groups at every stage of the policy- and decision-making process.[10] Indeed, it is impossible fully to describe the activities of Whitehall and Westminster without giving an adequate account of the part played by pressure groups. They have become inevitable and even desirable participants in the procedures of official consultation and as such they contribute to the building of public consent for the acts of Government. Their involvement in the policy- and decision-making process is shown diagrammatically in Fig. 6.1.

### Policy-germination

At the initial stage of policy-germination the main role of pressure groups is to identify problems and to get issues onto the political agenda. This is something which they can do rather well and which they are sometimes

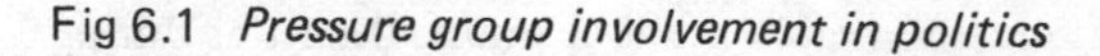
Fig 6.1 *Pressure group involvement in politics*

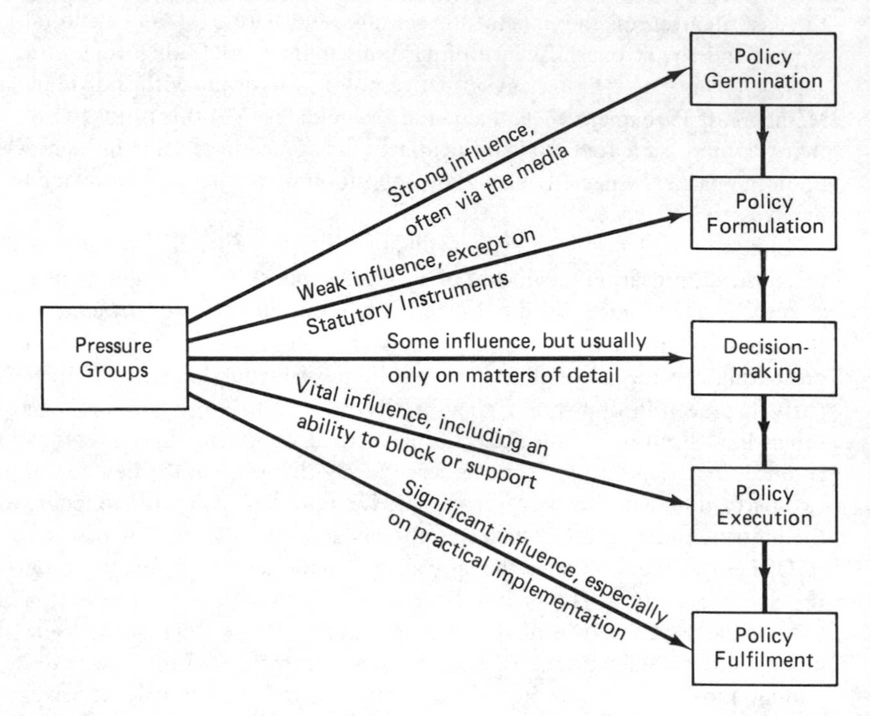


encouraged to do by Government Departments. This is because the latter often prefer to appear to be responding to external pressures rather than taking initiatives on their own account. For example, the National Society for Clean Air (previously the Smoke Abatement Society) was to a considerable extent instrumental in getting the problem of air pollution onto the political agenda in the 1950s. It then conducted a sustained campaign of publicity and persuasion which helped to bring about the passage of the Clean Air Act in 1956.

In playing their part at this early stage of the policy- and decision-making process, pressure groups depend very heavily upon their ability to excite the interest of the media. Without such media assistance many of their campaigns would never get off the ground at all. For example, the creation of the Department of the Environment in 1970 was to a considerable extent a political response to the pressures exerted over many years by the Conservation Society and other environmental groups. It was also a response to the general public interest in environmental matters which later found expression at the 1972 Stockholm Conference.

Pressure groups also need to persuade influential politicians of the good sense and timeliness of their particular causes. For example, the Road

Haulage Association (RHA) worked very closely with leading figures in the Conservative party when the latter were in Opposition between 1945 and 1951 and was able to persuade them of the case for the de-nationalisation of its industry. The result of this pressure was seen in the partial de-nationalisation of the industry by the Conservative Government soon after its victory at the 1951 General Election.

When pressure groups wish to get issues onto the political agenda of the Government of the day, the most effective approach is usually to persuade officials in the relevant Whitehall Department to take notice of a particular problem and then to follow up with expert and detailed advice, preferably including proposed solutions which would be both practicable and relatively non-controversial. A notably successful practitioner of this technique has been the National Farmers Union (NFU) which over the years from the 1947 Agriculture Act at least until British entry into the European Community in 1973 enjoyed an exclusive and almost symbiotic relationship with the Ministry of Agriculture. This relationship influenced the outcome of every annual farm price review and is also credited with having given rise to the 1957 Agriculture Act. However, it has subsequently made it more difficult for successive Ministers of Agriculture to embark upon new policy departures for environmental or other purposes.

**Policy-formulation**

Pressure groups also have influence, but not such an important role at the stage of policy-formulation. When a political party is in Opposition, policy formulation is mainly the work of its leading personalities who are assisted by officials from the party organisation. When a party is in Government, it is mainly the work of civil servants in the Departments concerned. Yet in both cases those who formulate policy are likely to consult pressure groups, provided the latter can be trusted to preserve sufficient confidentiality and are able to offer sufficiently expert advice and information.

The role of groups is especially significant when a policy is formulated with a view to the introduction of new legislation. For example, the Town and Country Planning Association has made various representations over the years and some of its ideas have been incorporated in legislation affecting the operation of the planning system. Equally, the Society of Conservative Lawyers had some real influence upon the policy formulated by the Conservative party in Opposition during the late 1970s which led to the subsequent passage through Parliament of the 1981 British Nationality Act. There is therefore a role for pressure groups at the stage of policy-formulation.

**Decision-making**

In a strict sense pressure groups have no direct involvement at the decision-making stage of the political process, since this is a matter essentially for elected politicians. Yet even such an apparently clear-cut statement does not fully reflect the various ways in which political decisions are actually taken in modern Britain. For example, many Ministerial decisions are really taken by civil servants acting in the name of Ministers, notably in the detailed and complex area of delegated legislation. Groups with the necessary expertise and access to officials can play an influential part in this aspect of decision-making. Examples can be found in the close and effective contacts between the Law Society and the Lord Chancellor's Department, the Building Societies Association and the Department of the Environment or the British Medical Association and the Department of Health and Social Security.

In so far as the introduction of new legislation also involves important decision-making of a kind, pressure groups play an influential part in that stage of the political process as well. For example, the 1982 Criminal Justice Act was influenced at least in important matters of detail by the persistent representations made during the committee stage by groups such as the Magistrates Association or the National Association for the Care and Resettlement of Offenders. Similarly, the Finance Bills, which pass through Parliament every year and which often contain legislative changes of considerable importance, can be influenced in matters of detail by pressure groups with interests to defend or causes to advance. In these various ways groups are involved to some extent at the decision-making stage.

**Policy-execution**

The real test of effective power for all modern Governments is whether or not they manage to execute their policies. Ministerial decisions or Acts of Parliament are not worth much more than the paper on which they are printed if they cannot be implemented in practice.

This is the stage at which the involvement of groups can be absolutely vital, since their active co-operation or passive acquiescence is often a condition of the satisfactory execution of policy. For example, in 1977 the National Union of Teachers refused to co-operate with the Labour Government when it sought answers to a questionnaire on aspects of the school curriculum from all local education authorities in England and Wales. Similarly, in 1981 the National Union of Mineworkers refused to accept the proposed closure of certain uneconomic pits which the National Coal Board had felt obliged to propose in order to stay within the financial limits set by the Conservative Government. In both cases group acquiescence in Government policy was a vital condition of policy execution. In the latter case, however, the Government of the day was eventually obliged to change its policy by increasing the cash limits on the National Coal Board by about £200 million in order to accommodate the extra cost of keeping open the uneconomic pits which had been scheduled for closure.

Formidable blocking power is also available to civil servants. If senior civil servants wish to delay or block the decisions of Ministers, there are many ways in which they can do so. The most gentle technique is simply to go slowly in the administrative implementation of Ministerial decisions. Another is to suggest further consultations on the detailed implementation of policy with the groups most directly affected. More drastic still is the tactic of deliberate non-co-operation which was practised in many parts of the public administration during the long civil service dispute in 1981. This did considerable damage to the efficiency of government and led to long delays in the collection of certain forms of public revenue.

Such examples emphasise the key point that one of the main tasks of Ministers and other decision-makers in the political process is to define the limits of what is 'politically possible' in a given situation at a given time. In making such definitions stick it is clear that the co-operation of pressure groups is an asset and their non-co-operation a serious liability in the execution of policy by any Government.

**Policy-fulfilment**

A similar point can be made about the stage of policy fulfilment in that few policies of central Government can be brought to fruition without the active co-operation or at least the passive acquiescence of the pressure groups most directly affected. Ministers and civil servants would commit serious mistakes if they were ever tempted to equate the political process solely with what happens in Whitehall and Westminster. In modern political conditions there are many external factors which can influence the success or failure of a given policy - for example, the effect of the world-wide commodity price increases in 1972-3 upon the counter-inflation policies of the 1970-4 Conservative Government, or the effect of the huge American deficit upon interest rates in the United States and elsewhere and hence upon the prospects for sustained economic recovery in Britain today. Such examples may appear to extend the scope of the present discussion beyond the sphere of conventional pressure groups. Yet it is undeniable that in our interdependent world political issues need to be considered in their wider context if we are to take full account of all the limitations upon modern Government.

Politicians may imagine, especially when they have been recently returned to office with what they regard as a clear electoral mandate to carry out their policies, that they have become the undisputed masters of the political scene. Yet they would do well to remember that in modern political conditions they are bound to depend upon the co-operation of pressure groups and the influence of other external forces for the fulfilment of their policies.

## 6.4 CONCLUSION

There are reasons for regarding the activities of pressure groups as broadly beneficial to the British political system and other reasons for regarding them as rather harmful. On the positive side, there are at least four points which can be made. Firstly, they can provide the Government of the day with expert information and advice which would not necessarily be available from other sources. Secondly, they can provide frameworks for public participation in the political process between General Elections by all who are unwilling or unable to channel their energies through one of the political parties. Thirdly, they help to define and focus public attention upon issues which may not be ripe for decision but which need nevertheless to be placed on the political agenda. Fourthly, they can provide a form of institutional ratification and public consent for the actions of Government which can assist Ministers in the difficult tasks of policy-execution and fulfilment.

On the negative side, there are at least three reasons for regarding pressure groups with suspicion if not distaste. Firstly, they tend to give too much weight in the political process to the importance of the concurrent majority (that is, the various sectional groups in our pluralist society) to the detriment of the numerical majority (that is, the part of the electorate which voted for the majority party in the House of Commons at a particular time). Secondly, they can become accomplices in the maintenance of a system of government which is based upon exclusive metropolitan circles of policy- and decision-making and which may be to the detriment of the millions who live and work outside such privileged quarters. Thirdly, they can reinforce the tendencies towards corporatism in our society which may work to the detriment of Parliament and elected local government.

In conclusion, we need to assess the role of pressure groups in parallel with our assessment of the political parties. Both categories of institution play vital roles of mediation and representation which contribute to the working of our political system. Whereas pressure groups are not democratically accountable in the way that political parties have to be, they do share common aspirations to reflect and defend the views and interests of their members. In this way they bring a measure of public consent to the working of the political process and help to endow it with a measure of legitimacy which it might not otherwise have. It is clear, therefore, that pressure groups are among the most significant sources of power, pressure and opinion in the British political system.

## SUGGESTED QUESTIONS

1. What are the main functions of pressure groups in British politics?
2. Which factors make some pressure groups more powerful than others?
3. At what stages in the political process do pressure groups exert their most effective influence?

## NOTES

1. In R. Rose (ed.) *Studies in British Politics*, 3rd edn (London: Macmillan, 1976) p. 343.
2. G. C. Moodie and G. Studdert-Kennedy, *Opinions, Publics and Pressure Groups* (London: Allen & Unwin, 1970) p. 60.
3. S. E. Finer, *Anonymous Empire*, revised edition (London: Pall Mall, 1966) p. 3.
4. In R. Kimber and J. J. Richardson (eds) *Pressure Groups in Britain* (London: Dent, 1974) p. 280.
5. 'Corporatism' is a term which is often used pejoratively by those who believe that democratic representation should be territorial (that is, based upon constituencies) rather than functional (that is, based upon the various sectional groups within society). For our purposes here it is taken to mean the tendency in modern politics for the Government to deal directly with the 'social partners' (i.e. employers' bodies and trade unions) to the detriment of the elected MPs in Parliament. See R. K. Middlemas, *Politics in Industrial Society* (London: Deutsch, 1979) for a fuller discussion of this subject.
6. 'Syndicalism' is a term which was used originally to describe the movement among industrial workers at the end of the nineteenth century (especially in France) of which the primary aim was the transfer of the means of production, distribution and exchange from capitalist owners to groups of workers at factory level. On the British experience see B. Holton, *British Syndicalism, 1900–14* (London: Pluto Press, 1976).
7. However, in 1984 Mr Scargill seemed to have more success in persuading many of his members to support strike action against the plans of the National Coal Board for the closure of 'uneconomic' pits.
8. J. J. Richardson and A. G. Jordan, *Governing under Pressure* (Oxford: Martin Robertson, 1979) p. 74.
9. See H. Pelling: *A History of British Trade Unionism* (London: Macmillan, 1963) and H. Pelling: *A Short History of the Labour Party* (London: Macmillan, 1965) for a fuller account.
10. See Chapter 13 for a fuller description of the policy- and decision-making process in Britain.

## FURTHER READING

Beer, S. H., *Modern British Politics* (London: Faber, 1969).
Blondel, J., *Voters, Parties and Leaders* (Harmondsworth: Penguin, 1974).
Eckstein, H., *Pressure Group Politics* (London: Allen & Unwin, 1983).
Field, F., *Poverty and Politics* (London: Heinemann, 1982).
Finer, S. E., *Anonymous Empire*, revised edn (London: Pall Mall, 1966).
King, R. and Nugent, N. (eds) *Respectable Rebels* (London: Hodder & Stoughton, 1979).
Kogan, M., *Educational Policy-Making* (London: Allen & Unwin, 1975).
Marsh, D. (ed.) *Pressure Politics* (London: Junction Books, 1983).
Moodie, G. C. and Studdert-Kennedy, G., *Opinions, Publics and Pressure Groups* (London: Allen & Unwin, 1970).
Richardson, J. J. and Jordan, A. G., *Governing under Pressure* (Oxford: Martin Robertson, 1979).
Rose, R. (ed.) *Studies in British Politics*, 3rd edn (London: Macmillan, 1976).
Wootton, G., *Pressure Groups in Britain* (London: Allen Lane, 1975).

# THE MEDIA

In considering the media in Britain, we are concerned with more than neutral channels of communication. We are examining influential participants in the political system, even though they have no formally recognised place in our constitutional arrangements. For better or worse we live in an age which is characterised by the widespread use of the various channels of communication for a broad range of political and other purposes. Politicians need the media and seek to use every opportunity to get their messages across. Equally, those who work in the media are not too shy to exert the significant influence over the political process which they can sometimes wield.

## 7.1 THE CURRENT SITUATION

**In the press**

The current situation in the British press is that there are four daily national newspapers of quality, five daily national newspapers of the popular variety, three Sunday national newspapers of quality and five Sunday national newspapers of the popular variety. There is only one major evening newspaper in London, *The Standard*, but there are a number of successful regional newspapers in other parts of the country, for example, *The Western Morning News*, *The Yorkshire Post*, *The Manchester Evening News* and *The Glasgow Herald*. There are a number of weekly newspapers which give prominence to political issues, for example, *The Economist*, *The Spectator*, *The New Statesman*, *The Listener* and *New Society*. There are also a number of more academic periodicals which deal with political issues, such as *Political Quarterly*, *Parliamentary Affairs*, *Government and Opposition* and *Public Administration*. Mention should also be made of the Communist daily newspaper, *The Morning Star*, the satirical and anti-Establishment periodicals, such as *Punch*, *Private Eye* and

*Time Out*, and the publications of the political fringe, such as *Militant*, *Socialist Worker* and *The Nation*.

There is, therefore, a wide variety of political and other points of view expressed in the British press and some of the most influential and widely read publications are not explicitly political at all, for example, *Woman* or *Woman's Own*. However, in recent years the common denominator has been the great difficulty for nearly all publications to earn enough money from sales and advertising to keep going in a bleak economic climate. The result has been that economic pressures and unsatisfactory industrial relations in the printing industry have brought about an increasing concentration of ownership as more and more companies have been forced to amalgamate or close. In Fleet Street in particular most attempts by management to introduce new technology in order to make existing publications economically viable have been fiercely resisted by the traditionally-minded print unions. Even new ventures have proved very expensive to launch and often impossible to keep going as economically viable concerns. In such circumstances it is not altogether surprising that seven multinational companies or very wealthy families own all the popular national newspapers in Britain and that the future prospects for the press point to greater concentration of ownership and fewer titles unless determined and radical steps are taken to modernise industrial practices. Even then the likely developments in broadcasting and telecommunications may well transform or even put paid to newspapers as we have known them. A table of the various national newspapers is set out in Fig. 7.1.

**In broadcasting**

The current situation in British broadcasting is that there are four television channels which provide services covering the entire country. On the one hand, there are the two channels used by the British Broadcasting Corporation (BBC1 and BBC2). The former channel is designed to appeal to the mass audience and attempts to entertain and inform its viewers, whereas the latter channel puts greater emphasis upon its educative responsibilities within the mix of programmes which it provides. On the other hand, there are the two channels used by Independent Television (ITV and Channel 4). The former competes for viewers directly with BBC1 and offers a mixture of entertainment and information programmes which are financed by the advertising which is carried, whereas the latter competes largely with BBC2 and tries to cater for a wider range of interests as well as acting as a 'publisher' for various programme makers.[1] While the BBC makes and broadcasts much of its own material and is financed from the proceeds of the licence fee levied upon nearly all who use a television set, Independent Television is brought to the viewing public by fifteen different

Fig 7.1 *Main national newspapers*

| *Title and Foundation Date* | *Publisher* | *Political Leaning* | *1982 UK Circulation (figures rounded)* |
|---|---|---|---|
| **(a) Quality dailies** | | | |
| *The Times* 1785 | Times Newspapers Ltd | Pro-Establishment | 305 000 |
| *Financial Times* 1888 | Pearson Longman Group | Independent Conservative | 204 000 |
| *The Guardian* 1821 | Guardian Newspapers Ltd | Moderate Left, Pro-Alliance | 421 000 |
| *Daily Telegraph* 1855 | Daily Telegraph Ltd | Pro-Conservative | 1 302 000 |
| **(b) Popular dailies** | | | |
| *Daily Express* 1900 | Express Newspapers Ltd | Pro-Conservative | 1 979 000 |
| *Daily Mail* 1896 | Associated Newspapers Ltd | Pro-Conservative | 1 861 000 |
| *Daily Mirror* 1903 | Reed International Group | Pro-Labour | 3 265 000 |
| *The Sun* 1969 | News Group Newspapers Ltd | Populist, Pro-Conservative | 4 179 000 |
| *Daily Star* 1978 | Express Newspapers plc | Populist, independent | 1 288 000 |
| **(c) Quality Sundays** | | | |
| *Sunday Times* 1822 | Times Newspapers Ltd | Moderate, Conservative | 1 268 000 |
| *The Observer* 1791 | The Observer Ltd | Moderate Left, Pro-Alliance | 793 000 |
| *Sunday Telegraph* 1961 | The Sunday Telegraph Ltd | Pro-Conservative | 784 000 |
| **(d) Popular Sundays** | | | |
| *News of the World* 1843 | News Group Newspapers Ltd | Populist, Pro-Conservative | 4 180 000 |
| *Sunday People* 1881 | Reed International Group | Populist, independent | 3 409 000 |
| *Sunday Mirror* 1915 | Reed International Group | Pro-Labour | 3 559 000 |
| *Sunday Express* 1918 | Sunday Express Ltd | Pro-Conservative | 2 780 000 |
| *Mail on Sunday* 1982 | Associated Newspapers Group | Pro-Conservative | 1 003 000 |

programme companies each with an exclusive franchise for a part of the country and for an agreed contractual period. The programme companies are supervised by and answerable to the Independent Broadcasting Authority (IBA) which publishes an annual report and is accountable to Parliament. All the news and much of the political information on Independent Television is provided by Independent Television News (ITN), a separate non-profit-making company established for the purpose and jointly owned by the programme companies.

On radio the BBC has four wavelengths (Radio 1, Radio 2, Radio 3 and Radio 4) which try to cater for the wide range of public interests and tastes. Radio 1 and Radio 2 provide mostly popular music and light entertainment, while Radio 3 caters for minority interests of a more highbrow and cultural variety and Radio 4 provides most of the news, information and comment upon current affairs. Whereas the four radio wave-lengths are national in scope and coverage, the BBC also provides local radio services from thirty local radio stations in all parts of the country (September 1983). These local radio stations are matched by forty-four independent local radio stations in all parts of the country (September 1983) which are financed from the proceeds of local advertising. Local radio of both kinds usually concentrates upon local and community issues, although there has to be a great deal of pop music and other popular programmes in the schedules in order to retain the listeners. There is considerable emphasis upon phone-in and other programmes of that kind which are designed to enlist considerable audience participation from the listeners. Many people would argue that this has been a healthy development for British democracy and it is noticeable that some of the most successful programmes on national radio follow the same principles of audience participation, for example, Any Questions, Election Call or You the Jury.

Concentration of ownership is less of a problem in the world of broadcasting than it is in the press, since the financial attractions of independent radio and television ensure that there are always new companies keen to bid for the available commercial opportunities. The real problems are caused by public resistance to adequate financing of public service broadcasting and political sensitivity about the content and bias of some programmes.

The financial problem arises from the way in which the BBC is financed through an annual licence fee (currently £46 for a colour set) levied upon nearly all who buy and use television sets. This method of financing is unpopular with many members of the public, especially old age pensioners, who dislike having to make such explicit payments for a service which many of them believe should be free at the point of use, that is, financed from general taxation. It is also awkward for the BBC in times of inflation when its income from licence fees does not rise in line with its costs.

The political problem arises from the fact that all broadcasters are jealous of their journalistic independence, yet they have to take account of political objections to the content and bias of some of their programmes. This means that programme producers, and especially senior executives of the BBC, have to strike a difficult and changing balance between professional integrity and political accountability. Of course, the problem is solved in part by the existence of the BBC Board of Governors and the Independent Broadcasting Authority which act as buffer bodies between the broadcasters and the politicians and between the programme-makers and the public. However, the difficulties seem likely to remain as long as people continue to assume that broadcasting in general and television in particular has such a pervasive and significant influence upon politics and society. The structure of television and radio in Britain is shown in diagrams and tables in Figure 7.2.

Fig 7.2 *Structure of television and radio*

**A. Television**

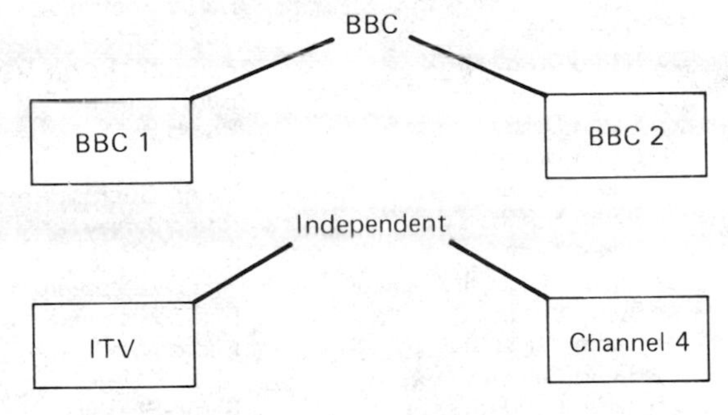


(a) *Regional production companies*

Border Television
Central Scotland Television
Channel Television
Central Television
Anglia Television
Thames Television
London Week-End Television
Tyne Tees Television
Granada Television
Television South
Television South-West
Harlech Television
Yorkshire Television
Grampian Television
Ulster Television

(b) *National production companies*

Independent Television News
Channel Four Television
TV am

**B. Radio**

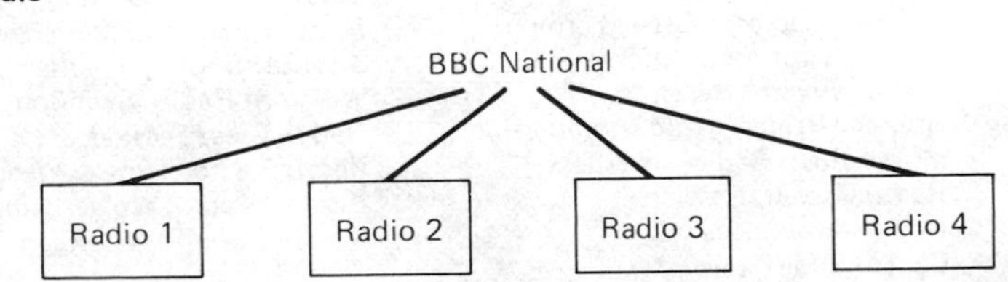

*Fig 7.2 cont.*

**BBC Local Radio**

Radio Bristol
Radio Cambridgeshire
Radio Cleveland
Radio Cornwall
Radio Cumbria
Radio Derby
Radio Devon
Radio Furness
Radio Humberside
Radio Kent
Radio Lancashire
Radio Leeds
Radio Leicester
Radio Lincolnshire
Radio London
Radio Manchester
Radio Merseyside
Radio Newcastle
Radio Norfolk
Radio Northampton
Radio Nottingham
Radio Oxford
Radio Sheffield
Radio Solent
Radio Stoke-on-Trent
Radio Sussex
Radio W.M.
Radio York
Radio Guernsey
Radio Jersey

Radio Aberdeen
Radio Highland
Radio Nan Eilean
Radio Orkney
Radio Shetland
Radio Solway
Radio Tweed

Radio Wales
Radio Northern Ireland
Radio Foyle

**Independent Local Radio**

North Sound Radio, Aberdeen
West Sound, Ayr
Downtown Radio, Belfast
BRMB Radio, Birmingham
2CR, Bournemouth
Pennine Radio, Bradford
Southern Sound, Brighton
Radio West, Bristol
Saxon Radio, Bury St Edmunds
CBC, Cardiff
Mercia Sound, Coventry
Radio Tay, Dundee
Network East Kent, East Kent
Radio Forth, Edinburgh
Devon Air Radio, Exeter
Radio Clyde, Glasgow
Severn Sound, Gloucester
Radio Broadland, Great Yarmouth
County Sound, Guildford
Radio Wyvern, Hereford
Humber Bridge Radio, Humberside
Moray Firth Radio, Inverness
Radio Orwell, Ipswich
Radio Aire, Leeds
Centre Radio, Leicester
Radio City, Liverpool
Capital Radio, London
LBC, London
Northside Sound, Londonderry
Chiltern Radio, Luton
Northdown Radio, Maidstone
Piccadilly Radio, Manchester
Gwent Broadcasting, Newport
Radio Trent, Nottingham
Hereward Radio, Peterborough
Plymouth Sound, Plymouth
Radio Victory, Portsmouth
Red Rose Radio, Preston
Radio 210, Reading
Radio Mercury, Reigate
Radio Hallam, Sheffield
Essex Radio, Southend
Signal Radio, Stoke-on-Trent
Swansea Sound, Swansea
Wiltshire Radio, Swindon
Radio Tees, Teeside
Metro Radio, Tyne & Wear
Beacon Radio, Wolverhampton
Marcher Sound, Wrexham

## 7.2 THE INFLUENCE OF THE PRESS

### Influence and bias

All the national newspapers have political reporters and commentators many of whom take distinctive lines on the issues of the day. However, in the popular national newspapers the main purposes are to entertain the readers and to please the advertisers with the result that coverage of political issues is usually not very extensive or prominent. Few readers of the popular press pay much attention to the political line taken by the papers which they read, not least because they are usually more interested in sport or scandal or soft pornography. The editors know this and usually allocate the column inches accordingly.

As a general rule, however, the influence of the popular press seems to vary inversely with the knowledge of its readers on a given subject. For example, when *The Sun* gave strong and unequivocal support to the Conservative party at the time of the 1979 General Election, this may well have had a significant influence upon the voting behaviour of its readers many of whom would not normally have voted Conservative or even been particularly interested in political issues. Equally, *The Daily Mirror*, which has consistently supported the Labour party at General Elections, may well have a significant influence upon the voting behaviour of its readers by persuading many of them to remain loyal to their usual Labour allegiance. Thus it may be that the relative scarcity of political news and comment in such newspapers and the relative ignorance of their readers about political issues actually contributes to the influence which such papers can have on the rare occasions when they pull out all the stops.

The quality national newspapers have a more subtle kind of influence mainly because it is politicians, civil servants and other political opinion-formers who pay most attention to them. In this way well-known political commentators, such as Samuel Brittan in *The Financial Times* or Peter Jenkins in *The Guardian* or Peregrine Worsthorne in *The Sunday Telegraph*, can have considerable influence upon sections of élite opinion. Similarly, leading articles, features and letters to *The Times* are still taken seriously in Westminster and Whitehall as indicators of the movement of élite opinion. Of course, these are examples of intra-élite opinion formation rather than mass persuasion. Yet in the exclusive and largely metropolitan parts of the British political system such organs can be disproportionately influential.

Some leading figures on the Left of British politics have argued that there is a persistent bias in the national press against the views and interests of the Left. It is certainly true to say that the *Daily Mirror* is the only national daily newspaper which has consistently supported the Labour party as a matter of editorial policy. All the other national newspapers can be divided between those which are still broadly in favour of the post-war consensus (for example, *The Sunday Times*, *The Observer* and *The Guardian*) and those which are invariably strongly pro-Conservative (for example, *The Daily Telegraph*, *The Daily Express* and *The Daily Mail*). Indeed, Tony Benn has written of both categories that 'the fundamental criticism of the British newspapers is not that they necessarily support the policies of the Conservative party, but that they support conservative policies whether carried out by a Conservative or a Labour Government.'[2]

No doubt some will agree and some disagree with such observations. Certainly it should not be supposed that the journalists working for newspapers which take a non-Left political line necessarily share the views of their editors or proprietors. Yet it seems clear that the influence of the advertisers and the political preferences of some of the contemporary press barons make it difficult to discount this Bennite criticism of the national press.

**Secrecy and censorship**

Another important characteristic of the British press is that it is more inhibited than in most other Western countries by the traditional secrecy of British government and the restrictive attitudes in Whitehall towards the disclosure of official information. Such secretive habits have been well established for years and are strongly reinforced by the continued existence of the 1911 Official Secrets Act which is meant to deter public servants (including politicians) from communicating and journalists from receiving any unauthorised or classified information. Indeed, Section 2 of the Act is drawn so widely that it could be used to prevent the disclosure even of the brand or quality of paper used in Whitehall lavatories. Paradoxically, the effect of such legislation has been largely to discredit the whole idea of official secrecy as it has been practised in this country over many years and to breed a cynical response from many public servants and journalists alike.

The same restrictive attitudes are reflected in the so-called 'D Notice' system which is meant to prevent the publication in the press of sensitive defence information by the simple expedient of issuing a written warning from an official committee upon which both journalists and officials are represented. Once again although the work of this committee inhibits the disclosure of sensitive information, it has also bred a deep cynicism among journalists who are not so restricted in many other Western countries.

Similarly restrictive attitudes are reflected in the libel, copyright and *sub judice* aspects of British law. These confer extensive powers of prior restraint and hence censorship in effect upon those who wish to prevent the publication of anything which they may deem to be sensitive material by the simple expedient of obtaining a High Court injunction. While there is an obvious need in any free society for a powerful and independent press which can expose the shortcomings of politicians and other public servants, it seems that the need has not been fully met in Britain.

**Freedom of information**

Various attempts have been made over recent years to deal with the problems of secrecy and censorship by introducing proposals designed to promote freedom of information. In 1978 a report by 'Justice', the British Section of the International Commission of Jurists, recommended the establishment of a Code of Practice on the disclosure of official information by all Government Departments and other public authorities supervised by the Parliamentary Commissioner for Administration.[3] At about the same time a Liberal MP, Clement Freud, introduced a Private Member's Bill designed to legislate for freedom of information along the lines of proposals made a year or so earlier by the Outer Circle Policy Unit.[4] Other MPs have also tried and failed to introduce legislation along similar lines.

In most cases those who have pressed for reform have wanted to see a right of access to official information enshrined in statute law and based upon the principle that the onus should be put upon public authorities to satisfy the Courts of the need for non-disclosure rather than upon ordinary citizens to argue for disclosure. This principle is the reverse of Section 2 of the 1911 Official Secrets Act which holds that all classified information must remain restricted unless its release has been specifically authorised. The reformers have also wanted to give citizens the right to see their personal files and to establish a reliable register or index of all official files, except those concerning the security of the state. They have favoured the establishment of some form of appeals procedure against refusals to supply official information and the introduction of a judicial remedy for aggrieved citizens in cases of proven non-compliance with the law. Only certain categories of specified material, including some defence and security matters, information involving commercial confidentiality and that which is safeguarded for reasons of privacy, was to have been exempt from the provisions of such legislation.

Apart from the inherent unwillingness of most Ministers and civil servants to respond positively to such proposals, the main argument used against them has usually been the extra cost to public funds which would be involved. Furthermore, in those countries where such legislation has been implemented – for example, Sweden and the United States – the actual experience has been that pressure groups and commercial interests have made the greatest use of it and sometimes for economic gain rather than reasons of principle to do with the assertion of civil rights. At bottom the idea provokes the fundamental antipathy of Ministers, civil servants and most public officials in Britain towards the disclosure of any official information other than that which is unavoidably forced upon them (such as through unauthorised leaks) or which is believed to be advantageous to their cause. There is little reason to suppose that any code of practice or new legislation could do much to change such attitudes in a political élite as congenitally secretive as the one in this country.

**The role of the Lobby**

The paradoxical aspect of the position in this country is that whereas there is so much emphasis upon secrecy and censorship in the formal legal arrangements, informally a great deal of official information is leaked to the media on what are called 'Lobby terms'.[5] This practice involves supplying accredited Lobby journalists (that is, those entitled to frequent the Members' Lobby and other restricted parts of the House of Commons) with privileged and unattributable political information on the strict understanding that there is no disclosure of sources or attribution of comments. The practice has spread beyond the precincts of the Palace of Westminster to every part of Whitehall so that every Department (including No 10 Downing Street and the Cabinet Office) has contacts with trusted journalists who are the privileged recipients of official information and guidance which is deliberately leaked to them. Indeed, most Ministers and some officials see it as an important part of their job to keep at least a few carefully chosen journalists well-informed of what is happening or about to happen in their areas of responsibility. Equally, the journalists concerned find it convenient to connive at this practice, since it ensures for them a steady flow of news and opinion on which they can base their stories in the press or in broadcasting.

The Lobby system has advantages for both the providers and the receivers of official information. Many journalists depend upon it as if it were part of their daily diet. For politicians it can be an effective way of defusing potentially difficult issues through judicious and timely leaks, so that when the information is released officially much of its adverse publicity impact has been removed. A good example of this technique would be the early leaking of unemployment figures which are going to be damagingly high or the leaking of rumours of a tough Budget so that the Chancellor can eventually get the credit for being more generous than people were led to expect. Ministers and occasionally officials authorised by Ministers can also use the Lobby system to fly kites for new policy initiatives in order to get some idea of how they might be received by the media or the public. Occasionally the system is used to pursue in the columns of the press or in radio and television studios policy arguments or personality conflicts which the politicians or officials concerned fear they may be losing behind closed doors in Whitehall or Westminster. Whether such techniques can be described as 'news management' is a moot point, since most experienced journalists are not easily fooled by politicians or their spokesmen and most political attempts to manipulate the media have not ultimately been successful.

## 7.3 THE POWER OF BROADCASTING

### The power of television

The power of television has affected many aspects of our society and in the political sphere notably the style and nature of political debate. As Anthony Smith has observed, television has become a well from which society draws many of its common allusions (illusions?) and an important source of social reference points.[6] This means that in considering the power of television, we need to look not so much at its impact upon voting behaviour (which until recently has been minimal) as its capacity to influence the way in which the political debate is conducted both between elections and during election campaigns.

In essence political issues are often treated on television as if they were simply another form of public entertainment. The respectable argument for this is that it serves to grab and hold what would otherwise be an uninterested and apathetic viewing public. However, while it may produce a greater degree of public awareness of some telegenic issues, it does not necessarily raise the level of public understanding and may even produce a bias against it.[7]

In so far as television has had a discernible electoral effect in Britain, it seems to have been one of reinforcement rather than conversion, although the early studies on this subject seemed also to suggest that the direct effects upon voting behaviour were rather slight either way. For example, Trenaman and McQuail in their study of the 1959 General Election showed that the main effect of television upon the first campaign to be given extensive coverage by the medium was simply to increase the store of information available to the electorate.[8] In a follow-up study of the 1964 General Election Blumler and McQuail showed that in addition to this factor, the only other discernible effect was to boost slightly the popularity of the Liberal party by giving it an abnormal degree of television exposure.[9] Television coverage of the newly-formed Social Democratic party in 1981 seemed to have a similar effect upon its success at

Parliamentary by-elections at that time. However, with the notable increase in voting volatility in the 1970s and early 1980s it seems plausible that the impact of television upon the outcome of elections is greater than it was in the late 1950s and early 1960s when the conventional wisdom on this matter was established.

Probably the most significant general effect of television upon British politics has been manifest in the style and methods of election campaigning. Since the 1964 General Election campaign the parties have held daily press conferences each morning during the campaign period. This development and the nightly news bulletins on BBC and ITN have had the effect of focussing public attention increasingly upon the party leaders and a few of their senior colleagues. The presence of television cameras and radio microphones on tour with the party leaders has increased the emphasis upon a presidential style of campaigning. This has diminished the role and importance of most ordinary Parliamentary candidates, except in very marginal seats or highly publicised by-elections. One practical consequence of this tendency towards presidentialism has been to diminish still further the value of public meetings as a form of political campaigning, although this is not always the case in sparsely populated rural areas or at important by-elections. A more general consequence of this media concentration upon the leading personalities of the campaign has been to increase the temptation for the party leaders to perform in front of the cameras rather than reason with the electorate.

Just as some on the Left are concerned about anti-Left bias in the national press, others have expressed the view that television too is far from being a neutral medium of mass communication. According to this argument, the political effect of television is no longer simply to reinforce existing values and preferences in society, but actually to set the hidden agenda of political discussion. For example, public faith in the impartiality of television news is said to be misplaced on the grounds that true objectivity can never be achieved by those who produce it. As the Glasgow Media Group expressed it, 'one must see the news as reflecting not the events in the world out there, but as the manifestation of the collective cultural codes of those employed to do this selection and judgemental work for society'.[10] In other words, the news is not really 'the news', but an arbitrary selection and presentation of certain information and opinion according to the unstated criteria of those who produce and edit the programmes.

If there really is such 'an ideology of news', as these sociologists have argued, the answer to the problem cannot sensibly be sought in the quest for a value-free alternative, since such a form of communication has never existed. It would seem that the critics of the present arrangements would only rest content if they and their ilk were able to decide the way in which news and views were presented on television. Yet if such a change were made, it is very likely that others of a contrasting political outlook would find reason to complain from their point of view. As it is, there are many on the conservative side of the argument who believe that they have cause to complain about the iconoclastic and even subversive nature of some television programmes produced by the media professionals now responsible for the news and other current affairs programmes.[11] If social reformers or academic critics wish to change the hidden agenda of British politics, they are really involved in trying to change the nature and values of British society. The programme-makers, for their part, can usually retort that they are merely holding up a mirror to reflect contemporary reality or a part of it. In the final analysis political change is principally a matter of politics and people should not be misled into thinking that it can be brought about simply by the manipulative skills of television professionals.

**The power of radio**

Radio is also a powerful medium which has its effect upon both politics and society. The programmes broadcast on the four national wavelengths serve in most cases to entertain the listening public. However, Radio 4 seeks to set a consistently high standard of political reporting and analysis and Radio 3 includes some programmes of a highly informative and even academic nature, such as Open University broadcasts. Nowadays the producers of current affairs programmes put quite a lot of emphasis upon audience participation - as in Points of View, You the Jury, Any Questions, etc. - and this is certainly one way of involving more people in the process of political discusssion. There is also daily coverage of what happens in Parliament which is based upon recorded extracts of what Ministers and others say in the House of Commons with occasional pieces from the Lords as well, However, the radio broadcasting of Parliamentary proceedings, especially Prime Minister's Question Time, does not seem to have enhanced public understanding or respect for our political process, since it has tended to exaggerate the rumbustious side of party politics at the expense of the more serious and low-key aspects of life at Westminster. Since it is impossible at present to convey the full variety and flavour of our Parliamentary proceedings, it is likely that the public will continue to have a distorted and unfavourable impression of how Parliament actually works.

The expansion of local radio has also had a significant effect upon the conduct of British politics. The local radio stations in all parts of the country have given an undoubted boost to local consciousness and the more colourful political personalities have thrived in the atmosphere thus created. Apart from heavy doses of popular music and other forms of light entertainment, the programmes include a considerable number of chat shows and phone-in programmes which provide opportunities for ordinary people to air their grievances and for politicians to demonstrate their activity and concern. Thus local radio has contributed greatly to the vitality of British politics.

**The impact of new technology**

It is already clear that new information technology is likely to have a very significant impact upon the media in Britain. The technology is based upon micro-electronics and fibre-optics which will make possible wide-band interactive communications between individuals, businesses and public agencies. It may also have social and political consequences which could be even more significant than those which have flowed from the activities of the press and the existing forms of broadcasting.

If everything goes well and the technology is developed along the benevolent lines foreseen by its most enthusiastic proponents, then we may see the development of a society which has been described by Kenneth Baker, Minister for Information Technology, as 'better informed . . . more relaxed, less formal, more mobile, less enamoured with structure, more skilled, less ridden with class and social differences and full of scope for more individuality'.[12] However, if things do not go well and the new technology is developed principally for manipulative purposes of social control, then individual freedoms could be eroded, social vitality could be stultified and totalitarian tendencies could increase to an alarming extent.

One technical possibility once wide-band interactive cable communications are available to every home in the land (and that day is bound to be a long way off) would be instantaneous public opinion polling on every conceivable political issue. Obviously, this would have serious consequences for our system of Parliamentary democracy, since, as Kenneth Baker himself has warned, 'the danger is that push-button politics will raise expectations that no political system can or should meet and increase popular frustration'.[13] The political decision-makers will therefore need to be circumspect when deciding how far and how fast to allow the realisation of some technical possibilities.

In the more immediate future the most important issues facing the decision-makers in this sphere are those concerned with the effects of cable communications technology upon broadcasting policy. At present broadcasting in Britain is regulated by the BBC and the IBA within the limits set by the relevant legislation. However, the advent and expansion of cable television could complicate and change the position in a number of significant ways.

At its best this new technology could provide an increased range of home entertainment, greater facilities for education and training at home, new opportunities for working, buying and selling direct from home, and new consumer services such as electronic mail and tele-banking. At its worst it could lead to a waste of scarce national resources, threats to privacy and social diversity, and damage to the quality of existing forms of broadcasting. Much will depend upon the kind of technology chosen, whether coaxial copper cable of the kind now used in the United States or an interactive switched system using laser technology and fibre optics of a kind now scarcely beyond the research and development stage. Even more will depend upon how the regulatory arrangements work out in practice.

The 1982 Report of the Hunt Committee recommended that a typical thirty-channel cable system should include 'must carry' broadcast services (that is, existing BBC and ITV programmes), interactive services of benefit to business and the consumer and a wide range of other services of special interest to various groups and localities.[14] It also recommended a statutorily-based form of national supervision rather than regulation of the cable operators to be achieved through the establishment of a new Cable Authority with the power to award franchises and to see that the technology is developed within certain, albeit liberal, ground-rules.

It is too early to tell exactly what impact this new technology will have upon British politics and society. However, in April 1983 the Thatcher Government announced its decision to go ahead with cable TV on the basis of a White Paper produced jointly by the Home Office and the Department of Industry.[15] The Government decided to promote the development of cable television and to control the new technology via a new statutory Authority, as recommended by the Hunt Committee. The Cable Authority will have two main roles: to award franchises to cable operators for the provision of cable services and to exercise statutory supervision of those services. Pending the passage of the necessary legislation and the establishment of the Authority, the Government was prepared to authorise up to twelve new cable systems as pilot projects each covering a maximum of about 100 000 homes, and to allow cable-relay operators to offer new programme services on their existing systems for a transitional period. In these ways it hoped to maintain the momentum of cable development in Britain.

Of course, there are other technological developments in the offing, such as Direct Broadcasting by Satellite (DBS), which could have social and political effects just as far-reaching as those of cable television.[16] For example, (assuming the adoption of common international standards) DBS could have the effect of enabling people in this country to tune in directly to television programmes broadcast from other countries and vice versa. The implications of such technological developments for traditional ideas of national identity could be quite significant. It therefore seems likely that national Governments, especially in closed or fragile societies, will need a great deal of persuasion before they agree to take a full part in such developments.

## 7.4 CONCLUSION

The power of the media in the British political system is in one sense greater but in another sense not so great as it was during the last century. It is greater in that television in particular has such a strong influence upon the contemporary context and style of British politics, as well as the underlying assumptions which help to shape our political culture. It is not so great in that the media cannot sway political opinion or topple Governments as the national press claimed to have done on some occasions in the nineteenth century.

Certainly television has had an unsettling and pervasive influence upon the British political system. For most politicians it has acted like a lamp to moths. For the public it has gained a false aura of impartiality in that most people tend to believe in the objectivity of what they see with their own eyes. For the opinion-formers it has provided extensive channels of powerful communication to millions of people who might not otherwise have been reached. On the other hand, it does bring with it dangers of bias, triviality and sensationalism which are not so readily acknowledged by those who work in the medium. It remains to be seen whether these dangers can be averted and the medium used in ways which would enhance the quality of our democracy, for example, for adult education and general consciousness-raising.

The overall contribution of the media to our political system can be summarised as the encouragement of greater public awareness of political issues among those who are otherwise excluded from the process of policy- and decision-making, and the influencing of the hidden agenda of politics through their choice of the issues and personalities which are brought to public notice at any time. The latter applies especially in the world of pressure group politics in which many different interests and causes compete for the attention of both the Government and public opinion. It is also true in the broader sense that political priorities are often influenced not so much by the intrinsic importance of different issues as by the nature and extent of the coverage given to them in the media.

Of course, the influence of the media extends beyond the sphere of politics, since it has a significant effect upon the values, assumptions, attitudes and behaviour of ordinary people. It has contributed to the materialism of modern society by reinforcing the widely-held assumption that individual satisfaction and social progress are to be measured principally in terms of goods purchased, services received or status attained. It has affected public attitudes towards Government and other public agencies by raising expectations that problems thus exposed will be swiftly solved. However, it has also raised the level of public awareness and prompted more urgent Government responses to some of the problems and injustices of the modern world.

In short, the media may have made it more difficult for Governments to govern, since they hold up a mirror to the flaws and shortcomings in our society and encourage a level of public demands upon the political system which no Government has been able fully to satisfy. Yet by their very nature the media are always more likely to be critics rather than buttresses of the politicians in power and it is right that this should be so in a political system which can be defined as a pluralist, liberal democracy.

## SUGGESTED QUESTIONS

1. Describe the structure and organisation of the media in Britain.
2. How influential is the British press?
3. In what ways do radio and television affect the course of British politics?

## NOTES

1. Figures published in September 1983 by the Broadcasters' Audience Research Board showed that the most popular national TV programmes are usually shown on ITV, for example, the soap operas *Coronation Street* (more than 10 million viewers) and *Crossroads* (more than 8 million viewers). The BBC has usually achieved its largest audiences with the *Nine O'Clock News* (more than 8 million viewers) and *Top of the Pops* (more than 8 million viewers) which are both broadcast on BBC1. Consistently popular programmes on BBC2 have included nature and wild life films, such as *Our Undersea World* (2.85 million viewers) and *The World About Us* (2.5 million viewers). The most popular programmes on Channel 4 seem to have been television drama, such as *I Married a Witch* and *Brookside* for which typical ratings have varied from 3.2 million to 1.9 million.
2. A. Benn, *Arguments for Democracy* (London: Jonathan Cape, 1981) p. 115.
3. *Freedom of Information* (London: Justice, 1978).
4. *An Official Information Act* (London: Outer Circle Policy Unit, 1977).
5. For a fuller discussion of the Lobby at Westminster see J. Margach, *The Anatomy of Power* (London: Star, 1981) pp. 125–55.
6. A. Smith, *The Politics of Information* (London: Macmillan, 1978), p. 5.
7. This point was made very well by John Birt and Peter Jay in *The Times* on 28 February, 30 September and 1 October 1975.
8. J. Trenaman and D. McQuail, *Television and the Political Image* (London: Methuen, 1961).

9. J. G. Blumler and D. McQuail, *Television in Politics* (London: Faber, 1968).
10. Glasgow Media Group: *Bad News* (London: Routledge & Kegan Paul, 1981) pp. 12–13.
11. For example, there was a wave of complaint at the height of the 1982 Falklands crisis when the BBC programme, *Panorama*, was focussed on one occasion almost exclusively upon the arguments and misgivings of Conservative critics and doubters at a time when the vast majority of Conservative MPs and, indeed, public opinion was in no mood to appreciate such 'anti-patriotic' programmes. The BBC has also been severely and publicly criticised on more than one occasion for programmes which included interviews with members of the IRA and which were screened in such a way as to appear to aid and abet the IRA cause.
12. K. Baker: 'Towards an Information Economy', speech to the British Association for the Advancement of Science, 7 September 1982.
13. Ibid.
14. Report of the Inquiry into Cable Expansion and Broadcasting Policy, Cmnd 8679 (London: HMSO, 1982).
15. See 'The Development of Cable Services and Systems', Cmnd 8866, (London, HMSO, 1983).
16. In 1983 the Home Office agreed that there should be four new television channels for Direct Broadcasting by Satellite, two under the control of the BBC and two under the control of the IBA. This form of television should be available to the viewers with the appropriate electronic equipment by 1986–7.

## FURTHER READING


Blumler, J. G. and McQuail, D., *Television in Politics* (London: Faber, 1968).

Curran, J. (ed.) *The British Press, a Manifesto* (London: Macmillan, 1978).

Curran, J. and Seaton, J., *Power without Responsibility* (London: Fontana, 1981).

Gilmour, I., *The Body Politic* (London: Hutchinson, 1969).

Glasgow Media Group, *Bad News* (London: Routledge & Kegan Paul, 1981).

Rose, R., (ed.) *Studies in British Politics*, 3rd edn (London: Macmillan, 1976).

Seymour-Ure, C., *The Press, Politics and the Public* (London: Methuen, 1968).

Seymour-Ure, C., *The Political Impact of Mass Media* (London: Constable, 1974).

Smith, A., *The Politics of Information* (London: Macmillan, 1978).

Trenaman, J. and McQuail, D., *Television and the Political Image* (London: Methuen, 1961).

Whale, J., *The Politics of the Media* (London: Fontana, 1977).

Worcester, R. M. and Harrop, M. (eds) *Political Communications* (London: Allen & Unwin, 1982).

CHAPTER 8

# PUBLIC OPINION

Public opinion means different things to different people and it has changed its meaning over the years. Whereas Jeremy Bentham defined it as 'a system of law emanating from the body of the people', Robert Peel defined it as 'that great compound of folly, weakness, prejudice, wrong feeling, right feeling, obstinacy and newspaper paragraphs'.[1] A. V. Dicey was more charitable when he defined it as 'the wishes and ideas as to legislation held by . . . the majority of those citizens who have . . . taken an effective part in public life'.[2] On the other hand, V. O. Key was more cynical when he defined it as 'those opinions of private persons which Governments find it prudent to heed'.[3]

Such diversity of definition reflects the different views taken at different times by different people, depending upon the society in which they lived and the political outlook which they had. In Britain in the nineteenth century public opinion was usually considered to be synonymous with the views of the relatively small number of people who were enfranchised and so able to have effective political influence, at least at election time. Nowadays it is generally accepted that public opinion includes the views and prejudices of all adults, no matter how shallow or fitful their involvement in politics. Thus for the purposes of this chapter we may define public opinion as the sum of opinions held on political issues by the entire adult population. The flow of public opinion is shown in diagrammatical form in Figure 8.1.

## 8.1 THE COMPOSITION OF OPINION

### Consensus and controversy

There is both consensus and controversy in British public opinion. Indeed, there are many different components of public opinion which vary from issue to issue and from time to time. As Richard Rose has put it, 'there is not a single public with which the Government seeks to communicate; there is a variety of publics distinguishable by their degrees of organisation,

Fig 8.1 *The flow of public opinion*

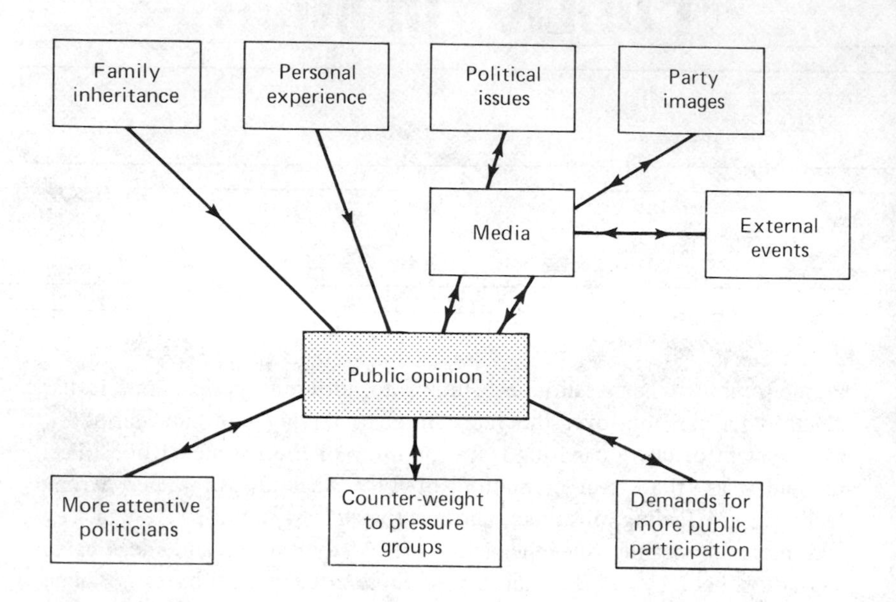


their policy preferences and their knowledge or interest in political issues'.[4] The composition of public opinion is therefore more akin to a mosaic than to a well-defined or predictable diagram.

In Britain for most of the period since the war, at any rate until the early 1970s, there was a remarkable degree of consensus in public opinion. This was reflected in the attitudes of the two major parties which both accepted the wartime commitment to full employment and the post-war commitment to the Welfare State. In these circumstances the political argument was confined very largely to disputes about the best way to allocate extra resources on a basis of differential expansion. Admittedly, there were some deep divisions of opinion about some issues, notably in the sphere of foreign policy, for example, the Suez expedition in 1956, the process of decolonisation in the late 1950s and early 1960s, and Britain's relationship with the European Community in the late 1960s and early 1970s. Yet such arguments tended to take place against a background of basic agreement upon many other issues of fundamental importance. In such a political climate it could be maintained that the most significant cleavage in public opinion was neither between Right and Left nor between rich and poor, but between informed and mass opinion. In other words, the real gulf was between the minority who were 'in the know' and the rest who were not.

**Informed opinion and mass opinion**

Informed opinion on political issues is opinion held by the minority of people who are 'in the know' and it is usually the result of a recognisably rational process of thought. Typically, it is the opinion of politicians at Westminster, civil servants in Whitehall, political journalists, pressure group spokesmen and some other limited categories, for example, those prominent in public corporations, local government, the law, the church, the City, etc. In view of the metropolitan character of British politics, it often derives disproportionately from interacting London élites, although it can be influenced quite heavily by ephemeral intellectual trends which often originate in Oxford or Cambridge. It is therefore essentially the opinion of the Establishment and its licensed critics.

Mass opinion, on the other hand, is often little more than ignorant sentiment, although it is usually based upon significant attitudes, beliefs and ideas which are founded upon popular experience. This means that it has often to be conjured up before it can be said to exist. As V. O. Key observed, 'public opinion does not emerge like a cyclone and push obstacles before it: rather it develops under leadership'.[5] The extent of public ignorance about the basic facts of politics has been a matter of record for some time. For example, in 1964 almost a quarter of a representative sample did not know that the coal industry had been in public ownership for nearly twenty years. In 1971 another opinion poll showed that only 13 per cent of those questioned could name the six member states of the European Community at a time when the British Government was engaged in widely publicised negotiations for British entry. In 1978 only 46 per cent of those questioned in a national poll could give the name of their MP and a poll in 1979 showed that 77 per cent of those questioned did not know what was meant by NATO – thirty years after the foundation of the North Atlantic Treaty Organisation.

Bearing in mind all the political communication which takes place in Britain today, it is perhaps a little difficult to understand why such a degree of public ignorance exists. The explanation could be that those politicians and others who have something to say are not saying it with sufficient clarity or repetition. It could be that the channels of communication in the mass media are defective for this purpose. It could even be that the public audience is perfectly able to hear, but not really prepared to listen.

Simple observation would suggest that politicians and other opinion-formers try to impart a great deal of fact and opinion to the general public, perhaps even too much for easy assimilation. It would also suggest that the media, especially television, are more pervasive and influential than before. Yet at the same time it is clear that these factors do not necessarily produce a well-informed or enlightened public opinion. This may be because the conduct of political argument on party lines is not the best way of explaining to the public many of the complicated issues involved in contemporary politics. It may also be because the imperatives of economic survival in Fleet Street and the fierce commercial competition throughout the media have discouraged editors and producers from giving sufficient coverage or explanation of many political issues. For example, the popular national newspapers are more noted for their coverage of sport, scandal and sex than for intelligent discussion of important political issues. The radio and television programme-makers are more concerned to compete for a mass audience and to win the battle of the ratings than to provide sufficient serious coverage of political news and views, at any rate during peak media hours.

As for the attitudes of the general public, much of the available evidence suggests that many people are largely uninterested in politics and bored or even annoyed when the communicators try to change their views. If we discount the various technical considerations which limit the effectiveness of the media, it would seem to be more a case of a public which is not really keen to listen than politicians and other opinion-formers who are not prepared to communicate.

It seems, therefore, that mass opinion on most political issues consists of a large component of ignorance, a considerable lack of interest, a certain amount of prejudice, an assortment of received ideas, a smattering of popular mythology and much rationalisation of personal experience. If this appears to be little more than a caricature, then it must be said that there is not much evidence from opinion polls or other sources to disprove it. It appears to be the political reality with which we must live until such time as it proves possible to change things.

## 8.2 THE FORMATION OF OPINION

### Inheritance and experience

Expert studies have shown that public opinion is formed from a myriad of private opinions, whether personal or group opinions. Such private opinions are usually formed quite early in life, very often when people first become aware of political issues. They tend to be derived principally from family inheritance and personal experience, although the influence of school, work, friends and neighbourhood all play a part as well.

In the 1960s Butler and Stokes wrote an important book in which they demonstrated the strength of family inheritance as a factor which influences voting behaviour and there is little reason to suppose that the significance of this factor has diminished very much since then.[6] Young people today still derive many of their attitudes and opinions from their parents and family influence remains one of the more constant factors in the development of every young generation. Of course, there are always some young people who reject the attitudes and opinions of their parents, either as part of adolescent rebellion or as a function of economic and social mobility. Yet on the whole family influence still plays a major part in the formation of public opinion and even the increase in one-parent families does not seem to have invalidated this factor to any significant extent.

As for the influence of personal experience, it is obvious that this has a major impact upon the formation of individual opinions. Few people form their opinions on political issues on a basis of purely rational or altruistic considerations, since that is a luxury which is usually available only to those whose material circumstances enable them to afford such Platonic detachment. For most people individual opinions are formed in the light of the fortune or misfortune which they experience during the course of their lives, whether at home, at work or at leisure. Indeed, it has been argued that it is really the formative experience of young adults which has the most lasting influence upon their opinions later in life. This is known as 'the cohort theory' of opinion formation and it certainly seemed to fit those who came of age in 1945 as well as those who did so during the late 1950s. However, more recent evidence seems to suggest that formative experience may have a diminishing effect over the years, since each successive cohort, on coming of age, is subject to a diminishing degree of generational solidarity as the electorate as a whole becomes more volatile.[7]

**Issues and images**

Public opinion is also formed by individual responses to political issues and party images. Much of the historical evidence suggests that people have tended to reconcile their political opinions with their party allegiances rather than the other way around. In the past neither policy nor ideology seemed to mean very much to the average British citizen whose political opinions appeared to be largely unaffected by such considerations. Yet more recent evidence suggests that political issues do have an impact upon the formation of public opinion and hence upon voting behaviour. For example, in addition to the adverse electoral impact upon the Labour party of the so-called 'winter of discontent' in 1979, Ivor Crewe has concluded that 'it was issues, not organisation or personalities, that won the (May 1979) election for the Conservatives'.[8] Indeed, even those who voted Labour often preferred Conservative policies, although evidently not enough to persuade them to align their votes with their policy preferences.

However, in considering the influence of political issues, we need to distinguish between the bread and butter issues of daily life (such as jobs, prices or pensions) upon which most people pronounce their opinions with justifiable confidence and the more esoteric issues of national policy (for example, money supply, exchange rates or theories of nuclear deterrence) upon which some people may hold opinions, but which tend to baffle or confuse the vast majority. In dealing with issues in the latter category, it is therefore sensible to rely upon the processes of Parliamentary democracy rather than to flirt with experiments of government by plebiscite or opinion poll.

Among the more ephemeral considerations which influence the formation of public opinion, the images of the parties and especially of their respective leaders constitute another important factor in modern political conditions. For example, in the 1950s the Conservative party had an image of competence in office and authority in Government which led many people to support it even when it may not have appeared particularly likeable or sympathetic in its handling of the political issues of the day. This party image was to some extent a reflection of the personal image of its leaders - for example, Winston Churchill, Anthony Eden or Harold Macmillan - who were respected and in some cases even revered for their achievements in office, even though their presence did not necessarily engender feelings of great warmth or real affection in the hearts and minds of the general public.

On the other hand, the Labour party has had an image over the years of compassion and concern for ordinary working people which has enabled it to retain the voting loyalties of much of the working class for longer than its performance in office might seem to have deserved. This too was partly a reflection of the personal image of its leaders - for example, Clement Attlee, Hugh Gaitskell and Harold Wilson - but mainly a tribute to the image of the party as the Parliamentary vanguard of the entire Labour movement. Although party images have been important in forming public opinion and influencing voting behaviour, the personal image of the leader does not seem to have been as vital to the Labour party as to the Conservative party, perhaps because the democratic aspirations of the former and the hierarchic habits of the latter have tended to draw a clear contrast between the two.

## 8.3 THE EFFECTS OF OPINION

### More deferential politicians

Public opinion in Britain has a variety of political effects. It is arguable that one effect has been to make most politicians more deferential to the wishes of the electorate. While this tendency may seem to have reached its zenith in the time of Harold Wilson (1963-76) who as Leader of the Labour party paid assiduous attention to opinion polls and other psephological evidence (such as by-election and local election results), it has remained significant at all times in post-war politics, especially when

General Elections are imminent. Certainly it has been true in the negative sense that leading politicians both in and out of office usually take considerable care not to put forward policies or to take positions which seem destined to encounter powerful opposition from public opinion. Even the redoubtable Margaret Thatcher, who more than any other post-war leader has sought to do what she believes to be right almost regardless of the political consequences, has adjusted party policy on some occasions in order to take account of the public response which could have been expected if she and her colleagues had pressed ahead with certain radical policies.[9]

This draws our attention to the elusive and controversial concept of 'political impossibility' which has played such an important part in so many political calculations by leading politicians over the years. In essence it can be defined as the influence upon political decision-makers of anticipated public reaction. Some have argued that this is a deleterious influence, since it can prevent the adoption of radical policies which may be justified as an appropriate response to many of our deep-seated national problems. Others have argued that this is a beneficial influence, since it can be seen as a contribution to our national cohesion especially during difficult periods of disappointment and relative decline when a less sensitive political approach could prove very damaging.

The argument is really between those who regard the conservatism of British public opinion as something of a saving grace, since it constitutes a significant obstacle to the ambitions of the zealots in each major party, and those who see it as a tragedy, since it often constitutes a virtually insuperable barrier to radical action. If the major priority is to guard against radical change, then the former view ought to be commended. If the major priority is to make radical change, then the latter view ought to prevail. In any event the outcome is likely to depend upon the personal temperament of the leading politicians who have to carry the major responsibilities of Government.

### A counterweight to pressure groups

Another important effect of public opinion has been the way in which it has provided a useful counterweight to the influence of pressure groups in the British political system. As we noted in Chapter 6, there are times when it becomes very difficult for any Government to resist the claims of certain powerful interest groups – for example, the National Union of Mineworkers or the British Medical Association – without appealing over the heads of the group concerned to the general public. This is essentially what Edward Heath sought to do when he called a General Election in February 1974 on the issue of 'who governs'? It is also what the 1979–83 Conservative Government sought to do when it introduced legislation to provide for secret ballots in trade union affairs. In each case the intention of Ministers was to appeal over the heads of obstructive interest groups to the wider public in an effort to fulfil their political purposes.

Indeed, whenever politicians of Right or Left invoke in support of their cause the views of the wider public, it is usually a sign that they have been obstructed or opposed by a small but powerful group which seeks to set its sectional interest above that of the general community. This is as true when Labour Ministers complain about the pernicious influence of the City of London as when Conservative Ministers criticise the abuse of trade union power. In each case they are seeking to defend the principle that general public opinion has more inherent legitimacy than any sectional group. On the whole there is no reason to oppose this principle, especially since general public opinion has a sounder record than sectional groups on most political issues. Yet every political system needs safeguards against the tyranny of the majority, since in most societies there have been times when majority opinion has been comparatively unenlightened and unduly biased against political change. Thus a balance has to be struck which allows fair opportunities for both majority and minority opinion, while retaining a democratic presumption in favour of the former.

**The influence of opinion polls**

Yet another effect of public opinion has been to give political opinion polls an influence out of all proportion to their intrinsic value. Such polls have become the most familiar and systematic expression of public opinion between General Elections. When sensibly interpreted, they can provide a useful navigational aid for politicians whether in Government or in Opposition. The systematic analysis of opinion poll data has enabled the parties to identify key target groups of voters (for instance, the wives of blue-collar workers in the case of the Conservative party) and then to concentrate and organise their communications with particular target groups in mind. Opinion polls also guide the Prime Minister of the day in making the decision about when to call a General Election and they can affect the morale of party activists if the findings are either very good or very bad for a particular party or its leader.[10] While opinion polls should not be used to determine policy- or decision-making, it is understandable that they should influence both the development and the presentation of policy, since (apart from by-elections and random anecdotal evidence) practising politicians have few other ways of ascertaining the state of public opinion between periodic General Elections.

Special considerations apply to the role of opinion polls during General Election campaigns. Some observers have argued that the polls produce a bandwagon effect which assists the party that seems to be on a winning streak. Others have argued for the backlash effect which leads doubting voters to rally to the party that appears to be the underdog. A few have argued that the publication of opinion polls should be banned altogether for the duration of General Election campaigns. Yet this would not be a realistic or effective course, since private polls could still be commissioned by the parties and the results would almost certainly be leaked to the media.

Richard Rose has come to some conclusions about opinion polls which are published during General Election campaigns.[11] These are that the vote for the governing party is usually over-estimated, the gap between the two major parties tends to close during the campaign, Conservatives are more likely than others to express a readiness to vote, there is no anti-Labour or pro-Conservative bias, the Liberal (or third party) vote tends to be underestimated, polls conducted closest to polling day are invariably the most accurate, and polls conducted nationally are normally more reliable than those conducted only in a limited area. There seems to be little reason to dissent from such reasonable conclusions.

**The advent of referenda**

Another effect of public opinion is the way in which the growing self-confidence and declining deference of the general public has led to more frequent demands for national referenda.[12] These demands have arisen on a variety of political issues, notably those which demonstrate that Parliamentary opinion is out of tune with public opinion - for example, on the emotive issue of capital punishment. Of course, national referenda have not been a defining characteristic of our constitutional arrangements in Britain and most MPs in all parties have been determined to see that this remains the position. Yet there is always a temptation for political demagogues or other publicity seekers to break ranks from their colleagues in Parliament by calling for national referenda on certain issues when they believe that the results would be in their favour.

The important and much publicised referenda on British membership of the European Community in 1975 and on devolution to Scotland and Wales in 1979 are still generally considered to have been special cases. The reason is that they were conducted on constitutional issues of major importance in which the very future of Parliament itself was intimately involved. They could therefore be regarded as exceptions to the general rule that we have Parliamentary rather than plebiscitary democracy in Britain. On the other hand, it would seem that once such precedents have been set and the public appetite for direct decision-making has been whetted, it may prove increasingly difficult for MPs in all parties to resist further demands for referenda on a wide range of political issues, especially when public feeling is running high, powerful cause groups are involved or a majority in the House of Commons is seen to be out of tune with the majority mood of the general public.

**The impact of public demonstrations**

Finally, we should not neglect the impact of public demonstrations as a powerful form of non-verbal and non-literate political communication. We should note the fact that at various stages in our history public protest, whether spontaneous or induced, has played an important part in the expression of public opinion. We need only instance Wat Tyler and the Peasants' Revolt in 1381, the Peterloo Massacre in 1819, the Chartist Movement in the 1840s, the Suffragette demonstrations in the early 1900s, the unemployment marches in the 1930s or the inner city riots in 1981. All provide examples of the power of public opinion, whether expressed lawfully or unlawfully and whether representing majority or minority views at the time.

Nowadays lawful public demonstrations are usually organised for publicity purposes by minorities who feel strongly about an issue and who may also feel excluded from the regular channels of influence and representation in our society. The fact that some people have recourse to such methods may cast doubt upon the validity of their arguments. Yet more often it reflects their assessment of the chances of attaining their objectives by more orthodox institutional means, such as official consultations in Whitehall. For example, those who believe in the merits of unilateral nuclear disarmament have chosen to squat outside Greenham Common air base or to march in large processions through London, since they do not believe that more conventional means of putting their case would have as much impact upon the decision-makers. Public demonstrations have always been a recognised way of seeking publicity for a grievance or support for a cause and most are conducted in a peaceful and law-abiding manner. Yet they do not always succeed in influencing political decisions in their chosen direction, since their impact upon the passive majority of public opinion is often adverse and occasionally counter-productive.

## 8.4 CONCLUSION

In summary, public opinion in Britain can be regarded as a source of political legitimacy, a counterweight to the influence of pressure groups, a form of political intelligence and increasingly perhaps as a 'Court of Appeal' in matters of strong public concern or major constitutional significance. However, its true value is limited by the fact that in complex issues of national policy it is usually not based upon sufficient knowledge or experience and is often more of a reflection than an inspiration for the positions taken by leading politicians and other opinion-formers. It is undoubtedly a dynamic factor in the working of the British political system, since it involves a constant and continuous process of two-way communication between the politicans and the people.

It is clear that political leadership therefore has a major part to play in the formation of British public opinion. Yet if such leadership is to be really effective, it will have to make itself felt beyond the limited confines of Westminster and Whitehall. Metropolitan élites will need to leave the corridors of power more often in order to make genuine and repeated contacts with the general public in all parts of the country. All opinion-formers will need to have a clearer idea of what they want to say and how best to communicate their message. The key figures in the media will need to offer more political news and views and to present such material in balanced and responsible ways. Schools and other institutions of learning will need to put more emphasis upon political literacy in all its forms. Yet even assuming a reasonable degree of success with all these endeavours, the politicians will still have to keep their fingers crossed and hope that the British people really want to play a full part in the political system.

## SUGGESTED QUESTIONS

1. What are the main components of public opinion in Britain?
2. How is public opinion formed in Britain today?
3. What are the effects of public opinion upon contemporary British politics?

## NOTES

1. Both quoted in A. H. Birch, *Representative and Responsible Government* (London: Allen & Unwin, 1964) p. 172.
2. A. V. Dicey, *Law and Opinion in England in the Nineteenth Century* (London: Macmillan, 1905) p. 10.
3. V. O. Key, *Public Opinion and American Democracy* (New York: Knopf, 1961) p. 14.
4. R. Rose (ed.) *Studies in British Politics*, 3rd edn (London: Macmillan, 1976) p. 254.
5. V. O. Key, *Public Opinion and American Democracy*, p. 285.
6. See D. E. Butler and D. Stokes, *Political Change in Britain*, 2nd edn (London: Macmillan, 1974) pp. 19–151.
7. See H. T. Himmelweit *et al.*, *How Voters Decide* (London: Academic Press, 1981) pp. 50–72.
8. In H. R. Penniman (ed.) *Britain at the Polls, 1979* (Washington DC: American Enterprise Institute, 1981) p. 282.
9. For example, during the 1979 General Election campaign Margaret Thatcher and her senior colleagues were obliged to abandon any ideas which they might have had of breaking the link between increases in

state pensions and increases in the cost of living and also to confirm their willingness to honour the so-called Clegg recommendations on pay comparability for the public sector, in both cases because of the anticipated public reaction to what they might have wished to do. Similarly, at the 1982 Conservative Party Conference Margaret Thatcher was obliged to reassure the wider public that the National Health Service was 'safe with us', even though she and her Treasury colleagues may have been tempted to adopt the recommendations contained in a report by the Central Policy Review Staff, one of which would have involved severe cuts in the National Health Service.

10. For example, Michael Foot, when leader of the Labour party, consistently trailed behind Margaret Thatcher in the opinion polls and even behind the ratings given to his party. One of the effects of his poor showing in the opinion polls was to damage the morale of his Parliamentary colleages and his party activists throughout the country. This, in turn, must have damaged the electoral fortunes of the Labour party to some extent.
11. In H. R. Penniman (ed.) *Britain at the Polls, 1979*, pp. 201-2.
12. See D. E. Butler and A. Ranney (eds) *Referendums, a comparative study of practice and theory* (Washington, DC: American Enterprise Institute, 1978) for a fuller discussion of the role of referenda in politics.

## FURTHER READING


Butler, D. E. and Ranney, A. (eds) *Referendums, a Comparative Study of Practice and Theory* (Washington, DC: American Enterprise Institute, 1978).

Butler, D. E. and Stokes, D., *Political Change in Britain*, 2nd edn (London: Macmillan, 1974).

Clemens, J., *Polls, Politics and Populism* (London: Gower, 1983).

Hodder-Williams, R., *Public Opinion Polls and British Politics* (London: Routledge & Kegan Paul, 1970).

Johnson, N., *In Search of the Constitution* (London: Methuen, 1980).

Macfarlane, L. J., *Issues in British Politics since 1945* (London: Longman, 1975).

Moodie, G. C. and Studdert-Kennedy, G., *Opinions, Publics and Pressure Groups* (London: Allen & Unwin, 1970).

Penniman, H. R. (ed.) *Britain at the Polls, 1979* (Washington, DC: American Enterprise Institute, 1981).

Rose, R., *Influencing Voters* (London: Faber, 1967).

Rose, R. (ed.) *Studies in British Politics*, 3rd edn (London: Macmillan, 1976).

Rush, M., *Parliament and the Public* (London: Longman, 1976).

Särlvik, B. and Crewe, I., *Decade of Dealignment* (Cambridge: Cambridge University Press, 1983).

Teer, F. and Spence, J. D., *Political Opinion Polls* (London: Hutchinson, 1973).

Worcester, R. M. and Harrop, M. (eds) *Political Communications* (London: Allen & Unwin, 1982).

# PART III
# PARLIAMENT

# CHAPTER 9

# THE MONARCHY

In formal terms the Monarchy is one of the institutions of Parliament. With a Queen on the throne every Government is 'Her Majesty's Government' and the Monarch still has an important, if largely formal, part to play in our constitutional proceedings. It is the Queen who opens every session of Parliament, who reads the speech from the throne on such occasions and who later in the year gives her Royal assent to Bills without which they could not become Acts of Parliament. Admittedly, the Monarch has long been regarded as one of the 'dignified' as distinct from the 'efficient' parts of the constitution (in Walter Bagehot's nineteenth-century terminology). Yet for all that it is still appropriate that we should consider the Monarchy in this part of the book.

## 9.1 POWERS AND FUNCTIONS

The powers which the Monarchy now possesses are more theoretical than real, since they are based upon no more than conventions and residual Royal prerogatives. This means that they can only be used within the confines of well-established custom and practice. If such conventions were ever broken by the Monarch, it would discredit and possibly do fatal damage to the institution of Monarchy itself.

### The choice of Prime Minister

Whereas George III chose and dismissed Prime Ministers almost at will, Elizabeth II is normally free to choose as Prime Minister only the elected leader of the largest single party in the Commons. It would only be in the special circumstances of a 'hung Parliament' - that is, when no single party has an overall majority in the Commons - that the Queen might be free to choose someone else, if there were to be another leading political figure with a better chance of forming a Government which could command the support of a majority in the Commons.

However, this has not always been the position even in modern times. In January 1957 when Anthony Eden became too ill to continue as Prime Minister, the Queen took advice from Sir Winston Churchill and the Marquess of Salisbury and invited Harold Macmillan to form a new Government. In October 1963 when Harold Macmillan became seriously ill and a successor had to be found, the Queen again took advice - this time from Harold Macmillan in hospital - before inviting Lord Home to form a new Government. In both cases a new leader of the Conservative party was said to have 'emerged' from the process of informal soundings which characterised the decision-making of the party in those days. On the latter occasion the behaviour of the so-called 'magic-circle' was strongly criticised by Iain Macleod and Enoch Powell who both refused to serve in Lord Home's Administration.

Since 1965 in the case of the Conservative party (and 1922 in the case of the Labour party) there have been more systematic arrangements to ensure that a new leader is rapidly elected to succeed one who retires or dies. The result is that the role of the Queen is now confined to choosing as Prime Minister whoever has already been elected as leader of the largest single party in the Commons. Of course, when there is a clear change of Government following a clear-cut result in a General Election, the Queen sends for the leader of the victorious party and invites him to form a new Government.

There has always been a possibility of a more significant role for the Monarch at a time of national crisis or when a General Election produces a 'hung Parliament'. An example of the first eventuality occurred in 1931 when George V was instrumental in encouraging the formation of the National Government under Ramsay Macdonald in order to get through the Commons the deflationary economic measures which were not acceptable to a significant part of the Parliamentary Labour Party. Another example occurred in 1940 when George VI had some influence upon the choice of Winston Churchill to succeed Neville Chamberlain as Prime Minister after the latter had been discredited by the significant number of abstentions within the Conservative party at the end of a crucial debate of confidence on the conduct of the war. An example of the second eventuality occurred in February 1974 when it seemed possible for a while that the Queen could have been drawn into political controversy by Edward Heath's attempt to retain power for the Conservatives by offering a pact to the Liberals after his Government had been defeated at the General Election. As things turned out, it proved impossible for the Liberal leader, Jeremy Thorpe, to persuade his party to do such a deal with the Conservatives. Thus a few days later Harold Wilson was duly invited by the Queen to form a minority Labour Government.

### Dissolution of Parliament

It is now a well-established convention that the Monarch can only dissolve Parliament at the request of the Prime Minister in office within the five-year maximum life-span of a Parliament. It is necessary to go back to the reign of Queen Anne to find the last example of a Monarch exercising this Royal prerogative in an independent way. Even in 1913, when it was argued by some that George V might have been within his constitutional rights to have dissolved Parliament in order to give the electorate a chance to pronounce upon the Liberal Government's Bill for Irish Home Rule which did not command all-party support in Ireland or in the rest of the United Kingdom, A. V. Dicey, the eminent constitutional expert, was not prepared to recommend such a step to the King.

Since that time various views have been advanced about the power of dissolution. One view, which was advocated by some after the General Election in 1950, holds that if the Prime Minister in office is not prepared to advise a dissolution in circumstances where it might be considered in the national interest to have one, then the Monarch is entitled to seek other leading figures who might be prepared to advise such a course. However, such a view did not prevail in 1950 and it has not prevailed ever since. The Monarch is therefore governed by the conventional view which holds that she is obliged to accept only the advice of the Prime Minister in office.

There may, however, be a valid distinction between the Monarch's constitutional right to refuse a dissolution on the grounds that it would lead to a premature and unnecessary General Election and the now unsustainable claim by any Monarch to the right to impose a dissolution contrary to the wishes of the Prime Minister in office. In practice, of course, either form of Royal initiative would run the serious risk of fatally discrediting the whole idea of constitutional Monarchy in this country. It would involve the Monarchy in apparently taking sides in the party battle and this would destroy its vital asset of political impartiality.

Notwithstanding the conventional wisdom on this matter, there are some conceivable circumstances in which the Queen might be justified in exercising the Royal prerogative of dissolution in defiance of the wishes of the Prime Minister in office. For example, if it became clear in the course of a 'hung Parliament' that a particular minority Government had outlived its usefulness and was simply standing in the way of a timely General Election which might produce a clear Parliamentary result, those who advise the Palace might be prepared to recommend a dissolution to the Queen. Such a course of action might also be considered if any Government broke the most basic of electoral rules, namely the five-year maximum life-span of a Parliament, without the necessary all-party support for doing so, as has existed, for example, in time of war.[1] However, it must be stressed that these are all hypothetical circumstances which would be most unlikely to arise in practice today.

In all such eventualities it is likely that the Monarch would win no more than a Pyrrhic victory, since such steps would almost certainly lead to a 'Monarch versus people' clash at the ensuing General Election which would probably be won by the aggrieved political party which claimed to represent the will of the people. Even if that were not the outcome, the Monarch would incur the lasting hostility of the aggrieved political party which could put in jeopardy the very continuation of our constitutional Monarchy. The practical conclusion, therefore, is that any Monarch in this country today has no sensible alternative to accepting the advice of the Prime Minister in office, whatever might appear to be the temptations of doing otherwise.

**Assent to legislation**

Royal assent to legislation is another aspect of the Monarch's prerogative which has become purely formal. Charles II managed to postpone or quash Bills of which he disapproved by the simple expedient of mislaying them. Queen Anne was the last British Monarch to veto legislation outright. George III and George IV both managed to delay legislation on Catholic emanicipation by letting it be known that they were not happy with the idea. However, today the Royal assent is a mere formality and any attempt to make it otherwise would precipitate a constitutional crisis.

**Creation of peers**

The Monarch has the power to create new peers and in certain cases it is believed that the Palace still has some influence over the final selection from the various names proposed. Certainly there was a time when the use of this particular Royal prerogative was formidable indeed. For example, in 1711 Queen Anne created twelve new peers precisely to ensure Parliamentary ratification of the Treaty of Utrecht. In 1831 even the threat of William IV to create new peers helped to ensure the passage of the first Reform Bill and in 1911 the willingness of George V to create as many as 400 new Liberal peers caused the hereditary majority of Conservatives in the upper House to give way to the Liberal majority in the House of Commons.[2]

In contemporary circumstances the creation of new peers by the Monarch has become little more than a constitutional formality. Appointments to the peerage are normally made twice a year when the names of the newly-created peers appear in the Honours Lists. The appointments are made on the basis of advice given and co-ordinated by the Prime Minister in office, although anyone can make suggestions which are then discreetly sifted and assessed by a small unit of civil servants attached to 10 Downing Street before the Prime Minister of the day makes any recommendations.

Since 1964 life peerages have been the usual order of the day, mainly because successive Prime Ministers have not felt generally inclined to recommend the creation of hereditary peerages to the Monarch. However, this is no more than a convention of recent times and as such it can always be modified or reversed. For example, immediately after the 1983 General Election William Whitelaw and George Thomas were made hereditary peers on the recommendation of Mrs Thatcher, the former in recognition of his distinguished service to the Conservative party and the nation and the latter in recognition of his distinguished period as Speaker of the House of Commons. In each case the Queen complied with the Prime Minister's wishes, as she is wont to do with other recommendations which are made to her in the normal way.[3]

**Granting of honours**

The Monarch is also formally involved in the granting of a range of honours, both civilian and military, to those whom it is customary for society to recognise and reward in this way. As with the creation of peerages, this usually happens twice a year when the Honours Lists are published, although there can be special investitures to recognise special events, for example, the honours awarded to some of those who took part in the 1982 Falklands campaign. On every occasion the system is a popular and effective way of recording public recognition of those who have made notable contributions to the well-being of British society and who have shone in various walks of life. It also adds lustre to the institution of Monarchy and provides regular opportunities for rewarding service to the community in a way which does not involve either bribery or corruption.

Nearly all such honours are awarded by the Monarch on the recommendation of the Prime Minister who is of course advised by a small civil service unit attached to No 10 Downing Street. Once again this unit sifts and assesses a wide range of recommendations made by MPs and others. However, a few honours have remained in the personal gift of the Monarch, for example, the Order of the Garter, the Order of the Thistle, the Order of Merit and the Royal Victorian Order. Usually these awards have no political significance and are simply a way of signifying the Monarch's personal recognition of an outstanding person, such as Mother Theresa, the Catholic charity worker in Calcutta, who was awarded the Order of Merit by the Queen on her visit to India for the 1983 Commonwealth Conference. Yet occasionally they do have political significance, as was the case when the Queen awarded the Royal Victorian Order to Sir Humphrey Gibbs for his personal loyalty to the Crown in continuing to act as Governor of Rhodesia long after that country had been declared unilaterally independent in 1965 by Ian Smith and the Rhodesian National Front.

**Public appointments**

The Queen plays a formal role in many public appointments, since all important positions in the civil service, the police, the judiciary, the BBC and the Church of England are filled in the name of the Monarch, not to mention of course the Ministerial appointments in every Government. Once again such appointments are usually made on the basis of advice given or co-ordinated by the Prime Minister often with the help of the small civil service unit attached to 10 Downing Street which processes the recommendations from all quarters. Senior appointments in the Diplomatic Service are made on the advice of the Foreign Secretary, in the armed services on the advice of the Defence Secretary, in the police on the advice of the Home Secretary and in the judiciary on the advice of the Lord Chancellor, although it must be added that all Prime Ministers take a close personal interest in all such recommendations to the Monarch.

In these circumstances it is not surprising perhaps that some concern has been expressed from time to time about the nature and scope of such patronage which is Royal in name but Ministerial in fact.[4] A number of politicians (notably Tony Benn) and some journalists have been concerned about the lack of prior public scrutiny or subsequent democratic accountability of such public appointments, not to mention the implications for public expenditure in the wide range of public bodies to which such people are appointed. Yet this kind of political patronage has not led the critics to attack the Monarch, since it is well understood that the Monarch is merely acting as a dignified rubber stamp for appointments which are not really within her control.

**Mercy and pardon**

The prerogatives of mercy and pardon are still vested in the Monarch who is entitled to exercise them on the advice of the Home Secretary. However, since the House of Commons voted in 1965 to abolish the death penalty on a provisional basis and since that decision has subsequently been confirmed in successive free votes, it now seems that this particular aspect of the Royal prerogative has fallen into disuse. Pardons are granted only after conviction and sentence in rare cases when there is some special reason why a sentence should not be carried out or a conviction should be expunged, for example, a discovery that the evidence on which a conviction was based is actually false. Thus the exercise of this aspect of the Royal prerogative has been both formal and rare.

**Other formal functions**

Several formal functions are exercised in the name of the Monarch, but actually by Ministers. These include major matters, such as the conclusion of international treaties, declarations of war, the introduction or amendment of colonial constitutions and the establishment of public corporations. In each case the Monarch is acting as a splendid and dignified veil for decisions which are actually taken by Ministers in the Government of the day.

In the conduct of foreign policy the Royal prerogative to conclude treaties enables Ministers to reach legally binding agreements with other Governments without having to secure the prior approval of Parliament. For example, the 1972 Treaty of Accession which took Britain into the European Community was signed by Edward Heath as Prime Minister in Brussels without the Government having had to secure the prior approval of Parliament at Westminster. Unlike the constitutional position in the United States where treaties negotiated by the Administration have to secure the 'advice and consent' of the Senate before they can become law, the position in Britain is that it is only if treaties have legislative consequences in the United Kingdom that the Government has to involve Parliament and even then this need only be done after treaties have been signed by Ministers on behalf of the Crown.

A declaration of war is made officially in the name of the Monarch, although in the nuclear age such formalities might be of little more than academic interest in certain circumstances if time were very short. In the event of a major war which directly affected this country, it would be for the Prime Minister and a few senior colleagues and advisers to take all the key decisions. Such decisions would merely be ratified by the Monarch as and when appropriate. In the case of the 1982 Falklands conflict Britain did not declare war upon Argentina, since there were technical and legal reasons for not doing so. Although the Queen was not therefore required to sign a declaration of war, she was kept informed by the Prime Minister at every stage of the conflict.

Colonial constitutions are promulgated or changed in the name of the Monarch. For example, the constitution of Zimbabwe, which British Ministers had negotiated with the representatives of all the parties at Lancaster House in 1979-80, was eventually promulgated in the name of the Queen and given statutory authority in the Zimbabwe Independence Act of 1980.

The creation of public corporations is also done in the name of the Monarch by granting Royal Charters to the bodies concerned. For example, the BBC became a public corporation by Royal Charter in 1926. The various New Towns - for example, Milton Keynes and Telford - which were built over the years since the war were established in a similar way, as were the new universities - for example Sussex and Essex - which were built in the 1960s and 1970s.

**Symbolic functions**

The Queen and other members of the Royal family play an important symbolic role in many different ways. For example, the Queen has made innumerable State visits during her long reign to countries in all parts of the world and she has played an important role at successive Commonwealth Conferences and in entertaining foreign Heads of State or Government when they visit this country. In all such activities she and other members of the Royal family are serving the national interest, as defined by the Government of the day. More generally, the Monarch plays an important symbolic role as Head of the Commonwealth. This has involved her and other members of the Royal family in travelling thousands of miles to different parts of the world to see and be seen by millions of people in the forty-eight member nations of the Commonwealth. It has also led her to attach considerable personal importance to her annual Christmas broadcasts to the people of this country and the rest of the Commonwealth.

At home the Queen and other members of the Royal family are also involved by custom and tradition, and sometimes at the instigation of the Government, in the promotion of good causes and in various forms of ceremonial designed to raise the morale and to reinforce the unity of the British people. For example, the Queen usually leads the nation in paying respect to the dead of two World Wars and other conflicts at the Cenotaph in Whitehall on Remembrance Sunday every year. She and other members of the Royal family also pay conspicuous visits to all parts of the United Kingdom, including notably those where the people have suffered from natural disasters (as at Aberfan in 1966) or been involved in social unrest (such as the inner city areas of London and Liverpool after the 1981 riots). In these and many other ways the Monarchy makes a valuable contribution to the underlying cohesion and morale of the British people.

**Unpublicised functions**

The Monarch also performs some unpublicised functions, the most notable of which are her regular and confidential contacts with every Prime Minister in office. On such occasions the Monarch still enjoys what Walter Bagehot once described as 'the right to be consulted, the right to encourage and the right to warn'.[5] In modern circumstances these rights are exercised during her private conversations with the Prime Minister every week when she is at Buckingham Palace and once a year for several days in the late summer when she is on holiday at Balmoral.

The Queen's experience of the affairs of state is now unrivalled in modern times, since in more than thirty years on the throne she has had eight different Prime Ministers and twelve different Governments. She has the undisputed right to see all state papers and in consequence she is almost certainly better informed about key political developments than anyone else in the land. Her private advice to all Prime Ministers must be invaluable in view of the length and variety of her experience of matters of state. Indeed, one former Prime Minister apparently accepted the analogy of paying a weekly visit to a psychiatrist and admitted that he could say things to the Queen that he could not say even to his closest political colleagues.[6] The functions of the Monarchy are summarised below in Figure 9.1.

Fig 9.1 *Functions of the Monarchy*

| *In Parliament* | *Political functions* |
|---|---|
| State opening of Parliament<br>Royal Assent to Bills<br>Dissolution of Parliament | Choice of Prime Minister<br>Creation of peers<br>Granting of honours<br>Public appointments |
| *Other formal functions* | *Quasi-judicial functions* |
| Conclusion of treaties<br>Declaration of war<br>Introduction or amendment of colonial constitutions<br>Establishment of public corporations | Prerogative of mercy<br>Prerogative of pardon |
| *Symbolic functions* | *Unpublicised functions* |
| Head of the Commonwealth<br>State visits abroad<br>Entertaining foreign Heads of State in U.K.<br>Patronage of good causes<br>Visits to all parts of U.K.<br>Military ceremonial<br>Religious ceremonial | Personal contacts with the Prime Minister<br>Confidential advice to the Government |

## 9.2 THE MONARCHY AND THE PUBLIC

### Public attitudes towards the Monarchy

Although the Monarchy is probably the most revered of our national institutions, it would be a mistake to exaggerate the degree of deference shown towards it by ordinary British people. It tends to appeal more to women than to men and to those of deferential disposition more than those who value social equality. A 1969 opinion poll demonstrated considerable public support for the Monarchy in that only 13 per cent thought it should be ended, 30 per cent thought it should continue as it was and 50 per cent thought it should continue but change with the times (7 per cent had no opinion).[7] A more recent opinion poll in 1980 showed that the continuing popular appeal of the Monarchy is derived to a significant extent from the fact that it is usually projected to the people as the 'Royal Family', which 80 per cent of those questioned thought to be 'a marvellous example to everyone of good family life'.[8] The same poll also showed that 90 per cent of those questioned preferred the British Monarchy to a Republic of the French or American type.

Furthermore, the criticism that the Monarchy is unduly privileged and fundamentally undemocratic cuts very little ice with anyone in Britain except a few dedicated republicans. Nearly all the British people realise quite well that the Monarchy is bound to be privileged financially and in other ways. Only 30 per cent of those questioned in the 1980 poll thought that the Monarchy cost the country more than it was worth and another poll the following year revealed that 76 per cent of those questioned thought that the benefits of the Monarchy outweighed the costs.[9] Thus it seems clear that public attitudes remain well disposed towards both the Queen and her family and that this public support is unlikely to evaporate as long as the Monarch and her advisers recognise the conventions which limit her constitutional position.

Since in our modern television age there is always a risk that familiarity will diminish the respect traditionally shown to the Monarch, the Queen and her advisers have been careful to preserve the vital elements of glamour and mystery which have long enhanced the position of the Monarchy in the eyes of ordinary people. We need only reflect upon the brilliant way in which the 1977 Silver Jubilee celebrations or the 1981 Royal Wedding were organised by the Palace to see that the Royal family and its advisers have lost none of their flair for publicity and spectacular ceremonial. Such glittering events, as well as the more homely Christmas broadcasts by the Queen to the nation and the Commonwealth, have done much over the years to tighten the bonds of sentiment and loyalty between the Royal family and the British public. On such a basis of affection and respect there seems little doubt that the British public will retain its positive attitudes towards the Monarchy for many years to come.

**Financial position of the Monarchy**

The Queen receives an annual sum of about £3.7 million (in 1983) from public funds and allowances are also paid to the Duke of Edinburgh, the Prince of Wales, the Queen Mother, Princess Margaret, Princess Anne and other active members of the Royal family. Half the revenue from the Duchy of Cornwall goes to the Prince of Wales (the other half goes to the Exchequer) while the Royal residences, aircraft and yacht are all maintained from public funds. The Royal family also has a large private fortune which has been inherited free of death duties, as well as valuable collections of jewellery, stamps and pictures, some of which are put on show to the public.[10]

This privileged financial position is scarcely challenged, since the vast majority of people in this country believe that the Queen and her family perform their official duties with exemplary charm and efficiency. The few notorious critics of the Monarchy, such as Willie Hamilton MP, tend to concentrate their criticism upon the cost of supporting the Royal household and the somewhat anachronistic image of some of the courtiers. In general, however, such critical views are not widely shared and successive Governments have not been criticised for seeing that the Monarchy is adequately supported to enable it to carry out its constitutional duties without financial or other embarrassment.

**Possible future problems**

It would appear that the position of the Monarchy in Britain is secure both in constitutional terms and in the hearts and minds of the British people. Yet this might not always be the case in future if the Monarchy were to be faced with awkward constitutional problems which required new or unconventional solutions. As Hugo Young has suggested, there are at least three possible scenarios which could put the Monarchy in a difficult position in future.[11]

One future possibility is that an unpopular Prime Minister might carry out a threat to call a General Election in mid-Parliament rather than agree under pressure from senior Cabinet colleagues either to change Government policy or even to resign the Premiership. In such circumstances the established political conventions would support the Prime Minister, even if there appeared to be sufficient support in the governing party for a change of policy or even for a new Premier. Whatever might be the private views of the Queen and her advisers, it seems clear that she would be obliged to grant the wish of the Prime Minister in office, however unpopular that might be with large sections of the governing party.

Another possibility is that a future Labour Government might be committed to the effective abolition of the House of Lords. In such an eventuality much would depend upon whether the Monarch considered that the new Government had a clear mandate for such a far-reaching constitutional change. If so, she would probably conclude that she had no alternative but to approve the creation of perhaps as many as 1000 new Labour peers whose sole task in the House of Lords would be to vote for their own abolition. Yet it is not absolutely certain that the Queen would act in this way, since she might be advised that the demise of the House of Lords foreshadowed the demise of the Monarchy itself. If that were to be the case, the only way out might be to hold a national referendum on the subject. However, she could not force such an idea on the Government and its realisation would require the approval of a majority in the House of Commons.

Yet another possibility, and one which is inherently more plausible, is that the outcome of a future General Election might well be another 'hung Parliament' in which no single party had an overall majority.[12] In such an eventuality the Queen would be expected to send initially for the leader of the largest single party in the Commons who would then have to see whether he could form a minority Government or arrive at some sort of understanding with one or more of the other parties. Either course would be quite plausible and it would only be in the unlikely event of complete Parliamentary deadlock that the Queen might be advised to send for another leading figure to form a viable Government rather than agree to an early dissolution very soon after the previous General Election.

The point is that in any of these circumstances the Monarch would have some very awkward decisions to take. The answer to the problem might be for her to allow another General Election very soon after the one which had created all the Parliamentary difficulty. It might be to charge a leading political figure with a conditional commission to form a Government only if he could establish that he would have the necessary Parliamentary support to do so. Whatever the outcome, the Queen might be obliged to play a decisive, even prominent role in the process of Government formation. This is not something which she or her private advisers would relish, since it might well cast doubt upon the traditional neutrality of the Monarchy in all party political matters. This, in turn, could damage the satisfactory relationship which has existed for so long between the Monarchy and virtually all sections of Parliamentary and public opinion in Britain.

## 9.3 **CONCLUSION**

The Monarchy still holds the supreme position at the apex of British society. Yet it does so at the expense of its previous claims before 1832 to wield real political power. Today it remains the quintessence of all that is most dignified and dazzling in our constitutional arrangements. It serves as a powerful symbol of continuity and community which is particularly valuable to the nation in difficult or troubled times.

The Monarchy provides an excellent example of the many paradoxes which abound in the British political system. It is an inherently conservative institution which facilitates change. Whatever else may be altered, the Monarchy appears to most people to be an unchanging landmark and point of reference. Such seemingly permanent institutions can make it easier for people to accept radical change in other areas of their existence, since they provide a measure of reassurance that at least some things remain the same. It therefore plays an important part in preserving the cohesion of the British political system and contributes significantly to the sentiment of underlying national unity which helps to hold society together. If it did not exist, it would probably have to be invented.

## SUGGESTED QUESTIONS

1. What are the functions of the British Monarchy?
2. Does the Monarch still have any real power in Britain today?
3. Analyse the relationship between the Monarchy and the British public.

## NOTES

1. The Parliaments elected in 1910 and 1935 were each extended by all-party agreement, in the former case until the so-called 'khaki election' in 1919 and in the latter case until the 1945 election which took place soon after the agreed ending of the wartime Coalition Government.
2. Some historians would argue that in 1831 the threat of the mob and in 1911 the threat of rebellion in Ireland also played a major part in persuading the Conservative peers to give way to the Government of the day in the Commons.
3. An even more recent departure from the modern norm was the granting of an hereditary Earldom to Harold Macmillan in February 1984, an honour which he had been offered when he ceased to be Prime Minister in October 1963 but which he had consistently refused to accept.
4. Among those who have expressed concern about this are A. Benn, *Arguments for Democracy* (London: Jonathan Cape, 1981) pp. 18–43, and P. Holland and M. Fallon, *Public Bodies and Ministerial Patronage* (London: CPC, 1978). See also Chapter 16, Section 16.3, of this book for a fuller discussion of QUANGOs.
5. W. Bagehot, *The English Constitution* (London: Fontana, 1978) p. 11.
6. This is a point made by Dr David Butler in correspondence with the author.
7. See *The Sunday Times*, 23 March 1969.
8. See *Now*, 8 February 1980 (a weekly news magazine which later ceased publication).
9. See *The Guardian*, 22 July 1981.
10. In 1983 the annuities payable to the Monarch and other members of the Royal family under the Civil List voted by Parliament amounted to about £4.5 million in total. Various estimates have also been made of the private wealth of the Royal family ranging from £10 million to £70 million.
11. *The Sunday Times*, 8 November 1981.
12. See D. E. Butler, *Governing without a Majority* (London: Collins, 1983) pp. 72–134, for a fuller discussion of the issues which could arise in a future 'hung Parliament'.

## FURTHER READING

Bagehot, W., *The English Constitution* (London: Fontana, 1978).
Benemy, F. W. G., *The Queen Reigns, She Does Not Rule* (London: Harrap, 1963).
Butler, D. E., *Governing Without a Majority* (London: Collins, 1983).
Marshall, G. and Moodie, G. C., *Some Problems of the Constitution*, 5th edn (London: Hutchinson, 1971).
Martin, K., *The Crown and the Establishment* (Harmondsworth: Penguin, 1963).
Morrison, H., *Government and Parliament* (Oxford: Oxford University Press, 1959).
Murray-Brown, J. (ed.) *The Monarchy and its Future* (London: Allen & Unwin, 1969).
Petrie, C., *The Modern British Monarch* (London: Eyre & Spottiswoode, 1961).
Rose, R. (ed.) *Studies in British Politics*, 3rd edn (London: Macmillan, 1976).
Wade, E. C. S. and Phillips, G. G., *Constitutional and Administrative Law*, 9th edn (London: Longman, 1977).

# THE HOUSE OF LORDS

The House of Lords, which Walter Bagehot described in 1867 as one of the 'dignified' as opposed to the 'efficient' parts of the constitution, has had a long and varied history during which it has displayed considerable institutional resilience. However, since the 1832 Reform Act its existence has been characterised by steadily declining political power, offset to some extent by its continuing political influence especially in the Conservative party.

The 1911 Parliament Act provided the statutory basis for the present limitations upon the power of the Lords. This piece of legislation was really a constitutional package deal which affected both the Lords and the Commons. Its three main components were that Money Bills should become law within one month of being sent to the Lords, that no other Bills could be delayed by the Lords for more than two years and that the maximum span of a Parliament should be reduced from seven to five years. Although the 1911 Act restricted the power of the Lords, it did nothing to change the composition or the functions of the Upper House. Subsequently, the 1949 Parliament Act further reduced the delaying power of the Lords to one year, but failed once again to deal with either its composition or functions.

Since then there have been three minor reforms affecting the House of Lords and one further attempt at major reform which failed. In 1957 daily allowances were introduced for travel to and attendance at the House of Lords. In 1958 the Life Peerages Act made possible the creation of life peers, including women peers in their own right. In 1963 the Peerage Act allowed hereditary peers to disclaim their titles and so make themselves eligible for election or re-election to the House of Commons.[1]

The one further attempt at major reform which failed was the ill-fated Parliament Number 2 Bill which was introduced by the Labour Government in 1968. This involved both a reduction in the total number of peers and an attack upon the hereditary principle. The essential proposals were that there should be a reformed second Chamber composed of 250 peers with voting rights who would be appointed by the Government of the day, together with a larger number of peers who would have the right to speak but not to vote. The existing hereditary peers who were not among those appointed to the voting category would be allowed to remain in the non-voting category, although their heirs would not have had even that limited right. The composition of the appointed membership would have been reviewed from time to time and altered when necessary in order to ensure that the Government of the day always had a voting majority over the principal Opposition party but not necessarily over all the other parties together. The reformed body would have had a delaying power of six months and a number of other revising and burden sharing functions in the legislative sphere. However, the proposals were abandoned by the Government in 1969 in the wake of a sustained and effective filibuster by backbenchers on both sides of the Commons led by Enoch Powell and Michael Foot.

## 10.1 **COMPOSITION OF THE LORDS**

At the end of 1982 nearly 1200 peers were eligible to attend the House of Lords, although the average daily attendance in 1981–2 was about 290 and a total of almost 800 peers attended at least once during the session. This pattern of attendance is possible because under a Standing Order adopted by the House in 1958 peers may apply for leave of absence for the whole or part of a session at any time during a Parliament and a considerable number do so. At the same time any peer who wishes to attend the House can do so at a month's notice, even if he has previously been granted leave of absence, provided only that he has received a writ of summons in the first place.

Of the total of nearly 1200 peers in the House of Lords, about 800 are hereditary peers and about 330 are life peers. There are also twenty-six Bishops (including the Archbishops of Canterbury and York) and nineteen Law Lords (including the Lord Chancellor and former Lords of Appeal). Fifteen hereditary peers have disclaimed their titles under the provisions of the 1963 Peerage Act. Therefore the House is still disproportionately hereditary in its composition, even though the life peers tend to play a fuller and more regular part in its proceedings.

### Hereditary peers

The vast majority of hereditary peerages were created during this century and a significant number of them during the time when Lloyd George was Prime Minister (1916–22). However, some peerages were created much longer ago and are still extant, for example, the Dukedom of Norfolk in

1403, the Earldom of Shrewsbury in 1442 and the Barony of Mowbray in 1283. Very few hereditary peerages have been created since 1964, because successive Prime Ministers since that time have been reluctant to recommend such honours to the Queen. Labour Prime Ministers have been ideologically opposed to the expansion of the hereditary peerage and most Conservative Prime Ministers have not wanted to appear provocative on the issue. Yet there were notable departures from recent custom and practice when in June 1983 William Whitelaw and George Thomas were created hereditary peers on the recommendation of Mrs Thatcher and in February 1984 when Harold Macmillan finally accepted the hereditary Earldom which he had previously declined on ceasing to be Prime Minister in October 1963.

It should not be assumed that all hereditary peers are mere 'backwoodsmen', since some of them have played a distinguished part in Government. For example, Lord Home was Foreign Secretary in the Governments of Harold Macmillan and Edward Heath, Lord Shackleton was a senior member of Harold Wilson's Government, and Lord Carrington was Defence Secretary in Mr Heath's Government and Foreign Secretary in Mrs Thatcher's first Government. The hereditary peerage has also produced some very able younger peers who have been useful and effective Ministers, for example, the Conservative Lord Gowrie or the Labour Lord Melchett.

**Life peers**

All life peers have been created since 1958 and the vast majority of them have been distinguished men and women from a wide variety of walks of life who have been so honoured in recognition of their political or public services. They may be former civil servants or diplomats who retired at the top of their profession, distinguished soldiers, sailors or airmen who rose to the highest military ranks, successful industrialists or prominent trade union leaders, distinguished scientists or university academics, renowned actors or other figures from the world of the arts and the media. At the end of 1982 there were forty-three women among their number which was an increase compared with earlier years, but still a rather small figure.

However, by far the largest single category of life peers is composed of former politicians from the House of Commons or the world of local government. In the former case these tend to have been either retired senior Ministers or previously very senior back-benchers whom the Prime Minister of the day has wished to reward with a seat in the Lords. In the latter case they tend to have been distinguished local government figures whose experience in local government has been recognised or thought to be an attribute to the deliberations of the Lords. In both cases we can agree with Ian Gilmour who observed that 'the House of Lords does something to reduce the hazards of a political career and embalms without burying a number of useful politicians'.[2]

**Party divisions**

More than one third of the total of nearly 1200 peers take the Conservative whip and about 220 are registered as Independents. This means that about half of all those eligible to attend can be reckoned to be in the Conservative camp, while many of the rest are often sympathetic to the Conservative cause. By comparison, the numbers of Labour and Liberal peers are small, even insignificant. At the end of 1982 there were about 130 Labour peers and about 40 Liberal peers, as well as one Communist peer (Lord Milford). In 1981-2 the fastest growing party in the Lords was the Social Democratic party which recruited about thirty peers almost entirely from the ranks of former Labour peers. Cross-benchers do not sit on either side of the House, but at the end of the Chamber facing the Woolsack. By convention they include the twenty-six Bishops and a number of fastidious Law Lords and other peers who do not wish to take any party whip.

Party divisions in the Lords are not normally as sharp or bitter as they can be in the Commons and this is apparent in the relatively relaxed and polite style of debate in the Upper House. Most of the legislative work and speech-making is done by perhaps sixty to eighty particularly active peers, although a larger number usually take part in divisions. There have been occasions over the years when the natural Conservative majority has sought to amend or delay Labour legislation of which it disapproved and a few occasions on which similar treatment has been meted out to Conservative legislation. However, as we shall see, the Conservative peers have usually been rather careful (at any rate in modern times) not to use even the limited constitutional power which has been left to them in ways which would embarrass Conservative Governments or provoke Labour Governments. This is because they have recognised that such action could lead to a major constitutional conflict and even perhaps the abolition of the upper House.

## 10.2 POWERS AND FUNCTIONS

**Powers**

The powers of the House of Lords have been steadily reduced over the centuries. Today they consist essentially of the power of legislative delay (that is, the ability to delay for about one year the passage of Bills approved by the Commons), the power of legislative revision (that is, the ability to amend and improve Bills inadequately considered by the Commons) and the power of well-informed deliberation (that is, the ability to debate the issues of the day in a more knowledgeable and less partisan way than is often the case in the Commons).

The procedures of the 1911 and 1949 Parliament Acts, which confirmed the supremacy of the Commons over the Lords, have been used very rarely. The 1947 Parliament Bill became the 1949 Parliament Act under the procedures and powers which had been laid down in the 1911 Parliament Act. In 1974–6 the then Labour Government encountered temporary deadlock with the Conservative majority in the Lords over both the Trade Union and Labour Relations Amendment Bill and the Aircraft and Shipbuilding Industries Bill. In the latter case there had been complicated procedural arguments in the Commons about the 'hybridity' of the Bill which had cast doubts upon its constitutional validity and which had encouraged the Conservative peers to insist upon certain amendments which the Labour Government could not accept.[3] Although both Bills were reintroduced under the provisions of the 1949 Parliament Act, they subsequently became law in a form to which the Lords agreed after the Labour Government in the Commons had decided to make further amendments which went some way to meet the objections of the Conservative majority in the upper House. In 1981 the Conservative Government also ran into legislative difficulties with the Lords, including some of its own supporters, over certain clauses about rural transport in what later became the 1981 Education Act. However, the difficulties were eventually resolved in a manner consistent with the wishes of the Government.

All the evidence demonstrates that the powers of the Lords in relation to the Commons are no longer of decisive significance. On the whole the effect of the 1911 and 1949 Parliament Acts has been to inhibit the Lords in the exercise of even the limited degree of power which the law and conventions still allow. That is why most of those who have wanted to reform the Lords have really been seeking to strengthen the position of the upper House. It is also why any such reform is unlikely to be accomplished when so many members of all parties in the Commons are so strongly attached to the predominant position of the lower House. In such circumstances it is difficult to see how those who press for reform of the Lords will ever manage to overcome the objections of those who want to leave things as they are or to frustrate the purposes of those who favour the outright abolition of the upper House.

**Functions**

Paradoxically, the functions of the Lords appear to have grown over the years in modern times as their constitutional power has been steadily reduced. The clearest exposition of the functions of the Lords was provided by the Bryce Commission in 1918.[4] It identified four main functions for the upper House: legislative delay, legislative revision, the initiation of non-controversial legislation and well-informed deliberation upon the issues of the day.

To the four functions which were identified by the Bryce Commission, we must add the judicial function and the scrutiny functions. The former function is performed by the Law Lords in not more than two relatively small Appellate Committees in nearly all cases. The latter are performed by peers from all parties who are appointed to committees specially established for the careful consideration of Private Bills and the scrutiny of delegated legislation flowing from Government Departments in Whitehall and the European Community institutions in Brussels.

Fig 10.1 *Functions of the House of Lords*

*Legislative functions*

Legislative delay
Legislative revision
Initiation of non-controversial legislation

*Deliberative function*

Well-informed debate on the issues of the day

*Judicial functions*

Hearing of appeals in the Appellate Committee
Hearing of appeals in the Judicial Committee of the Privy Council

*Scrutiny functions*

Private Bill Committees
Joint Committee on Statutory Instruments
Select Committee on the European Communities

**Legislative delay**

In theory, the function of legislative delay is performed by the Lords when they refuse to approve legislation already passed by the Commons. In practice, since 1911 this function has been performed only sparingly, because the Conservative majority in the upper House has been well aware of the danger that excessive use of this power could hasten the day when a future Labour Government might decide to abolish the Lords altogether. For example, when the Conservative majority in the Lords opposed the 1947 Parliament Bill which was intended to reduce their delaying power from two years to one year, their opposition was little more than a political gesture and they did not really persist. Accordingly, the Bill duly became law two years later under the provisions of the 1911 Parliament Act.

In 1969 when the Conservative majority in the Lords insisted upon amendments to the House of Commons (Redistribution of Seats) Number 2 Bill, which was designed to free the Home Secretary, James Callaghan, from the legal obligation to lay before Parliament the reports of the Parliamentary Boundary Commissions, the Bill was lost. This was an action which the Conservative peers were perfectly justified in taking, since the Labour Government was involved in a cynical attempt to ensure that it fought the following General Election on outdated constituency boundaries which would improve Labour's electoral chances. The Bill was not reintroduced by the Labour Government in the following session and the recommendations of the Boundary Commissions were eventually implemented by the new Conservative Government after the 1970 General Election.

In the 1974–9 Parliament the Conservative majority in the Lords sought only rarely to use its constitutional delaying power, notably when seeking to exclude ship repairs from the nationalisation provisions of the 1975 Aircraft and Shipbuilding Industries Bill. The legislation was reintroduced in the following session and subsequently became law in 1976 after the Labour Government had agreed to omit the ship-repairing clauses as the price of getting the Bill with the consent of the Lords in good time. The Government could only have got the Bill in its original form if it had relied upon the provisions of the 1949 Parliament Act and this would have entailed a further delay until the end of the session which it was keen to avoid. Thus although the majority in the Commons can always get its way in the end if it really wants to do so, in some cases at least modern Governments have chosen to take account of objections made by the Lords and to respect the power of legislative delay still available to the upper House.

**Legislative revision**

The function of legislative revision performed by the House of Lords has long been necessary, especially when dealing with complex or controversial Government Bills. This is mainly because MPs very often make inefficient use of the time in Standing Committees when they are supposed to scrutinise and debate Bills line by line and clause by clause. The result is that there is often a need for legislative revision which falls upon the House of Lords where many of the necessary amendments and new clauses are introduced by Ministers on behalf of the Government. Sometimes this arises from second thoughts by Ministers on points which have been debated during the Committee stage in the Commons. Sometimes it is a response to continuing pressure from interest groups involved with the legislation. Sometimes it is simply a matter of doing in the Lords what should have been done in the Commons, if there had been enough time to do so and if all parties when in Opposition did not spend so much of the available time in Committee simply filibustering on the early clauses of Bills. This is therefore a function performed by the Lords which is essential to maintaining the quality of the legislative output of Parliament. If the upper House did not perform this function, the Commons would have to do so and this would oblige them to change their procedures and practices in ways which many in the lower House would prefer not to do.

**Initiation of non-controversial legislation**

The initiation of legislation which is largely non-controversial in party political terms is another useful function performed by the House of Lords. This has the effect of relieving the Commons of at least some of the legislative burden at the beginning of every session of Parliament. Indeed, it has been estimated that since 1945 about one quarter of all Government Bills have been introduced in this way.

This procedure is particularly appropriate with legislation which is both complex and technical, but which is not a source of fierce party political controversy, such as Bills on data protection or energy conservation. It is also popular with many of their Lordships who like to get away from London to their estates or grouse moors well before 12 August every year, an aspiration which can be thwarted if the upper House has to deal with too much legislation coming from the Commons during the second half of each session.

**Deliberative function**

The deliberative function of well-informed debate upon the issues of the day is another worthwhile aspect of the activities of the House of Lords. This is because the standard of debate and argument in the upper House is often very high and because the issues are usually approached in a serious and relatively dispassionate way. Indeed, the Lords can often find time to debate important and topical issues which might never get an airing in the more partisan and busy conditions of the Commons. In such debates the Lords can also draw upon the wealth of knowledge and experience which is available among their number, especially the life peers who include Fellows of the Royal Society and others of great intellectual and professional distinction. This is therefore one of the activities of the Lords which can have considerable influence in Whitehall and Westminster and often upon the climate of informed opinion in the country.

**Judicial function**

Formerly there was no restriction on the participation of lay peers in the judicial proceedings of the House of Lords. However, after the O'Connell case in 1844, in which their intervention would have had the effect of overturning the decision of the Law Lords (that is, the Lord Chancellor, the Lords of Appeal and such peers as held or had held high judicial office in a superior Court), it became an established convention that they should not take part in the judicial work of the House. Because of the ensuing shortage of peers who had held high judicial office, the 1876 Appellate Jurisdiction Act provided for the appointment of two Lords of Appeal and declared that appeals to the Lords should not be heard unless at least three Law Lords were present. In 1948 the Lords authorised (on a temporary basis at first) the hearing of appeals by an Appellate Committee drawn from the eleven appointed Law Lords and the other senior legal figures already mentioned. After a time this innovation became permanent, so that nearly all appeals to the House of Lords are now heard by the Law Lords sitting as either one or two Appellate Committees, depending upon the number of cases to be heard.[5]

Judgements on appeal to the Lords are still delivered by members of the Appellate Committee meeting in the Chamber, but since 1963 this has taken the form of written opinions from each individual judge. Usually appeals are heard by a Committee of five judges and decisions are reached by majority. The judgements of the Law Lords have great authority and have influenced the development of English law over the years. For a long time the Law Lords regarded themselves as bound by legal precedents established in their earlier decisions, but since 1966 they have been prepared occasionally to modify that doctrine by departing from their previous decisions when it has appeared right to do so. This is, therefore, another vital function of the House of Lords, albeit one which is usually exercised by only a small Committee of Law Lords.

**Scrutiny functions**

Finally, there are the very important scrutiny functions of the House of Lords. These are exercised by special Committees established for the careful consideration of Private Bills and the scrutiny of delegated legislation flowing from Government Departments in Whitehall and from the European Community institutions in Brussels.

In the former category, Private Bills (which are Bills to alter the law relating to a particular locality or to confer rights or relieve liabilities from a particular person or class of persons) may be assigned to a committee of five peers for their detailed consideration once the legislation has been through the earlier stages of public notification and Second Reading. Such Private Bill Committees have some of the attributes of quasi-judicial proceedings in that the promoters and opponents of Private Bills are usually represented by legal counsel and may call evidence in support of their arguments. Once this Committee stage is successfully concluded, the Bill is reported to the House where its subsequent stages are similar to those of a Public Bill.

In the latter case of delegated legislation, the original Act may confine to the Commons the responsibility for the Parliamentary control of the Statutory Instruments concerned, for example, as with all fiscal measures. However, in most other instances the Lords have the same power of control as the Commons. Nevertheless it is rare for the Lords to exercise a legal veto over such subordinate legislation and on those occasions when they have attempted to do so, there have often been adverse consequences for the Upper House. For example, in 1968 when the Lords unwisely rejected an Order under the 1965 Southern Rhodesia Act which contained provision for economic sanctions against the illegal regime in that territory, it caused the Labour Government to propose that the power of the Lords to veto Statutory Instruments should be abolished.

In most cases when general Statutory Instruments are laid before Parliament, they come under scrutiny by the Joint Committe on Statutory Instruments which consists of seven peers and seven MPs. The duty of the Committee is to consider whether the attention of Parliament should be drawn to a particular Statutory Instrument on any of a number of different grounds, for example, that it would impose a charge upon public funds, that it would be retrospective in effect, that it had been unjustifiably delayed or that there was doubt as to whether it would be *intra* or *ultra vires*. In short, the Committee may report on a Statutory Instrument on any technical ground which does not impinge upon its merits or the policy behind it. Very few of the Statutory Instruments are referred to Parliament in this way for further debate, although all those subject to the negative procedure and those subject to the positive procedure which are reported upon unfavourably, can be 'prayed against', that is made the subject of a critical motion put down by MPs or peers for debate on the floor of either House. The main effect of this procedure, in which peers play a full part, is to keep Whitehall officials up to the mark by discouraging them from drafting sloppy or unjust delegated legislation.

As for Parliamentary scrutiny of European secondary legislation, committees of each of the two Houses have been established since 1974 with scrutiny functions similar to those of the committees which deal with national Statutory Instruments. The House of Lords Select Committee on the European Communities matches the House of Commons Select Committee on European Secondary Legislation. Both of these committees are constantly involved in the scrutiny of European Commission proposals received by Parliament and both may report to their respective Houses with recommendations that particular proposals be debated, in the case of the Lords on the floor of the House. Thus the Lords play their full part in this important aspect of Parliamentary control as well.

It is readily apparent that this is a wide range of functions and that if the House of Lords were not performing them, some other institution would need to do so. Of course, there is always room for argument about how well or badly the Lords perform their functions, just as there is a continuing debate about whether or not they should be entrusted with additional functions. Among the further tasks for the Lords which have been canvassed from time to time are the detailed control of public administration, the territorial representation of the regions and the functional representation of the main economic and social interests, notably labour and capital.

Whatever the range of powers and functions with which the Lords may be entrusted, Janet Morgan was surely right to point out that 'it is only by monitoring their own behaviour and remaining sensitive to their image in the world outside that they can avoid infringing a web of sanctions explicitly formulated or implicitly understood'.[6] However, all these matters fall within the scope of the discussion about the whole future of the Upper House to which we shall turn in the following section.

## 10.3 PROPOSALS FOR CHANGE

### Labour proposals

Traditionally, the Labour party has been less interested in reform than in abolition of the House of Lords. However, under the influence of R. H. S. Crossman when Leader of the House of Commons, the 1964-70 Labour Government did propose a far-reaching and complicated reform of the Upper House which was embodied in the 1968 Parliament Number 2 Bill to which reference has already been made.[7] Since that time the Labour party in the Commons has shown no real interest in reforming the House of Lords and Labour policy has reverted to the idea of total abolition. Only the caution of Mr Wilson (as he then was) and Mr Callaghan as Labour Prime Ministers in the 1970s, together with robust opposition from Labour peers like Lord Shackleton, has prevented the party from putting its abolitionist policy into practice.

### Conservative proposals

Traditionally, the Conservative party has been quite interested in reforming the House of Lords, since it has seen such ideas as a way of putting the Upper House on a more secure constitutional basis. Winston Churchill and L. S. Amery were among those who flirted in the 1920s with the idea of turning the Lords into a more functional body capable of directly representing both sides of industry as well as the hereditary peerage.[8] The Marquess of Salisbury, as the Conservative Leader in the Lords in the late 1940s and early 1950s, concentrated upon encouraging his noble colleagues to exercise political self-restraint, especially when facing a radical Labour Government. Thus it was not until the 1970s that serious reform proposals were once again forthcoming from the Conservative side.

In 1977 Lord Carrington, then Conservative Leader in the House of Lords, proposed the creation of a reformed second Chamber whose members would have been elected by proportional representation from large regional constituencies. His argument was that such a Chamber would reflect public opinion rather differently from the Commons, since the type of constituencies, the method of representation and the date of the elections would all have been different from those of the lower House. His main objective was to produce a reformed second Chamber with sufficient democratic legitimacy to survive and prosper as a constitutional check or counterweight to the House of Commons.

In 1978 a Conservative committee chaired by Lord Home produced another set of proposals which recommended that the membership of the Lords should be reduced to about 400, of which one-third would have been nominated by the political parties and two-thirds elected on a basis of proportional representation from about 250 large territorial constituencies. Neither of these proposals or anything resembling them has since been implemented. This is partly because Margaret Thatcher has never given a high priority to Lords reform and partly because the majority of the Conservative party has gone cold on anything involving proportional representation.

**Alliance proposals**

As might be expected from parties which do not do particularly well out of the political system at present, both the Alliance parties favour the principle of House of Lords reform as part of a larger package of electoral and constitutional reform. The position of the Liberal party is that the present upper House should be replaced with a new democratically elected second Chamber which would include representatives of the nations (for example, Scotland and Wales) and the regions (for example, Yorkshire or Cornwall), as well as some members of the European Parliament.[9]

At present the Social Democratic party is not fully committed to any binding policy statements on the future of the House of Lords. However, it has published a so-called Green Paper in which Social Democratic views on this subject have been expressed.[10] In this document it was proposed that the present House of Lords should be replaced with a new second Chamber with no hereditary element, but consisting of regional members elected for a fixed term by new regional assemblies, together with life-members appointed by the Government of the day. The new institution would have a delaying power of up to two years when dealing with Parliamentary legislation. The indirectly-elected regional members would have full voting rights and number about 250. The appointed life-members would have the right to speak but not to vote. Together the two categories would make up a reformed Chamber of perhaps 500 members.

## 10.4 CONCLUSION

The debate between those who would like to reform the House of Lords and those who would like to abolish it seems certain to continue. If the Conservative party remains in office, it seems unlikely that changes will be made. If the Alliance parties were to win decisive influence in a future

Parliament, it is more likely that reforms will be made, perhaps as part of a larger package of electoral and constitutional reform. If the Labour party were to win a working majority in the Commons, it is very likely that steps would be taken towards the eventual abolition of the House of Lords and the introduction of unicameral government in Britain.

The choices facing those who now consider the future of the House of Lords are either to reform and strengthen it or to leave it as it is or to abolish it. The Conservative party ought logically to have a strong interest in the reform of the Lords in order to strengthen its constitutional position against attack from a future Labour Government. The Alliance parties have a clear interest in reform of the Lords as part and parcel of the wider electoral and constitutional reforms which they favour. Only the Labour party ought logically to have an interest in the preservation of the House of Lords on exactly the present basis, since that could strengthen the argument for its eventual abolition.

Many years ago Peter Bromhead wrote that 'so long as the House of Lords continues by the exercise of voluntary restraint to perform a restricted function in the exercise of political power, there is . . . little reason for altering either its powers or its composition'.[11] Such a complacent view might still make sense today, provided everyone were content that the House of Lords be left alone as a dignified and relatively unimportant anachronism. Yet plainly not everyone is content with such a position, so it seems likely that changes will be made sooner or later. In these circumstances the most interesting question is whether such changes in the House of Lords will be made in isolation or as components of a larger package of electoral and constitutional reform affecting other political institutions as well. Only time will tell.

## SUGGESTED QUESTIONS

1. Analyse the composition of the House of Lords in Britain today.
2. How well does the House of Lords perform its various functions?
3. Assess the respective cases for reforming or abolishing the House of Lords.

## NOTES

1. The 1963 Peerage Act was the direct result of the efforts of Tony Benn, then Viscount Stansgate, who was determined to change the law which before that time had disqualified peers from standing for election to the Commons.
2. I. Gilmour, *The Body Politic* (London: Hutchinson, 1969) p. 302.

3. A hybrid Bill is defined in Erskine May (p. 862) as 'a public Bill which affects a particular private interest in a manner different from the private interests of other persons or bodies of the same category or class'.
4. Report of the Bryce Commission, Cd 9038; (London: HMSO, 1918).
5. The only appeals heard by the House as a whole are those which happen to be ready between the beginning of the Michaelmas legal term and the autumn Parliamentary 'overspill', that is, between the beginning of October and the brief period from the end of October when the House often has to sit to complete its consideration of Bills sent from the Commons.
6. J. P. Morgan: *The House of Lords and the Labour Government, 1964–70* (Oxford: Clarendon Press, 1975) p. 8.
7. See the introductory paragraphs of this chapter for a description of this Bill.
8. See L. P. Carpenter, 'Corporatism in Britain, 1930–45' in the *Journal of Contemporary History*, no 11 (1976) pp. 9–14; and references to 'Industry and the State' published in 1927 by Harold Macmillan and others.
9. See the Liberal Programme 1982, p. 6.
10. See the Social Democratic Green Paper no. 3 entitled *Decentralising Government* and published in the summer of 1982.
11. P. A. Bromhead, *The House of Lords and Contemporary Politics* (London: Routledge & Kegan Paul, 1958) p. 16.

## FURTHER READING

Bagehot, W., *The English Constitution* (London: Fontana, 1978).

Bromhead, P. A., *The House of Lords and Contemporary Politics* (London: Routledge & Kegan Paul, 1958).

Crick, B., *The Reform of Parliament*, revised edn (London: Weidenfeld & Nicolson, 1968).

Gilmour, I., *The Body Politic* (London: Hutchinson, 1969).

Jennings, W. I., *Parliament*, 2nd edn (Cambridge: Cambridge University Press, 1969).

Menhennet, D. and Palmer, J. *Parliament in Perspective* (London: Bodley Head, 1967).

Morgan, J. P., *The House of Lords and the Labour Government, 1964–70* (Oxford: Clarendon Press, 1975).

Morrison, H., *Government and Parliament* (Oxford: Oxford University Press, 1959).

Wade, E. C. S. and Phillips, G. G., *Constitutional and Administrative Law*, 9th edn (London: Longman, 1977).

CHAPTER 11

# THE HOUSE OF COMMONS

Unlike the Monarchy or the House of Lords, the House of Commons still has real power in the British political system, provided it is willing and able to use it. Yet the nature of its power is different from what it was in the nineteenth century when most of the traditional notions about the House of Commons were established. The modern House of Commons is neither the Government of the country nor even the principal place where most of the legislation is conceived. It is essentially the stage upon which the party political battle is fought, the sounding-board for popular representation and redress, the proving ground for Ministers and shadow Ministers, and the principal forum within which legislation and other actions of Government are criticised and assessed between periodic General Elections.

The essential purposes of the House of Commons have not changed significantly since the last quarter of the nineteenth century. W. I. Jennings described them as being 'to question and debate the policy of the Government and in doing so to bring home . . . the unpopularity (or popularity) of a particular line of policy'.[1] L. S. Amery described them as being 'to secure full discussion and ventilation of all matters . . . as the condition of giving its assent to Bills . . . or its support to Ministers'.[2] Such descriptions are still broadly valid today.

## 11.1 COMPOSITION OF THE COMMONS

The present House of Commons is composed of 650 members elected on a uniform franchise from single member constituencies of about 67 000 electors on average. The Speaker and his three deputies, who are all elected to Parliament like other MPs, take no partisan part in debates or votes (unless a vote is tied), since they are responsible in the Chair for seeing that the rules of order are maintained. Of the remaining 646 MPs at present (in November 1983) 395 are Conservative, 207 Labour, seventeen Liberal, fifteen Ulster Unionist (of various kinds), six Social Democratic, two Scottish Nationalist, two Welsh Nationalist (Plaid Cymru), one Social Democratic and Labour (SDLP) and one Provisional Sinn Fein.

**Characteristics of the MPs**

The characteristics of the MPs who make up the House of Commons are highly varied. All sorts and conditions of men and a few women (twenty-three in November 1983) are to be found among the total membership. Using figures derived from the results of the 1983 General Election, we can illustrate the point. For example, 96 per cent of the Conservative and 57 per cent of the Labour MPs came from middle-class or professional occupations, while only 4 per cent of the Conservative and 43 per cent of the Labour MPs came from working-class occupations. Of all MPs 79 per cent had had higher or further education and 36 per cent had been to university at Oxford or Cambridge. Of the Conservative MPs 60 per cent had been educated at private schools, as had 16 per cent of the Labour MPs. Thus MPs as a whole could be described as a kind of élite in occupational and educational terms, at least when compared with the rest of the population. Yet it should be noted that this is the case in virtually all comparable Parliamentary assemblies throughout the world.

In view of these characteristics, it is reasonable to observe that the composition of the Commons is not strictly representative of the electorate as a whole.[3] Quite apart from the obvious under-representation of women (who account for more than 50 per cent of the elecotrate, but only about 3 per cent of the MPs) and of those who vote for national third parties (that is, the Liberals and Social Democrats as already discussed in Chapter 3), certain categories in the electorate are not directly represented at all, for example, blacks, Asians and those under 24 or over 80 years old. On the other hand, certain occupational groups tend to be over-represented, for example, lawyers, consultants and company directors in the Conservative party and lecturers, journalists and public sector workers in the Labour party. However, many MPs develop a wide range of interests during their time in the House and this can turn them into very adequate 'virtual representatives' of otherwise under-represented categories in the electorate.[4]

**Front-benchers**

Paid office-holders in the Government (who are entitled to sit on the front bench) make up about 100 of the total Conservative MPs. The figure includes the fourteen Government Whips who draw Ministerial salaries but do not speak in debates or run Government Departments. This so-called payroll vote (that is, those who can normally be relied upon to support the Government) is supplemented by about forty Parliamentary Private Secretaries (PPSs) who do not sit on the front bench but who are connected with the Government in that they perform various unpaid tasks for individual Ministers. The present Conservative Cabinet has twenty-one members of whom eighteen are drawn from the Commons, since the Lord President of the Council, the Lord Chancellor and the Chancellor of the Duchy of Lancaster now sit in the Lords (November 1983).

On the Opposition side the so-called Shadow Cabinet is made up of twenty senior members of the Labour party. It is composed of the Leader, the Deputy Leader, the Opposition Chief Whip, the Chairman of the Parliamentary Labour Party, the Leader of the Opposition in the Lords and fifteen others from the Commons who are elected each year by the Parliamentary Labour Party. However, when the Conservative party is in Opposition, the members of the Shadow Cabinet are all appointed by the Leader. Junior to the Shadow Cabinet there are about forty to fifty other Opposition spokesmen who are appointed by the Leader to share the front-bench duties of shadowing the various areas of Government activity. In addition, there are about ten Opposition Whips, including the Opposition Chief Whip and his Deputy who, together with the Leader of the Opposition, receive additional salaries from public funds for their front-bench responsibilities.

**Back-benchers**

The other 420 or so MPs are all back-benchers who have no direct involvement with the Government or the tasks of front-bench Opposition.[5] Some are senior, have been in the House a long time and wield a good deal of influence within their own parties. A few carry weight in the House as a whole. However, most back-benchers are relatively junior, have been in the House less than ten years and try to make their way as well as they can. Usually this means that they seek to attract the attention and approval of the party Whips by playing an active part in proceedings both in the Chamber and 'upstairs' in Committee.

When their party is in Government, the principal duty of back-benchers is to support it with their votes and, to a lesser extent, with their voices in question time and debate. When their party is in Opposition, the principal task is to attack the Government on every available occasion both in the Chamber and in Committee 'upstairs'. Occasionally, some back-benchers will choose a more notorious path and become rebels within their own party. Some others will become professional mavericks or eccentrics. Yet such behaviour is not normally recommended for those who wish to secure Ministerial office, unless they are particularly lucky or clever in their choice of topics on which to defy party orthodoxy.

The life of a back-bencher in the modern House of Commons is usually more fun in Opposition than in Government. In the former case, this is because there are many more opportunities to take a prominent part in the party battle and to catch the attention of the party leadership. In the latter case, back-benchers have to tread the narrow path between sycophancy and rebellion and they may often conclude that all the Whips really want is their presence in the Division Lobbies at the appointed time. Certainly junior back-benchers in the major parties on both sides of the House invariably have cause to complain about the privileges given to Privy Councillors (that is, senior back-benchers most of whom have held senior Ministerial rank at an earlier stage in their careers) and to the spokesmen of all minor parties, since both categories are always more likely to be called in debates and to catch the Speaker's eye at Question Time. This is mainly a reflection of the power of the seniority principle which governs the pecking order at Westminster and in most other Parliaments around the world. However, it is also a reflection of the well-established Westminster convention that the Speaker always tries to ensure a hearing for minority points of view and indeed for dissidents within each of the major parties. For example, a back-bencher who intends to abstain or to vote against his party will normally be given a chance to explain his intentions during the course of the debate.

**Pay and conditions**

All MPs receive a Parliamentary salary from public funds (about £16 100 a year in 1984), together with a range of Parliamentary allowances for secretarial help, research assistance, travel to and from their constituencies, etc. Ministers receive various salaries according to their level in the Government (ranging in 1984 from about £40 400 for the Prime Minister to about £21 400 for an Under Secretary), as well as a portion of their Parliamentary salaries (about £10 600 in 1984) in recognition of the fact that they have the same duties towards their constituents as have their back-bench colleagues.

Apart from the Speaker and his three deputies, the only MPs not in the Government who have additional salaries paid from public funds are the Leader of the Opposition (about £27 700 in 1984), the Opposition Chief Whip (about £21 300 in 1984) and the Opposition Pairing Whip (about £13 400 in 1984). These financial arrangements symbolise the long-standing commitment to the concept of constitutional Opposition and give financial expression to the traditional idea of 'Her Majesty's Loyal Opposition'. Indeed, Britain was the first Parliamentary democracy to make such arrangements for leading members of the Opposition in recognition of their constitutional duty to oppose the Government of the day.

The conditions of work for MPs have improved over the last decade or so, although many of the arrangements still reflect the lingering amateurism which characterises so many of the traditional habits and assumptions of politicians at Westminster. For example, when the Chamber was rebuilt after the last war, it was decided to leave the size and shape as it had been before, namely rows of opposed benches and a total seating capacity for no more than about three-quarters of those entitled to take a seat. This was done in order to reinforce both the adversary nature of the proceedings and the conversational, occasionally intimate atmosphere of many debates.

Equally, there is still a shortage of suitably equipped office premises for all MPs and many have to make do with a desk, a telephone and a filing cabinet in a room containing several of their colleagues. This has been the case partly because of the understandable political fears of many MPs about the likely public response if they were to vote large sums of public money 'to feather their own nests'.[6] However, it is mainly a reflection of the fact that every Government seems to prefer the traditional idea of a House of Commons composed of amateur and part-time MPs rather than professional and full-time politicians able to deal with the Executive on a more equal terms. Furthermore, many MPs now have such a burden of constituency work and committee responsibilities that they spend little of their time in the Chamber, except when present for Questions or for the particular debates in which they hope to speak. The perverse result is that many MPs have had to perform an increasingly varied and arduous range of modern political duties in physical conditions which have been largely unchanged since the late nineteenth century.

## 11.2 PRINCIPAL POWERS

The powers of the House of Commons are diffuse, variable and somewhat indeterminate. They are not set out in any single document or defined in any Court rulings. In cases of dispute the most reliable guide is Erskine May, the reference book which covers the whole of Parliamentary procedure according to precedents established over the centuries by successive Speakers and recorded by successive Clerks of the Commons.

### Theory and practice

In theory, the House of Commons has very great power in our constitutional arrangements. This could be said to include the power to make and unmake Governments, to topple Prime Ministers, to safeguard the liberties of British citizens, to bring to light and remedy injustices and even to legislate itself out of existence or the country into a dictatorship.

In practice, the power of the Commons is usually subsumed in the power of the Government of the day which rules through Parliament as long as it retains the voting support of its majority in the Commons. It is therefore misleading to refer to the powers of the Commons in any way which implies that such powers are separate or distinct from those of modern party Government. In normal Parliamentary conditions when one of the major parties has an overall working majority in the Commons, the power of the House as a representative institution is wielded mainly by the official Opposition in its constant efforts to draw attention to the shortcomings of Government policy and to criticise, delay and occasionally obstruct the course of Government legislation. However, there is also an important, if delicate role for Government back-benchers as representatives of those in the electorate who voted for the party in office and as occasional critics of Government policy when they believe that it is falling short of party commitments or public expectations.

Only on very rare occasions since the war has the power of the House of Commons really made itself felt. One famous example was in May 1940 when the result of a vital confidence debate led Neville Chamberlain to resign as Prime Minister and so make way for Winston Churchill to succeed him. A more recent example was in March 1979 when at the end of another confidence debate the Opposition parties united to defeat the Callaghan Government and so precipitated the General Election of May 1979. On the whole, however, such examples of Parliamentary power have been rare in modern times and most Governments have got their way in Parliament most of the time, at any rate on the issues which really mattered.

**The power of influence**

In most normal circumstances the House of Commons has to rely upon the power of influence, that is, influence upon the politicians in Government, influence upon the policies of Government and influence upon political opinion in the country. Effective influence in the Commons is frequently exerted in a discreet manner before the event, whether in party committees or private conversation. On the other hand, the exercise of overt Parliamentary power is usually confined to the rare occasions when the authority of a Minister or the Government as a whole is in jeopardy. For example, when it became clear at the beginning of April 1982 that Ministers in the Foreign Office and the Ministry of Defence had lost the confidence at any rate of the vast majority in the Conservative party in the immediate aftermath of the Argentinian invasion of the Falklands, Lord Carrington and most of his Ministerial team at the Foreign Office resigned and John Nott at the Ministry of Defence offered his resignation, even though it was refused at the time by the Prime Minister. In crude and capricious Parliamentary conditions this was a graphic example of the power of the House of Commons.

The case of the defeat of the Callaghan Government in March 1979 exemplified something rather different. In that case the Government had really sown the seeds of its own defeat when it had brought forward its proposals for legislation on devolution which were acceptable neither to a significant minority of its own back-benchers nor to any of the minor parties. This was bound to be disastrous at a time when it was possible for the Government to continue in office only as long as it proceeded on a basis which was broadly acceptable to all these disparate political elements.

Over the period since 1945 such occurrences have been rare. On most occasions the electorate has voted and the electoral system has worked in such a way as to ensure that one of the major parties has had an overall majority in the Commons large enough to withstand the normal erosion which takes place through death and retirement during the normal span of a Parliament. In such circumstances the power of the Commons has not normally been manifested in successful attempts to censure Ministers, still less to defeat Governments. Instead it has been exercised as the power of influence through the constant contacts between Ministers and their own back-benchers and through the constant interplay between Governments striving to get their business through Parliament and Oppositions striving to criticise and sometimes prevent them from doing so.

## 11.3 MAIN FUNCTIONS

In 1867 Walter Bagehot suggested that the House of Commons needed to do the following: 'elect a Ministry, legislate, teach the nation, express the nation's will and bring matters to the nation's attention'.[7] If we were to put these functions into modern terms, we could say that the House of Commons has to provide most of the Ministers for any Government, to scrutinise and pass legislation, to give a lead to public opinion on the great issues of the day, and to seek redress for the grievances and concerns of ordinary people. There are, of course, other vital functions performed by the modern House of Commons, notably Parliamentary control of the Executive and party political conflict on the Parliamentary stage. Yet the essential contribution of the House to the British political system has not changed very much since the time when Bagehot made his authoritative pronouncement.

### Representation and redress

The oldest function of Members of Parliament is to represent the interests of their constituents and to seek the redress of their grievances. This function, which has been performed ever since the establishment of Parliament in the thirteenth century, is still a vital task of MPs in modern conditions. If MPs did not speak and intervene on behalf of ordinary people when they feel frustrated by the bureaucracy of central or local government or cheated of their democratic rights as citizens, many people might conclude that our form of democracy was a sham and withdraw from it their loyalty and respect. On the other hand, with the benefit of conscientious constituency MPs most people are more likely to appreciate the value of our Parliamentary democracy. The fulfilment of this function by MPs is therefore one important reason why our political system has survived so long, notwithstanding many grander disappointments and disasters over the years.

**The party battle**

Another function of Members of Parliament is to act as party political publicists, whether in defence of their party when it is in office or in criticism of the Government when their party is in Opposition. The party battle, which has become notably more polarised over recent years, is now criticised from many different quarters. However, there are points to be made in its favour. It encourages the electorate to take an interest in national politics, to consider at least two sides to every political argument and to give a democratic verdict every four or five years at General Elections. Without the political drama of the party battle at Westminster and in the media, it is likely that the political process would lose much of its vitality and the influence of the non-political bureaucracy would increase.

While it must be acknowledged that many people pay little or no attention to politics at all, without the stimulus of the party battle there might be even less public interest and even more public apathy. Certainly the evidence shows that the relative success or failure of the Opposition parties in criticising the Government of the day and in putting forward their own alternative proposals does have a significant effect upon public opinion and upon the voting behaviour of at least the more attentive voters. Opposition parties may not always get all the publicity which they would like, but they can often be successful in sowing the seeds of doubt and resentment about the performance of the party in office.

**The legislative process**

Another well-recognised, but not always well-understood function of Members of Parliament is the scrutiny and approval of legislation. It is the function which most members of the public mention when asked about the activities of Parliament. Over recent years it has absorbed an increasing amount of Parliamentary time as the scope and complexity of modern government has increased and as the public has come to expect more and more of every Government. Only in the last two or three years have there been some signs that public expectations may be moderating and even this may not constitute a lasting trend.

The legislative process in the Commons begins with First Reading. This is the name of the formal stage at which printed copies of a Bill are laid on the Table of the House and made available in the Vote Office for all MPs and other interested parties to read and consider.

After an appropriate interval, this is followed by Second Reading when a debate takes place for about six hours during which the broad purposes of the Bill are discussed and at the end of which a vote is taken to show whether or not the House approves of the Bill. This is the time when the senior Minister in charge of the Bill sets out the broad arguments for it, the chief Opposition spokesman sets out the broad arguments against it (unless the Bill is wholly uncontentious, in which case detailed criticism and constructive suggestions are more likely to be forthcoming), interested back-benchers on both sides of the House make national or constituency points and junior Ministers and Opposition spokesmen wind up the debate during the final hour by attempting to take up or answer the various points made by others during the course of the debate. At the end of such debates on all Government Bills the voting is whipped, which means that MPs are expected to vote as their party has decided they should, unless they have powerful reasons for doing otherwise, for example, conscientious objections to the Bill or overriding constituency reasons.

Assuming that a Bill is approved by the House at Second Reading, it is then usually referred to a Standing Committee 'upstairs' (that is, in one of the Committee rooms of the House) where it is debated in detail by a Committee of between sixteen and fifty MPs chosen to reflect the party balance in the House as a whole. This means that a typical Standing Committee may be made up of one or two Ministers in charge of the Bill, a Government Whip and perhaps a dozen or more back-benchers on the Government side, ranged against a variety of Opposition MPs whose composition depends upon the nature and extent of political interest in the Bill, but who will always include one or more Opposition spokesmen and an Opposition Whip who between them carry much of the burden of proceedings at the Committee stage.

The task of a Standing Committee is to debate a Bill clause by clause and line by line. This usually involves the Opposition members putting down a large number of detailed amendments, some of them probing amendments and some seeking to alter the Bill in significant matters of detail. This requires the Ministers in charge of the Bill to answer each separate debate and, if necessary, to persuade their own back-benchers to vote against amendments unacceptable to the Government which the Opposition is not prepared to withdraw. Once all the debates on amendments and on each clause 'stand part' have been concluded, new clauses can be proposed and debated, provided they fall within the scope of the long title of the Bill. In the case of a complex and controversial Bill, the later stages in Committee often have to be time-tabled, if the Government can get the necessary 'Guillotine' vote at the end of a brief debate in the Chamber. This does at least ensure that all parts of the Bill are discussed, however briefly, during the Committee stage and that the passage of the Bill through Committee is not unduly delayed by Opposition filibustering. Yet even with the benefit of this time-tabling procedure, some Bills may involve a Committee stage of 100 hours or more

After an appropriate interval, the Bill is then returned to the floor of the House where it goes through the stages of Report and Third Reading. These are usually taken together and may last for six hours or more. The Report stage is the time when the House as a whole (that is, those who did not serve on the Standing Committee) can debate and vote upon both the amendments which may have been passed during the Committee stage and any new amendments or new clauses which may be accepted for further debate on the floor of the House. However, it is out of order for opponents of a Bill to go over ground already traversed during earlier stages of the legislative process. Third Reading, which follows immediately, is usually no more than a brief and fairly repetitive debate on the general merits or de-merits of a Bill. It is concluded by yet another vote on the main principle of the Bill in which MPs vote according to the guidance of the party Whips on party political lines.

After that the House of Commons has usually concluded its scrutiny of a Bill, unless subsequently the House of Lords insists upon any substantial amendments. If this happens, the Commons has later to consider them. If all the Lords' amendments are approved by the Commons, the lower House simply sends a message to the upper House notifying its agreement. If, however, the Lords' amendments are not acceptable to the Commons, the lower House sends a message containing its reasons for disagreement and possibly some counter-amendments. It is then for the Lords to decide whether to persist with its opposition or to give way gracefully in the light of the 1911 and 1949 Parliament Acts. On nearly all occasions since the war their Lordships have considered discretion to be the better part of valour.

Since the vast majority of Lords' amendments are inspired by the need for technical or drafting improvements to Bills, nearly all of which are made by Ministers in the light of criticisms voiced during earlier stages of the legislative process, such amendments cause no difficulties in the Commons. They merely underline the usefulness of having a bicameral legislative procedure. Once it is out of the Lords, a Bill is virtually in its final form and awaits only the formality of Royal Assent. The whole process from First Reading to Royal Assent normally takes between six months and one year, although it can be speeded up dramatically in cases of emergency legislation, for instance, Bills to deal with terrorism or civil disorder when it is possible to complete all stages of the legislative process within twenty-four hours if necessary.

**Parliamentary control**

Yet another vital function of Members of Parliament is to control the activities of the Executive. This is probably the most necessary but also the most difficult function which has to be carried out by the House in modern conditions. Traditionally, it was assumed that Ministerial accountability to the Commons at Question Time and in debate was broadly adequate to ensure Parliamentary control of the Executive. However, with the steady extension of Government activity over the last forty years and more, it became clear that such a traditional approach was not sufficient and needed to be supplemented by other institutional devices if central Government and other public agencies were to be properly monitored and controlled by the elected representatives of the people.

Thus the system of Parliamentary Select Committees, which can be traced back to its origins in the nineteenth century, had to be reformed and extended in successive attempts by the House of Commons in particular to achieve some genuine Parliamentary control of the Executive in modern conditions. Following the latest stage of reform in 1979, there is now one of these all-party and non-partisan committees for each Departmental area of central Government activity, as well as a number of non-Departmental committees which have survived from previous Parliaments.[8] These Select Committees, each of which is usually composed of between nine and eleven MPs who reflect the party political balance in the House, meet regularly to oversee and investigate their particular areas of Departmental activity. In the course of their investigations they can call for persons and papers, and their findings are normally contained in substantial reports written for the benefit of the House as a whole. In normal circumstances they have no legislative role, although on a few occasions they have been used as Parliamentary mechanisms for the exploration of policy ideas at the pre-legislative stage.[9] While they do not match in any way the scope and power of Congressional Committees in the United States, they do represent the first systematic and comprehensive attempt in Britain to improve Parliamentary control of the Executive.

It remains a matter of considerable controversy whether or not the Westminster Parliamentary system, which is so dominated by the forces of party discipline and the habits of voting on party lines, can ever exercise truly effective Parliamentary control of the Executive. As Bernard Crick has warned, we should not read too much into the idea of Parliamentary control in Britain, since in this country it means 'influence not direct power, advice not command, criticism not obstruction, scrutiny not initiative, and publicity not secrecy'.[10] Yet even these forms of Parliamentary control should not be underrated in a political system which has never been characterised by clear-cut and unambiguous power relationships. The functions of the House of Commons are summarised in tabular form in Figure 11.1.

Fig 11.1 *Functions of the House of Commons*

*Representation and redress*

On behalf of constituents
On behalf of causes

*The legislative process*

First Reading
Second Reading
Standing Committee
Report Stage
Third Reading

*The party battle*

In the Chamber
In Committee 'upstairs'

*Parliamentary control*

Oral questions
Written questions
Select Committee investigations
Delegations to see Ministers
Letters to Ministers

## 11.4 THE PROSPECTS FOR REFORM

The prospects for reform of the House of Commons are limited by the fact that the power of Parliament is usually a euphemism for the power of Government ruling through Parliament and by the fact that there is an inherent tension between the interests of the Executive and those of the Legislature, in other words between actual and potential Ministers and all back-benchers. In most normal circumstances when the governing party has an overall majority in the Commons, any reform (that is to say, strengthening) of the power of the Commons is likely to mean a weakening of the power of the Government. The only changes which could alter this state of affairs would be the implementation of electoral reform involving some kind of proportional representation or constitutional reform involving some kind of codified constitution. Since those who benefit most from the present Parliamentary arrangements seem unlikely to agree to such far-reaching changes, it is easy to see why the cause of substantial Parliamentary reform has made such a little headway in recent years.

### Select committee developments

In the 1960s and 1970s the main focus of Parliamentary reform was upon the extension and strengthening of Select Committees. Between 1965 and 1969 there was considerable impetus in this direction under the aegis of Richard Crossman, Leader of the House for some of that time. However, these developments in the power and scope of Select Committees were nipped in the bud between 1969 and 1971 when some of the committees (for example, Education and Science, Agriculture, and Scottish Affairs) were terminated largely because their activities had become somewhat embarrassing to Government.

In spite of these set-backs, the later 1970s saw a steady growth in the number and scope of Select Committees and arguably in their impact upon the political process as well. Certainly there were some celebrated cases during the period of the 1974–9 Labour Government when Select Committee reports had considerable influence upon the general political debate at Westminster. For example, the General Sub-Committee of the Expenditure Committee produced a series of reports which contained powerful criticism of Treasury policy. Similarly the Trade and Industry Sub-Committee produced some controversial reports on Government financial support for British Leyland and Chrysler UK. Such committee work made its mark upon the general party battle, because it dealt with topical and highly political aspects of policy and involved weighty criticism of the Executive on a bi-partisan basis which proved embarrassing to the party Whips and the 'rebel' MPs alike. Such consequences emphasised the inherent tension between effective Parliamentary control and traditional party government in Britain.

After the 1979 General Election, the Conservative Government agreed to the establishment of a reformed structure of Select Committees consisting of fourteen Departmental committees and five (now six) non-Departmental committees which were allowed to survive from previous Parliaments. It is too soon to tell whether this structure of Select Committees will do more for Parliamentary control than the arrangements which applied before. At present it seems unlikely that the real influence of such committees will be much greater than before. This is because the procedure in the Commons is still dominated by the two front benches working through their respective party whips and through what are described as 'the usual channels' – that is, direct and informal contacts between Ministers and Opposition spokesmen. It is also unlikely because there is a distinct possibility that the Departmental committees may become little more than privileged interlocutors and possibly even defenders of the Departments which they are supposed to monitor and control (an outcome known as 'agency capture' in the United States).

**Other procedural reforms**

On the whole the prospects for Parliamentary reform do not look very good, unless it is supposed that there will be other measures of wider electoral and constitutional reform as well. As S. A. Walkland has pointed out, 'Parliamentary reform cannot be effective in a vacuum or . . . within the confines of the present political structure of the House'.[11] The underlying political conditions do not seem to have changed since that observation was made, so it remains doubtful whether the Parliamentary reformers can be justifiably optimistic about their prospects of progress.

Some of the minor procedural reforms made in recent times did not amount to very much or last very long. For example, the attempt to make it conventional in Second Reading debates that back-bench speeches between 7p.m. and 9p.m. should be limited to ten minutes had to be quietly buried after a brief and unsatisfactory trial period. On the other hand, the mixed procedure which was introduced for some public Bills may prove to have been a worthwhile and durable modification of existing procedure. The idea is that in cases of technical and largely non-controversial legislation the first three sessions of the Standing Committee stage are conducted on an investigative basis (similar to a Select Committee) before reverting to the normal committee procedure for the rest of that stage of the legislative process. At the time of writing this mixed procedure has been used on four separate occasions.[12]

There are, of course, some more far-reaching Parliamentary reforms which might be made one day. These include the idea of imposing an obligation on the House to debate all major Select Committee reports, the setting aside of one day a week when the House sits exclusively for committee work and the time-tabling from the beginning of more debates on Government legislation in order to ensure that such Bills are thoroughly considered in their entirety.[13] Other proposals that have already been broadly accepted by the Government of the day include the idea that Departmental Estimates should be examined each session by the appropriate Select Committees and that Opposition debating time (known as Opposition Days) should be reduced in number in order to allow more time in the Chamber for debates on public expenditure, defence, the European Community and Scottish affairs.[14]

However, perhaps the most significant reform proposals in recent years were made by the Armstrong Committee on Budgetary Reform.[15] Among these proposals was the idea that the Commons should consider the revenue and expenditure aspects of the annual Budget together on the basis of a provisional Treasury document published several months in advance of the actual Budget in the spring in order to take fuller account of Parliamentary views and other relevant developments. The 1979-83 Thatcher Government went some way towards accepting this idea which was also endorsed by the Treasury Select Committee. In a reply to that Committee the Government agreed to a substantial increase in the information available to the Commons by including estimates of revenue, expenditure and borrowing for the following financial year in the annual economic forecast published by the Treasury every November.[16] It also agreed to provide more information about public expenditure plans for the following year, as well as guidance on the implications of any future changes in the structure of taxation and National Insurance contributions which might be implemented in the following Budget. This procedure was duly brought into effect for the first time in November 1982.

**Broadcasting possibilities**
Finally, there is the possibility that all the proceedings of the House of Commons might eventually be broadcast live on radio or television, as now happens in some other countries. This ideas has been under discussion in Britain at least since the early 1960s, but so far there has been nothing more adventurous than a limited experiment in the late 1970s with live radio transmission of Prime Minister's Question Time and occasional live broadcasts of a few major debates on matters of particular press and public interest, such as the May 1978 debate on the Parker Report on nuclear fuel reprocessing at Windscale or the April 1982 debate at the outset of the Falklands crisis.

The present position (1984) is that the producers of radio programmes normally use edited extracts from tape recordings of proceedings in the Chamber as the raw material for programmes which are transmitted after the event, such as 'Today in Parliament' or 'The Week in Westminster'. There is no televising of Parliamentary proceedings other than the ceremonies of the State opening by the Queen at the beginning of every session. Frequent attempts have been made over the years to provide for the televising of normal Parliamentary proceedings in the Chamber, but so far there has not been enough support from both the front benches and the back benches to bring this about. In November 1983 Austin Mitchell, a Labour MP with media connections, managed to get the Commons to approve a Ten Minute Rule Bill to this effect, which suggests that opinion in the present House of Commons may be shifting slightly in that direction. Yet so far no definitive decisions have been taken and the actual installation of TV cameras to cover proceedings in the Commons is probably still some way off.[17]

## 11.5 CONCLUSION

In summary, the House of Commons has a range of powers and functions which can be fomidable or merely nominal, depending upon the party balance and the personal inclinations of the 650 MPs. In most normal circumstances, when the governing party has an effective overall majority, the Government of the day is able to dominate the House, provided only that it retains the confidence of its back-benchers.

In the rarer circumstances when the Parliamentary results of a General Election have been very close or inconclusive (for example, after both 1974 elections), the Government of the day is vulnerable not only to dissatisfaction on its own back benches but also to defeat at the hands of the combined Opposition parties. It was Parliamentary conditions of this kind which forced James Callaghan to embark upon the so-called Lib-Lab Pact in March 1977 and which later led to the Parliamentary defeat of the Labour Government by the combined Opposition parties in March 1979.

There are many paradoxical aspects of the House of Commons which ought to discourage sweeping generalisations. All that can really be said is that the House carries out its various tasks with varying degrees of efficiency and success. It is reasonably effective as a forum for popular representation and public redress. It is best known as a dramatic stage for party political conflict. It is quite good at the detailed scrutiny of legislation (except when the Opposition decides to filibuster), but rather bad at modifying legislation against the wishes of the Government as made known by the whips. It is gradually becoming more effective as a mechanism for the supervision and control of the Executive, although in this respect it is never likely to be able to emulate the power and independence of the United States Congress.

In short, while the House of Commons is theoretically supreme in the constitutional arrangements of this country, in practice it is usually controlled by the Government of the day in most normal Parliamentary circumstances. This position is unlikely to change unless and until there are far-reaching reforms of our procedural, electoral and constitutional arrangements. Furthermore, such changes are unlikely to be made unless a future General Election produces another 'hung Parliament' in which the Government of the day is forced to do a deal on all these matters with the Opposition parties. Even then it may well be possible for the governing party to thwart such changes by following a policy of 'divide and rule'. Thus nothing is absolutely certain when considering a political institution as inherently powerful but also unpredictable as the British House of Commons.

## SUGGESTED QUESTIONS

1. To what extent do the members of the House of Commons reflect the views and interests of the British electorate?
2. How well does the House of Commons perform its four main functions?
3. What changes need to be made to improve Parliamentary control of the Executive?

## NOTES

1. W. I. Jennings, *Parliament*, 2nd edn (Cambridge: Cambridge University Press, 1969) pp. 7–8.
2. L. S. Amery, *Thoughts on the Constitution* (Oxford: Oxford University Press, 1947) p. 12.
3. See J. Blondel, *Voters, Parties and Leaders* (Harmondsworth: Penguin, 1974) pp. 130–57; and A. Mitchell, *Westminster Man* (London: Thames Methuen, 1982) pp. 141–55.

4. 'Virtual representation' was best defined by Edmund Burke who wrote in a letter to Sir Hector Langrishe in 1797 that it was representation 'in which there is a communion of interests and a sympathy in feelings and desires between those who act in the name of any description of people (i.e. MPs) and the people in whose name they act (i.e. particular sections of the general public), though the trustees (the former) are not chosen by them'.
5. Indeed, it is significant that less than one-third (31 per cent) of the present House of Commons (November 1983) has had direct experience of Government, that is, has been a Minister or a Whip at any time.
6. In December 1983 the House of Commons voted to approve a plan for the refurbishment of buildings on Bridge Street, Westminster, which are intended to provide about 280 new units of office accommodation for MPs.
7. W. Bagehot, *The English Constitution* (London: Fontana, 1978) p. 170.
8. In the 1979–83 Parliament there were the following Select Committees: Agriculture: Defence; Education, Science and the Arts; Employment; Energy; Environment; Foreign Affairs (including a Sub-Committee on Overseas Development); Home Affairs (including a Sub-Committee on Race Relations); Trade and Industry; Social Services; Transport; Treasury (including a Sub-Committee on the Civil Service); Scottish Affairs; and Welsh Affairs. There were also six non-Departmental Select Committees which derived from some of those established in previous Parliaments: Parliamentary Commissioner for Administration; Public Accounts; Statutory Instruments; European Legislation; Consolidation Bills; and Procedure (Supply). The arrangements for all Select Committees are co-ordinated by a small Liaison Committee composed of the various Chairmen.
9. For example, in the 1970s Select Committees were occasionally asked by Government to look into possible ideas for fiscal legislation, for example, Corporation Tax in 1970–1, Tax Credit in 1972–3 and Wealth Tax in 1974–5.
10. B. Crick, *The Reform of Parliament*, revised edn (London: Weidenfeld & Nicolson, 1968) p. 80.
11. In S. A. Walkland and M. Ryle (eds) *The Commons Today* (London: Fontana, 1981) p. 294.
12. For Bills on Deep Sea Mining, Special Education, Criminal Attempts and Mental Health.
13. See the First Report from the Select Committee on Procedure, 1977–8, HC 588–I; (London: HMSO, 1978).
14. See the First Report from the Select Committee on Procedure (Supply), 1980–1, HC 118–I; (London: HMSO, 1981).
15. See W. Armstrong *et al.*, *Budgetary Reform in the UK* (Oxford: Oxford University Press, 1980).
16. *The Financial Times*, 6 August 1982.
17. However, the House of Lords seems to be favourably disposed towards television coverage of its proceedings and may well approve an experiment of this kind in the near future.

## FURTHER READING

Bagehot, W., *The English Constitution* (London: Fontana, 1978).
Bromhead, P. A., *Britain's Developing Constitution* (London: Allen & Unwin, 1974).
Butt, R., *The Power of Parliament*, 2nd edn (London: Constable, 1969).
Crick, B., *The Reform of Parliament*, revised edn (London: Weidenfeld & Nicolson, 1968).
Jennings, W. I., *Parliament*, 2nd edn (Cambridge: Cambridge University Press, 1969).
Judge, D. (ed.) *The Politics of Parliamentary Reform* (London: Heinemann, 1983).
Marshall, E., *Parliament and the Public* (London: Macmillan, 1982).
Mitchell, A., *Westminster Man* (London: Thames Methuen, 1982).
Morrison, H., *Government and Parliament* (Oxford: Oxford University Press, 1959).
Norton, P., *The Commons in Perspective* (Oxford: Martin Robertson, 1981).
Rush, M., *Parliament and the Public* (London: Longman, 1976).
Taylor, E., *The House of Commons at Work*, 9th edn (London: Macmillan, 1979).
Walkland, S. A. (ed.) *The House of Commons in the Twentieth Century* (Oxford: Clarendon Press, 1979).
Walkland, S. A. and Ryle, M. (eds) *The Commons Today* (London: Fontana, 1981).

# PART IV
# CENTRAL GOVERNMENT

CHAPTER 12

# PRIME MINISTER AND CABINET

The term 'Prime Minister' was no more than a tenuous convention from the time of Robert Walpole (1721–42) to the time when Lord North insisted that his Administration resign *en bloc* in 1782. Indeed, on a number of occasions during the eighteenth century the most powerful politician of the day, Lord Chatham, was actually the leading Secretary of State rather than the Prime Minister in Administrations led by others, such as Lord Pelham or Lord Newcastle. Until the beginning of William Pitt's Administration in 1784, all 'Prime Ministers' were chosen because of their good relationships with the Monarch and they survived in office only because of their ability to manage the House of Commons.

The term 'Cabinet' is older in origin and was first used during the reign of Charles II. At that time the king used to summon a few favoured members of his Privy Council for consultations in his private apartments and such people became known as members of his 'Cabinet'. For a time they were also known as the 'Cabal' which happened to be an acronym for the names of those involved - Clifford, Arlington, Buckingham, Ashley and Lauderdale.

The office of Prime Minister and the institution of the Cabinet evolved together throughout the nineteenth century. Until the 1832 Reform Act the Prime Minister and Cabinet were as answerable to the Monarch as they were to Parliament. The extension of the franchise in 1832 meant that the Prime Minister and Cabinet became answerable to and dependent upon shifting majorities in the House of Commons. Further changes occurred after the 1867 Reform Act as the growing power of nationally organised political parties began to limit the independence of individual MPs. One of the consequences was the increased political stature of the major party leaders, such as William Gladstone and Benjamin Disraeli, who alternated as Prime Minister for nearly twenty years. In 1878 the title of 'Prime Minister' was recorded officially in a public document for the first time when Benjamin Disraeli signed the Treaty of Berlin on behalf of the British

Government. Another equally important development during this period was the growth of the power of the Cabinet in relation to the House of Commons. By the time of Lord Salisbury's second Administration (1886-92) Britain had moved essentially from Parliamentary government of the classic type to Cabinet government of the modern type, i.e. government through Parliament rather than government by Parliament.

The role of Prime Minister and Cabinet has not changed fundamentally since the beginning of the twentieth century. However, statutory recognition of the office of Prime Minister was not formally complete until 1937 when the Ministers of the Crown Act provided the Prime Minister of the day with a salary and a pension from public funds. Yet to this day the powers and responsibilities of the Prime Minister are not defined by statute. Like the institution of the Cabinet, the office of Prime Minister provides a classic example of the importance of conventions in British constitutional arrangements.

In contemporary political circumstances the Prime Minister and the Cabinet together constitute the supreme decision-making body in the British political system. Yet their decisions are ultimately subject to Parliamentary approval in the sense that they can be challenged by debate and vote, whether or not legislation is entailed. They can also be challenged in the Courts, at least in respect of the administrative consequences of their decisions. In political terms the most effective sanctions against Cabinet decisions of which people may disapprove are a decisive back-bench revolt in the governing party or the verdict of the electorate at the subsequent General Election. The Prime Minister and Cabinet are also influenced in an imprecise but real way by the views of their own back-benchers in the House of Commons, the need to take account of the Opposition's demands which can affect the progress of Government business in Parliament, their relations with party activists, pressure groups and the media, and their assessment of public opinion on any given issue. All these factors tend to qualify and refine the power and authority of the Prime Minister and Cabinet.

## 12.1 THE MACHINERY OF CABINET GOVERNMENT

### Composition and functions

The Cabinet in modern Britain has been composed of between nineteen and twenty-four senior Ministers (including the Prime Minister) who meet every Thursday morning around the large table in the Cabinet room at No 10 Downing Street. It subsumes a large network of committees, both Ministerial and official, and it depends for its efficient operation upon the work of the Cabinet Secretary and about 200 civil servants in the Cabinet Office. The latter is the administrative nerve-centre of central Government and responsible for recording all Cabinet and Cabinet committee decisions and then communicating them to those who need to know in the various Whitehall Departments.

Certain very senior Ministers always have a place in every Cabinet, for example, the Chancellor of the Exchequer, the Home Secretary and the Foreign Secretary. Some other Ministers have a place by dint of the geographical area of the country which they represent as Ministers, for example, the Secretaries of State for Scotland, Wales and Northern Ireland. Occasionally some important Ministers - for instance, the Secretary of State for Transport - are included in the Cabinet in one Government and excluded from it in another Government, depending upon the competing claims of other Ministries and the personal preferences of the Prime Minister of the day. In a few rare cases a senior Minister may belong to the Cabinet, but draw no public salary for it in view of the upper limit on the permitted number of such paid positions (currently twenty-three). The Government Chief Whip is not a member of the Cabinet, but invariably attends all Cabinet meetings.

The Cabinet meets formally once a week on Thursdays for about two and a half hours at a time, although extra meetings are often arranged as and when the need arises. Owing to its size there is usually no question of all its members taking an active part in all its discussions. Some may remain silent because their Department is not involved in the issue under discussion. Some may not get a chance to speak about an issue because they have to be away on the day in question, in which case another Minister from their Department will deputise if need be. Indeed, it is just as well that the Cabinet proceeds in this way, since if every Cabinet Minister spoke on every item of Cabinet business, the agenda would never be covered in the time available. At the invitation of the Prime Minister other non-Cabinet Ministers attend Cabinet meetings when necessary, but only remain in the room for the period when the item or items affecting their Department are under discussion.

Cabinet committees are an essential and integral part of Cabinet activity. They are usually composed of the relevant subject Ministers and other senior Ministers who are representative of Cabinet opinion. They are normally empowered to take decisions on behalf of the entire Cabinet and only in cases of serious disagreement are matters referred back to the full Cabinet for final resolution. Few substantial issues are taken by full Cabinet which have not already been dealt with in some way by a Cabinet committee. Thus one of the main purposes of Cabinet committees is to reach decisions whenever possible without having to put issues to the full Cabinet. However, when Cabinet committees cannot reach agreement or when the issues under consideration are too important to be left to a Cabinet committee, the whole Cabinet has to argue things out in order to reach agreed conclusions upon which the Government can act.

Cabinet committees can conveniently be divided between Standing committees - such as the Economic Committee, the Home and Social Affairs Committee, the Overseas and Defence Committee, and the Legislation Committee - and the *ad hoc* committees which are usually classified under the 'Miscellaneous' heading and which remain in being only as long as necessary to resolve a particular issue of policy. Many of the Standing committees and their sub-committees are chaired by the Prime Minister, since they deal with the most important issues of policy. Decisions reached in such committees do not normally require subsequent ratification by the Cabinet as a whole. 'Miscellaneous' committees are normally chaired by a senior Cabinet Minister and may meet for one, several or many discussions, depending upon the scope and complexity of the issues which have to be decided. For example, in recent years such committees have dealt with the replacement of the Polaris force with Trident, the abolition of the GLC and other Metropolitan Councils, the imposition of spending cuts on Departmental Ministers, the de-indexing of benefits and the annual Rate Support Grant to local authorities. It is fairly normal for the decisions of such committees to require subsequent ratification by the full Cabinet or one of its standing committees. However, in both cases the key to the method of working is that such committees are empowered to take decisions on behalf of the whole Cabinet and they do so without any political or constitutional difficulties in most cases.

Senior civil servants and the military Chiefs of Staff are not members of the Cabinet. Yet they have occasionally participated in some Cabinet committee discussions - for example, in the special circumstances of the 1982 Falklands crisis when the Chief of the Defence Staff and a few very senior civil servants from the Cabinet Office and the Foreign Office played a part in what the press called the 'War Cabinet'. In the broader framework of Cabinet government in general, junior Ministers play a frequent and useful part in Cabinet committees where they can relieve senior Ministers of some of the burdens of collective decision-making. Indeed, junior Ministers are the work-horses of the Cabinet committee system and they can often make or mar their reputations when performing this aspect of their Ministerial duties. The structure of Cabinet committees is shown in tabular form in Figure 12.1.

**Support in Whitehall**

Meetings of the Cabinet and its committees would not proceed as smoothly as they usually do if it were not for the fact that most Ministerial meetings are prepared and supported by official meetings of senior civil servants from the various Departments concerned. It is this parallel structure of official committees which keeps Government business moving along and

### Fig 12.1 *The structure of Cabinet committees*

| Committee Initials | Chairman | Functions |
|---|---|---|
| | **A. ECONOMIC AND INDUSTRIAL** | |
| EA | Margaret Thatcher (Prime Minister) | Economic strategy, energy policy, changes in labour law, the most important EEC matters |
| E(EX) | Margaret Thatcher | Exports policy |
| E(NI) | Margaret Thatcher | Public sector strategy and oversight of the nationalized industries |
| E(NF) | Nigel Lawson (Chancellor of the Exchequer) | Nationalised industry finance |
| NIP | Nick Monck (Treasury official) | Official committee on nationalised industry policy |
| E(PSP) | Nigel Lawson | Public sector and public service pay policy |
| E(DL) | Nigel Lawson | Disposal and privatisation of state assets |
| E(PU) | Norman Tebbit (Trade & Industry Secretary) | 'Buy British' policy for public purchasing |
| E(CS) | Peter Rees (Chief Secretary) | Civil Service pay and contingency plans for Civil Service strikes |
| E(OCS) | Peter le Cheminant (Cabinet Office official) | Official committee for preparing contingency plans |
| PESC | John Anson (Treasury official) | Committee of finance officers handling the annual public expenditure survey |
| | **B. OVERSEAS AND DEFENCE** | |
| OD | Margaret Thatcher | Foreign affairs, defence and Northern Ireland |
| | **B.** | |
| OD(O) | Sir Robert Armstrong (Cabinet Secretary) | Permant secretaries group working to OD |
| OD(E) | Sir Geoffrey Howe (Foreign Secretary) | EEC policy |
| EQ(S) | David Williamson (Cabinet Office official) | Committee of deputy secretaries steering OD(E) |
| EQ(O) | David Hannay (Foreign Office official) | Official committee on routine EEC business |
| OD(SA) | Margaret Thatcher | Committee on the South Atlantic, the so-called 'War Cabinet' of 1982 |
| OD(FOF) | Margaret Thatcher | Committee on the future of the Falklands |
| Northern Ireland Group | Lord Whitelaw (Lord President) | Preparation of future initiatives |
| | **C. HOME, LEGISLATION AND INFORMATION** | |
| L | John Biffen (Leader of the House) | Future legislation and Queen's speech |
| H | Lord Whitelaw | Home affairs and social policy, including education |
| CCU | Lord Whitelaw | The Civil Contingencies Unit of the Cabinet Office which plans for the maintenance of essential supplies and services during industrial disputes |
| H(HL) | Lord Whitelaw | Reform of the House of Lords |
| HD | Leon Brittan (Home Secretary) | Home (i.e. civil) defence |
| HD(O) | David Goodall (Cabinet Office official) | Official committee shadowing HD |
| HD(P) | David Heaton (Home Office official) | Updating of central and local government civil defence plans |

Source: *The Times*, 30 April 1984.

C.

| | | |
|---|---|---|
| TWC | Sir Robert Armstrong | Transition to War Committee which updates the 'War Book' for the mobilization of Whitehall and the Armed Forces in a period of international tension |
| ECM | Peter le Cheminant | Monthly meeting of Whitehall establishment officers on industrial and personnel policy |
| M10 | Bernard Ingham (No 10 Press Secretary) | Weekly meeting of chief information officers |
| M10(E) | Bernard Ingham | Special group for handling economic information. Now meets infrequently because of persistent leaking |

D. INTELLIGENCE AND SECURITY

| | | |
|---|---|---|
| MIS | Margaret Thatcher | Ministerial steering committee on intelligence which supervises MI5, MI6 and GCHQ and fixes budget priorities |
| PSIS | Sir Robert Armstrong | Permanent secretaries' steering group on intelligence: prepares briefs for ministerial group |
| JIC | Sir Antony Duff (Cabinet Office official) | Joint Intelligence Committee which prepares assessments for ministers collating intelligence from all sources and circulating them weekly in the 'Red Book' |
| JIC(EA) | Sir Antony Duff | Economic intelligence assessments |
| SPM | Sir Robert Armstrong | Security and policy methods in the Civil Service |
| Official Com'tee on Security | Sir Robert Armstrong | Permanent secretaries' group on internal security |

D.

| | | |
|---|---|---|
| Pers'nel Security Com'tee | Sir Robert Armstrong | Official group supervising the working of positive vetting, polygraphs, etc. |

E. AD HOC

| | | |
|---|---|---|
| MISC 3 | John Dempster (Lord Chancellor's Dept official) | Public records policy |
| MISC 7 | Margaret Thatcher | Replacement of the Polaris force with Trident |
| MISC 14 | Nigel Lawson | Policy innovations |
| MISC 15 | Formely head of Think Tank: post now defunct | Official group for briefing MISC 14 |
| MISC 21 | Lord Whitelaw | Ministerial committee which meets each autumn to fix the level of rate and transport support grant for local authorities |
| MISC 32 | David Goodall | Deployment of the Armed Forces outside the Nato area |
| MISC 42 | David Goodall | Military assistance (e.g. training of personnel) for the armed services of friendly powers |
| MISC 51 | David Goodall | Commodities needed for strategic purposes, eg oil |
| MISC 58 | John Dempster | Liberalizing the declassification of official documents |
| MISC 62 | Lord Whitelaw | The 'Star Chamber' for forcing spending cuts on departmental ministers |
| MISC 79 | Lord Whitelaw | Alternatives to domestic rates: rate-capping |
| MISC 83 | David Goodall | Internal constitutional arrangements for the Falklands |
| MISC 87 | Nigel Lawson | De-indexing of benefits |
| MISC 91 | Margaret Thatcher | Choice of ALARM anti-radar missile |
| MISC 95 | Margaret Thatcher | Abolition of the GLC and the metropolitan counties |

makes it possible for the Cabinet and its committees to dispatch a great deal of Government business in a comparatively short period of time on each occasion. Cabinet Office officials often chair these official committees which are intended to maximise the areas of potential inter-Departmental agreement and to define, if not minimise, the areas of potential disagreemet. Since each Department has a tendency to respect the interests of every other Department and since there is an established Whitehall hierarchy with 10 Downing Street and the Treasury at the top and the smaller or newer Departments - for example the Department of Transport or the Department of Energy - at the bottom, it follows that the outcome of inter-Departmental discussions at official level often reflects the balance of bureaucratic power in Whitehall. This may facilitate the decision-making process at Cabinet level, but it can also make for smooth, inter-Departmental compromises which can lower the quality or reduce the effectiveness of the decisions eventually taken. In other words, a significant price can be paid for the collegiate conventions of Whitehall and the idea of collective responsibility.

However, the outcome of Cabinet discussions and of inter-Departmental discussions at official level is also affected by the relative standing and authority of the various Ministers whose Departments are involved with any issue at a given time. Thus if the Chancellor of the Exchequer and the Chief Secretary have recently won battles with their Cabinet colleagues over the management of the economy and the control of public spending, the Treasury will be even more formidable than usual in its dealings with other Departments. Equally, if Foreign Office Ministers have been proved wrong and had to resign over sensitive issues - such as the Argentinian attack on the Falklands in April 1982 - then the Foreign Office will find its authority in Whitehall somewhat diminished. The only sure rule of thumb in central British Government is that it is usually wise to enlist the support of Downing Street in any inter-Departmental battle.

In the process of Cabinet government the Cabinet Office has a vital role to play in ensuring fast and efficient communication of Cabinet decisions to all who need to know of them throughout Whitehall. The Cabinet Office, which consists mainly of civil service 'high flyers' seconded from other Departments, communicates Cabinet decisions in the form of extracts from Cabinet minutes to those parts of the Government machine which have to act upon them. This means that in the first instance such decisions are communicated to the Private Offices of the Ministers concerned which then relay them within their respective Departments.

The minutes of the Cabinet and Cabinet committees are drawn up by officials of the Cabinet Office under the direction of the Cabinet Secretary. It is open to the Prime Minister and, indeed, any Minister to see the minutes in draft, to point out errors and ask for suitable amendments. Yet this has to be done within forty-eight hours and such requests are not very frequently made and infrequently granted. In short, senior Cabinet Office officials keep a tight administrative grip upon this aspect of Cabinet government.

From 1971 to 1983 the Cabinet was also assisted in its deliberations by the Central Policy Review Staff (CPRS). This was set up by Edward Heath as a small advisory body within the Cabinet Office designed to give intelligent and dispassionate advice to the Cabinet on matters of policy affecting the entire Government. Under the initial direction of Lord Rothschild it seemed to achieve this objective and proved itself to be a useful source of independent and sometimes heretic advice to Ministers. Yet subsequently it seemed to lose some of its effectiveness. This was partly because senior officials in the Treasury and Cabinet Office disapproved of some of its work on public expenditure and political priorities in the early 1970s and partly because in the late 1970s the Labour Government tended to use it too much as a short term, inter-Departmental trouble-shooter and to put it too much in the political limelight by publishing many of its reports to Ministers.

The final straw which probably brought about the demise of the CPRS was the fact that some people in Whitehall could not be relied upon to preserve the confidentiality of some of its more sensitive reports to Ministers during the 1979–83 Conservative Government. One notorious example in the autumn of 1982 involved the unauthorised disclosure of a CPRS report which questioned the future ability of the Government adequately to finance much of the Welfare State and notably the National Health Service. This caused some considerable embarrassment to Mrs Thatcher and her Ministers and it was therefore not altogether surprising when Mrs Thatcher decided to abolish it soon after the Conservative victory at the 1983 General Election.

**10 Downing Street**

In addition to the formal structure of the Cabinet government just described, successive Prime Ministers have had other sources of advice available to them at 10 Downing Street. Lloyd George really began this practice with his so-called 'Kitchen Cabinet' during the First World War and it has continued in one form or another ever since. Winston Churchill during the Second World War had the help of Lord Cherwell; Clement Attlee after the war had Francis Williams; Harold Macmillan had John Wyndham, Harold Wilson had Marcia Williams and Margaret Thatcher has had her own personal advisers, including Sir Alan Walters and Sir Anthony Parsons.

Since 1964 there has also been a Policy Unit of one kind or another in 10 Downing Street consisting normally of fewer than a dozen advisers brought in to serve the Prime Minister personally and to assist in any way thought appropriate. The personnel of such a Unit vary from Government to Government, depending upon the outlook and inclinations of the Prime Minister of the day. For example, James Callaghan depended quite heavily upon Dr Bernard Donoghue, a former academic at the London School of Economics, for advice on issues of domestic policy, whereas Margaret Thatcher has had advice and support from Sir John Hoskyns, a former businessman, and Ferdinand Mount, a former journalist on *The Spectator*.

Whether such advisers are installed in a Policy Unit or work more informally for the Prime Minister of the day, their contributions to the really big issues of Cabinet government are probably no more than marginal in most cases. Yet as long as other Cabinet Ministers are either disinclined or discouraged from enlisting the assistance of comparable staff of their own, it may be that such advice and support gives a small additional advantage to the Prime Minister of the day in dealing with some items of Cabinet business.

## 12.2 THE POWER OF THE PRIME MINISTER

The Prime Minister of the day could be described as the most powerful person in Britain. Certainly the reality of Prime Ministerial power has been recognised for some time by practising politicians and academic observers alike. Yet the nature and extent of such power is a matter of continuing controversy and there remain some significant constraints upon its exercise, no matter who occupies the premises at 10 Downing Street.

### Conflicting interpretations

There have been at least two strongly conflicting interpretations of Prime Ministerial power in Britain. On the one hand, Harold Wilson, one of the longest-serving peace-time Prime Ministers, has concluded that 'the predominantly academic verdict of overriding Prime Ministerial power is wrong.'[1] In making this forthright comment Lord Wilson was probably reflecting upon his own experience of having to preside over a number of Labour Cabinets which contained powerful and determined personalities.

On the other hand, Lord Morley in his biography of Sir Robert Walpole (but with William Gladstone very much in mind) wrote as long ago as 1889 that 'the flexibility of the Cabinet system allows the Prime Minister to take upon himself a power not inferior to that of a dictator, provided always that the House of Commons will stand by him'.[2] This view has had its strong adherents ever since, including Sir Anthony Eden (later Lord Avon) who wrote in his Memoirs that 'a Prime Minister is still nominally *primus inter pares* (first among equals), but in fact his authority is stronger than that'.[3]

One way of assessing these conflicting interpretations is to examine the various aspects of Prime Ministerial power in order to see which of the two schools of thought is best supported by the facts. However, even at this stage of the argument it is tempting to agree with the common sense view expressed by Herbert Asquith more than fifty years ago, when he wrote that 'the office of Prime Minister is what its holder chooses and is able to make of it'.[4] In the light of the entire history of the office, it is difficult to dissent from such a concise view expressed by one of its most distinguished occupants.

**The power of patronage**

The Prime Minister has the power of political patronage. This is manifested principally in the power of appointment to and dismissal from Ministerial posts in Government. Once a party leader has accepted the Royal commission to form a new Government, he can fill the 100 or so Ministerial posts as he sees fit. However, in terms of practical politics there are always a number of senior figures in any party who virtually select themselves for Ministerial office and some others whom it would be imprudent for any new Prime Minister to exclude. Other considerations which come into play in the course of Government formation are regional balance, ideological balance and age balance, as well as political debt and personal allegiance. Thus although the Prime Minister can do virtually as he likes when making Government appointments (and increasingly so as time goes by), his freedom of manoeuvre is always limited in practice by common prudence and political calculation.

Equally, the Prime Minister can always ask for the resignation of any member of his Government on the grounds that the Minister concerned is not up to the job or is too old or that the office is needed for someone else. However, the most usual motives for Ministerial dismissal at Cabinet level are either to remind the governing party and the public of the reality of Prime Ministerial power by having a 'reshuffle' or to put a more personal stamp upon the Government at the highest level by getting rid of Cabinet Ministers who are widely known to have been in fundamental disagreement with the Prime Minister at one time or another. For example, in September 1981 Mrs Thatcher sacked three Cabinet Ministers (Lord Soames, Sir Ian Gilmour and Mark Carlisle) at least two of whom had displeased her in this way and appointed three new ones (Norman Tebbit, Nigel Lawson and Lady Young) at least two of whom were thought to be close to her own political outlook. Such power of dismissal can sometimes be used more capriciously than the power of appointment, but in both cases Prime Ministers are well advised not to abuse their power, as Harold Macmillan did in the notorious 'night of the long knives' in 1962 when he dismissed about one third of his Cabinet and some of the unlucky Ministers first learned of their fate from the media.

The Prime Minister of the day also has a wider and more general power of political patronage which stems from his right to advise the Monarch on many of the public appointments made in the name of the Crown. This means that a considerable number of important positions in the higher reaches of the British Establishment are effectively in the gift of the Prime Minister of the day when they fall due for appointment or re-appointment. For example, Permanent Secretaries in Whitehall Departments, Bishoprics in the Church of England, the Governorship of the Bank of England, the Chairmen of nationalised industries and key appointments to a host of other public bodies all depend to a considerable extent on finding favour with the Prime Minister of the day, although other Ministers also make such recommendations within their own Departmental spheres. In view of the highly influential nature of many of these positions, such appointments can have considerable, wider significance. For example, the appointment of a former clearing-bank chairman to be Governor of the Bank of England or the appointment of an expatriate Scottish businessman to be successively chairman of the British Steel Corporation and the National Coal Board fall into this category. This Prime Ministerial patronage, whether exercised positively or negatively, directly or indirectly, is a formidable aspect of Prime Ministerial power.

**Power within the Government**

It goes without saying that the Prime Minister of the day normally has considerable power within the Government. Indeed, many would argue that a strong Prime Minister has the ability to dominate the Government by setting both its strategic purposes and its political priorities. This is done in a number of different ways, all of which are facets of Prime Ministerial power. It is achieved through the Prime Minister's control of the Cabinet agenda, his right to establish and pick the members of Cabinet committees, his practice of chairing the most important Cabinet committees, his right to summarise the sense of Cabinet meetings, his preferential access to the best available advice both in the civil service and outside, his freedom to take an overall and non-Departmental view of political issues, his pre-eminent position in the eyes of the media, his power of appointment and dismissal and, above all, his leadership of the governing party in the House of Commons.

As already indicated, this is a subject of continuing controversy, since the available evidence usually comes from witnesses or participants who were committed in favour of or against the Prime Minister concerned and since most outside observations are inevitably speculative and second-hand in view of the considerable degree of official secrecy in which the process of British government is shrouded. The honest investigator is left with not much more than a series of impressions of one Prime Minister as compared with another or of the same Prime Minister at different times. The real dilemma is that those who might be reliable and objective witnesses of the political drama do not normally gain access to the theatre, whereas those who were privileged to be on stage are not normally the most reliable witnesses when they eventually go on public record often many years after the events in question. Thus no firm or definitive conclusions can sensibly be drawn about this aspect of Prime Ministerial power, although it seems reasonable to add that in the modern political world Prime Ministers are not called 'Prime Minister' without good reason.

**Power in Parliament**

The Prime Minister of the day usually has formidable power in Parliament. This is partly because the power of appointment and dismissal can do so much to determine the political fortunes of the MPs in his own party and partly a reflection of the Prime Minister's leading role in the gladiatorial battle between the two sides of the House at Question Time. Clearly the extent and nature of such power has varied from time to time, depending upon the personal position of the Prime Minister and the political habits of his party. For example, much depends upon the extent to which the Prime Minister can rely upon the loyalty and support of his Parliamentary colleagues. Much depends upon the efficiency and subtlety of the Government Whips. Much depends upon the personal standing of the Prime Minister in the eyes of the media and the general public.

On the whole Conservative Prime Ministers seem to have been more powerful in relation to their Parliamentary followers than Labour Prime Ministers in relation to theirs. This is mainly a reflection of the contrasting origins, organisation and habits of each of the major parties. Whereas the Conservative party has been traditionally both hierarchically organised and deferential towards its leaders, the Labour party has tended to be more democratic in its aspirations and more egalitarian in its outlook. On the whole this has made it somewhat easier for Conservative Prime Ministers to preserve their authority than for Labour Prime Ministers to preserve theirs, although the contrast should not be exaggerated.

In general, all peace-time Prime Ministers in this century have usually exercised effectively dominant power within their own Parliamentary parties for as long as they have continued to hold their high office and have been able to count upon the loyal support of the great majority of their own back-benchers. On the other hand, once they have left 10 Downing Street and have been reduced to the status of Leader of the Opposition, they have become more vulnerable to challenges from their rivals, especially in the Conservative party which traditionally has been rather unsentimental in its attitude towards losers.

**Party political power**

The Prime Minister of the day can have great power over the fortunes and destiny of the party which he leads. In the Conservative party this stems from the usually dominant position of the party leader which is enhanced when combined with the office of Prime Minister. In the Labour party the situation is usually not so clear-cut, since Prime Ministerial power has to be shared to some extent with the Parliamentary party, the trade unions and the constituency parties. In such circumstances Labour Prime Ministers have not always been able to get their way in discussions within the National Executive Committee of the party, since nearly all the other members of the Committee usually have their own particular power-bases within the Labour movement which enable them to take independent lines, if they so choose. Furthermore, whereas the authority of Conservative Prime Ministers is generally recognised, if occasionally resented, at all levels of the party which they lead, the paramount position of Labour Prime Ministers is not always recognised and often challenged by their party colleagues both in private and in public.

In no case is the party political power of the Prime Minister more significant than in the exclusive right to recommend to the Monarch the time of dissolution within the five-year maximum span of a Parliament. The exercise of this aspect of Prime Ministerial power can have lasting effects, for good or ill, upon the political fortunes and destiny of the party concerned. A few examples will illustrate the point. Clement Attlee decided to call a General Election in 1951 even though the Labour Government which he led still had an overall majority of five in the Commons and more than three years of its Parliamentary term still to run.[5] The result was a narrow victory for the Conservative party and the beginning of thirteen years of Conservative rule. Edward Heath decided to appeal to the country by holding a General Election in February 1974, even though the Conservative Government which he led still had a comfortable majority in the Commons and nearly eighteen months of its Parliamentary term left to run. The result was a narrow victory for the Labour party and the beginning of more than five years of Labour rule.

However, James Callaghan appeared to err in the other direction when he decided not to call a General Election in October 1978 against the advice and instincts of nearly all his senior colleagues and contrary to the confident expectations of many of the most powerful trade union leaders. The main political consequence was that the Labour party missed what was probably its best opportunity to win another term of office at a time when there was relative industrial peace and some evidence of economic revival. When the General Election eventually took place in May 1979, it was against a background of the so-called 'winter of discontent' among the trade unions and the defeat of the Government in the Commons in the vote of confidence of March 1979. The result was the election of a Conservative Government on the basis of the largest swing since 1945. Thus, in this and many other cases, it can be argued that this particular aspect of Prime Ministerial power has had very significant political consequences.

**National power**

In contemporary political conditions the Prime Minister of the day has considerable national power in the sense that he has considerable national status and prestige, even allowing for de-mystified public attitudes and widespread public cynicism. Of course, the symbols of Prime Ministerial power should not be confused with the substance, but they are nevertheless important as part of the aura of power which surrounds all heads of Government in modern conditions. Certainly this particular aspect of power is strongly emphasised by the sycophantic attention which many in the media devote to nearly every facet of Prime Ministerial activity. It is also dramatised by the modern tendency for British Prime Ministers to attend frequent summit meetings with their opposite numbers from other countries. As such it is a notable aspect of the tendency towards presidentialism from which the British political system is not immune.

Furthermore, the national power of the Prime Minister is enhanced every time there is a real crisis or a requirement for particularly swift and effective national leadership. This is especially true in time of war, but it is also true in relation to matters of national security in time of peace. For example, it is usually the Prime Minister who has to act decisively in the event of a spy scandal in Government or a major industrial crisis which threatens essential services. Equally, in foreign affairs it is the Prime Minister who has to give a clear lead when British national interests are seriously threatened, as Sir Anthony Eden did at the time of Suez in 1956 or as Margaret Thatcher did at the time of the Falklands conflict in 1982. Similar considerations would also apply in the awful event of full-scale war involving the possibility of a nuclear exchange between this country and the Soviet Union. Although this aspect of Prime Ministerial power is minor in comparison with that of the American President or Soviet General Secretary, it is likely to remain the most awesome facet of Prime Ministerial responsibility as long as Britain continues to retain an independent nuclear weapons capability.

## 12.3 THE ROLE OF THE CABINET

It is difficult to consider the role of the Cabinet in Britain in a manner which separates it from consideration of the office of Prime Minister. Yet there are some important points which can be made about the ideas of Cabinet government and collective responsibility which also serve to illuminate some of the limitations upon the exercise of Prime Ministerial power.

John Mackintosh provided a useful framework for analysis when he wrote that the major tasks of the Cabinet are 'to take or review the major decisions (of Government), to consider (though not necessarily at the formative stage) any proposals which might affect the future of the Government, and to ensure that no Departmental interests are overlooked, thus giving the work of the Government a measure of unity'.[6] It will be worthwhile, therefore, to consider each of these aspects in turn.

### Major decision-making

The Cabinet is the major decision-making body in British Government. It plays this central role, because there is no other institution as well-placed or qualified to meet the need for decisive arbitration at the apex of central Government. After all there is no Chief Executive in British central Government and all executive power is vested by Act of Parliament in the various Departmental Ministers. Thus, whatever its shortcomings, the Cabinet has to act in this capacity in order to make a reality of the principle of collective responsibility.

Some have argued that in modern times it has usually been the Prime Minister of the day who has taken all the really important decisions, albeit usually after appropriate consultations with a small number of senior Ministerial colleagues. There is evidence to support this view in the 1947 decision to develop a British nuclear weapon capability, the 1956 decision to invade the Suez Canal Zone and the 1982 decision to recapture the Falklands. Yet even such apparently Prime Ministerial decisions had to be cleared with a few senior Ministerial colleagues and subsequently endorsed by the entire Cabinet.

There are several reasons why the Prime Minister of the day usually comes out on top in the decision-making process. The main reason is that in every modern Cabinet the Prime Minister has been more than simply first among equals. This happens partly for the reasons already given in the section on Prime Ministerial power, but also because the civil service prefers to deal with Ministers in an hierarchical way. This enables senior civil servants to appeal to the Prime Minister in certain cases when they have been overruled or frustrated by other Ministers. Indeed, the same practice is adopted by Ministers themselves when seeking to outflank their colleagues.

As it happens, nearly every Cabinet in modern times has divided quite conveniently into two parts: a 'first eleven' of very senior Ministers who carry real weight and authority in the Government and a 'second eleven' who, although in charge of Departments or holding Cabinet rank, count for much less. Indeed, Winston Churchill sought at one time in the early 1950s to formalise this division by nominating a few 'Overlords' from among his most senior Cabinet colleagues to supervise and co-ordinate the work of clusters of other Ministers, including Cabinet Ministers. Subsequently, in the late 1960s Harold Wilson also experimented with the idea of creating an 'inner Cabinet' composed of fewer than half a dozen of the real political heavyweights in the Cabinet. No such formal arrangements have worked particularly well in the past, but informal divisions along such lines seem to have evolved in every Cabinet.

It seems that in every Cabinet it is the Prime Minister who usually holds most of the high cards in dealings with his Cabinet colleagues. He can manipulate the membership of Cabinet committees in order to exclude those who are most likely to challenge his preferred course of action or to include those who can be relied upon to support it. He can also exploit the possibilities of continuous bilateral consultations between No 10 Downing Street and particular Departments in order to divide and rule the potential opposition to his policies in Cabinet. Furthermore, if he chooses to forge an axis with the Chancellor of the Exchequer, there are few occasions on which the two of them can be defeated by their Cabinet colleagues.

In any case the doctrine of collective responsibility means that the invidious choice facing any member of the Cabinet who is really unhappy about an important Government decision, is either to threaten resignation with the risk that the Prime Minister may choose to accept it or to bite his lip and risk losing personal credibility in the eyes of his Department and his Cabinet colleagues if it is known that he is out of sympathy with the decision actually taken. Clearly this is not an attractive choice. Yet most Cabinet Ministers faced with this dilemma have chosen the latter course on most occasions.

In the Conservative party it is necessary to go back to Anthony Eden in 1938 or Peter Thorneycroft in 1958 to find examples of senior Cabinet Ministers who chose to resign over significant policy differences with the Prime Minister of the day.[7] In the Labour party it is normal to refer to Aneurin Bevan in 1951 or George Brown in 1968. Yet in most of these rare and celebrated cases clashes of personality played a part as well. In more recent times there has been a tendency in both Conservative and Labour Cabinets for disaffected members of the Cabinet to convey their disapproval of certain aspects of Government policy either via unauthorised private conversations with Lobby journalists or in carefully coded public speeches designed to be just within the formal bounds of collective responsibility while marking out important differences intended to distance them from the prevailing political orthodoxy. The use of such techniques can be regarded as a tribute to the durability and flexibility of collective responsibility. Yet it is also worth noting that on two recent occasions it led to the dismissal of the Cabinet dissidents concerned.[8]

Thus the Cabinet is still the forum within which all the major decisions of Government are ratified, if not actually taken. It is therefore the body in whose name the Government takes its major decisions, even when the actual decision-making is done by Cabinet committees. It can be a formidable brake upon Prime Ministerial power and individual Ministerial initiative. Yet it seems to have had a rather limited creative role in modern times, at any rate in all but emergencies and other exceptional circumstances.

**Review of key problems**

Another important role of the Cabinet is the review of key problems which can affect the future of the Government. To the outside observer this would appear to be an activity upon which any Cabinet worthy of the name ought to concentrate. After all, where else but around the Cabinet table should there be serious and timely discussion of such vital subjects as the growing scarcity of cheap and easily recoverable forms of energy, the apparently intractable problems of long-term unemployment or the impact of low economic growth upon the future of the Welfare State? Yet sadly the truth seems to be that this aspect of the Cabinet's responsibilities has often been neglected in favour of more urgent political issues.

In recent years every regular Cabinet agenda has included an item on the following week's Parliamentary business (when Parliament is in session), an item which permits the Foreign Secretary or the Prime Minister to give a brief report on current international developments affecting Britain and often an item which allows the Chancellor of the Exchequer to report on the febrile state of the economy as indicated by the latest official statistics. Of course, any member of the Cabinet may apply to the Cabinet Secretary to have a particular item included on the agenda of a future meeting, but it is not uncommon for such requests to be turned down and the matter referred to an appropriate Cabinet committee at the behest of the Prime Minister who is in effective control of the Cabinet agenda. On most occasions when the Prime Minister does this, he is merely acting as a good chairman by seeking to get decisions taken at as low a level as possible. However, in the case of a real emergency or if a Cabinet Minister is not prepared to accept the decision of a Cabinet committee, the Prime Minister ensures that the matter is put immediately on the agenda of the full Cabinet. Any other response would lead to a deterioration in the general atmosphere of the Cabinet which can not be in the Government's interest. In general, therefore, the preparation and timing of Cabinet decisions is to a considerable extent susceptible to the influence of the Prime Minister and this gives him a real advantage in any Cabinet battle.

The fact that successive Prime Ministers and senior officials in the Cabinet Office have not encouraged the Cabinet as a whole to discharge its responsibility for strategic review of this kind can be attributed to a number of different reasons. Firstly, it is doubtful whether regular Cabinet meetings are the appropriate occasions to attempt this task, since senior Ministers are always very busy and short of time – they have Parliamentary matters to deal with, Departmental business to manage and a variety of public engagements to fulfil. Secondly, the Cabinet exists mainly to settle or endorse the major decisions which have already been carefully prepared in Whitehall and which may even have been taken (in effect at any rate) by the Prime Minister and a few senior colleagues and advisers in advance of regular Cabinet meetings. In these circumstances it is not surprising that the Cabinet has such a poor record in this respect.

Just occasionally, of course, the Cabinet does get an opportunity for intensive and extensive discussions of this kind. This happened with the discussions in the Churchill Cabinet about British withdrawal from Egypt in 1954, the discussions in the Macmillan Cabinet about European policy in the late 1950s, the discussions in the Heath Cabinet about policy towards Northern Ireland in 1972–3 and the discussions in the Callaghan Cabinet in 1976 when it was necessary to agree upon a considerable package of public expenditure cuts to satisfy the conditions of the IMF loan to Britain. Yet apart from such comparatively rare instances, most Cabinet decisions are largely pre-ordained and even somewhat ritualistic. The Cabinet retains the supreme decision-making power in our political system, but it has usually been a disappointment to those who have looked to it for deep or intense discussions on the key issues of the day.

**Inter-Departmental co-ordination**

Yet another important role of the Cabinet is to ensure inter-Departmental co-ordination of the development of Government policy. In the eyes of many well-informed observers this has been the most notable role of the Cabinet in recent years. It is obviously a key aspect of Cabinet activity, since it helps to impart a degree of coherence and unity to Government policy and so reinforces the doctrine of collective responsibility. Indeed, it could not really be otherwise, since senior Ministers cannot be expected to be bound by Cabinet decisions affecting their spheres of responsibility if their Departmental interests and political points of view have not been adequately taken into account. Such inter-Departmental co-ordination helps to guard against the taking of political decisions by one Department which may have unintended consequences that do collateral damage to the interests of other Departments. It is also intended to contribute to the administrative efficiency of Government in that it can help to avoid both unnecessary duplication of effort in Whitehall and the creation of unintended gaps in the scope of official action.

More generally, it is clear that single-party Government in Britain needs to be united Government if the political system is to work satisfactorily. The Cabinet is the main institutional expression of this unity and it is therefore vital that its decision-making procedures should contribute to rather than detract from the essentially collegiate nature of Government in Britain.

## 12.4 CONCLUSION

Considerable controversy continues to surround the issues raised by Cabinet government in Britain. There is, therefore, no consensus of opinion among academic observers or practising politicians.

Some may agree with John Mackintosh who wrote that 'the weight of evidence does suggest that British Prime Ministers are in a position of very great strength as against their colleagues and within the whole framework of British government'.[9] Others may agree with George Jones who wrote that 'the Prime Minister is the leading figure in the Cabinet whose voice carries most weight, but he is not the all-powerful individual which many have recently claimed him to be'.[10] However, Robert Blake probably came to the most sensible conclusion when he wrote that 'the powers of the Prime Minister have varied with the personality of the Prime Minister or with the particular political circumstances of his tenure'.[11] On the whole this last interpretation seems to accord most closely with the historical evidence. It allows for the fact that there have been times when Prime Ministers have carried all before them - as in the immediate aftermath of General Election victories – and times when powerful Ministers or the Cabinet collectively have asserted their authority over weak, lazy, sick or discredited Prime Ministers. Such are the vagaries and realities of politics.

Although we have been looking in this chapter at two distinct components of the British political system, the fortunes of the Prime Minister and the Cabinet are nearly always closely linked. Whatever their respective roles and capabilities, neither can function satisfactorily without the consent and co-operation of the other. In so far as each is limited in the exercise of political power, the constraints are essentially political rather than constitutional, practical rather than theoretical. It is the other actors in the political process - the political parties, pressure groups, the civil service, the media and public opinion - which keep both the Prime Minister and Cabinet in check. It is the passage of events and the verdict of the electorate which usually seal their fate.

## SUGGESTED QUESTIONS

1. Describe the structure and organisation of Cabinet government in Britain.
2. How powerful are Prime Ministers in modern Britain?
3. Can Cabinets counter-act the tendency towards 'presidentialism' in British central Government?

## NOTES

1. H. Wilson, *The Governance of Britain* (London: Weidenfeld & Nicolson, 1976) p. 8.
2. Quoted in R. Blake, *The Office of Prime Minister* (London: OUP, 1975), p. 50.
3. A. Eden, *Full Circle* (London: Cassell, 1960) p. 269.
4. H. H. Asquith, *Fifty Years of Parliament*, vol. II (London: Cassell, 1926) p. 185.
5. On the other hand, it can be argued that Clement Attlee did not really have any choice, since his senior Cabinet colleagues had either died (for example, Ernest Bevin and Stafford Cripps) or were exhausted after eleven years continuously in Government (for exampler, Herbert Morrison and Hugh Dalton) and since he was under pressure from some of his political colleagues, notably Hugh Dalton, to go to the country at that time in any case.
6. J. P. Mackintosh, *The British Cabinet*, 3rd edn (London: Stevens, 1977) p. 414.
7. In April 1982 Lord Carrington and his Ministerial colleagues at the Foreign Office resigned because of the Government's failure to foresee or prevent the Argentinian invasion of the Falklands and not because of any fundamental policy difference with the rest of the Government.
8. Mrs Thatcher dismissed Norman St John Stevas in December 1980 and Sir Ian Gilmour in September 1981. The former was said to have been guilty of flippancy and loose talk to the press, whereas the latter was deemed to have been guilty of political heresy in the eyes of the Prime Minister and her staunchest supporters.
9. In A. King (ed.) *The British Prime Minister* (London: Macmillan, 1969) p. 198.
10. Ibid, p. 190.
11. R. Blake: *The Office of Prime Minister*, p. 51.

## FURTHER READING

Blake, R., *The Office of Prime Minister* (Oxford: Oxford University Press, 1975).

Butler, R. A., *The Art of the Possible* (London: Hamish Hamilton, 1971).

Crossman, R. H. S., Introduction to W. Bagehot, *The English Constitution* (London: Fontana, 1978).

Gordon-Walker, P., *The Cabinet* (London: Fontana, 1972).

Jennings, W. I., *Cabinet Government*, 3rd edn (Cambridge: Cambridge University Press, 1959).
King, A. (ed.) *The British Prime Minister* (London: Macmillan, 1969).
Mackintosh, J. P., *The British Cabinet*, 3rd edn (London: Stevens, 1977).
Morrison, H., *Government and Parliament* (Oxford: Oxford University Press, 1959).
Rose, R. and Suleiman, E. (eds) *Presidents and Prime Ministers* (Washington, DC: American Enterprise Institute, 1980).
Wilson, H., *The Governance of Britain* (London: Weidenfeld & Nicolson, 1976).

CHAPTER 13

# POLICY- AND DECISION-MAKING

In this chapter we are concerned only with the policy- and decision-making process of British national politics. We may define policy as a deliberate course of action or inaction worked out by the leading figures of the major political parties with the help of others in order to define their political purposes and, to some extent, the methods by which they intend to achieve them. We may define decision-making as an act by a Minister (or a civil servant in the name of a Minister) to select a particular course of action or inaction on a matter of public policy. Such definitions may seem rather general. Yet if they are to reflect the various realities of modern British politics, this is bound to be the case.

At the outset it is also worth heeding Richard Neustadt's observation that 'in Britain governing is meant to be a mystery'.[1] This can be attributed to a number of different factors. Firstly, there is the pervasive official secrecy of British Government, which derives from the 1911 Official Secrets Act and is firmly established as one of the ruling conventions of activity in Whitehall. Secondly, there is the tendency for all Ministers and civil servants to exploit the fact that their privileged access to official information is a form of real power in any political system. Thirdly, there are the limitations imposed upon all enquiries in this area by the fact that those who might be able to dispel the mystery are usually inhibited from doing so by the requirements of official secrecy, while those who would be willing to do so are not usually given sufficient access to the evidence.

For these and other reasons it is not easy to identify all the characteristics of the policy- and decison-making process, let alone to draw all the right conclusions about what actually happens. Yet an attempt must be made in the following pages. The process is shown diagrammatically in Figure 13.1.

Fig 13.1 *The policy- and decision-making process*

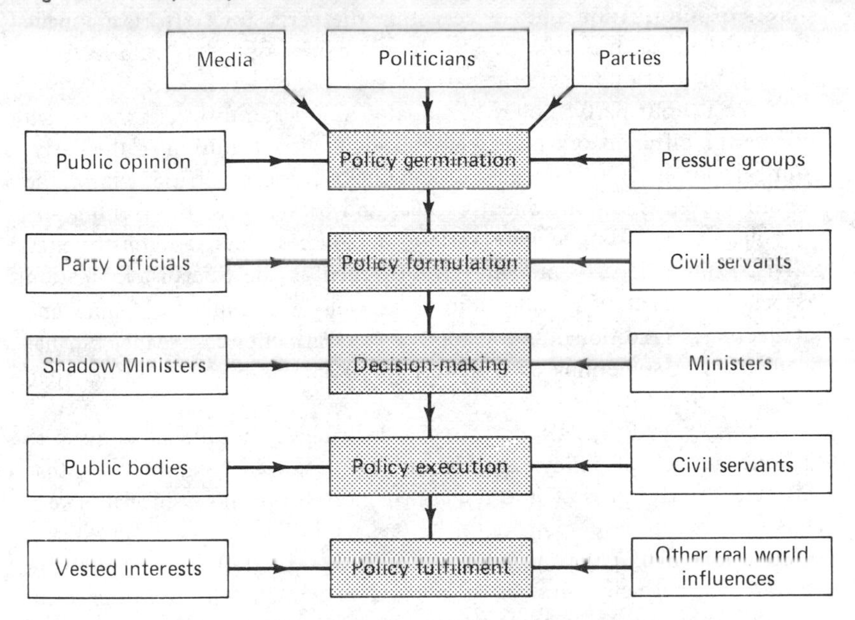


## 13.1 STAGES IN THE PROCESS

In many ways it is somewhat artificial to divide the policy- and decision-making process into a number of discrete stages, since in real life there is always a good deal more overlap and confusion than such a neat presentation would suggest. However, it is a useful way of clarifying how the process works and of identifying the key participants and procedures. In default of a better method we shall proceed in this way.

### Policy germination

The process begins with the stage of policy germination. This usually takes place when a party is in Opposition and its leading figures are communing with themselves and a few Parliamentary colleagues, party activists and well-disposed pressure groups.

In the Conservative party what usually happens is that the leadership identifies a problem or set of problems arising from its previous experience in office or its observation of the current economic and social scene and so decides upon the need for a new policy or the reconsideration of an old policy in a particular area. Then it has to see whether there are the necessary sources of information and advice within the party fold to embark upon the formulation of policy proposals. If it seems clear that there are, the leadership will probably press ahead by setting up a policy group on that basis. On the other hand, if it is clear that there are not sufficient sources of information and advice within the party fold, efforts are made to enlist the assistance of sympathetic and expert outsiders who have the time and inclination to help the party in such policy work.

In the Labour party, policy germinates in a rather different way which reflects the different organisational and ideological tradition of the party. Political power and influence over policy is more diffuse within the Labour movement. Consequently, ideas and pressure for the germination of policy come from a wide variety of sources, such as constituency activists, internal party pressure groups (such as the Socialist Education Association), affiliated trade unions, as well as friendly academics and intellectuals. Traditionally, the role of the Parliamentary leadership has been to act as something of a brake upon policy germination rather than an accelerator of it.

In both cases the developments just described may be characterised as the pure models of policy germination. Yet it should be emphasised that this stage of the process is often much more hit-or-miss, since it is very dependent upon developments in the real world which usually produce a reactive model of policy germination or sustained campaigns by pressure groups which usually produce an absorptive model. It can also be influenced by the media in their presentation of events, their selection of issues and their interpretation of public opinion on the issues in question. Perhaps most commonly of all, it is influenced by reference to or self-conscious contrast with the line taken by the party when last in office.

At this stage of the process the key questions are who defines the problems to be solved, who sets the priorities for the policy work and by what criteria are the various policy groups established? When a party is in Opposition, it is really the leading politicians who take charge of the various policy groups who have the greatest influence at this stage of the process. When a party is in Government, different considerations apply, since it is the school of experience which leads to the germination of most policy ideas once the initial burst of ideological zeal has been exhausted.

**Policy formulation**

The next stage in the process is that of policy formulation. By this we mean the translation into coherent policy proposals of the ideas which have germinated in the ways just described. This is a stage which also takes place more systematically in Opposition than in Government, although both situations will need to be examined.

In the Conservative party, policy formulation is usually the work of party officials and others who draft the papers in which policy proposals are contained. Of course, such people work under the careful direction and control of the chairman of the policy group concerned and indirectly of the senior politician or politicians who are given the responsibility for policy co-ordination. For years this work has been done by the employees of the Conservative Research Department which has been a relatively small but rather competent organisation staffed mainly by bright young graduates. However, since the Department was absorbed directly into Central Office in 1980 its role has not been so prominent in this or other aspects of party work.

In the Labour party, the work of policy formulation is done by analogous people employed in the party's Research Department. They work under the direction and control of the leading politicians most closely involved with the policy groups, but within the structure of policy committees and sub-committees established under the auspices of the National Executive Committee. Thus, except for the final drafting of the most important policy documents (such as the Party Manifesto), this work is done mainly by people who will not be directly involved in carrying out its policy implications when the party is in office.

In Government, of course, the policy formulation stage can be rather different, since Ministers have the benefit of official information and advice provided by their Departments. Nevertheless the essential work of drafting and re-drafting the proposals which may or may not find their way into the party Manifestos, is still done mainly by party officials and others working within the structure of party policy groups.

In the Labour party, the structure of such groups tends to be as elaborate when the party is in Government as when it is in Opposition, since the National Executive Committee still provides the framework for what sometimes amounts almost to a rival policy-making process with which the Parliamentary leadership may have to struggle in order to get its way. However, Ministers remain free to choose when deciding which of many policy commitments proposed by the National Executive Committee they will accept and which they will reject for inclusion in the party Manifesto. When in Government they also retain considerable flexibility and discretion in deciding upon the methods and the timing for the implementation of even the most unambiguous policy commitments.

In the Conservative party, the structure of such groups tends to be less elaborate when the party is in Government than when it is in Opposition. This is because there is no equivalent of Labour's National Executive Committee with which to contend and because Ministers retain almost exclusive control of the policy-formulation stage of the process. Thus a variety of policy groups are established which are normally chaired by members of the Commons or the Lords and serviced by party officials or others within the party fold. In the first instance the actual work of policy-formulation is usually done by the party officials who act as secretaries to the policy groups, although they tend to work under the close supervision and control of the relevant policy group chairmen. The policy proposals are then likely to be considered by the groups and often redrafted or refined in the light of such discussions. They are then further considered by the relevant Minister or Ministers and in all important cases referred to the Prime Minister for approval before a decision is taken about their inclusion or exclusion from the party Manifesto.

**Decision-making**

The next stage in the process is that of decision-making. On all important or politically sensitive issues this is the work of Ministers or Shadow Ministers, as the case may be.

In Opposition, the requirements and procedures are quite simple. Usually all that is necessary is that the Shadow Cabinet should meet to accept or reject the policy proposals put to it which have been formulated, re-formulated and refined in the ways already described. Of course, there are some issues which require lengthy discussion in the Shadow Cabinet and which cannot be resolved at a single meeting. Yet in most cases by the time that policy formulations reach this stage in the process, the actual decisions are taken with a reasonable degree of expedition, not least because the Leader of the Opposition and his closest colleagues will have taken care to prepare the ground before the meeting.

In Government, this stage in the process is both more varied and more complex. Some Government decisions can be taken quite expeditiously by individual Ministers acting within their particular spheres of responsibility. Some are taken by groups of Ministers within one Department. However, nearly all the important Government decisions affect a variety of Departmental interests and therefore have to be taken by Cabinet committees composed of Ministers (and occasionally senior civil servants) from each of the Departments concerned and normally chaired by a senior Cabinet Minister or, in some cases, the Prime Minister.

It is difficult to make any useful or definitive generalisations about decision-making at meetings of the Cabinet and its committees. It would appear that in full Cabinet decisions are normally taken quite expeditiously and that it is only when the Cabinet has to deal with the most difficult and contentious political issues - for example, public expenditure cuts - that it has to return on several occasions to the same subjects. This really underlines the trouble that officials take to prepare the ground for Cabinet decisions and the considerable efforts which all Prime Ministers make to facilitate Cabinet decision-making by holding bilateral meetings with the Ministers most closely concerned in advance of meetings of the full Cabinet.

When it becomes necessary to use a Cabinet committee to make a decision on a particular subject, the terms of reference are usually supplied to the chairman by the Prime Minister or, occasionally, by the Cabinet as a whole. It is then for the chairman of the committee to hold as many meetings as necessary in order to reach a decision which can be recommended to the Cabinet as a whole often within an agreed period of time. In the later stages of the 1964–70 Labour Government it became conventional that no member of the Cabinet who was not on a particular Cabinet committee, challenged the decisions of that committee without the prior approval of the Prime Minister or the chairman of the committee concerned. Indeed, the whole rationale for Cabinet committees is that they should be able to take decisions on behalf of the Cabinet as a whole without normally having to submit them to a further formal stage of decision-making in full Cabinet. Only if they work in this way can they truly be said to save the time and energy of the entire Cabinet. Yet it also remains true that the convention of collective responsibility and the tradition of Cabinet government entitles all Cabinet Ministers, if they are sufficiently determined, to pursue a particularly sensitive or important issue in full Cabinet if they insist on doing so.

Some Prime Ministers have found it necessary to lay down strict ground-rules for Cabinet decision-making (such as the one already mentioned) when the members of a particular Cabinet are not sufficiently amenable to Prime Ministerial leadership and guidance. Others have not found it necessary to act so formally, because for various reasons to do with politics or personalities they have been able to dominate and control their Cabinet colleagues. In all cases the nature of the decision-making is likely to depend upon the balance of power and experience within a Cabinet, so there can be no definitive generalisations.

**Policy execution**

The next stage in the process is that of policy execution. This is the stage at which Whitehall excels, provided the decision has been clearly taken and clearly minuted. The real difficulties tend to occur later on.

Policy execution normally follows immediately after the three stages already described. However, so far as civil servants are concerned, its roots can be traced back to an earlier stage in the process. Once the broad objectives of party policy have been set and in many cases enshrined as Manifesto commitments, it is for senior civil servants in the various Whitehall Departments to prepare position papers designed to assist Ministers to implement their policies in Government. This aspect of civil service work begins during or even before every General Election campaign, when the various Departments prepare different files of guidance for incoming Ministers according to the different political commitments made by the different parties. Thus new Labour Ministers may have advice on their desks as to how best to implement their policy of nationalisation, while new Conservative Ministers may have comparable advice on their policy of denationalisation. The advice may be sanguine or cautious, but it is usually intended to suggest the most effective ways of executing the policies of the incoming Government, while confronting Ministers with the practical consequences of their political commitments.

From then on the initiative is with Ministers and their behaviour varies according to their personal drive and political inclinations and the extent to which the party commitments in their particular Departmental spheres are given priority by the new Government. If a Minister is charged with the execution of a policy which is given a high political priority and if the commitment is clearly expressed in the party Manifesto or other formal statements by the party leader, then it will usually be a straightforward matter of taking the appropriate Ministerial decisions for the initiation of administrative action or the introduction of new legislation, whichever is appropriate. On the other hand, if a Minister has to execute a policy which has been given a low political priority, then he will probably have little alternative to preparing the ground with suitable administrative action or putting in his Departmental bid for a future place in the legislative time-table. In anticipation of progress he can, of course, improve his Department's prospects by stimulating interest in Parliament and the media and by mobilising support in relevant pressure groups and public opinion. If he does all these things successfully, he will increase the chances of making a mark for himself and his Department at a later stage in the Parliament.

Assuming, therefore, that the appropriate decision has been taken within the Cabinet structure, the stage of policy execution is initially the responsibility of the Cabinet Office which has to communicate the decision to all Departments and other bodies which need to know about it. For example, if a decision concerns a nationalised industry, it will be communicated by the Cabinet Office to the relevant Department (for example, the Department of Transport in the case of British Rail, the Department of Energy in the case of the National Coal Board or the Department of Industry in the case of the British Steel Corporation) which will then be responsible for seeing that the decision is conveyed to the Chairman and Board concerned. If the decision involves matters of local government responsibility (such as planning, housing, land use, etc.), it will be communicated to the Department of the Environment for onward transmission to the local authorities in England and to the Scottish, Welsh and Northern Ireland Offices in so far as the decision affects people living in those parts of the United Kingdom. All such civil service communication is carried out between the Cabinet Office and the appropriate Ministerial Private Offices which are then responsible for the further communication within their Departments. It is, therefore, complementary to the direct communication between Ministers which takes place in the relevant Cabinet committees and on other more informal occasions in the House of Commons and elsewhere.

If a Cabinet decision has legislative implications, it becomes the responsibility of the Minister or Ministers who will have to pilot the legislation through Parliament. However, the Department or Departments concerned will have to work very closely with the legal experts from the Office of Parliamentary Counsel who act as legislative draftsmen for the entire Government. Indeed, the role of these Parliamentary draftsmen can be of crucial significance, since the precise wording of Bills can sometimes be as important as the fundamental principles involved.

If the execution of a Government decision requires new primary legislation, then it begins with the vital pre-Parliamentary stage within Whitehall. This involves extensive consultations between civil servants in the Departments concerned and the relevant experts and interested groups both within and outside the web of government. Such detailed consultations may continue for many months on the basis of draft legislative proposals and it is not unknown for the results of all this work to be rejected by the Legislation Committee of the Cabinet and for the Ministers and civil servants concerned to be told to start again or even to shelve the project until a later date. Thus by the time that a proposed Government Bill is ready for inclusion in the Queen's Speech at the beginning of a Parliamentary session in November, it can usually be assumed that its content has been so fully discussed with the relevant experts and interested groups that the result should be acceptable and workable law.

Alternatively, the execution of a Government decision may only require new secondary legislation, in other words a Statutory Instrument issued under the authority of an existing Act of Parliament. Once again there are detailed consultations within Whitehall with a wide range of relevant experts and interested groups. Indeed, such consultations are doubly important in this case, since the subsequent procedures for Parliamentary scrutiny of Statutory Instruments when published are widely agreed to be cursory and inadequate.

However, if the decision falls within the sphere of the lawful administrative discretion provided for Ministers by legislation already on the Statute Book, the Minister concerned normally acts in an executive capacity and then communicates directly with the individuals or bodies concerned via Departmental circular or by ordinary letter or memorandum. In some cases the decision may entail the delegation of executive responsibility to statutory bodies which already have lawful powers in certain specified areas, such as local authorities or public corporations. Yet in most cases it is a matter of Departmental action carried out directly on behalf of the Minister concerned by the civil servants in his Department. As we shall see in Chapters 14 and 15, this means that it is usually impossible to maintain a credible distinction between policy and administration and that the execution of policy is often as important as the decision actually taken.

**Policy fulfilment**

The final and most problematic stage in the process is policy fulfilment. Recent British history suggests that it is the stage at which the failures of successive Governments have been most marked. Among the reasons for this may be that Governments have tried to do too much, pursued often mutually contradictory objectives, had to share power with formidable interest groups, found themselves constrained by expected or revealed public opinion and been obliged to work within the limiting framework of established policy assumptions and uncompromising realities in the outside world. Faced with such difficulties, successive Governments have sought to ensure the fulfilment of their policies by using one or more of the following political techniques.

First of all, there is the technique of accommodation. This is a standard Whitehall technique whereby Governments seek to neutralise any threats to their policies by the simple expedient of accommodating critical points of view and absorbing critical people. It may take the form of co-opting troublesome or obstructive individuals onto official consultative committees or appointing them to positions of responsibility on public bodies or simply holding privileged discussions with powerful groups with a view to incorporating at least some of their ideas or concerns into Government policy. It is certainly one of the most effective and well-tried methods of dealing with outside critics or adversaries of Government policy and turning them into compliant or at least pacified semi-insiders. Yet it is not usually enough to ensure the fulfilment of policy.

Another technique is that of manipulation. This is really little more than a sinister term for the well-tried art of political persuasion and it includes such often-practiced methods as systematic news management, that is, the attempt to influence public opinion via careful and deliberate guidance of the media. This technique has been used with varying degrees of success at least since the early 1950s by successive Governments which sought to adjust the timing of their decisions on economic policy in such a way as to maximise the chances that a gullible electorate would reward them with re-election. The technique, which usually took the form of a degree of deliberate reflation of the economy perhaps a year or two before an expected General Election, could be said to have worked in 1959 and 1966. However, it has been of diminishing utility and effectiveness since the early 1970s and it is now doubtful whether it would work at all in current economic circumstances.

Another technique is that of public opinion mobilisation. This is really a matter of seeking the support of the 'silent majority' to redress the political balance against the disproportionate influence of the vociferous and articulate minorities. As an exercise in political leadership, it is no easier than the other techniques already mentioned and can be more difficult in view of the problems involved in trying to hold public opinion constantly to one particular line and then translating that fixity of purpose into actual voting behaviour when it is needed. Such difficulties are illustrated by the familiar tendency for many people to give strong support in public opinion polls to the general idea of incomes restraint, but then to act individually or collectively in flagrant contravention of the general principle. Nevertheless there are various ways in which this technique can be applied. These may involve the use of powerful rhetoric, constant repetition of simple points, persuasive argument designed to appeal to the man in the street, symbolic gestures designed to evoke a favourable public response and even specially commissioned political advertising and opinion polls. However, none of these methods has proved decisively effective, so responsible politicians in Government have usually had to rely upon the more traditional methods of rational argument and emotional appeal.

Finally, there is the technique of political shock treatment which involves confronting the public with the full implications of failing to support Government policy. In a sense this is a technique which has been used by the Thatcher Government in its efforts to change public attitudes permanently and radically in the vital area of economic productivity and industrial performance. It is certainly a technique which has been successful in the past at times of clear and imminent danger - as in 1940 when Britain stood alone against Nazi Germany - and it may also have worked during the 1982 Falklands conflict when public opinion rallied strongly behind the British armed forces. Yet there can be no certainty that it will work in normal circumstances during times of peace, so Governments would be wise not to count upon it.

## 13.2 KEY ASPECTS

### Continuity and discontinuity

It should be clear from the foregoing description that policy- and decision-making in Britain is essentially a continuous process which proceeds from week to week, month to month, year to year and even Government to Government. This is mainly because the crucial problems have remained very much the same over several decades, regardless of which party has been in office. It is also because the civil service has a natural preference for continuity, which is to be expected from any permanent and institutionalised bureaucracy.

For about twenty-five years after the Second World War the continuity of Government policy stemmed from the high degree of broad political consensus which began with the Coalition Government during the war. Subsequently this continuity was reinforced by Governments of both major parties in the 1950s and early 1960s which eschewed any really radical policies and chose to remain within the broad framework of the post-war consensus. It was not until the early 1970s that this consensus began to crumble and the familiar continuity from Government to Government was diminished.

On the other hand, if we focus on discontinuity, we see that all Governments since the war have taken some highly political decisions which produced a number of major new departures of policy. The decision taken in 1947 by Clement Attlee and a few of his senior colleagues to develop an independent nuclear weapons capability for Britain was one powerful example. Another was the decision taken in 1956 by Anthony Eden and a small group of senior Ministers to send British forces to invade the Suez Canal Zone. Another was the decision taken in 1960 by Harold Macmillan and a few close advisers to open negotiations with a view to full British membership of the European Community. Another was the decision to devalue the £ taken in 1967 by Harold Wilson and a few senior colleagues and advisers. Another was the decision taken in 1972 by Edward Heath and a few senior colleagues to impose direct rule from Westminster upon Northern Ireland. Yet another was the decision taken in 1976 by James Callaghan, Denis Healey and a few senior advisers to apply to the International Monetary Fund for a massive loan to assist the British economy. All these were decisions which entailed notable discontinuities of policy.

Such decisions were precipitated in most cases by developments over which the Government of the day had little or no control. On the whole they did not stem from independent conclusions independently arrived at, but rather from the imperatives of external developments. For example, the 1947 decision to develop an independent nuclear weapons capability for Britain stemmed largely from the unwillingness of the American Congress to allow the Truman Administration to share American nuclear weapons information with other countries. The 1956 decision to send British forces to the Suez Canal Zone stemmed largely from the threatening behaviour of President Nasser which in its turn had been provoked by the refusal of the American Government to help finance the construction of the Aswan Dam. The 1960 decision to open negotiations with the Six with a view to full British membership of the European Community derived mainly from the failure of the British Government a year earlier to negotiate a wider European Free Trade Area with the same countries. The decision to devalue the £ in 1967 flowed more or less inevitably from the previously serious pressure upon our currency in the foreign exchange markets and persistent problems with our balance of payments. The decision in 1972 to impose direct rule from Westminster upon the people of Northern Ireland stemmed mainly from the Government's sense of exasperation with the unwillingness of the Protestant majority to make any real concessions to the Catholic minority in the vital sphere of civil rights. The decision in 1976 to apply for a massive loan from the International Monetary Fund could be attributed mainly to the lack of international confidence in the previous economic policies of the Labour Government.

Although most of these discontinuities were forced upon Ministers by the pressure of mighty events or the imperatives of what they believed to be their national duty, there have been many other decisions taken at the highest political level which have represented deliberate discontinuities of policy for party political or ideological purposes. Decisions of this kind have been increasingly evident over the last two decades. They have stemmed from the tendency of each major party, when in Opposition, to return to ideological first principles in order to formulate radical and often uncompromising policies for implementation on returning to Government. The effect of this kind of policy- and decision-making has been to lead each major party, on coming into Government, to claim that it has a popular mandate for every commitment made in its Manifesto, no matter how damaging or daft it might be to implement such a policy when in office. This pattern has produced sharp discontinuities of policy for which Ministers have taken party political credit, at any rate until such time as the passage of events or the school of life has demonstrated just how mistaken such policies really were.

The only people who relish deliberate discontinuities of this kind are the ideological zealots in each of the two major parties who tend to come into their own when their party is in Opposition. Their approach to policy- and decision-making can be justified only on certain conditions which are difficult to fulfil. When their party is in Opposition, they must mobilise the great majority of public opinion in support of their radical ideas. During the General Election campaign, they must make their political intentions crystal clear. In Government, they must succeed in explaining what they are doing to the satisfaction of at least the politically-attentive section of the public. If even one of these vital conditions is not satisfied, the authority of Government suffers in consequence.

The underlying problems in Britain have not changed very much over the years, except in so far as the problems of Government have probably become harder to solve since the first oil crisis in 1973–4. However, the initial responses of each major party on coming into office have contrasted more and more sharply as each has attempted to be more radical than its predecessor in Government. Inevitably, this has produced considerable discontinuities of policy which, in their turn, have led to considerable disappointments for the zealots in each major party as they have been obliged to come to terms with the realities of Government.[2] Unfortunately, it has also led each major party, when in Opposition, to conclude that the real answers to such problems are to be found in even sharper and more deliberate discontinuities of policy. Thus we seem to have moved in Britain since the war from a period when policy- and decision-making was characterised by broad consensus and continuity which matched the continuity of our national problems to a period since the early 1970s when policy- and decision-making has been characterised by considerable discontinuities, even though the underlying problems have remained very much the same. It may be that leading politicians in all parties are now moving, however reluctantly in some cases, towards a new policy consensus which will produce continuity on a new basis in future. Yet it seems just as likely that we shall have to live in conditions of considerable discontinuity as long as developments in the real world and the political responses to the chain of events continue as before.

**Strengths and weaknesses**

There are both strengths and weaknesses in the policy- and decision-making process in Britain. It is neither one of the best nor one of the worst processes of its kind in the liberal democratic societies. It has some characteristics which are universal and some which are peculiar to Britain. In any case it ought to be assessed on its merits.

The most obvious strength is the ability of the process to translate party political commitments into Government action or legislation. This derives principally from the way in which the electoral system is capable of turning a minority of the votes cast into a majority of the seats won by the victorious party. Thus it enables a particular interpretation of the popular will to be transformed into executive or legislative action by the Government of the day usually without encountering any insuperable obstacles, at any rate in Whitehall and Westminster.

Another strength of the process is its efficiency in turning Ministerial decisions into administrative action or legislation. This is a tribute largely to the efficiency of the senior administrative grades in Whitehall and their capacity for ensuring effective public administration. It means that the writ of Ministers runs effectively throughout Whitehall and its satellite institutions, although not so effectively in the quasi-autonomous spheres of public corporations and local government.

Yet another strength of the process is its ability to withstand abrupt and radical changes of policy. Any institutions of government which have this ability to accommodate changes of political direction so quickly and completely must be very robust. What is more, such changes can be made without any significant shift of administrative personnel, in contrast to what happens in some other countries.

On the other hand, there are some notable weaknesses in the process which might be considered to outweigh the strengths just enumerated. In the first place, it can be argued that the robust flexibility of the process permits too many abrupt and often damaging discontinuities of policy. As has already been pointed out, these stem from the frequent determination of politicians in office slavishly to implement their party political commitments and from the increasing polarisation of the attitudes and policies of the two major parties.

Paradoxically, another weakness of the process is that there is also too much unimaginative continuity of thinking in Whitehall. This reflects the success of senior civil servants in bringing virtually all Governments back to the path of Whitehall orthodoxy within two or three years of every General Election. It also reflects the gyroscopic tendency of the British civil service which Shirley Williams has described as 'a beautifully designed and effective braking mechanism'.[3]

Another weakness of the process is that it encourages both Ministers and civil servants to pay too much attention to short-term political considerations at the expense of the quest for fundamental long-term solutions to the nation's most serious and intractable problems. While this is partly a function of the five-year maximum span of any Parliament, it is mainly due to the congenital tendency of all modern politicians to give what is urgent priority over what is important in a democracy which expects quick results.

Another weakness of the process is that both Ministers and civil servants tend to rely too heavily upon a rather narrow range of official information and advice. This is because Ministers rely almost exclusively upon civil servants and because civil servants in their turn are usually too dependent upon the information and advice stored in the Departmental files or supplied by a predictable range of established interests.

Another weakness of the process is that of governmental over-load.[4] In other words, Ministers and senior civil servants often have too much to do in too little time. This can be attributed to a number of different causes, among which are the increase over the years in the scope and the complexity of modern government, the growth of the international dimension of decision-making (for example, the European Community, the Commonwealth, the Economic Summits, etc.), the impact of modern mass communications which has led Governments to feel that they must respond instantly to any developments, allegations or rumours publicised by the media, and perhaps the Parkinsonian tendency in all administration for tasks to grow and staff to multiply simply in order to justify a larger budget and increased status for senior bureaucrats.

Yet another weakness of the process could be said to be the relatively limited scope for either Parliamentary or public participation. This is mainly because central Government in Britain is essentially élitist and secretive with a marked tendency to exclude everyone other than the chosen few whose involvement has been traditionally acceptable to Ministers and civil servants. Among the company of the excluded, the vast majority of back-benchers in Parliament feel it most acutely. Yet it is difficult to see how the problem can be solved within the traditional conventions of Parliamentary government in Britain.

## 13.3 POSSIBLE IMPROVEMENTS

This is not the place to canvass in any detail the wide range of possible improvements which have been proposed in order to deal with the weaknesses of the policy- and decision-making process in Britain. It is sufficient to mention a few of the more familiar suggestions which have been made in recent times.

### Increased support for the Opposition

Some people have argued that there should be increased support for the Opposition. To this end they have suggested the creation of a small, but capable Department of the Opposition to advise and inform the Opposition parties and so keep their policies more closely in touch with the realities of the outside world as seen from Whitehall. If this were agreed, it would be an important political and constitutional development, since the uneven quality of party policy can be attributed to some extent to the ignorance and insularity of much policy-making in Opposition and since the dominance of Parliament by the Government of the day can be attributed at least in part to the superior support and advice which Ministers enjoy.

Another way of achieving the same objective of 'educating' the Opposition would be to give all Opposition politicians much fuller and more frequent access to official information and advice. This already happens to some extent in the case of Privy Councillors (former Ministers of senior rank) who can see restricted information on privileged terms. It also happens during the Standing Committee stage of many complicated Government Bills when the MPs concerned are supplied with detailed Departmental briefs on every clause and proposed amendment. However, it could perhaps be extended to more MPs on more occasions if Ministers and civil servants would agree to do so.

Yet another way of achieving the same objective would be to provide the political parties with substantial support from public funds, perhaps in proportion to the votes which they receive at General Elections or the money which they raise by their own efforts. This would enable parties in Opposition to employ many more advisers and research staff and so ensure that their front-bench spokesmen were more fully briefed. However, it would not of itself guarantee a better standard of Opposition, since that must also depend upon the motivation and the capabilities of the politicians concerned.

**Wider advice for Ministers**

Another proposal which has been put forward is that there should be a more open approach towards civil service recruitment and staffing, so that a wider range of advice would be available to Ministers from a wider range of official sources. If this could be arranged, it would probably have a positive effect, since the quality of policy- and decision-making in British Government seems to have been adversely affected on occasions by the rather narrow outlook and cautious assumptions of many senior civil servants.

Some would take this idea a good deal further by opening up the senior grades of the civil service to permit the employment in each Department of perhaps ten to twenty politically appointed officials who would serve in Government on fixed term contracts at market rates of pay.[5] The theory is that such temporary officials would be able to offer Ministers support and advice which would be more in keeping with the prejudices and purposes of the politicians concerned. Yet it is not clear whether such a change would raise the quality of Government decision-making or provide Ministers with advice which is not available to them now, at any rate in those Departments which already include political advisers to Ministers as is the case in a number of instances today.

**Structural changes in Whitehall**

Another proposal which has been made from time to time is that there should be structural changes in Whitehall in order to make the centre more powerful in relation to the various individual Departments. This has led some people to propose the creation of new central Departments, such as a fully fledged Prime Minister's Department or an enlarged and reconstructed Cabinet Office.[6]

The advocates of such changes believe that they would strengthen the position of the Prime Minister in the policy- and decision-making process and encourage all senior Ministers to pay more attention to Government policy as a whole rather than their own more narrow Departmental interests. However, it seems rather doubtful whether such changes are really necessary, since most well-informed observers agree that a strong Prime Minister is more than able to dominate the purposes and priorities of the Government and that the process of policy- and decision-making already has many of the attributes of a presidential system of government. In so far as there is a real problem of excessive 'Departmentalism' in

Whitehall, it ought to be solved by more effective and timely use of Cabinet committees rather than structural changes in the organisation of central Government.

**Greater role for Parliament**

Finally, some people have been attracted by the idea that Parliament should be given a greater role in the policy- and decision-making process. This would almost certainly mean the further development of the existing Select Committees in ways which would be designed to get them more deeply involved in the formative stages of policy-making. For example, it might mean encouraging Select Committees to consider legislative proposals at the pre-legislative stage or to influence decisions on taxation and public expenditure before they are finally taken by Ministers.

In general, such contributions from back-benchers would probably be enhanced if Parliament were to strengthen its own independent sources of information and advice by establishing new institutions to support an enhanced role in the policy- and decision-making process. In this context the General Accounting Office and the Office of Technology Assessment which assist the US Congress might provide possible models for new institutions in this country. Yet even if such changes were made, there would remain some considerable and perhaps insuperable difficulties in making more assertive Parliamentary practices compatible with the traditional procedures and assumptions of Parliamentary government in Britain.

## 13.4 CONCLUSION

A balanced conclusion to the issues raised in this chapter would seem to be that the policy- and decision-making process works rather well, but only within the limited confines of Whitehall and Westminster. Outside the walls of these bureaucratic and political citadels the process is not particularly effective at securing either the understanding or the consent of the general public. Even the pressure groups and others who are consulted by Ministers and civil servants do not really believe in most cases that they have much more than a marginal influence upon either the process or the outcome of politics in Britain. Whatever may happen in exceptional circumstances, it is normally the senior politicians and their close advisers who take the decisions which really matter and who do so according to their own political criteria.

In the longer term the best hope of improving the process may lie in the current tendency for politicians deliberately and steadily to reduce public expectations of what central Government and other public agencies can really deliver. Indeed, this may be essential, since if practices were to continue as before (for instance, during the 1950s and 1960s), we might experience growing public disenchantment or even alienation from the entire political system. Although Britain is a mature and robust Parliamentary democracy, it would be foolish to take unnecessary and gratuitous risks with the political system, especially since there appear to be better ways of doing things which could improve the chances of securing public satisfaction and political success.

## SUGGESTED QUESTIONS

1. Describe the policy- and decision-making process in British central Government.
2. Where does real power lie in the policy- and decision-making process?
3. How could the policy- and decision-making process be made more democratic and accountable to the general public?

## NOTES

1. Quoted in R. Rose (ed.) *Policy Making in Britain* (London: Macmillan, 1969) p. 292.
2. This pattern fitted the 1966–70 Labour Government, the 1970–4 Conservative Government and the 1974–9 Labour Government. Arguably, the Conservative Government under Mrs Thatcher since 1979 may have created a new pattern of determined consistency of policy, although there are those who would maintain that its Ministers have known how to trim when they needed to do so.
3. In W. Rodgers *et al.*, *Policy and Practice, the Experience of Government* (London: Royal Institute of Public Administration, 1980) p. 81.
4. Lord Hunt of Tanworth, a former Cabinet Secretary who had served four Prime Ministers, elaborated this point in a lecture given to the Chartered Institute of Public Finance and Accountancy on 9 June 1983.
5. See Sir John Hoskyns, 'Whitehall and Westminster, an Outsider's View' in *Fiscal Studies*, November 1982.
6. Both Lord Hunt and Sir John Hoskyns have addressed this question. The former merely outlined four possible options and expressed no strong personal preference as betweeen a full-blown Prime Minister's Department, a strengthened Cabinet Office, a strengthened Central Policy Review Staff (possibly amalgamated with the Policy Unit at 10 Downing St) and a strengthened Prime Minister's Office. The latter advocated what he described as 'a small new Department responsible for the development and over-seeing of the Government's total strategy across all Departments, integrating policy and politics into a single whole'. He thought it would incorporate the CPRS and might emerge as a reconstructed Cabinet Office.

## FURTHER READING

Ashford, D. E., *Policy and Politics in Britain* (Oxford: Blackwell, 1981).
Blondel, J., *Voters, Parties and Leaders* (Harmondsworth: Penguin, 1974).
Bruce-Gardyne, J. and Lawson, N., *The Power Game* (London: Macmillan, 1976).
Butler, R. A., *The Art of the Possible* (London: Hamish Hamilton, 1971).
Crossman, R. H. S., *Inside View* (London: Jonathan Cape, 1972).
Mackintosh, J. P. (ed.) *People and Parliament* (Farnborough: Saxon House, 1978).
Richardson, J. J. and Jordan, A. G., *Governing under Pressure* (Oxford: Martin Robertson, 1979).
Rodgers, W. *et al.*, *Policy and Practice, the Experience of Government* (London: Royal Institute of Public Administration, 1980).
Rose, R. (ed.) *Policy Making in Britain* (London: Macmillan, 1969).
Smith, B., *Policy Making in British Government* (Oxford: Martin Robertson, 1976).

# CHAPTER 14

# MINISTERS AND DEPARTMENTS

Britain is a country with a long tradition of centralised government. Some of the public offices of central Government have been in existence for centuries. For example, the first Lord Chancellor was appointed by Edward the Confessor, the Exchequer developed in the twelfth century and the office of Lord President of the Council dates from 1497. Some of the Departments of central Government are now over 200 years old. For example, two of the most prestigious Departments were established in 1782 when George III created a Department for Foreign Affairs and a Department for Home and Colonial Affairs (now the Home Office).

Since the mid-nineteenth century Departments of central Government have been created, reorganised and dissolved. For example, the Board (Department) of Education was established in 1870 with a Minister directly responsible to Parliament for the whole area of public education. The Board (Department) of Agriculture and Fisheries was converted into a Ministry in 1919 after the struggle to feed the nation during the First World War. The Air Ministry was created in 1937 to organise the national response to the growing threat from German air power. More recent examples include the Department of the Environment which was established in 1970 as one of the super-Departments designed to secure better co-ordination in Whitehall and the Department of Energy which was established in 1974 as a response to the energy crisis at that time.

However, few of these Departmental arrangements last for ever. For example, the 1974–9 Labour Government split the super-Departments into several smaller Departments – the Department of Transport was re-established as a separate Department outside the Department of the Environment and the Department of Trade and Industry was split into a Department of Industry, a Department of Trade and a new Department of Prices and Consumer Affairs. Equally, the 1979–83 Conservative Government abolished the Civil Service Department and redistributed its functions between the Treasury and the Cabinet Office, while the present Conservative Government has recreated the Department of Trade and Industry but transferred some of its functions to an enlarged Department of Transport. Thus there has been both change and continuity in the organisation of British central Government.

## 14.1 THE WORK OF CENTRAL GOVERNMENT

Throughout the entire period of Departmental government in Britain there has been only one serious examination of the overall structure of central Government. This was carried out by a committee chaired by Lord Haldane which reported to Lloyd George's Government in 1918.[1] The two main recommendations of its report were that Departmental boundaries should be based upon functional criteria (such as Health, Agriculture, Defence, etc.) and that the Cabinet should be kept as a compact policy-making body at the apex of central Government. Neither recommendation has been implemented fully or deliberately over subsequent years. Thus it has been quite common for Departments based upon function to coexist with some based upon tradition (such as the Home Office) and others based upon geography (for example, the Scottish Office or the Northern Ireland Office). Furthermore, Cabinets have had as few as five members (Winston Churchill's War Cabinet in 1940) or as many as twenty-four members (Harold Wilson's Cabinet in 1975).

A limited attempt at Departmental reorganisation was made by Edward Heath's Government in 1970. This stemmed from careful preparation in Opposition and was set out in a White Paper published soon after the Conservative election victory.[2] It marked the culmination of a trend in the 1960s towards the creation of super-Departments, the adoption of a managerial style of government and deliberate attempts to strengthen the central co-ordinating Departments in relation to the rest of Whitehall. However, only the emphasis upon the so-called central Departments (such as the Treasury and the Cabinet Office) really substantiated the rhetoric about a new managerial style of government.

### Departmental structure

The Departmental structure in Whitehall today consists of eighteen main Departments, including the three legal Departments.[3] In political terms the most important are the Treasury, the Foreign Office and the Home Office. Yet in terms of the public spending for which they are responsible the Department of Health and Social Security and the Ministry of Defence are the most significant. In formal terms there is no Prime Minister's Department, although the staff at 10 Downing Street and in the Cabinet Office provide effective civil service support for the Prime Minister of the day.

There are a few non-Departmental Ministers other than the Prime Minister, such as the Lord President of the Council, the Leader of the House of Commons and the Chancellor of the Duchy of Lancaster. These senior Ministers are often assigned key tasks of co-ordination in central Government, for example, the chairmanship of Cabinet committees or the control of Government information policy. Such offices are also a convenient way for the Prime Minister of the day to include close political colleagues in the Cabinet without burdening them with Departmental responsibilities. The structure of Departments in central Government is shown diagrammatically in Figure 14.1.

Fig 14.1 *The structure of central Government*

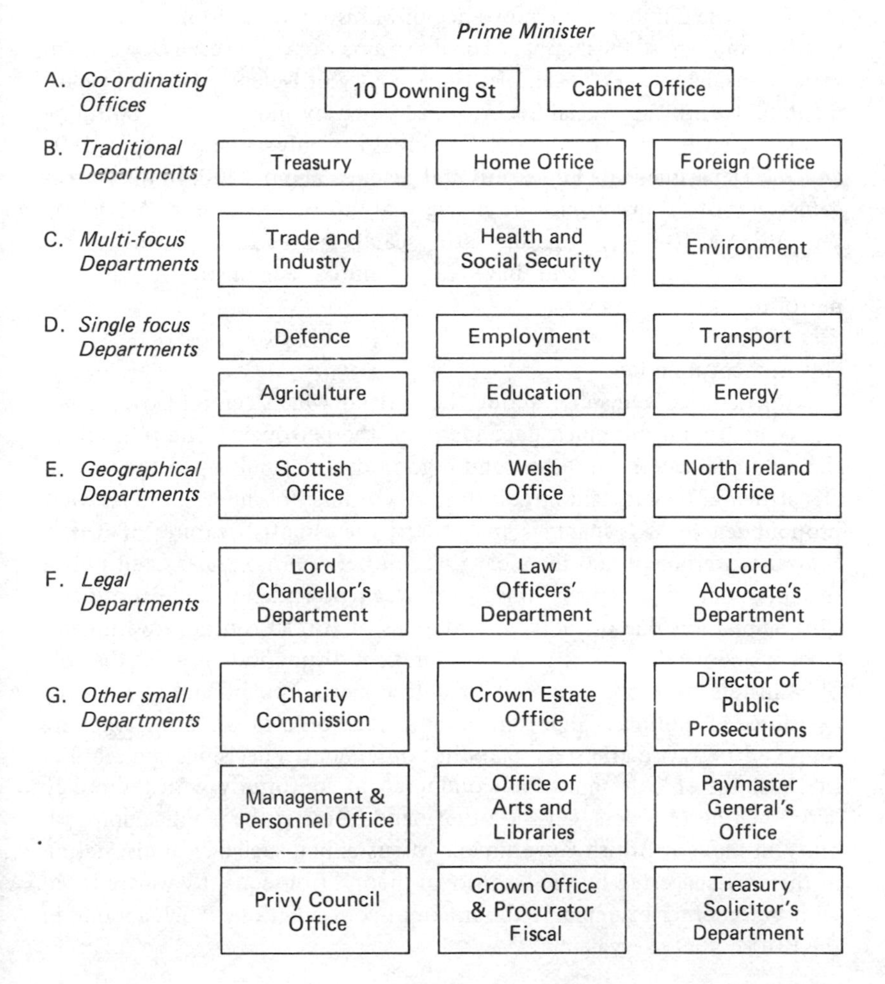

Within each major Department the normal Ministerial pattern is for the Department to be headed by a Secretary of State or Minister of Cabinet rank, supported by at least one Minister of State at the second level and perhaps two or more Under Secretaries at the third level. Obviously, there are variations in this pattern which depend mainly upon the nature and scope of each Department's responsibilities. For example, the Department of the Environment has one Cabinet Minister, two Ministers of State and four Under Secretaries, whereas the Welsh Office has only a Cabinet Minister, one Minister of State and one Under Secretary. The Treasury is distinctive in many ways, not least in having two Cabinet Ministers - the Chancellor of the Exchequer and the Chief Secretary - and normally the backing of the Prime Minister as well (who is also known formally as the First Lord of the Treasury).

Just as the number and importance of Ministers varies from one Department to another, so the number of civil servants working in each Department varies considerably. For example, the Ministry of Defence and the Department of Health and Social Security each employ more than 90 000 non-industrial civil servants, whereas the Treasury only employs about 3800 and the Department of Education and Science about 2400. In the former category, both Departments are amalgamations of a number of previously separate Departments. In the latter category, both Departments are essentially supervisory and have only limited administrative tasks to perform.

**Government functions**

It is difficult to generalise about the way in which central Government works in Britain. So much depends upon the personality and outlook of the senior Ministers concerned and a good deal depends upon the various Departmental habits and traditions. According to the traditional view propounded by W.I. Jennings and others, the essential features of British central Government are 'the clear division between politicians and public servants and the close relationship between policy and administration'.[4] This emphasises one of the key paradoxes of British central Government. On the one hand, there is a clear theoretical distinction between the role of Ministers, who are supposed to determine the policy and take all the decisions of political importance, and that of civil servants, who are supposed to advise Ministers, take the consequential decisions and see that the business of Government is conducted in conformity with the policy laid down by Ministers. On the other hand, there is the practical impossibility in modern British Government of sustaining such a clear distinction in the way suggested by the traditional theory. Consequently we are faced with yet another example of the inherent contradictions which abound in the British political system.

Most Ministers have to work very hard, often for between twelve and eighteen hours a day. There are official papers to be read and approved, Ministerial correspondence to be read and signed, frequent meetings to attend both within their own Departments and bilaterally with other Departments or 10 Downing Street, meetings of the Cabinet and its commitees to attend, meetings to be held with outside bodies and the representatives of various pressure and interest groups, Parliamentary commitees to attend, Parliamentary questions to be answered, Parliamentary debates in which to take part, official visits to be made to various parts of the country and abroad, foreign visitors to be welcomed and entertained, journalists and others in the media to be briefed, and constituents and party activists to be kept content. Such an inventory provides no more than a superficial and incomplete sketch of the range of Ministerial activities, since it is impossible to give a definitive description of a working life which is inherently so varied and unpredictable.

Civil servants, notably those in the senior administrative grades in Whitehall, do their best to ensure that Ministers are adequately briefed on all matters with which they have to deal. Yet at the same time they try to see that Ministers are not over-burdened with unnecessary paper-work or meetings and decisions which can be handled at official level. This means that one of the key roles of senior civil servants and especially those who work in Ministerial Private Offices is that of 'gate-keeper' in the information-gathering and decision-making process of central Government. Every day such civil servants have to decide whether to refer matters to Ministers for political determination or whether to deal with issues themselves within the confines of established Government policy. Although there is a natural tendency for civil servants to err on the side of caution by referring all politically sensitive matters to Ministers, their 'gate-keeper' role gives them considerable influence and power within central Government and the veil of official secrecy behind which they work makes it hard to evaluate just how satisfactorily they perform in their key positions.

Perhaps the most characteristic aspect of activity in Whitehall is the work which is done in the extensive network of inter-Departmental committees both at political level in the form of Cabinet committees and at official level in the form of civil service committees made up of civil servants from the Departments concerned. Since many of the issues with which central Government has to deal are too broad and complex to be handled within the sphere of a single Department, the process of inter-Departmental co-ordination by officials is vital to a great part of the policy- and decision-making. It is of great assistance to Ministers, most of whom are usually too busy with many other duties to be able to devote as much time as they would wish to the preparation of policy decisions. It also puts a considerable burden upon the Prime Minister and a few senior Cabinet colleagues who chair the main Cabinet committees. It may be that the process of Cabinet government would not work without the support of such inter-Departmental co-ordination at official level, but it is not certain that the quality of decision-making is necessarily improved by relying on such procedures.

Another important aspect of the work of British central Government is the frequent and extensive involvement of civil servants in Departmental consultations with client or pressure groups. Nowadays nearly every Department finds it useful and expedient to consult widely with such groups not so much about which policy to adopt as about the detailed effects and implications of policy already determined by Ministers. For example, the Ministry of Agriculture works in very close conjunction with the National Farmers Union (NFU) in accordance with the statutory duties of consultation laid down in the 1947 and 1957 Agriculture Acts. Equally, the Department of Trade and Industry keeps in frequent contact with the Confederation of British Industry (CBI) and the various Chambers of Commerce and Trade Associations, the Department of Employment keeps in touch with the Trade Union Congress (TUC) and other representatives of organised labour, and nearly all other Departments make it their business to keep in touch with the various interest and cause groups active within their spheres of Departmental responsibility. Indeed, such regular procedures of Departmental consultation between Departments and pressure groups have become an established and necessary part of the political process in Britain. Any Government which spurned or neglected them would lay itself open to serious criticism in Parliament and in the vociferous sections of the general public.

## 14.2 THE ROLE OF MINISTERS

The role of Ministers in central Government can be simply defined as the taking of decisions on matters of policy within their respective spheres of responsibility and the defence of that policy in Whitehall, Westminster and in the country at large. Within their Departments Ministers act essentially as political jurymen who take decisions on the basis of advice supplied to them by their more expert civil servants. Of course, Ministers are always free to ignore or discard such advice, but this does not happen very often. Civil servants do not usually recommend courses of action or inaction which they know would be unacceptable to their Ministers at the time. Ministers for their part often do not have the time or the inclination to question or reject most of the suggestions which are put to them. Only very strong Ministers or those who are engaged upon implementing clearly established party policy usually manage to dominate their Departments.

Every Government since the war has contained a few senior Ministers who have been able, more often than not, to get their way with officials, with their Ministerial colleagues and in Parliament. One example of such a Ministerial 'heavyweight' was Ernest Bevin, who was Minister of Labour in the wartime Coalition Government and Foreign Secretary in the post-war Labour Government. Another example was Duncan Sandys, who was successively Commonwealth Secretary and Defence Secretary in Conservative Governments in the 1950s. Another was Denis Healey, who was Defence Secretary from 1964–70 and Chancellor of the Exchequer from 1974–9. Another is Viscount Whitelaw, who was Leader of the House of Commons and Northern Ireland Secretary in the 1970–4 Heath Government, Home Secretary in the 1979–83 Thatcher Government and is now Leader of the House of Lords in the present Government. It is not easy to define what qualities such Ministers have had which have earned them the accolade of 'political heavyweights'. Force of character and political experience undoubtedly play an important part, but Prime Ministerial backing has also been a powerful factor.

**Ministerial responsibility**

Ministerial responsibility is the key concept in British central Government. It has endured since the nineteenth century because it still has advantages for Ministers and civil servants alike. Ministers benefit from the fact that it puts them in a privileged position in which they are the main beneficiaries of civil service advice. Civil servants benefit from the fact that it gives them considerable influence over Government policy- and decision-making without any formal need to accept public responsibility for the outcome.

Within a Department the senior Minister is theoretically responsible for everything which happens and can be held to account by Parliament for acts of omission as well as commission. For example, the resignation of Lord Carrington and most of his Ministerial colleagues in the Foreign Office in April 1982 was a recognition of his Department's failure to foresee and prevent the Argentinian invasion of the Falklands. On the other hand, John Davies did not resign as Secretary of State for Trade and Industry in 1971 in the wake of the Court Line collapse or in 1972 after the failure of Vehicle and General, even though in both these celebrated cases it could have been said that Ministerial responsibility was involved. Thus there are no hard and fast rules which determine the nature or extent of Ministerial responsibility in all cases and the outcome depends upon an unpredictable mixture of precedent and political circumstance in each case as it arises.

The chain of responsibility in a Government Department is hierarchical, which means that civil servants and junior Ministers alike report to the senior Minister at the head of the Department and it is he who has to take the ultimate responsibility for their action or inaction. Of course, there have been times when junior Ministers have been so out of sympathy with the policy of their Department or the Government as a whole that they have felt bound to resign. Yet on the whole junior Ministers stay at their posts and only tender their resignations if they are obliged to do so in the course of a Ministerial reshuffle organised by the Prime Minister of the day.

Indeed, it seems that individual Ministerial responsibility has been blurred and eroded in modern times by the size and complexity of modern government. This means that it has been effectively impossible for any senior Minister to be aware of, let alone to control, everything which happens in his Department. For example, thousands of planning appeals have to be decided every year by the Secretary of State for the Environment, many of them important and nearly all of them complicated and contentious. Yet no Minister in that position can possibly hope to consider all of them personally, so civil servants effectively take the decisions in the Minister's name in all but a few outstanding cases. Thus in most cases individual Ministerial responsibility has really become little more than an empty constitutional shibboleth, a convenient fiction for Parliamentary and civil service purposes, but a doctrine which is now put strictly into practice only in exceptional cases.

However, collective Ministerial responsibility is somewhat closer to reality even in modern political conditions in that it is a constitutional notion which reflects the collegiate and usually cohesive nature of single-party Government in Britain. It is really a way of expressing the fact that all Ministers, Whips and, indeed, Parliamentary Private Secretaries are bound by Government policy and are expected to stand by it and to speak and vote for it at any rate in public.

While no politician can really be expected to believe totally in everything which he has to support in public, those whose activities are covered by collective Ministerial responsibility are expected to speak and vote in support of the Government on all occasions. If they feel unable or unwilling to do so on a particular issue, they are supposed to resign. However, this convention has not always been fully observed, notably by Parliamentary Private Secretaries in relation to areas of Government policy outside the spheres of responsibility of the Ministers whom they assist. There have also been times when it has been effectively impossible to enforce the convention of collective responsibility and on a few occasions it has had to be suspended altogether.[5] It is also unwise for those covered by collective responsibility to test the boundaries of the permissible too obviously or too often, since by doing so they are quite likely to be dismissed by the Prime Minister of the day. On the whole, therefore, collective Ministerial responsibility is more of a convenient shield for politicians in office than a mechanism of real Parliamentary accountability.

### Parliamentary accountability

In theory, the proper constitutional check upon the power of the Executive in Britain is to be found in Ministerial accountability to Parliament. This is supposed to be achieved in three ways. None of these is adequate on its own, but taken together there are some safeguards for the public interest.

Firstly, there are the opportunities for MPs to hold Ministers to account during proceedings in the Chamber of the House of Commons, that is, at Question Time, during debates and following Ministerial statements. However, the scope for real Parliamentary control in such proceedings is limited by the ability of most competent Ministers to answer points in the House without revealing any new or substantial information. Experience shows that such proceedings are often rather an empty ritual and that genuine Parliamentary control has largely given way to party-political point-scoring.

Secondly, there are the opportunities for MPs to probe Ministerial thinking and Government policy-making during Select Committee investigations and the Committee stage of Government Bills. These have proved to be more effective mechanisms of Parliamentary control. However, in the former case the usefulness of such investigations is limited by the general unwillingness of both front benches to act upon the findings and in the latter case the legislative scrutiny by the Opposition has to be set against the voting power of the Government majority at the Committee stage of all Government Bills in a normal Parliament. Once again such proceedings provide a form of Parliamentary accountability, but not genuine Parliamentary control.

Thirdly, there are the various opportunities for MPs to use the power of Parliamentary publicity to dramatise the errors of Ministers or the shortcomings of Government policy. The principal effect of this form of Parliamentary accountability over the years has been to encourage habitual caution on the part of civil servants and to reinforce the tendency for Whitehall Departments to play safe in the conduct of Government business. Indeed, it is the capricious and unpredictable quality of such Parliamentary accountability which has led both Ministers and officials to treat it with wary respect. It has had a marked influence upon attitudes and working practices in Whitehall and has discouraged bold or imaginative decision-making by Ministers. It has, therefore, been purchased at quite a high price in terms of the quality of decision-making in British central Government.

Thus if we examine the various forms of Parliamentary accountability, we discover that none of them has proved to be any guarantee of effective or responsible government. The lack of proper accountability has been most marked in the many areas of policy covered by Statutory Instruments, the secondary legislation which is drafted by civil servants in the name of Ministers and lawfully implemented under the authority of existing Statutes. In effect, legislation of this type is no longer within the realm of effective Parliamentary control. Although there is a Joint Committee of the Lords and Commons which has the task of overseeing the spate of secondary legislation which pours out of Whitehall, the problem has really become unmanageable for Ministers and back-benchers now that there are more than 2000 Statutory Instruments issued each year. The volume of such secondary legislation and the shortcomings of existing Parliamentary procedures for dealing with it are such that genuine Parliamentary accountability in this area is really unattainable.

The other notable area in which Parliamentary accountability is clearly defective is that of European legislation. Under the 1972 European Communities Act the British Government is obliged to implement automatically the regulations issued by the EEC Commission, notably in the sphere of the Common Agricultural Policy, and to find appropriate national means of carrying out the directives which flow from decisions taken by the Council of Ministers. In 1974 the House of Commons established a special Select Committee to sift European legislation and to make recommendations as to whether or not the various items were sufficiently important to merit a debate on the floor of the House. However, as things have turned out, it has not always proved possible for the House to find time to debate even some of the most important draft legislative proposals before they are considered by the Council of Ministers and the rest of the directly applicable European legislation becomes law without any consideration of its merits by MPs at Westminster.

One answer to the problem of insufficient Parliamentary accountability in this area of executive action is to entrust the task to the directly-elected European Parliament. Yet this cannot be a complete answer at present, since in most sectors of policy it is the national Parliaments which retain the exclusive power to legislate and to hold their Ministers to account. In the longer term only a great leap forward towards full political integration in Europe or a dramatic step backwards towards complete British withdrawal from the European Community is likely to solve these particular problems of Parliamentary accountability.

When reflecting generally upon the post-war history of Parliamentary accountability in Britain, we must conclude that it has been more notable for the tendency of Ministers to escape the shackles of real accountability than for the ability of Parliament to impose its will and control upon Ministers.[6] While there were the celebrated cases of the Crichel Down Affair in 1954 and the Argentinian invasion of the Falklands in 1982 each of which led to the resignation of the Cabinet Minister most directly accountable, such cases have proved to be exceptions to the general rule in modern times that Ministers and civil servants can make grievous mistakes without ever really being subjected to fully-fledged Parliamentary control. Ministers are accountable in the sense that they have to answer to Parliament, but not in the sense that they are controlled by it.

## 14.3 THE PROBLEMS OF CENTRAL GOVERNMENT

The problems of central Government vary from Department to Department and from time to time. However, the key question which has to be faced by all Governments is whether or not Ministers are really in full control of their Departments. In this section we shall examine some of the problems which make it difficult to give a convincing, affirmative answer to this question.

**Ministerial work-load**

One major problem of central Government is the heavy work-load which senior Ministers have to bear, especially the Cabinet Ministers in charge of the largest Departments, such as Health and Social Security, Defence, or Trade and Industry. The very size, scope and complexity of such Departments militates against the idea that a senior Minister should be able to dominate or control every aspect of his Department's activities. Yet that is what he is expected to do in spite of the extra demands upon his time which are imposed by modern political circumstances. Indeed, in view of the collegiate nature of Cabinet government in Britain, it is a problem which afflicts all senior Ministers to a greater or lesser extent.

One way of alleviating this burden upon Ministers would be to reduce the size of the public sector which accounts for about 45 per cent of the Gross National Product. This ought to reduce the area of activities for which Ministers are held directly or indirectly responsible. Another way would be to reduce the range of tasks which senior Ministers are expected to perform, for example, by relieving them of their constituency duties (as in France) or their administrative tasks (as in Sweden where this aspect of Departmental work is entrusted to separate public agencies). However, it seems most unlikely that any radical changes of this kind will be made in Britain, not least because neither back-benchers nor civil servants would be likely to support such ideas. Back-benchers still like to think that Ministers have to keep their feet on the ground at least partly because they have to deal with very much the same constituency problems as other MPs. Civil servants often find it convenient that Ministers are acquainted with the problems of public administration, not least because it emphasises the practical consequences of policy decisions.

The problem of Ministerial work-load is also exacerbated by some of the conventions of government in Britain, notably the assumption that Ministers will consult widely and systematically before taking major decisions or introducing new legislation. Admittedly, many of these consultations with interest groups and relevant experts are conducted by civil servants on behalf of Ministers. Yet Ministers always have to lay down the ground-rules for such discussions and often have to take the leading part in the most important cases. A balanced solution to the problem would take account of all these factors, but no matter which ideas are adopted, Ministers will always require great personal energy and strong political will to overcome the difficulties.

**Departmental policy**

Another major problem of central Government is the continuously powerful influence of established Departmental policy. This may not make itself felt very much during the first year or two of a new Government's term of office, but it can assume considerable importance as time goes by when the political momentum of the party in office has begun to falter. This problem has been particularly noticeable in the well-established Departments, such as the Home Office or the Foreign Office, in which the senior civil servants often hold consistent, collective views on matters of policy which can outlast the life of a single Government. However, the outcome of such quiet struggles between Ministers and civil servants is never a foregone conclusion. Much depends upon whether Ministers individually and collectively are determined to carry out their policies and to impose their authority upon Departments. If they are so determined, both the realities of political power and the conventions of Whitehall will enable them to get their own way whatever the Departmental preferences of senior civil servants. If they are not, then Departmental policy usually triumphs in the end.

The strength of Departmental policy is enhanced by the conventions of Ministerial and civil service life. In the former case, it has been customary for Prime Ministers to change Ministers and move them from post to post quite frequently, partly to assert their Prime Ministerial authority and partly to broaden the Ministerial experience of their most promising Parliamentary colleagues. This has produced an average tenure of Ministerial office of about two years in post-war British Governments with the result that most Ministers are precluded from making anything more than a temporary impact upon the political issues with which their Departments have to deal. In the latter case, it has been customary to move civil servants in the administrative grades even more frequently from one job to another within and sometimes between Departments. In many instances this means that key administrative staff may stay in post for only a year or two with the result that they do not have time to develop a real expertise of their own in the relevant policy areas. This happens mainly for reasons of career development and is largely for the benefit of those who have been identified as 'high fliers' early in their civil service careers. The inevitable consequence is that even the best civil servants rely heavily upon what is in the Departmental files, in other words the accumulated wisdom of Departmental policy. Such tendencies can only be overcome by sustained political will on the part of senior Ministers and significant changes in civil service personnel policy.

### The quality of advice

Another problem of central Government is the quality of official information and advice available to Ministers. While such material is a source of strength for Ministers in relation to the Opposition and all back-benchers, it does not necessarily strengthen their position within their own Departments. This is because many of the politicians who become Ministers are likely to be posted to Departments about which they know little or nothing and which deal with areas of policy of which they have had little or no previous experience. Once in office, many Ministers may be wary of appointing personal advisers from outside the civil service and they may even be prohibited from doing so by the senior Minister concerned or by the Prime Minister. The result is that unless Ministers are engaged in the implementation of clear Manifesto commitments or other forms of unambiguous party policy, they are not provided with an alternative view of the issues before them and are obliged to rely upon conventional advice from their Departmental civil servants.

This is an unfortunate state of affairs for two reasons. Firstly, the best answers to many of the most difficult problems of central Government are unlikely to be found either in the liturgy of party Manifestos or in Departmental filing cabinets. Secondly, the policy- and decision-making process is unnecessarily deprived of a good deal of high quality information and advice from 'outsiders' who are both expert in their field and independent of Government. The problem will need to be rectified if the quality of policy- and decision-making is to be improved.

## 14.4 CONCLUSION

Well-qualified observers of British politics and distinguished practitioners have argued for years about whether Ministers are really in control of their Departments. As long ago as the 1850s Lord Palmerston wrote to Queen Victoria that 'Your Majesty will see how greatly such a system (of government) must place in the hands of the subordinate members of public Departments (i.e. civil servants) the power of directing the policy and the measures of the Government, because the value, tendency and consequences of a measure frequently depend as much upon the manner in which it was worked out (i.e. administered) as the intention and spirit with which it was planned.'[7] This was one of the earliest and most perceptive statements of the now familiar argument that the power to administer can be as important in the process of government as the power to decide. In other words, civil servants can have as much effective power as Ministers, even though the constitutional conventions may not admit it.

On the other hand, Herbert Morrison wrote in the 1950s that 'if the Minister in charge (of a Department) knows what he wants and is intelligent in going about it, he can command the understanding, co-operation and support of his civil servants'.[8] This statement from a senior Labour politician with long Ministerial experience could be interpreted as an affirmation of Ministerial dominance in Whitehall. Yet it could also be interpreted as a back-handed compliment to the power of the civil service and a warning that the Whitehall bureaucrats tend to fill any power vacuum which may be left by Ministers. Clearly it is necessary to refine the conventional statement that Ministers decide the policy and civil servants simply carry it out. The contemporary reality is more subtle and shaded, since the traditional model takes insufficient account of the administrative constraints in central Government.

In modern political conditions it is, of course, possible for Ministers to exercise clear leadership, but this becomes much less likely as each General Election recedes further into the past. Senior Ministers may believe that they are in complete charge of their Departments. Yet civil service control of official advice to Ministers, the long time-scale and complexity of policy- and decision-making in government, and the limited scope for effective political intervention in the problems of modern society all tend to reduce the impact of Ministerial leadership. The broad conclusion must be that Ministers may be in charge of their Departments, but only within the limits set by established administrative procedures and uncompromising political realities.

## SUGGESTED QUESTIONS

1. Describe the work of British central Government.
2. What is the role of Ministers in British central Government?
3. Are the problems of British central Government capable of solution within the existing institutions and conventions?

## NOTES

1. See Report of the Committee on the Machinery of Government, Cd 9230 (London: HMSO, 1918).
2. See 'The reorganisation of central Government', Cmnd 4506 (London: HMSO, 1970).
3. The Lord Chancellor's Department, the Law Officers' Department and the Lord Advocate's Department.

4. W. I. Jennings, *Cabinet Government*, 3rd edn (Cambridge: Cambridge University Press, 1959) p. 133.
5. For example, in 1931 there was an open 'agreement to differ' in the National Government on the issue of tariff reform and in 1975 during the EEC Referendum campaign Labour Cabinet Ministers were allowed to argue against each other on public platforms.
6. See A. H. Birch, *Representative and Responsible Government* (London: Allen & Unwin, 1964) pp. 141–8; and J. Bruce-Gardyne and N. Lawson, *The Power Game* (London: Macmillan, 1976) pp. 10–37.
7. Quoted in H. Parris, *Constitutional Bureaucracy* (London: Allen & Unwin, 1969), p. 114.
8. H. Morrison, *Government and Parliament* (Oxford: Oxford University Press, 1959) p. 311.

## FURTHER READING

Birch, A. H., *Representative and Responsible Government* (London: Allen & Unwin, 1964).

Bromhead, P. A., *Britain's Developing Constitution* (London: Allen & Unwin, 1974).

Brown, R. G. S. and Steel, D. R., *The Administrative Process in Britain*, 2nd edn (London: Methuen, 1979).

Bruce-Gardyne, J. and Lawson, N., *The Power Game* (London: Macmillan, 1976).

Jennings, W. I., *Cabinet Government*, 3rd edn (Cambridge: Cambridge University Press, 1959).

Kaufman, G., *How to be a Minister* (London: Sidgwick & Jackson, 1980).

Kellner, P. and Crowther-Hunt, N., *The Civil Servants* (London: Macdonald, 1980).

Mackintosh, J. P., *The British Cabinet*, 3rd edn (London: Stevens, 1977).

Marshall, G. and Moodie, G. C., *Some Problems of the Constitution*, 5th edn (London: Hutchinson, 1971).

Morrison, H., *Government and Parliament* (Oxford: Oxford University Press, 1959).

Parris, H., *Constitutional Bureaucracy* (London: Allen & Unwin, 1969).

CHAPTER 15

# THE CIVIL SERVICE

In Britain the standard definition of a civil servant is still the one which was formulated by the Tomlin Commission in 1931, namely 'a servant of the Crown employed in a civil capacity who is paid wholly and directly from money voted by Parliament'.[1] In July 1983 this definition covered about 643 000 people in all. Of this total about 128 000 were industrial civil servants employed in the Royal Ordnance factories, Royal Naval dockyards and other Government premises. The remaining 515 000 were non-industrial civil servants, about one quarter of whom worked in central London while the other three quarters worked in the local and regional offices of central Government in all parts of the country.

In this chapter we are concerned only with the civil servants who work in central London (popularly known as 'Whitehall' for these purposes) and specifically with those in the higher administrative grades. We are dealing, therefore, with the administrative élite at the heart of British central Government. The civil service numbers to 1 April 1988 are shown in tabular form in Figure 15.1 on pages 230–1.

## 15.1 COMPOSITION AND FUNCTIONS

The eighteen main Departments vary greatly in size and character from the Department of Energy with about 1100 civil servants to the Ministry of Defence with about 99 000. Indeed, the three largest Departments – Defence, Health and Social Security and the Inland Revenue (under the aegis of the Treasury) – account for about half the total of non-industrial civil servants. In a typical Whitehall Department about two-thirds of the civil servants are involved in the administrative tasks of government, while the remaining one-third perform a wide range of technical, scientific and support functions. In Whitehall as a whole about 4000 civil servants are involved in the policy- and decision-making process, although of these only about 2000 at the really senior levels have close and frequent contacts with Ministers. It is this small administrative élite which sets the

Whitehall conventions and determines the character of the civil service in Britain today.

**The personnel**

In the higher administrative grades the traditional preference for experienced generalists still holds sway and influences the character and quality of the civil service at every level. There are three main reasons for this.

Firstly, the civil service is still under the influence of the 1854 Northcote–Trevelyan Report which defined the role of civil servants as being 'to advise, assist and to some extent influence those who are set over them from time to time'. This still means that in the higher administrative grades no great value is placed upon the possession of specialist skills, except perhaps the skill of administration which is thought to be acquired best by experience on the job.

Secondly, there is a traditional disdain for professional expertise which was expressed by Lord Bridges (once Secretary to the Cabinet) when he defined a good civil servant as one 'who knows how and where to find reliable knowledge, can assess the expertise of others at its true worth, can spot the strong and weak points in any situation at short notice and can advise on how to handle a complex situation'.[2] This still means that in the higher administrative grades no great value is placed upon the possession of expertise, again with the exception perhaps of the expertise of administration. As the saying goes, the experts are supposed to be on tap but not on top.

Thirdly, there is the traditional tendency for the young recruits into the administrative élite to come disproportionately from those with a middle-class background and an arts degree at Oxford or Cambridge. Certainly this was true when the composition of the civil service was examined for the Fulton Committee in 1967.[3] It appeared still to be true in the mid-1970s when the matter was investigated by the Labour party.[4] Figures provided by the Civil Service Commission in 1978 showed that 63 per cent of the direct entrants into the administrative grades came from Oxford or Cambridge Universities.[5] Figures for similar entrants in 1981 showed a clear bias in favour of people with arts or social science degrees, since thirty-five were arts graduates, sixteen social science graduates and only three were graduates in science or technology. Figures for the 1982 intake of administration trainees showed that of the twenty-four successful entrants into the Home Civil Service, fourteen had graduated from Oxford, three each from Cambridge and London, and one each from Bristol, Exeter, Keele and Sheffield.[6]

Thus the sort of people who get to the influential positions at the senior levels of the civil service are very much the product of the values and outlook of their predecessors who selected them. The main consider-

## Fig 15.1 *Civil Service numbers to 1.4.1988*

| | 1 4 84 | 1 4 85 | 1 4 86 | 1 4 87 | 1 4 88 |
|---|---|---|---|---|---|
| **Agriculture, Fisheries and Food** | | | | | |
| Ministry of Agriculture, Fisheries and Food | 11 493 | 11 450 | 11 400 | 11 340 | 11 260 |
| Intervention Board for Agricultural Produce | 623 | 610 | 590 | 566 | 560 |
| **Chancellor of the Exchequer** | | | | | |
| Inland Revenue | 69 850 | 70 200 | 69 300 | 66 300 | 62 900 |
| Customs and Excise | 25 150 | 25 350 | 25 100 | 24 900 | 24 700 |
| Department for National Savings | 8 050 | 8 025 | 7 900 | 7 875 | 7 590 |
| HMSO | 4 000 | 3 700 | 3 500 | 3 460 | 3 440 |
| Treasury | 3 830 | 3 580 | 3 545 | 3 510 | 3 465 |
| Royal Mint | 977 | 965 | 981 | 970 | 960 |
| Central Office of Information | 949 | 952 | 955 | 945 | 935 |
| Registry of Friendly Societies | 129 | 129 | 129 | 127 | 120 |
| Government Actuary | 64 | 64 | 64 | 64 | 64 |
| National Investment and Loans Office | 52 | 52 | 52 | 52 | 52 |
| **Education and Science** | | | | | |
| Department of Education and Science | 2 402 | 2 472 | 2 437 | 2 417 | 2 392 |
| **Employment** | | | | | |
| Department of Employment | 31 048 | 30 238 | 29 995 | 29 211 | 28 505 |
| Health and Safety Commission/Executive | 3 742 | 3 662 | 3 652 | 3 644 | 3 644 |
| Manpower Services Commission | 22 229 | 21 677 | 21 297 | 21 297 | 21 297 |
| Advisory Conciliation and Arbitration Service | 645 | 639 | 632 | 629 | 629 |
| **Energy** | | | | | |
| Department of Energy | 1 110 | 1 106 | 1 085 | 1 062 | 1 033 |
| **Environment** | | | | | |
| Department of the Environment | 6 668 | 6 588 | 6 488 | 6 408 | 6 343 |
| Property Services Agency | 27 502 | 26 986 | 26 347 | 25 693 | 25 296 |
| Ordnance Survey | 2 815 | 2 948 | 2 934 | 2 920 | 2 906 |
| **Foreign and Commonwealth Office** | | | | | |
| Foreign and Commonwealth Office | 9 437 | 9 373 | 9 214 | 9 109 | 9 026 |
| Overseas Development Administration | 1 793 | 1 565 | 1 545 | 1 525 | 1 500 |
| **Home Office** | | | | | |
| Home Office | 35 767 | 36 645 | 38 205 | 40 135 | 41 144 |
| **Lord Chancellor** | | | | | |
| Lord Chancellor's Department (including Public Trustee Office) | 10 125 | 10 195 | 10 195 | 10 170 | 10 000 |
| Land Registry | 6 725 | 6 845 | 6 910 | 6 910 | 6 950 |
| Public Record Office | 406 | 406 | 413 | 419 | 425 |
| **Northern Ireland** | | | | | |
| Northern Ireland Office | 200 | 196 | 191 | 188 | 186 |
| **Scotland** | | | | | |
| Scottish Office | 9 800 | 9 909 | 9 791 | 9 622 | 9 542 |
| Scottish Courts Administration | 879 | 879 | 879 | 879 | 879 |
| General Register Office, Scotland | 283 | 266 | 268 | 278 | 274 |
| Registers of Scotland | 754 | 800 | 832 | 854 | 889 |
| Scottish Record Office | 132 | 128 | 125 | 122 | 118 |
| **Social services** | | | | | |
| Department of Health and Social Security | 90 709 | 90 000 | 89 500 | 88 850 | 87 850 |
| Office of Population Censuses and Surveys | 2 162 | 2 152 | 2 132 | 2 102 | 2 155 |
| **Trade and Industry** | | | | | |
| Department of Trade and Industry | 12 738 | 12 733 | 12 733 | 12 733 | 12 733 |
| Export Credits Guarantee Department | 1 840 | 1 840 | 1 835 | 1 835 | 1 830 |
| Office of Fair Trading | 320 | 313 | 313 | 313 | 313 |
| **Transport** | | | | | |
| Department of Transport | 14 220 | 14 528 | 14 713 | 14 511 | 14 174 |
| **Welsh Office** | | | | | |
| Welsh Office | 2 195 | 2 206 | 2 206 | 2 206 | 2 206 |
| **Small Departments** | | | | | |
| Cabinet Office | 518 | 518 | 518 | 518 | 518 |
| Charity Commission | 329 | 329 | 320 | 320 | 320 |
| Crown Estate Office | 114 | 116 | 117 | 118 | 119 |
| Director of Public Prosecutions | 237 | 242 | 241 | 240 | 240 |
| Law Officers' Department | 22 | 22 | 22 | 22 | 22 |
| Lord Advocate's Department | 22 | 22 | 22 | 22 | 22 |
| Management and Personnel Office | 1 194 | 1 184 | 1 174 | 1 164 | 1 154 |

| | | | | | |
|---|---|---|---|---|---|
| Office of Arts and Libraries | 49 | 49 | 49 | 49 | 49 |
| Paymaster General's Office | 870 | 873 | 912 | 938 | 967 |
| Privy Council Office | 33 | 33 | 33 | 33 | 33 |
| Crown Office and Procurator Fiscal Service | 966 | 980 | 1 000 | 1 020 | 1 040 |
| Treasury Solicitor's Department | 471 | 467 | 463 | 458 | 453 |
| **Defence** | | | | | |
| Ministry of Defence | 200 000 | 179 000 | 176 000 | 173 000 | 170 000 |
| Contingency Margin | 1 360 | 2 000 | 4 000 | 6 500 | 7 500 |
| **Total** | 630 000 | 608 208 | 605 255 | 600 554 | 592 723 |

Source: *The Government's Expenditure Plans, 1984-5 to 1986-7*; Cmnd 9143 - I (London: HMSO, 1984).

ation is to find promising young men and women with what is described as 'a good all-round intellect'. Good judgement and reliability are qualities which are highly valued, as well as clarity of expression and an ability to work smoothly with others. On this basis the administrative grades of the civil service still attract some of the best qualified and most able young people in every generation. Yet as long as such young people continue to form an élite which is such an accurate reflection of the older élite which selected them, the traditional character of the civil service is likely to be self-perpetuating.

**Main functions**

The main functions of the higher administrative grades in the civil service can be summarised as: informing and advising Ministers, helping them to formulate policy or make decisions, carrying out the subsequent administrative tasks, representing Ministers in meetings with other Departments, pressure groups and members of the general public, and managing the bureaucracy of central Government. It is convenient to look at each of these aspects in turn.

Civil servants are the main source of information and advice for Ministers. When a Minister needs to know something or has to prepare for a meeting, to make a speech, to answer questions in Parliament or to appear on the media, it is the civil servants in his own Department (and sometimes from other Departments as well) who provide the necessary briefing and advice. Usually this is provided in writing in the form of background papers and other internal memoranda. However, this is often supplemented (or even replaced) by oral information and advice at specially convened Departmental meetings, since this is often quicker in an emergency and in any case some Ministers prefer to be briefed in this way. On the whole civil servants do not produce original information for these purposes, since they do not have the time or the aptitude for such research. They act essentially as filters and interpreters of existing information which they derive either from the Departmental filing cabinets or from the range of experts to whom they have ready access.

Civil servants help Ministers to formulate policy and to make decisions by presenting them with option papers which encompass a range of possibilities and policy recommendations. They also provide the information and advice against which Ministers can test the soundness or otherwise of their own ideas and their party political commitments. The habitual complexity of the role of civil servants in the policy- and decision-making process has already been described in Chapter 13.[7]

Civil servants carry out the administrative tasks of central Government in accordance with the political guidelines laid down in earlier Ministerial decisions. If this is not possible in certain cases because new situations have arisen, reference is usually made to the appropriate Minister or group of Ministers for further policy guidance. Even though the administration of policy can be as important as the actual policy decisions, civil servants are trained to avoid behaving in such a way as to pre-empt or nullify the decisions of their political masters. On the whole they seek faithfully to carry out the policies which they have helped Ministers to formulate and the decisions which they have helped Ministers to make.

Civil servants have an important role as representatives of Ministers at meetings in Whitehall and elsewhere. These may be meetings with Ministers or officials from other Departments, with the spokesmen of pressure groups or with members of the general public. On occasions civil servants may speak on behalf of Ministers within the carefully defined limits of existing Departmental policy, for example, when giving evidence to a Select Committee or taking part in the discussions of an inter-Departmental Cabinet committee. On other occasions within Whitehall civil servants may not state the position precisely as their Ministers would have done, since they may be involved in an exercise of Departmental 'kite-flying' or 'devil's advocacy' in order to test or probe some aspect of the conventional wisdom. There is normally a clear distinction between the flexibility which may be allowed to them within the privacy of Whitehall meetings covered by the provisions of the Official Secrets Act and the rigid way in which they are expected to reflect Government policy in meetings with outsiders. Of course, some meetings between civil servants and outside groups are held on a confidential basis and on those occasions the officials concerned may feel free to be reasonably frank and expansive with knowledgeable outsiders whom they know they can trust. However, it takes a long time for outsiders to build up such trust in the eyes of Whitehall and on the whole official information is exchanged or communicated only to those who have a well-established 'need to know'.

Perhaps the main function of civil servants in the higher administrative grades is to see that the bureaucracy of central Government is managed in such a way as to ensure the greatest practicable efficiency and effectiveness in the civil service. This is an aspect of civil service activity which has been accorded much greater importance in recent years as a result of the determination of the Thatcher Government to reduce civil service numbers and to increase the efficiency of those who remain.

Ever since the implementation of the Northcote–Trevelyan reforms in the second half of the nineteenth century, the Permanent Secretary of each Department has had to take direct personal responsibility for the management of his Department and to act as the Accounting Officer of his Department in dealings with the Public Accounts Committee and the Comptroller and Auditor-General. However, in practice most of the day-to-day management tasks within Whitehall Departments have been delegated to other civil servants at lower levels in the various Departmental hierarchies, while the important matters of civil service pay and conditions are handled centrally by the Treasury and the Management and Personnel Office which is now within the Cabinet Office. Indeed, the efficient management of Whitehall Departments is regarded by the present Conservative Government as being of such importance that all senior Ministers have been urged by the Prime Minister to play a direct part in the management of their Departments. It would seem that efficient management of the bureaucracy of central Government is now considered too important to be left solely to senior civil servants, no matter what may be the practical difficulties for Ministers when they try to implement this policy.

## 15.2 KEY ASPECTS

There are many key aspects of the civil service in Britain and in this chapter it is sensible to concentrate on those which have a significant effect upon the British political system. Accordingly, we shall begin by considering some of the most important Whitehall conventions before going on to weigh up the strengths and weaknesses of the burearucracy of British central Government.

### Whitehall conventions

Perhaps the strongest convention in Whitehall is that the principal purpose of senior civil servants is to advise Ministers on matters of policy and to assist them in their dealings with Parliament and public. This means that they look up (to Ministers), not down (to the administration of their Departments), as one senior civil servant has put it.[8] The tasks of bureaucratic management and control have therefore tended to be seen as rather tedious and unattractive chores by many of the most talented officials who have reached the top of the civil service over the years. Notwithstanding the attempts made following the 1968 Fulton Report and again by the present Conservative Government to instil more managerial attitudes into senior civil servants, the results have appeared to be rather patchy and ephemeral. This is because the policy demands of Ministers must always come first and because the whole Whitehall machinery is still designed principally to serve Ministers in their dealings with Parliament and the public.

Another related convention is that civil servants invariably take their instructions only from their superiors in their own Departments or directly from their Ministers (where that is appropriate) and not from anyone else. This means that their lines of authority are strictly vertical and that to get anything done in a Whitehall Department it is usually necessary for Ministers or civil servants acting on their behalf to give the initial instrucions. This tends to put a disproportionate burden upon Ministers and their immediate civil service assistants in Ministerial Private Offices. It also makes it less likely that Departments will be able to respond to events quickly or imaginatively if they do not get a clear and decisive political lead from Ministers.

Another familiar Whitehall convention is that the administration of policy should be carried out according to the highest standards of probity and equity, preferably avoiding all forms of political embarrassment for Ministers. This has put a premium in the civil service upon a defensive and cautious approach to policy- and decision-making in Whitehall and has meant that undue emphasis has been laid upon seeing that neither Parliament nor the media nor the general public get any more than minimal opportunities to identify any shortcomings or failures in Government policy. Correct conduct in government is bought at the price of minimal administrative flexibility and very limited opportunities for local management initiatives, for example, in local DHSS offices.

Another well-established convention is that the Government of the day should have at all times a coherent and defensible position on all the policy issues with which it has to deal. Of course, this is really the minimum requirement for satisfactory Cabinet government so long as it is based upon the principle of collective responsibility. Yet it means that a great deal of civil service time and effort is spent upon producing agreed solutions with which all Departments can concur, often without paying much regard to whether such solutions are the most appropriate or rational in the circumstances. Thus coherence and defensibility is sometimes bought at the price of missed opportunities to adopt simpler or more radical solutions to the problems with which central Government is faced.

In short, all the civil service conventions in Whitehall are really consequences of habitual adherence to the dual principles of Ministerial responsibility and Parliamentary accountability. The former dictates that civil servants should regard the support of Ministers as their principal and overriding task. The latter ensures that civil servants are habitually cautious and unimaginative in the advice which they offer. Thus Whitehall conventions really derive from Westminster conventions and the political imperatives of our system of Parliamentary government.

**Strengths and weaknesses**

The British civil service has both strengths and weaknesses which stem from the nature of British central Government and the people who take part in it. In many cases the weaknesses are essentially the counterparts of the strengths which have been widely recognised by impartial and knowledgeable observers over the years. The same realities can be regarded from two contrasting angles and it is therefore unwise to be dogmatic in making an assessment.

One obvious strength is the intellectual and administrative ability of the higher administrative grades. This reflects the high entry standards and the considerable attractions of a career in the administrative civil service for many of the ablest students from our best universities. It also reflects the fact that an élite group of administration trainees are identified each year as 'fliers' and put into a special fast stream for accelerated promotion to positions of responsibility. Such people are given early opportunities to enhance their reputations and to leaven their intellectual abilities with the yeast of wide-ranging practical experience in various parts of the civil service. The result is the formation and constant renewal of a small cadre of highly trained and exceptionally able practitioners of the art of public administration whose forte is the ability to see that the decisions of Ministers are satisfactorily implemented at any rate within the spheres of Whitehall and Westminster.

On the other hand, it can be argued that the particular kind of ability demonstrated by this administrative group is too élitist and too generalist to be really beneficial to the process of modern government. For example, some unfavourable contrasts have been drawn with the qualities of comparable officials in the higher grades of the French civil service, since the latter are selected from cadres with both intellectual ability of the highest order and more technical training usually acquired at the *École Nationale d'Administration* or one of the other *Grandes Écoles*.[9] Equally, some of those on the Left of British politics have consistently criticised the narrow and unrepresentative composition of the British administrative élite and argued that its members should be recruited from a much more varied economic and social background.[10]

Another characteristic of the British civil service which has usually been identified as a strength is its traditional impartiality and facility for working quite satisfactorily with Governments of contrasting political persuasions. Of course, individual civil servants retain their own private political views, but professionally they are always prepared to carry out the policies of the Government of the day without obstruction or complaint, no matter what their private misgivings may be. Thus resignations from the civil service on policy grounds are very rare and in virtually every case the canons of political impartiality are scrupulously observed.

On the other hand, there are those critics of the civil service who interpret this vaunted political impartiality as little more than patient and practised obstruction of the political purposes of democratically elected Governments. Frustration and complaints of this kind have been expressed on both the Left and the Right of the British political spectrum. On the Left, Tony Benn and others have made such points in speeches and articles reflecting upon the experience of the 1974–9 Labour Government.[11] On the Right, Sir John Hoskyns has criticised civil servants for withholding the last 5 per cent of commitment to any Government in order to preserve their political neutrality and their credentials for serving a future Government of a different political persuasion.[12] It seems clear from such evidence that the civil service is at least even-handed in this aspect of its behaviour. Yet from the point of view of party political zealots such determined impartiality is bound to be a matter for criticism, especially when it is thought to have obstructed the political purposes of democratically-elected Governments.

Another admirable characteristic of the British civil service which is generally held to be a strength is its sense of dedication to public duty. This concept of public duty assumes that central Government must be scrupulously fair in its dealings with all other bodies and that it must be clearly accountable to the political and financial control of Parliament backed by the professional expertise of the Comptroller and Auditor-General.

On the other hand, the dedication of civil servants to their sense of public duty can also be regarded as a limiting factor by those who might wish to be more controversial or to take more risks in matters of public policy. For example, some senior civil servants have sometimes appeared to regard it as part of their public duty to defend the conventional wisdom of established Departmental policy, even to the extent of persuading Ministers to change their minds if there is a clash between the two. This can be illustrated by the Home Office in the 1950s when its senior civil servants successfully defended their Departmental policy of retaining capital punishment for murder notwithstanding the abolitionist views of at least two Conservative Home Secretaries during that period. It can also be illustrated by the Foreign Office in the 1960s when the senior civil servants there successfully convinced Foreign Secretaries in both

Conservative and Labour Governments of the wisdom of their Departmental policy to take Britain into the European Community.

As for the almost complete lack of corruption in the civil service, this must obviously be regarded as a virtue of British central Government. With very few exceptions British civil servants are people of the highest personal integrity who do not succumb to the temptations of bribery and corruption which damage the reputation of Governments in many other countries.[13]

Obviously, no one would argue seriously that the almost total absence of corruption in the British civil service is anything other than a strength. Yet it might be argued that the price which we have had to pay for the probity and rectitude of civil servants over the years is the attitude of stuffy and unadventurous caution which has been criticised by some who would like to look to the civil service for more spark and imagination. However, such a criticism would almost certainly be misplaced and mistaken in view of the fact that in the British political system it is for politicians and Ministers to take initiatives and for the civil service to carry them out with probity, efficiency and integrity.

Other criticisms are made of the British civil service which include the disinclination of senior civil servants to look at the problems of Government sufficiently in the long term or in the round. The charge is that they seem to concentrate too much upon immediate issues within their respective Departmental spheres. In so far as this is true, it stems from a natural bureaucratic instinct to play safe and from working habits which attach considerable importance to the orderly division of labour between Departments. Furthermore, in a system of government which is so heavily influenced by the political considerations of Ministers, it is perhaps naive to expect civil servants to set themselves broader or more distant targets than those of the politicians whom they serve.

Perhaps the most significant weakness in the British civil service has been its unwillingness or inability fully to embrace radical policies, or at least radical departures from previous policies, with sufficient enthusiasm to make them work. Civil servants demonstrate this tendency by filtering or diluting nearly all new ideas which do not fit into the received wisdom of the time. This does not mean that they always obstruct new or heretic ideas, since, when such initiatives come from Ministers, the policies are faithfully carried through with almost total commitment. However, it does mean that everything depends upon the source of the new ideas. If fresh thinking stems from Ministers, it is usually accepted, albeit sometimes with considerable reluctance. If it comes from anyone else, no matter how expert or enlightened, it is invariably dismissed as heresy.

The main explanation for this aspect of civil service behaviour seems to be that while civil servants are trained faithfully to carry out Ministerial policy, whatever it may be, they are nearly always reluctant to entertain new ideas which might disrupt or challenge the conventional wisdom of the time. A subsidiary explanation may be that many Ministers are too preoccupied, lazy or narrow in their political outlook to welcome such ideas and too ambitious or beholden to the leadership to be willing to take many risks.

This problem would not matter very much if the Prime Minister of the day and the most senior members of the Cabinet had more frequent opportunities for fresh thinking and intelligent reflection while in office or if there were better institutional arrangements in Whitehall to ensure that the conventional wisdom of any Government was constantly challenged from within. Yet on the whole this does not happen and it is left to the Government's critics in the Opposition or the media to 'think the unthinkable'. Unfortunately, this does not usually assist the process of policy- and decision-making very much, since all Governments have a tendency to close ranks against new or challenging ideas which are not their own. In short, political exorcism is not an adequate response to political heresy.

## 15.3 METHODS OF CONTROL

There are a number of different methods of controlling the civil service. All of them are used to a greater or lesser extent, but none of them has been sufficient on its own. It has, therefore, proved necessary to use them all in combination in the continuing attempts to achieve real and lasting control.

### Ministerial responsibility

The classic method of controlling the civil service is based upon the doctrine of Ministerial responsibility. This may have been effective during the second half of the nineteenth century when the scope and complexity of central Government was very small compared with today. However, in modern conditions its efficacity is more dubious as a number of expert witnesses have pointed out.[14]

In theory, Ministerial responsibility is supposed to mean that Ministers can account for everything which happens or fails to happen within their respective spheres of Departmental responsibility. In practice, modern central Government has become so large and complex that no Minister, however hard-working, can possibly achieve such an ideal. Indeed, as Michael Heseltine pointed out soon after becoming Secretary of State for the Environment in 1979, 'I had general advice on every policy issue, but no analysis of how each part of the (Departmental) machine operated, why it operated in that way and how much it cost'.[15] Without such basic information, let alone the necessary managerial experience and inclination to make use of it, most senior Ministers in modern times have been unable to control their Departments in anything like the true meaning of the term.

Admittedly, the Thatcher Government has sought to introduce throughout Whitehall a new Management Information System for Ministers (MINIS) which is supposed to set out the objectives, priorities, costs and results of every part of each Department's activities, so that waste and duplication can be eliminated and efficiency and effectiveness enhanced.[16] However, this approach has not appealed to all senior Ministers, some of whom have disputed that such managerial activity constitutes the best use of their time and energy. Thus as long as Ministerial responsibility continues to be interpreted by some senior Ministers in the traditional way, there is unlikely to be full and effective Ministerial control of modern central Government.

**Bureaucratic hierarchy**

Another traditional method of controlling the civil service is based upon the idea of bureaucratic hierarchy. This dates back to the second half of the nineteenth century and the reform of the civil service which flowed from the Northcote-Trevelyan Report of 1854. It is based upon the traditional idea that while Ministers are responsible for policy, senior civil servants are responsible for managing the administration which carries out the policy.

In theory, such a division of labour in Whitehall appears to be logical and ought to work quite well, since every Permanent Secretary at the head of a Department is also the Accounting Officer for his Department and thus directly answerable to the Public Accounts Committee of the House of Commons for every item of public spending attributed to his Departmental budget. In practice, however, the most senior civil servants at the top of the Departmental hierarchies are normally preoccupied with their role as policy advisers to Ministers and disinclined to spend much of their time on the tedious but necessary tasks of managing the administration. Yet it must be added that the conventions of civil service behaviour can be modified and that most senior civil servants have responded energetically to the clear wishes of Ministers in the present Government that more of their time and effort should be devoted to the exercise of tighter bureaucratic control over the administrative machine of central Government.

**Administrative efficiency**

Another method of controlling the bureaucracy is based upon the principle of administrative efficiency and the related idea that it ought to be possible to apply in the civil service some of the business efficiency techniques which are used in the private sector. Certainly this was one of the main thrusts of the Fulton Report in 1968, which advocated the introduction of 'accountable management' into the civil service, and the idea has been promoted intermittently by successive Governments ever since. It has included the attempted application of business techniques, such as the achievement of a given level of administrative output with less financial input, the comparison of different administrative methods to achieve a given policy objective, and the use of cost-benefit analysis in the process of administrative decision-making.

Such techniques imported from the private sector are not necessarily transferable to the civil service where the goals, constraints and criteria of success or failure are very different. In the private sector the principal goal is usually profit, the constraints are largely imposed by market conditions and the criteria of success or failure include the assessments made by investors and the rate of return on the capital and labour employed. In the civil service, on the other hand, the goals tend to be changeable and ill-defined, the constraints include considerations of equity and the public interest as well as the requirements of Parliamentary accountability, and the criteria of success or failure depend very much upon the priorities and prejudices of transient senior Ministers. Thus it is hard to see how it would be sensible to run the civil service as if it were Marks & Spencer or GEC, although there seem to be some useful lessons which could be learned from the most efficient private companies.

In spite of the inherent difficulties of this approach, the Thatcher Government has demonstrated that it is possible to make some progress in this direction. The so-called 'Rayner scrutinies' (named after Lord Rayner, Mrs Thatcher's original adviser on efficiency in Government) identified potential financial savings in some of the routine support services in Whitehall, for example, typing pools, messenger services and car transport. The scrutiny of Goverment research and development establishments also revealed potential financial savings of at least 15 per cent and the review of the non-office activities of Government - such as HM Coastguards and the Property Services Agency - indicated further potential financial savings.[17] On the other hand, not all such Rayner scrutinies have been a success, mainly because there have been occasions when such proposals have been deemed to be politically unacceptable. For example, in 1981 it was suggested in one such scrutiny that certain payments made through Sub-Post Offices to pensioners and others should be made fortnightly rather than weekly or in some cases no longer made at all. This idea stirred up such strong opposition in Parliament and among the general public that the Government felt obliged to drop the proposal.

Another way of achieving similar purposes has been for Ministers to seek to use the Government Accountancy Service in more aspects of civil service work. Admittedly, this approach has not yet been carried very far, since there are no more than about 500 fully qualified accountants in post in Whitehall (not including the 600 or so who work for the Exchequer and Audit Department and the National Audit Commission). Although the present Government is clearly determined to accord a high priority to the use of such techniques in order to increase efficiency throughout the civil service, it seems equally clear that there will always be limitations upon what can be achieved in this way for the reasons already given.

**Judicial scrutiny**

Yet another method of controlling the civil service is that of judicial scrutiny by the Courts and other quasi-judicial bodies (for instance, administrative Tribunals). The attraction of this method is that it should make it possible to provide a framework of standards for good administrative practice without introducing too much legalism into the methods used.[18] Yet it is doubtful whether the system of administrative law in this country is sufficiently developed to achieve such a purpose. So far the Courts have taken only limited steps in this direction, notably when the doctrine of *ultra vires* has been applied to cases brought against certain local authority decisions.[19] This form of control has not been applied very much to central Government, since it would conflict with the principle of Ministerial responsibility and since its full application would require the introduction of a codified constitution interpreted in this area of the law by a powerful administrative division of the High Court.

From the point of view of the ordinary British citizen, the most notable step in this direction was taken when Parliament decided in 1967 to establish the Parliamentary Commissioner for Administration (the so-called Ombudsman) with statutory authority to investigate public complaints of maladministration in central Government Departments and (later) in the National Health Service as well.[20] Although the Ombudsman has always been limited by the fact that he has no powers of general initiative or legal enforcement, his office has been able over the years to rectify faulty procedures in the civil service and occasionally to lead Whitehall Departments to make *ex gratia* payments by way of compensation to citizens with established and justifiable grievances. His powers of publicity and persuasion, backed by the support which he usually gets from the House of Commons Select Committee which monitors his work, have provided a significant addition to the range of methods available for the control of the civil service in Britain.

## 15.4 POSSIBLE FUTURE DEVELOPMENTS

There are a number of possible future developments which could occur in the management and control of the civil service. Some of them would be logical extensions of what is already happening. Others would involve major changes and new departures. All are likely to be difficult to achieve in the British civil service.

**Ministers as managers**

One possible future development, which would be a logical extension of trends already begun during the Thatcher Government, would be for Ministers to act as senior managers in their respective Departments. However, so far the application of this idea has been no more than patchy and there can be no certainty that it will outlast the period of the Thatcher Government.

It implies that all Ministers should take a much more direct and personal interest in the actual management of their Departments and spend a good deal of their time acting as if they were the chief executives of large public corporations. Such an approach might be practicable for Ministers in charge of the smaller Departments, such as the Department of Energy or the Department of Education and Science. It is bound to be more difficult in the larger Departments, such as the Ministry of Defence or the Department of Health and Social Security, especially when the senior Ministers concerned have more pressing priorities in the policy sphere.

Furthermore, the idea could be said to imply the appointment of more Ministers in nearly every Department (something which is limited by the 1937 Ministers of the Crown Act), the creation of smaller Departments by breaking up the various super-Departments (for example, the Department of Trade and Industry) and deliberate progress towards simpler forms of public administration and reduced Government activity in general. The idea might also be easier to implement if Ministers could be relieved of many of the burdens of Parliamentary accountability and the responsibilities of constituency representation (as in France). However, since few of these conditions are likely to be met, the idea will probably not be implemented to any significant extent.

**Officials as managers**

Another possible future development, which would also be a logical extension of trends begun by the Thatcher Government, would be for senior officials to spend more of their time and energy upon managing their Departments. This idea was originally advocated in the 1968 Fulton Report and it has been promoted very strongly by the Thatcher Government as a manifestation of its commitment to greater efficiency and effectiveness in the civil service.

As stated in the 1981 Government White Paper on this subject, 'an integral part of the Government's policy is to tackle the underlying obstacles to efficiency (in the civil service) by creating the right conditions for managers to manage and by bringing on and rewarding those who are successful.'[21] This approach has involved sharpening the responsibilities of line managers in the civil service, ensuring the provision of better management information, insisting that Departments pay for common services in Whitehall, putting greater emphasis upon managerial skills in the training of civil servants, and encouraging officials at all levels to make their own proposals for ways of increasing the efficiency of the bureaucracy.

However, there have been some difficulties in getting this managerial ethos established in the civil service. One reason, suggested by Sir Robert Armstrong, Secretary to the Cabinet, is that 'civil servants have tended to find policy work more glamorous and more interesting than management work'.[22] Another reason is that whereas it may be possible to measure the inputs of money and manpower which are used by the civil service to administer a given policy, it is much more difficult to measure the output of some Government programmes in a useful way. These problems are inherent in the process of government, which is why the Treasury and Civil Service Select Committee of the House of Commons did not feel able to recommend more than 'greater devolution of management (within Departments), but strengthened central review of the effectiveness and efficiency with which management operates'.[23]

In responding to the Select Committee, the Thatcher Government made it clear that it wanted to see all Departments following three basic principles. These were 'that objectives for policy and administration should be clear, that responsibility for attaining objectives and for the management of resources in so doing should be defined, and that the information needed to exercise the responsibility should be provided.'[24]

Whether or not it proves possible to implement such principles to their full extent in Whitehall, the strong insistence of the Thatcher Government upon the role of officials as managers may have a number of wider consequences. It may mean that Ministers will need to seek more policy advice from enlarged Ministerial Private Offices or specially seconded political advisers if their senior Departmental officials have to spend more of their time on the tasks of Departmental management. It may mean significant changes in the recruitment and training of civil servants, especially those destined for senior administrative positions who will need to demonstrate appropriate managerial skills at an early stage in their careers. It could even mean the introduction of a form of two-tier recruitment with some officials destined for a managerial role within their Departments and some for the more traditional civil service tasks of providing policy advice for Ministers.

**Structural reform**

Another idea for the future is that there could be a reform of the Whitehall structure which differentiated between the bulk of civil service work, which tends to be administrative, if not mechanical in character, and the work of the civil service élite which is mainly concerned with the provision of policy advice to Ministers. Such a reform would align the Whitehall structure much more closely with the administrative pattern in Sweden and West Germany where the Ministries are often quite small bureaucracies concerned exclusively with policy advice for Ministers, while the execution of policy is entrusted to much larger administrative agencies which enjoy considerable institutional autonomy. It is uncertain whether such an administrative pattern would work satisfactorily in Britain, since the existing structure and conventions of Whitehall are well established.

If such an idea were put into effect, it would not be very different from the practice of 'hiving off' sections of Whitehall Departments which has been tried on several occasions over the last two decades. For example, the Heath Government came to power in 1970 determined to reorganise the structure of central Government and it did this at least in part by 'hiving off' some Departmental activities into quasi-autonomous agencies, such as the establishment of the Civil Aviation Authority in 1971 and the Manpower Services Commission in 1973.

Another kind of structural reform which has been attempted by Conservative Governments is the idea of 'hiving in'. This involves giving a semi-independent existence to specific sections of some Whitehall Departments and then expecting them to function more or less commercially on the basis of their own trading accounts. During the Heath Government of 1970–4 this was done with the establishment of the Procurement Executive within the Ministry of Defence in order to co-ordinate the weapons purchases of our armed forces and the Property Services Agency within the Department of the Environment in order to manage and maintain all Government buildings. On the other hand, the 1979–83 Thatcher Government decided to abandon its plans to do the same thing with the Royal Ordnance Survey when a wide range of influential opinion made it clear to Ministers that this could have had deleterious effects by lowering the standards and reducing the services provided by that excellent institution.

Yet another kind of structural reform has been put into effect by the Thatcher Government. This is based upon the idea of transferring operations, in whole or in part, from central Government into the private sector, so that they can be performed under private contract and thus reduce the burden of public expenditure. For example, the Ministry of Defence has put many of its cleaning requirements out to private contractors, the Property Services Agency has had some minor maintenance work on the Government Estate done by private contractors, and Health Authorities in all parts of the country have been encouraged to have their hospital catering, cleaning and laundry done by private firms under contract. In such cases the objective has been either to get better value for money from the existing public provision or to negotiate cheaper contracts with firms in the private sector. However, the latter approach has not always been beneficial in the longer term, since private firms sometimes secure the contracts on a loss-leader basis and since their standards of quality and reliability are sometimes too low for the specialist tasks involved.

In general, the present Conservative Government has been determined since May 1979 to reduce the overall size and cost of the civil service. In May 1979 there were 732 000 civil servants and the numbers have been steadily reduced to attain the Government's target of 630 000 by April 1984. The result is that Britain now has a smaller civil service than at any time since 1945. Over the period from 1979–80 to 1982–83 the reduction in numbers was achieved mainly by improving efficiency (55 per cent of the total), dropping or curtailing functions (20 per cent of the total), privatisation including contracting out (10 per cent of the total), hiving off to new or existing public sector bodies (2 per cent of the total) and some reductions in work-load as a consequence of policy changes. Further reductions in civil service manpower are planned and it was announced in November 1983 that the total is to be reduced to 593 000 by 1988 mainly by transferring the Royal Ordnance factories into the private sector. The continuation of this policy will have the effect of reducing manpower over the period 1984 to 1988 in the Department of Health and Social Security from about 91 000 to about 88 000 and in the Inland Revenue from about 70 000 to about 63 000, while increasing it in the Home Office from about 36 000 to about 41 000 over the same period.[25]

**Judicial control**

Yet another idea for the future, which has been advocated by those who are attracted by Continental or American models of government, is that the civil service in Britain should be subjected to comprehensive judicial control in a formal way. This would require the establishment of a fully-fledged system of administrative law, including the use of special administrative Courts on the pattern of the *Conseil d'État* in France or the *Bundesverfassungsgericht* in West Germany. Such far-reaching legal and institutional changes could not be made in Britain unless there were prior all-party agreement upon the overriding need for them. In present and foreseeable political circumstances it seems most unlikely that such agreement would be forthcoming, so the idea is likely to remain largely academic for the time being.

## 15.5 CONCLUSION

It is reasonable to conclude that the higher grades of the civil service wield considerable power and influence within British central Government. Yet such senior officials are by no means necessarily the dominant forces in their Departments. Ministers are still in charge and their constitutional authority is not questioned by civil servants. Officials are there to guide, assist and advise their Ministers, not to control them. As Denis Healey has observed, 'a Minister who complains that his civil servants are too powerful is either a weak Minister or an incompetent one'.[26] In other words, if the relationship between Ministers and civil servants works as it is supposed to do, there need be no problem of over-mighty officials.

However, there is still a problem caused by the ethos and conventions of Whitehall which can frustrate the intentions of Ministers (especially junior ones) and lower the quality of policy- and decision-making in Government. This is because the top 2000 or so in the bureaucracy of central Government tend to form a self-conscious network within the 'village' atmosphere of Whitehall.[27] They are apt to share common assumptions about policy, to put a high value on consensus solutions to political problems and to close ranks against heretics or outsiders. Many of them consider themselves to be engaged essentially in the orderly management of decline. This often implies an elegant, laconic and honest pessimism about the prospects for national recovery. It does not suggest an obsession with power, but rather an honourable, if slightly weary sense of public duty.

In these circumstances we can conclude that the civil service in Britain is neither master nor servant in our political system. It is more like the bureaucratic ballast which helps to keep the ship of state on an even keel.

## SUGGESTED QUESTIONS

1. Is the composition of the British civil service well suited to the needs of the time?
2. Are the civil servants really running the country?
3. What are the most appropriate and effective ways of controlling the civil service in Britain?

## NOTES

1. Report of the Tomlin Commission, Cmnd 3909 (London: HMSO, 1931).
2. Lord Bridges, *Portrait of a Profession* (London: CUP, 1950) p. 25.
3. See Report of the Fulton Committee, Cmnd 3628 (London: HMSO, 1968) which showed that in 1967 21 per cent of the administrative grades came from social class 1 (professional and proprietorial), 46 per cent from social class 2 (intermediate and non-manual), and 23 per cent from social class 3 (white-collar and skilled manual). Only 10 per cent came from the families of semi-skilled or unskilled manual workers which then constituted over one quarter of the total working population.
4. Research published by the Labour party in 1975 showed that of the entrants into the administrative grades in 1975 76 per cent of the males and 82 per cent of the females came from families in social classes 1 and 2 and that 48 per cent of the males and 56 per cent of the females came from public, direct grant or other fee-paying schools, and that 61 per cent of the males and 52 per cent of the females came from Oxford or Cambridge Universities; see B. Sedgemore, *The Secret Constitution* (London: Hodder & Stoughton, 1980) pp. 148–53.
5. See P. Kellner and N. Crowther-Hunt, *The Civil Servants* (London: Macdonald, 1980) pp. 121–3.
6. *The Times*, 7 March 1983.
7. See Chapter 13, Section 13.1 from 'Policy germination' to end of section.
8. See D. Howells, 'Marks & Spencer and the Civil Service: a Comparison of Culture and Methods' in *Public Administration*, Autumn 1981.
9. For example, in the Report on the Civil Service by the House of Commons Select Committee on Expenditure, 1977, HC 535.
10. See. B. Sedgemore, *The Secret Constitution* (London: Hodder & Stoughton, 1980) pp. 11–48.
11. See A. Benn: 'Manifestos and Mandarins' in W. Rodgers *et al., Policy and Practice, the Experience of Government* (London: Royal Institute of Public Administration, 1980) pp. 57–78.
12. See. J. Hoskyns: 'Whitehall and Westminster, an outsider's view' in *Fiscal Studies*, November 1982.
13. Cases, such as the Poulson Affair, in which civil servants were implicated in corrupt practices have been very rare in modern times.
14. See H. Young and A. Sloman, *No, Minister* (London: BBC, 1982) pp. 19–31.
15. *Sunday Times*, 16 December 1979.
16. MINIS is described in paras 23–6 of the Third Report of the Treasury and Civil Service Select Committee of the House of Commons, 1981–2, HC 236–I.
17. From June 1979 to April 1983 133 Departmental scrutinies and 6 multi-Departmental reviews were carried out in association with Lord Rayner. These identifed total potential savings and extra income of £400m a year and £56m once and for all. By April 1983 firm decisions had been taken to implement recommendations which would achieve savings and extra income of £180m and £29m once and for all (Hansard, 11 April 1983).

18. See G. Drewry, *Law, Justice and Politics* (London: Longman, 1975) pp. 75–6 for elaboration of this point.
19. For example, in the 1981 case of Bromley Council *v.* the Greater London Council in which the Law Lords ruled that the GLC had gone *ultra vires* by subsidising London Transport fares to such an extent, thus precepting very heavily upon the rates of the outer London Boroughs.
20. See Chapter 18 Section 18.5, subsection on 'The Ombudsman' for a fuller description of the Ombudsman and his role in the judical scrutiny of the civil service.
21. 'Efficiency in the Civil Service', Cmnd 8293 (London: HMSO, 1981) para. 16.
22. Quoted in 'Efficiency and Effectiveness in the Civil Service', Third Report from the Treasury and Civil Service Select Committee of the House of Commons, 1981–2; HC 236–I, para. 21.
23. Ibid, para. 73.
24. Government observations upon the Third Report of the Treasury and Civil Service Select Committee, 1981–2; Cmnd 8616, para. 25.
25. See Hansard, 8 November 1983, Col. 92 and 17 November 1983, Cols 554–6.
26. Quoted in H. Young and A. Sloman, *No, Minister*, p. 25.
27. See H. Heclo and A. Wildavsky, *Private Government of Public Money* (London: Macmillan, 1981).

## FURTHER READING


Bourn, J., *Management in Central and Local Government* (London: Pitman, 1979).

Brown, R. G. S. and Steel, D. R., *The Administrative Process in Britain*, 2nd edn (London: Methuen, 1979).

Chapman, R. A., *The Higher Civil Service in Britain* (London: Constable, 1970).

Garrett, J., *Managing the Civil Service* (London: Heinemann, 1980).

Heclo, H. and Wildavsky, A., *Private Government of Public Money* (London: Macmillan, 1981).

Keeling, D., *Management in Government* (London: Allen & Unwin, 1972).

Kellner, P. and Crowther-Hunt, N., *The Civil Servants* (London: Macdonald, 1980).

Parris, H., *Constitutional Bureaucracy* (London: Allen & Unwin, 1969).

Rodgers, W. *et al.*, *Policy and Practice, the Experience of Government* (London: Royal Institute of Public Administration, 1980).

Russell-Smith, E., *Modern Bureaucracy, the Home Civil Service* (London: Longman, 1974).

Sedgemore, B., *The Secret Constitution* (London: Hodder & Stoughton, 1980).

Self, P., *Administrative Theories and Politics*, 2nd edn (London: Allen & Unwin, 1977).

Smith, B. and Stanyer, J., *Administering Britain* (Oxford: Martin Robertson, 1980).

Young, H. and Sloman, A., *No, Minister* (London: BBC, 1982).

# PART V

# OTHER PUBLIC INSTITUTIONS

# THE PUBLIC SECTOR

In this chapter the term 'public sector' is defined to include public corporations, fringe bodies - that is Quasi-Autonomous Non-Governmental Organisations (QUANGOs), - and other public bodies (for example, Water Authorities and Health Authorities).[1] It does not include the Departments of central Government, which were dealt with in Chapters 14 and 15, or the institutions of local government, which will be dealt with in Chapter 17. In view of the scope and complexity of the public sector in Britain, this chapter concentrates mainly upon the problems posed by public corporations, since these have been at the heart of the political debate for many decades. The various institutions in the public sector are shown diagrammatically in Figure 16.1.

Fig 16.1 *The composition of the public sector*

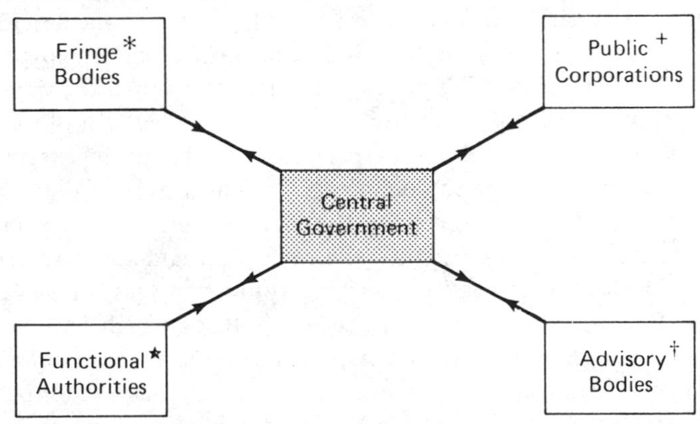


* Notably several hundred QUANGOs
+ Notably about 20 nationalised industries
★ Notably the Water Authorities and the Health Authorities
† Notably Advisory Committees, Royal Commissions and Departmental Committees

## 16.1 PUBLIC CORPORATIONS

In Britain there have been many different forms of public ownership and control which have been tried over the years. For example, in the second half of the nineteenth century the early Socialists advocated municipal control of commercial activities and those who were pressing for 'gas and water Socialism' considered local authorities to be the best mechanism for controlling public utilities. Before the Second World War more than two-thirds of electricity distribution and about one-third of gas distribution was under municipal control, as is the case in some Continental countries today. Over the years a number of municipal authorities also provided passenger transport services, civic amenities and other local services through their direct labour departments. However, since the war the policy of nationalisation under Labour Governments and the existence of rate-payer resistance under Conservative Governments led to a marked decline in this particular form of public enterprise with the result that it is no longer very significant today.

Since the war other forms of public ownership or control have included administrative control by a Whitehall Department headed by a Minister directly responsible to Parliament (for example, the Post Office until 1969); financial control by a state holding company, such as the Industrial Reorganisation Corporation in the late 1960s or the National Enterprise Board in the late 1970s; and financial influence within important parts of the private sector through the establishment of a state-owned financial institution, for example, the Post Office Giro Bank established in 1969.

However, in spite of the wide variety of institutional models which have been tried over the years, the clearest tendency has been the development of public corporations. Thus by 1982 such institutions employed about 1 759 000 people (about 7.5 per cent of those in work at the time), their contribution to GDP was about £26 115m (about 11 per cent of the total), and they accounted for about 17 per cent of total fixed investment in Britain.[2] They have come to dominate four vital sectors of the economy, namely energy, transport, steel and communications. They have included well-established institutions, such as British Rail and the National Coal Board, as well as some relatively new institutions, such as British Telecom and the British National Oil Corporation (both of which have been the subject of measures of denationalisation under the present Conservative Government). They are still important as both customers and suppliers of the private sector and they still have a profound and pervasive influence upon the economy and the politics of Britain.[3]

### Common characteristics

Public corporations in Britain have a number of common characteristics.[4]

They have been established by Acts of Parliament as statutory bodies responsible for the production of goods or the provision of services in specified areas of activity. They are publicly owned in the sense that any securities which they may issue give no powers to lenders and usually pay fixed rates of interest, although in some successful cases they are expected to pay public dividends to the Treasury.[5] They are subject to Government control via the indirect mechanisms of required rates of return on capital, external financial limits on spending and borrowing and, periodically, Ministerial appointments of their Chairmen and Board members. In return they enjoy varying degrees of day-to-day independence from central Government in operational matters in that their employees are not civil servants and their financial arrangements are at least semi-autonomous in the eyes of the Treasury.

**Essential problems**

There are a number of essential problems which have bedevilled public corporations in Britain over the years. These stem to a considerable extent from the conflicting pressures which gave rise to their establishment in the first place, including notably the ideological impetus provided by the Labour party after 1918 and the pragmatic need for a degree of national economic planning first recognised during the Depression in the 1930s. During the Second World War, in particular, there was a growing acceptance by the Coalition Government of final responsibility for the macro-economic management of the economy and by 1944 for the overall level of employment as well. It was against this background that the post-war Labour Government took further giant strides towards state ownership and political control of what were then considered to be the 'commanding heights' of the economy. It did this for the sake of the employees of the industries concerned in order to improve their pay and conditions. It did so in the cause of Socialist economic planning in order to improve the chances of national recovery after the war. Above all, it did so in fulfilment of Clause IV of the 1918 Labour party constitution which had called for the 'common ownership of the means of production, distribution and exchange'.

Yet as time went by, it became clear that the theory of public corporations was seriously flawed in practice. To begin with, the theory assumed that major matters of economic policy could be kept separate from the day-to-day concerns of management and that Ministers and members of the Boards could play distinct and complementary roles which would not conflict. In practice, we can now see that these were always heroic or naive assumptions, since central Government is inevitably involved for macro-economic and political reasons in the key decisions of public corporations.

This is partly a reflection of their economic weight and importance in the national economy, but mainly because their quasi-autonomous decisions can have a significant impact upon the wider political interests of any Government.

Furthermore, whereas the Socialist ideal which had inspired the establishment of public corporations was intended to permit the state to take over vital industrial undertakings on behalf of the people, all too often the subsequent reality was characterised by trade union demands for the state to rescue backward or ailing undertakings mainly for the sake of keeping their employees in work. This has diminished the ideal of public ownership in the minds of many people and presented successive Governments with intractable political problems.

The problems of dealing with the public corporations have not been made any easier by their notable diversity. This has been most clearly reflected in their widely differing economic fortunes. For example, at different stages during the last two decades British Airways, British Gas and British Telecom have each had an impressive economic record, whereas British Rail, the National Coal Board and the British Steel Corporation have each had enormous economic difficulties which have impaired their commercial performance. The former provide examples of expanding industries which have been capable of providing good returns on capital and labour employed, whereas the latter provide examples of traditional industries which have been afflicted with structural and attitudinal problems normally associated with industries in decline. Thus useful observations about public corporations are best made with specific reference to particular cases and with the basic understanding that the fortunes of particular industries have varied considerably over the years.

The public corporations have also suffered over the years from the fact that their very existence has been the subject of bitter and lasting political conflict between the two major parties. Today the non-interventionist tendency in the Conservative party, which appears to be in the ascendant, holds that the size of the public sector ought steadily to be reduced by a policy of steady and deliberate 'privatisation' and denationalisation over several years.[6] On the other hand, the zealous wing of the Labour party holds that the public sector ought to be extended by a deliberate policy of further nationalisation to include many of the largest and most successful firms in the private sector. The battle between these two ideological tendencies is still unresolved and seems likely to harm the economy for some time to come.

However, perhaps the central problem of the public corporations has been the difficulty of establishing an 'arm's length' relationship between them and the Government of the day. This must involve an attempt to reconcile managerial freedom for the Boards with the constant temptation for Ministers to interfere with either the boundaries of the public sector or the ground-rules or both.

Traditionally, the public corporations have been charged with twin statutory duties: to break even taking one year with another and to operate in the public interest. Yet these duties have often been incompatible and it has usually been the latter which prevailed. This might have been acceptable if there had been a clear and lasting consensus among the political parties about what constituted the public interest in cases of this kind. However, such a consensus has not existed, because of the inherent conflict between the interests of those employed by public corporations and the interests of the wider national community which has supported them via the Exchequer.

A White Paper in 1961 was the first statement of Government policy since the war to emphasise that public corporations should not be run as if they were social services, but rather should pay their way at least over a five-year period.[7] It also restated the classic view of Herbert Morrison that public corporations should remain at arm's length from the Government of the day. This was taken to mean that Ministers in sponsoring Departments should not interfere with the decisions of the Boards, that any political intervention which did occur should be specified clearly in writing and that the financial requirements imposed upon the Boards should be adjusted if the Government of the day were to insist that a public corporation should take on additional burdens of a social character, such as subsidised pricing or regional bias in investment decisions.

A subsequent White Paper in 1967 took this line of argument one stage further by emphasising that public corporations should be regarded as commercial undertakings and should gradually eliminate all non-commercial practices, such as internal cross-subsidies and pricing according to historic costs.[8] Yet at the same time the then Labour Government insisted that the public corporations should comply with its prices and incomes policy and to this end allowed them to interpret their financial requirements quite flexibly. This was a clear example of the sort of political ambiguity which has made it so difficult to manage public corporations with any real degree of lasting success.

Experience over many years has demonstrated the great difficulties of implementing an arm's length relationship between public corporations and the Government of the day. All too often the former have been required by the Treasury to reduce or defer their investment programmes for the sake of national macro-economic policy, notably Government decisions to limit or reduce public sector borrowing. On other occasions they have felt obliged to subordinate their commercial judgement to the political objectives of Ministers. For example, there have been occasions when the National Coal Board has wanted to close non-economic pits, but the Government of the day has insisted that they be kept open for regional or social reasons. There have been other occasions when the British Steel Corporation was expected to invest heavily in new plant and equipment at the instigation of Ministers only to find that the forecast expansion of the market did not materialise. Under the present Conservative Government the nationalised gas and electricity industries have been bullied by Ministers into putting up their prices by more than their own commercial judgement suggested simply in order to increase the revenue which they provide for the Exchequer. In all such cases the nation as a whole has tended to get the worst of both worlds.

This unsatisfactory relationship was well summarised in a 1976 NEDO Report.[9] It pointed out that the relationship was characterised all too often by 'a lack of incentives for adequate or improved performance' which then produced 'a minimising environment with few rewards for real success and negligible sanctions against failure'. In effect, Ministers have paid lip-service to the arm's length relationship and then departed from it whenever it seemed politically expedient to do so.

## 16.2 METHODS OF CONTROL

Since 1976 there have been some significant developments in the way in which successive Governments have sought to control the public corporations. In that year the Labour Government was obliged by the International Monetary Fund to introduce a system of rigorous cash limits on all forms of public spending and this included tighter financial controls upon the public corporations. This system has been refined and extended subsequently by the Conservative Government with the result that the Boards of public corporations have been caught in a vice between the tight financial policy of the Government and the adverse effects of the economic recession. Two of the most unfortunate consequences for the public corporations have been that their prices have often had to be increased faster than the rate of inflation to enable them to meet the Government's tight financial targets and their capital investment programmes have had to be reduced to enable them to remain within the external limits on their spending and borrowing. Thus although it might be said that the Boards still have the freedom to operate at arm's length from the Government of the day, the economic and financial climate within which they have recently had to function has reduced their capacity to do so.

In these circumstances the methods of control fall into three categories. These are Ministerial responsibility, Parliamentary accountability and other mechanisms of control. We shall examine each one briefly in the paragraphs which follow.

**Ministerial responsibility**
The most orthodox method of control has always been Ministerial responsibility. This takes the form of frequent consultations between Ministers and the Boards of public corporations on major matters of policy, such as investment planning, pricing decisions, pay negotiations and significant environmental issues, such as an airport runway extension or the siting of a new power-station. In this relationship Ministers have always sought to preserve the fundamental distinction between day-to-day management decisions in which they usually try not to intervene and long-term strategic decisions in which they usually have to be involved. Such access to inside information and frequent high-level contact can tempt Ministers to blur this distinction, although it does not really make it possible for them to usurp the role of management even if they feel inclined to try.

When Ministers decide to intervene, they have the statutory right to do so by issuing directives to the Board of the public corporation concerned. However, more often than not they are tempted to influence Board decisions in various informal ways not provided for in the statutes. Such methods are known as 'lunch-time directives' and usually involve confidential attempts by Ministers over lunch to persuade the Chairman concerned to modify the decisions of his Board in a manner conducive to the interests of Government policy. Examples of this technique might include Ministerial pressure on British Rail to keep open non-economic branch lines, on the Post Office or British Airways to buy British equipment, on the Central Electricity Generating Board to modify its power-station ordering programme and on the British Steel Corporation or the National Coal Board in connection with factory or pit closures. Under the present Conservative Government there seems to have been somewhat less of a conflict of interest, perhaps because in several notable cases - for example, the National Coal Board or British Rail - the public corporations concerned are now run by Chairmen who largely share the Government's viewpoint.

However, on many occasions in the past the Chairmen of public corporations have tended to interpret their statutory duties more narrowly than Ministers. This has often challenged the politicians either to do nothing about unpopular Board decisions and so risk public opprobrium or to intervene in Board decisions and so damage their working relationship with the management concerned. On the whole Ministers have preferred to take the latter risk, since the general public has more votes than the Boards concerned.

**Parliamentary accountability**
Another method of control, which is really the corollary of Ministerial responsibility, is provided by accountability to Parliament. However, this

has been imperfect in practice, since Ministers have consistently refrained from answering detailed questions in Parliament about the day-to-day decisions taken by the management of public corporations. All they usually say in reply is that they will 'draw the matter to the attention' of the relevant Chairman and Board. Nevertheless this form of accountability should not be completely dismissed, nor should the investigations by Select Committees or the occasional debates upon the annual reports of public corporations be regarded too lightly, since they are always taken seriously by the management concerned. Not even the most powerful and self-confident Chairman relishes the prospect of Parliamentary criticism, so even straightforward correspondence from MPs on behalf of their constituents is usually dealt with as helpfully and expeditiously as possible. Such a form of accountability may be indirect and imperfect, but it is not as ineffective as the purists might tend to believe.

**Other mechanisms**

From time to time other mechanisms of control have been used or suggested. Some have argued that there should be Efficiency Audits of the public corporations. Indeed, under the 1980 Competition Act the Thatcher Government encouraged the Monopolies and Mergers Commission to conduct special investigations into selected public corporations.[10] Others have pressed for regular debates in Parliament on the reports and accounts of the various public corporations, although the busy time-table of the Commons has not permitted this to happen more than once in a while. Occasionally, the Government of the day has established a Royal Commission or a special committee to conduct a detailed review of a public corporation and to lay the basis for future changes in policy or structure or both. However, the implementation of such recommendations usually requires the passage through Parliament of subsequent legislation and in very many cases such reports have been ignored or shelved by Government.

In normal circumstances perhaps the most reliable but undramatic mechanism of control is the simple expedient of an MP writing directly to the Chairman of the public corporation concerned in order to secure detailed information, air public grievances or tender operational advice. Certainly this method has often proved more effective than recourse to the appropriate Consumer Councils set up to monitor the various public corporations – for example, the Electricity Consumer Council or the Post Office Users' National Council – which have been shown to be little more than statutory watch-dogs with rubber teeth. However, in the final analysis none of these mechanisms really secures fully effective control, so the public and its elected representatives continue to be deprived of effective ways of bringing public corporations to book when they reveal serious shortcomings or failures.

## 16.3 FRINGE BODIES

In one of the most authoritative surveys of fringe bodies in the United Kingdom Geoffrey Bowen identified 252 such institutions which he defined as 'organisations which have been set up or adopted by Departments and provided with public funds to perform some function which the Government wishes to have performed, but which it does not wish to be the direct responsibility of a Minister or a Department.'[11] Such bodies are popularly known as QUANGOs, that is, quasi-autonomous non-governmental organisations. However, as Anthony Barker has pointed out, 'every list of QUANGOs is as long as a piece of string, because of the difficulties of definition and clarification'.[12]

In 1974-5 institutions of this kind employed about 184 000 people and were responsible for about £2367m of public funds. They covered a wide range of institutions including, for example, the British Library, the Equal Opportunities Commission, the Gaming Board, the Gas Consumers Council, the Trinity House Lighthouse Service, the Wales Tourist Board and the White Fish Authority. On the other hand, the definition excluded all Departmental advisory committees, the Royal Household, the armed services, the National Health Service, the institutions of Parliament, the judiciary, central Government Departments and local authorities.

A little later the Pliatzky Report revealed that in 1978-9 there were 489 institutions which corresponded to Geoffrey Bowen's definition, employing about 217 000 people and responsible for about £5800m of public funds.[13] Until Ministers in the Thatcher Government began consciously to prune this part of the public sector, it seemed to have been expanding in an apparently inexorable way. Thus such 'Government at arm's length' had become one of the defining characteristics of the British political system.

### Common characteristics

On closer inspection it is clear that fringe bodies have a number of characteristics in common. They derive their existence from Ministerial decisions and are therefore answerable to Ministers. Their creation normally requires legislative approval by Parliament and most of them produce annual reports which have to be laid before Parliament and can be debated there. They are usually financed by grants in aid, but may sometimes be given the power to raise their own statutory levies. Their Chairmen and Boards are appointed by Ministers for fixed terms of office and can be dismissed by Ministers at the end of such terms. They recruit their own staff who are not normally civil servants, although their pay and conditions are often comparable with those of the civil service. Their annual accounts are audited either commercially or by the National Audit Commission. In short, they are an identifiable sub-species of the public administration in Britain.

**Advantages and disadvantages**

Those who have investigated this grey area of the public sector have identified a number of advantages and disadvantages in the existence of fringe bodies. On the positive side, the following points can be made in their favour. They permit certain activities of importance to the state to be conducted outside the confines of central Government Departments yet within the Whitehall orbit. They permit such activities to be conducted free from direct or frequent interference by Parliament and therefore largely insulated from the party battle at Westminster. They enable Parliament to pass what is essentially framework legislation in some areas with the confidence that any practical problems which may arise can be solved in administrative fashion. They make it easier to achieve a broad continuity of administration in certain areas of the public sector and to resolve recurrent conflicts of interest in a largely apolitical way. They relieve Departmental civil servants of many administrative burdens and enable the Departments of central Government to be smaller than they would otherwise need to be. They provide useful opportunities for the dispensation of political patronage in a political system which is not really blighted by such practices.

On the other hand, the following negative points can be made against such institutions.[14] There is a lack of clarity or agreement about how many such bodies there really are and which should be included in any standard definition. The growth of such bodies has produced an institutional proliferation in the British political system which has proved expensive to administer and difficult to control. The appointments to such bodies provide a growing scope for Ministerial patronage which is unhealthy in a political system which has long been renowned for its relative lack of political patronage or corruption. There is a lack of proper democratic control over these bodies and the Ministerial appointments to them and a lack of democratic financial control over the public funds which they spend. For example, there is no Parliamentary Select Committee to oversee their activities or to 'advise and consent' to the public appointments involved.

It seems that in so far as appointments to these institutions represent an unacceptable amount of Ministerial patronage and in so far as their growth over the years has represented an unwelcome extension of effectively unaccountable public administration, the recent wave of political criticism may have been justified and steps should probably be taken to control their growth and their impact upon the rest of the political system. On the other hand, the vast majority of these institutions ought to be tolerated and understood, since they are no more than one manifestation of the scope and complexity of modern government.

## 16.4 OTHER PUBLIC BODIES

In considering other public bodies, we shall refer to Royal Commissions and Departmental Committees of Inquiry, as well as the myriad of advisory committees which assist the process of government in Whitehall. We shall also give a brief description of the special purpose authorities, notably the Water Authorities and the Health Authorities.

### Royal Commissions and Departmental Committees

The appointment of a Royal Commission or Departmental Committee to inquire into a particular problem or set of problems is an act of the Executive which requires no prior Parliamentary approval, although it is often a Ministerial response to political pressures. As Lord Benson and Lord Rothschild have put it, 'its purpose is first to ascertain all the relevant facts, next to assemble the facts fairly and impartially and finally to form balanced conclusions'.[15] The Commission or Committee usually calls for evidence and views from interested individuals and bodies both inside and outside the web of central Government. It may also undertake or sponsor its own research into the problems under consideration. The reports and the evidence of such bodies are normally published for anyone to read, although this is not the case with some internal inquiries dealing with highly confidential matters of concern to central Government, for example, reviews of arrangements concerned with national security.

Over the period 1954-69, twenty-four Royal Commissions and more than 600 Departmental Committees were appointed. Most of them were disbanded when their inquiries were complete, although a few have been appointed on a permanent basis, for example, the Royal Commission on Environmental Pollution or the Law Commission. Among the major Commissions or Committees of more recent years have been the Fulton Committee on the Civil Service 1966–8, the Redcliffe-Maud Commission on Local Government 1966-9, the Kilbrandon Commission on the Constitution 1969-73, the Bullock Committee on Industrial Democracy 1975-7, the Wilson Committee on Financial Institutions 1977–80 and the Scarman Committee of Inquiry into the Brixton Disorders in 1981. When such prestigious bodies report, it is for the Minister most directly concerned or the Government as a whole to decide whether the various recommendations are acceptable and if so, when and how they should be implemented.

Over the years all Governments have found that Royal Commissions and Departmental Committees can be very useful as institutional mechanisms to lay the basis for subsequent Government action or legislation in controversial areas which need thorough and impartial investigation before any important decisions are taken. They have also found the establishment of such bodies to be a convenient device for putting off decisions on vexed and difficult questions about which there is little or no political agreement. Indeed, in some cases the establishment of such a body has proved to be one way of burying a tricky issue altogether.

**Advisory committees**

As for the myriad of advisory committees which exist to assist Departments with the day-to-day process of public administration, these demonstrate the extent to which continuous consultations, whether formal or informal, have become essential to the process of modern government. As we noted in Chapter 6 on pressure groups, such advisory committees meet the needs of central Government for expert information and advice and the needs of sectional interests for access to Government and influence on policy. Thus they provide an important means by which Governments can seek to gain and retain the consent of the governed, at any rate those most directly affected by the consequences of current or prospective policy.

Such advisory committees are particularly useful to Departments in the detailed preparation of technical Statutory Instruments. The need for such an arrangement arises because Acts of Parliament have put statutory responsibilities upon Ministers in particular Departments to consult specified advisory bodies when drawing up detailed legislation. For example, under the 1964 Police Act the Home Secretary must consult the Police Council on regulations concerning the administration and conditions of service in police forces throughout the country. Equally, under the 1975 Social Security Act the Secretary of State for Health and Social Security must consult the National Insurance Advisory Committee on regulations to do with National Insurance.

There are also many examples of such consultations on a non-statutory basis, such as those which have taken place within the framework of the National Economic Development Council which has provided a forum for regular meetings between the Government and what is conventionally described as 'the two sides of industry'. In most cases considerable mutual benefit has been derived from these various mechanisms of consultation, although they have occasionally been boycotted by the trade unions when the latter have been particularly displeased with certain aspects of Government policy, for example, in the aftermath of the controversial decision in

1984 to withdraw trade union membership rights from those working for GCHQ at Cheltenham and elsewhere.

**Water Authorities**

Until the reorganisation of the Water Authorities in 1974, water supply in England and Wales had been the responsibility of 198 separate water undertakings, sewage treatment and disposal had been dealt with by about 1400 local Councils and twenty-four joint Boards, and water conservation had been the responsibility of twenty-nine river Authorities. In 1974 this complex system was replaced by a simpler one involving ten Regional Water Authorities, each within hydrologically determined boundaries and each responsible for all aspects of water treatment and supply within its area. Thus today a wide variety of water supply and sewage disposal functions are administered by large, integrated organisations which are essentially managerial in their approach and commercial in their behaviour.

The present institutional structure has both advantages and disadvantages. The main advantage is that the public water supply is now the responsibility of large, modern Authorities which can effectively guarantee to deal safely and satisfactorily with any meteorological or hydrological conditions. The main disadvantages are that the local authorities have resented losing their previous responsibilities in this area and have lobbied ever since to get them back, that the Water Authorities have become remote and apparently unresponsive to consumer concerns, and that the price of water and sewage services has risen rapidly since the new Authorities have been in existence. Furthermore, the scale and importance of these vital services has given the workers in them great power which they have sometimes used quite ruthlessly in pay bargaining with the employers and the Government. On balance, therefore, the disadvantages of the present structure appear to outweigh the advantages and no doubt that is one reason why the Labour party is committed to returning these services to the control of local authorities. It remains to be seen whether further reorganisation will produce more satisfactory results.

**Health Authorities**

The National Health Service (NHS), which had been in three separate parts since its foundation in 1948, was also the object of reorganisation in the early 1970s. The pressures for a unified service had been growing for a decade or more when in 1970 Richard Crossman, then the Secretary of State for Health and Social Security in the Labour Government, proposed a reorganised structure of ninety Area Health Authorities in England. Later the same year the matter was reconsidered by the incoming Conservative Government and after a further White Paper on NHS reorganisation in 1972, a new institutional structure was established by Act of

Parliament in 1974. Even though there was another change of Government in the latter year, the incoming Labour Government reluctantly decided to go ahead with the NHS reorganisation which had been initiated by its Conservative predecessor.

The unified structure which came into being in 1974 involved four levels of administration in England: the national level with the Secretary of State in overall charge of the service, the regional level with fourteen Regional Health Authorities responsible for overall management and resource allocation within national guidelines, the area level with ninety Area Health Authorities co-terminous with local authority boundaries to facilitate co-operation with the personal social services, and the district level with 206 District Health Authorities responsible for the day-to-day management of the service.

It soon became apparent that a veritable administrative wedding-cake had been created and that the service as a whole was suffering from too many layers of administration. The first Thatcher Government therefore legislated in 1982 to abolish the area level of administration in an attempt to secure a more streamlined and responsive institutional structure. The change was also made as a conscious attempt to tilt the balance of decision-making towards greater local autonomy for the District Health Authorities and to reduce administrative costs. The present Government has decided to make some further changes this time in the ethos of the National Health Service following acceptance of the 1983 Griffiths Report. The changes are designed to introduce more managerial attitudes into the service and to achieve better value for money.

## 16.5 FUTURE PROSPECTS

### Myths and realities

None of the problems of the public sector is made any easier to solve by the myths which permeate this area of public policy. For example, there is the myth that there can be a clear distinction between policy and administration with Ministers responsible for the former and the Boards of public corporations responsible for the latter. There is the myth that public corporations can act simultaneously as public trusts in the national interest and ordinary commercial undertakings. There is the myth that there can be either full Ministerial control of public corporations or complete managerial autonomy for their Boards.

The reality, on the other hand, is that all Governments and public corporations are condemned to relationships of inherent ambiguity and that the disadvantages of coping with the present ambiguity may well be outweighed by the disadvantages of seeking either to nationalise or to denationalise on a significant scale. In these circumstances the most sensible objectives for all Governments and public corporations should probably include the gradual amelioration of the tensions inherent in their relationships and the implementation of practical schemes for fruitful co-operation between the public and private sectors.

**Future guidelines**

Against this controversial and complicated background it is difficult to be sure about the future of the public sector in Britain. Even allowing for the fact that the present Conservative Government seems strongly committed to a policy of further denationalisation and a future Labour Government will probably be strongly committed to a policy of nationalisation, a few guidelines for the future of the public sector may be discernible.

Firstly, it is clear that in our mixed economy there are certain goods and services which must be provided by the public sector if they are to be provided at all, mainly because the private sector is unlikely to be willing to do so. For example, it is unlikely that loss-making postal or train services would be provided by private enterprise, so they have to be provided by the Post Office and British Rail on a subsidised basis if they are to be provided at all.

Secondly, there are considerations of national security which make it virtually unavoidable that the public sector should undertake certain projects. For example, if Britain is to remain in the forefront of some very expensive advanced technologies, such as aerospace or nuclear power, it is necessary for there to be powerful public sector undertakings capable of developing and manufacturing such high cost and high risk equipment. It was recognition of this reality which led in 1954 to the creation of the United Kingdom Atomic Energy Authority (UKAEA) and in 1971 to the reorganisation of Rolls Royce Ltd, in each case by a Conservative Government. Even in the United States, where such activities are undertaken by the private sector, they usually require the financial and political backing of the state through the medium of enlightened public procurement policy.

Thirdly, there will continue to be a good deal of argument about whether or not there are other ways in which public goods and services could be provided more effectively. For example, some argue that rural transport needs can best be met by a liberalisation of public vehicle licensing, so that private operators are free to carry passengers in more flexible ways. Others suggest that rural postal services can serve also as rural transport for people in sparsely populated outlying areas. However, in most cases of this kind the real problem is that the services are most unlikely to be profitable, so the question arises as to whether they are to be run at a loss and if so, how they are to be subsidised. In short, public service and corporate profit are usually difficult to reconcile, so Governments have to decide which they are going to favour. It is usually very difficult to maintain a satisfactory combination of the two.

## 16.6 CONCLUSION

We have seen in this chapter that the most notable characteristics of the public sector in Britain are its considerable size and diversity. Public corporations are different from fringe bodies which are different from other public institutions. Even within the more closely defined sphere of the public corporations there are considerable variations of institutional form and corporate performance.

In constitutional terms the main significance of the public sector has been the way in which its importance within the national economy has led to the development of a hybrid institution - the public corporation - which has turned out to be a disappointment to many on the Left and a bogey for many on the Right. This Morrisonian model has proved difficult to manage and even more difficult to control. Few people seem to have derived much direct benefit from it over the years, with the possible exception of some public sector employees. Nearly everyone else seems to have been frustrated or thwarted by this kind of institution and it has caused real problems for Ministers in sponsoring Departments. A 1978 Government White Paper stressed the need for trust, continuity and accountability in the relationship between central Government and the public corporations.[16] Yet it is clear from the record over the years that there has not normally been sufficient trust between Ministers and the management of public corporations, that continuity of policy for the public corporations has been prejudiced by the long-running party battle over the boundaries and ground-rules of the public sector, and that real public accountability has been vitiated by the anomalies and contradictions of the Morrisonian model.

The present Conservative Government seems determined to reduce the size of the public sector by denationalising those public corporations, whether in whole or in part, for which buyers can be found in the private sector. On the other hand, the Labour party still seems determined to extend the scope of the public sector, when it has the political power to do so, by nationalising or renationalising parts of the private sector. The Alliance of Liberal and Social Democratic parties appears to favour a middle way which would involve the encouragement of co-operation between the public and private sectors. Thus the outlook is uncertain and the only reasonable forecast is that the size and nature of the public sector in Britain will not remain constant for very long.

## SUGGESTED QUESTIONS

1. Assess the contribution of public corporations to Britain in the twentieth century.
2. To what extent can or should public corporations be controlled by Ministers?
3. Is the public sector an asset or a liability in Britain today?

## NOTES

1. A useful guide to the public bodies for which Ministers have a degree of accountability is *Public Bodies 1983* (London: HMSO, 1983). This lists the nationalised industries, certain public corporations (e.g. the Bank of England), non-Departmental public bodies and National Health Service Authorities. It is produced and brought up-to-date each year by the Management and Personnel Office under the auspices of the Cabinet Office.
2. See Central Statistical Office, *National Income and Expenditure*, 1983, Tables 1.10 and 10.3, and *Economic Trends*, February 1983, Appendix 1, Table 1.
3. For example, the public sector's purchases from the private sector in 1982 amounted to about £9000m, while its sales to the private sector of goods and services amounted to about £11 000m in the same year.
4. NB. These generalisations refer essentially to the nationalised industries and do not apply to all public corporations, some of which were created by Royal Charter, for example, the British Broadcasting Corporation.
5. For example, the British Steel Corporation, British Shipbuilders, the National Enterprise Board and the Scottish and Welsh Development Agencies have all received finance from the Government in the form of public dividend capital and have therefore been expected to pay dividends to the Exchequer at approximately market rates of interest after making allowance for varying trading conditions.
6. From June 1979 to November 1983 the Thatcher Government raised about £2590m in proceeds from the sale of public sector assets. These sales included shares in BP, land and buildings owned by the Property Services Agency, leases on motorway service areas, shares in British Aerospace and Britoil, and the entirety of Amersham International. Further asset sales are planned for the next four years at a rate of about £2000m a year - for example, British Telecom and British Airways - with the express purpose of increasing competition, reducing the size of the public sector, and lowering the levels of public borrowing and taxation which might otherwise be necessary to finance the planned levels of public spending over the period, including support for the remaining nationalised industries.
7. 'The financial and economic obligations of the nationalised industries', Cmnd 1337 (London: HMSO, 1961).
8. 'Nationalised industries, a review of economic and financial objectives', Cmnd 3437 (London: HMSO, 1967).

9. 'A study of UK nationalised industries' (London: National Economic Development Office, 1976) p. 40.
10. Recent examples have included investigations into the London letter post, the Severn–Trent Water Authority, the Central Electricity Generating Board and British Rail commuter services in London and the South-East.
11. G. Bowen *Survey of Fringe Bodies* (London: Civil Service Department, 1978).
12. A. Barker (ed.) *QUANGOs in Britain* (London: Macmillan, 1982) p. x.
13. L. Pliatzky 'Report on non-Departmental public bodies', Cmnd 7797, (London: HMSO, 1980).
14. See *What's wrong with QUANGOs* (London: Outer Circle Policy Unit, 1979).
15. Lord Benson and Lord Rothschild, 'Royal Commissions, a memorial' in *Public Administration*, Autumn 1982.
16. 'The nationalised industries', Cmnd 7131 (London: HMSO, 1978).

## FURTHER READING


Bacon, R. and Eltis, W., *Britain's Economic Problem* (London: Macmillan, 1976).

Barker, A. (ed.) *QUANGOs in Britain* (London: Macmillan, 1982).

Cartwright, T. J., *Royal Commissions and Departmental Committees in Britain* (London: Hodder & Stoughton, 1975).

Dell, E., *Political Responsibility and Industry* (London: Allen & Unwin, 1973).

Foster, C. D., *Politics, Finance and the Role of Economics* (London: Allen & Unwin, 1971).

Grove, J. W., *Government and Industry in Britain* (London: Longman, 1962).

Levitt, R., *The Reorganised National Health Service* (London: Croom Helm, 1976).

Pryke, R., *The Nationalised Industries, Policies and Performance since 1968* (Oxford: Martin Robertson, 1981).

Redwood, J. and Hatch, J., *Controlling Public Industries* (Oxford: Blackwell, 1982).

Rhodes, G., *Committees of Inquiry* (London: Allen & Unwin, 1975).

Robson, W. A., *Nationalised Industry and Public Ownership* (London: Allen & Unwin, 1962).

Thompson, A. W. J. and Beaumont, P. B., *Public Sector Bargaining* (Farnborough: Saxon House, 1978).

Thornhill, W., *The Nationalised Industries* (London: Nelson, 1968).

Tivey, L., *Nationalisation in British Industry* (London: Jonathan Cape, 1973).

# CHAPTER 17

# LOCAL GOVERNMENT

It is important to distinguish at the outset between local government, which can be defined simply as directly elected local authorities, and local administration which includes the regional and local offices of central Government, the local offices of public corporations and the local administration of justice. In this chapter we shall concentrate upon directly elected local authorities, in other words primary local government.

## 17.1 STRUCTURE AND COMPOSITION

The structure of local government is different in the different parts of the United Kingdom. It is represented diagrammatically in Figure 17.1.

### England and Wales

The structure of local government in England and Wales was reformed by the 1972 Local Government Act which came into effect in 1974. It reduced the previous mosaic of about 1400 local authorities to six Metropolitan authorities (outside Greater London which had been reformed by the 1963 Greater London Act), forty-seven County authorities (for example, Devon, Kent, Norfolk, Dyfed, etc.), thirty-six Metropolitan District authorities within the Metropolitan counties (of which the largest was Birmingham with a population of more than 1 million), and 333 District authorities within the Counties (representing areas with populations ranging from 60 000 to 100 000 in most cases). Thus a total of about 420 local authorities replaced the previous 1400 or so and the interdependence of town and country became the guiding principle of the structure of local government.

At the most local level the former Parish Councils were retained and their powers were increased to a limited extent. About 300 former Urban Districts and small Boroughs became Parish Councils. Parishes of more than 200 inhabitants were required to elect a Council, whereas those with fewer than 200 inhabitants were encouraged to practise the direct democracy of

Fig 17.1 *The structure of local government in the United Kingdom*

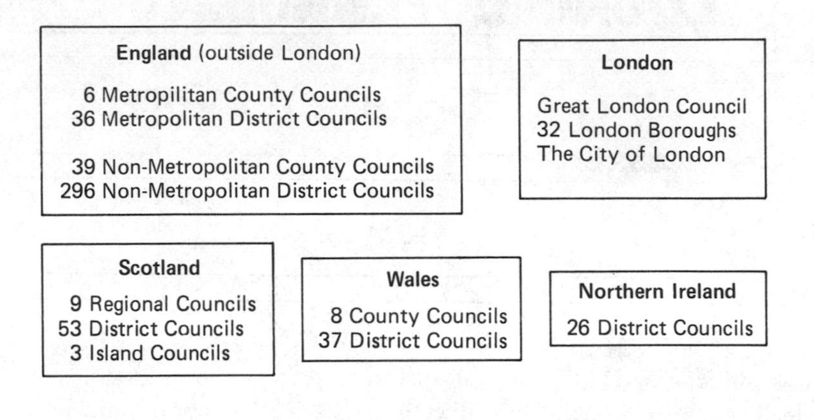


parish meetings. The 1972 Act also established separate local government Boundary Commissions for England and Wales. These bodies have kept the structure of local government under review and are empowered to propose boundary changes from time to time in order to take account of population movements and other social changes.

In October 1983 the present Conservative Government brought forward proposals for reorganising local government in Greater London and the other Metropolitan Counties.[1] These involved the abolition of the Greater London Council and the other six Metropolitan authorities (Greater Manchester, Merseyside, South Yorkshire, Tyne and Wear, West Midlands, and West Yorkshire) and the reallocation of their functions to Borough and District Councils, statutory joint Boards and other existing public bodies. The intention is to legislate for this reorganisation in the 1984-5 session of Parliament and for the change-over to take place on 1 April 1986. The Thatcher Government believes that the abolition of these upper-tier authorities will streamline local government in the Metropolitan areas, remove a source of conflict with central Government, save money after incurring some transitional costs, and provide a simpler and more accountable structure of local government.

## Scotland

The present structure of local government in Scotland was determined by the 1973 Local Government (Scotland) Act which came into effect in 1975. This involved the creation of nine Regional Authorities (with populations ranging from about $2\frac{1}{2}$ million in Strathclyde to fewer than 100 000 in The Borders) and fifty-three District Authorities within the larger regions. The division of functions between the two levels of local government is similar to that in England and Wales, except that the three island areas (that is, Orkney, Shetland and the Western Isles) are each single, all-purpose authorities.

**Northern Ireland**

The present structure of local government in Northern Ireland was largely determined by the 1972 Local Government (Northern Ireland) Act which came into effect in 1973. It created a single level of local government by establishing twenty-six District Councils based upon the main population centres. The Districts vary considerably in area and resources with populations ranging from about 13 000 to about 350 000. Under a subsequent reorganisation of local government in 1977, which was precipitated by the way in which the Protestant majority groups had abused their positions of local power, the District Councils were left with minimal functions, such as cleaning and sanitation, markets and abattoirs and recreational facilities.

All the more important functions of local government are carried out either by centralised Boards under the Northern Ireland Office (dealing with housing, police, fire services, electricity supply) or by area Boards (dealing with health and personal social services, education and libraries) or directly by the Northern Ireland Office (that is, town and country planning, water and sewage services, roads and car parks, vehicle registration and licensing). Apart from their severely circumscribed direct functions, local Councillors have some indirect influence which they can exercise when they sit as nominees on the various area Boards and some consultative influence when they hold formal discussions with Ministers and officials in the Northern Ireland Office.

The 1979-83 Conservative Government secured Parliamentary approval for the 1982 Northern Ireland Act which provided for the establishment of a unicameral elected Assembly with deliberative, scrutiny and consultative functions in relation to the government of Northern Ireland. The first elections to the Assembly were held in October 1982 and it met for the first time in November 1982. The Assembly has opportunities, within what was intended to be a scheme of 'rolling devolution', to express views at an early stage upon proposed legislation for Northern Ireland and generally upon the government of Northern Ireland. According to the original plan, it was envisaged that at a later stage it might be possible for the Ministers from the Northern Ireland Office, who now form the Executive which reports to the Assembly, to be augmented or replaced by locally elected politicians. It was thought that it might be possible at an even later stage for the Assembly, with the approval of the overwhelming majority of its members and of both communities (that is, Protestants and Catholics), to be given fully devolved powers, including direct control of the Executive. However, things have not worked out so well in practice, since only the

Democratic Unionists and the Alliance Party members are participating (in March 1984) and the work of the Assembly has not extended beyond its advisory and consultative functions in relation to draft legislation and to some executive action proposed by the Ministers of the Northern Ireland Office.

**Councillors and officials**

The composition of local authorities in England and Wales can be summarised by saying that each County Council has between sixty and 100 elected Councillors and each District Council has between thirty and eighty elected Councillors. In both cases Councillors are elected for fixed four-year terms. At present those elected to the Greater London Council, the London Borough Councils, the County Councils and the non-Metropolitan District Councils are elected *en bloc*, whereas in the Metropolitan District Councils one-third of the Councillors are elected every third year. For electoral purposes the Counties are divided into single member constituencies, whereas the Districts and London Boroughs are divided into wards represented by between one and three Councillors depending upon geographical area and population.

At every level of local government the chairman of the Council is elected annually by his fellow Councillors. In those Districts which are predominantly urban, the chairman takes the honorary title of Mayor and presides in that capacity over Council proceedings. However, the real power in all Councils is wielded by the leader of the majority political group and to a lesser extent by the chairmen of the key committees, for example, education, finance, housing, social services, etc. Most Councils have a Policy and Resources Committee (or its equivalent) which normally includes the chairmen of all the main committees and acts as a sort of 'Cabinet' for the local authority. Councillors of all political persuasions usually serve on more than one committee and the membership of committees reflects the relative strengths of the political parties in the local authority concerned. Since many local authorities are politically dominated by one party or another, this usually means that the key committees are controlled by the majority party in the particular locality.

Councillors are no more representative of the general public than are Members of Parliament. To be eligible for election, however, they must live or work in the local authority area concerned. In general, there is not a great deal of statistical evidence about their socio-economic composition. However, a survey conducted in 1964 revealed that only 12 per cent of Councillors were women, only 19 per cent were blue-collar workers and the average age was 55 years.[2] In 1977 the Robinson Report confirmed that the general characteristics of Councillors had not changed very much, since they were still predominantly male, middle-aged and middle-class.

although the proportion of women had risen slightly to 17 per cent.[3] However, in the Labour party in local government there seems to have been an increase in the number of younger Councillors, many of whom could be described as belonging to the 'new professional Left', that is, those who do white-collar jobs in the public sector or who are virtually full-time politicians living off their allowances as Councillors and sometimes working as employees of a neighbouring local authority.

Local authority officials are the other vital element in local government. In general, they assist Councillors in much the same way as civil servants assist Ministers. However, there are some significant contrasts with the civil service, especially in the fact that the key officials in local government are normally well-qualified as professionals in the particular sphere of activity in which they are engaged. For example, Chief Education Officers are often former teachers, Directors of Social Services are often former social workers and Chief Planners are often qualified planners, surveyors or architects. They can, therefore, have a considerable influence upon the policy of their local authorities by using their professional skills and experience in their work with elected Councillors.

On the other hand, the main similarity between local government officials and civil servants in central Government is that both are expected to remain politically neutral and faithfully to carry out the policies of their political masters. In local government the principal effect of such political neutrality is that most policy decisions are heavily influenced by the technical and expert advice of the officials concerned. Of course, the decisions are always taken by the Councillors, but there can be occasions when they appear to be acting as little more than the political spokesmen for the officials.

## 17.2 POWERS AND FUNCTIONS

The powers and functions of local government in England and Wales are set out in the relevant statutes and notably the 1972 Local Government Act. Such Acts specify the powers which are to be exercised by the various levels of local government and there is a clear understanding that all powers which are not statutorily designated for local authorities remain the preserve of central Government, assuming that Parliament has provided such statutory powers in the first place. Indeed, central Government is always able to modify or even abolish local government in this country, provided it has the political will to do so and the necessary majorities for the legislation in both Houses of Parliament. The distribution of local authority powers and functions is shown in tabular form in Figure 17.2.

Fig 17.2 *The distribution of local authority powers and functions*

| | *County Councils* | *District Councils* |
|---|---|---|
| *Metropolitan* | Planning: Structure planning<br>Transport planning with control of Passenger Transport Authorities<br>Some development control<br>Highways, traffic and transportation<br>Refuse disposal<br>Consumer protection<br>Fire service<br>Museums and art galleries[2]<br>Parks, open spaces[1,2]<br>Police | Education<br>Social services<br>Libraries<br>Museums and art galleries[1,2]<br>Housing<br>Planning: Most development control and local plan-making<br>Refuse collection<br>Environmental health<br>Parks, open spaces[1]<br>Coastal protection |
| *Non-Metropolitan* | Education<br>Social services<br>Libraries, museums and art galleries[2]<br>Planning: Structure planning<br>Transport planning but no responsibility for transport operation<br>Highways, traffic and transportation<br>Refuse disposal<br>Consumer protection<br>Fire service<br>Parks, open spaces[1]<br>Coastal protection[1]<br>Police | Housing<br>Planning (as Metropolitan districts)<br>Refuse collection<br>Environmental health<br>Museums and art galleries[1,2]<br>Parks, open spaces[1]<br>Coastal protection[1]<br>Municipal bus services |

*Notes*: 1 These are concurrent powers exercised by both county and district councils.
2 These services are often grouped together in Leisure Services Committees and Departments.

*Source*: H. Elcock, *Local Government* (London: Methuen, 1982).

**Statutory duties**

Local authorities are given statutory duties in Acts of Parliament. The Westminister legislation sets out what the statutory duties shall be in each case. This means that local authorities have to perform certain functions which Parliament has assigned to them and they carry out their duties in strict accordance with the terms of the legislation. For example, the 1944 Education Act stipulated that local authorities should be responsible for providing public education for all children in their areas who are within the statutory age range for school education. Equally, the 1972 Chronically

Sick and Disabled Persons Act laid statutory duties upon local authorities to provide care for all such people within their areas in the various ways prescribed in the legislation. Even when the statutes provide some latitude for local authorities as to exactly how they should carry out their statutory duties, subsequent advice and circulars from central Government usually ensure that minimum standards of provision are set.

**Discretionary powers**

Local authorities are also given discretionary powers in Acts of Parliament. Once again the Westminster legislation sets out in each case the areas and the extent to which such powers may be exercised. This means that local authorities are endowed with discretionary powers to provide certain services, provided they wish to do so and assuming they can raise the necessary finance. For example, the 1969 Children and Young Persons Act gave local authorities the discretionary powers to do all sorts of caring and compassionate things for young people in trouble, but failed to make the necessary extra financial provision without which it has proved effectively impossible to implement large sections of the Act. Indeed, far from being chastened by this experience, many local authorities have urged central Government to give them various discretionary powers in other sectors of provision for which they are statutorily responsible, so that they can improve their chances of making economies and so remain within the financial limits set by central Government. Thus the discretionary powers, which used to be seen as a way of extending local provision of national services, are now regarded by many local authorities as a convenient way of saving money, since they allow them to reduce or withdraw such services.

**Division of functions**

At the time of writing the six Metropolitan authorities outside Greater London have statutory responsibilities for transport, highways, police, fire services, Court administration, overspill housing, strategic planning, consumer protection and refuse disposal.[4] The thirty-six Metropolitan District authorities outside Greater London have statutory responsibilities for education, public libraries, personal social services, housing, local planning, environmental health, minor roads, licensing of public houses and places of entertainment, and the registration of births, marriages and deaths. The two levels of local government in the Metropolitan areas share responsibilities for museums and art galleries, parks and open spaces, municipal swimming baths, regional airports and land acquired for development. However, in practice most of these tasks are performed at the lower level.

In the non-Metropolitan areas the County Councils have the same statutory responsibilities as the Metropolitan authorities, but with the addition of education, public libraries and personal social services. This leaves the non-Metropolitan District authorities with the same responsibilities as the Metropolitan Districts, although without education, public libraries and personal social services.

Assuming the present Government's proposals for reorganising local government in Greater London and the other Metropolitan authorities come into effect in April 1986, it is envisaged that the Borough and District Councils will take on the vast majority of the functions now provided by the Metropolitan authorities and that only police, fire services, education (in inner London) and public transport will be transferred to statutory joint Boards, while the few remaining functions (for example, land drainage and flood protection and some arts sponsorship) will be transferred to other existing public bodies.[5]

## 17.3 RELATIONS WITH CENTRAL GOVERNMENT

The relations between local and central Government have seldom been easy or unambiguously defined. In the nineteenth century there was a lengthy search for a system of local government which would be both efficient and democratic, although not necessarily for a relationship designed to be mutually beneficial. Throughout the twentieth century there have been notable occasions when the usual habits of co-operation between local and central government have broken down and thus given rise to serious misunderstanding and conflict. In general, however, local authorities have faithfully performed their statutory duties and acted in accordance with the statutory constraints laid upon them by Parliament.[6]

### Constitutional relations

The constitutional relations between local and central government in Britain have varied greatly over the centuries. Between 1688 and 1835 the effective independence of local government could hardly have been greater, since there was virtually no central Government interference or control. On the other hand, since the 1835 Municipal Corporations Act the power and influence of central Government has grown steadily and there has been an apparently remorseless tendency towards the centralisation of power. However, this should not be thought surprising in a unitary state, such as Britain, in which all the legal power of local government has always derived from Acts of Parliament and in which local government has had to rely largely upon local elections and local pride to buttress its sense of legitimacy in dealing with central Government.

Today the constitutional relationship between local and central government is described by Ministers as a partnership and by Councillors, occasionally, as almost a central dictatorship. In Whitehall and Westminster not much more than lip-service is paid to the idea of partnership, partly because local authorities are often controlled by local politicians from the Opposition parties but mainly because local government is dependent upon central Government for about half its income and, indeed, for its very existence in constitutional terms.

There is, therefore, a paradoxical aspect to the relationship between local and central government which is explained partly by the historical fact that until modern times virtually all civil government in Britain was local government (for example, through Justices of the Peace), partly by the important tradition that national services should be provided locally, and partly by the tendency for central Government to act via the agency of local government rather than directly via its own regional and local organisation. It might have been more logical and sensible to have clear-cut statements and constitutional rules about the division of powers and responsibilities between local and central government. Yet as Professor Day has argued, 'the British political system is not one which readily accepts polar solutions and in the event some compromise (between local and central government) is likely'.[7] In this case the compromise which has been reached is to accord to local government a clearly subordinate position in its constitutional relationship with central Government, while recognising its co-ordinate position with central Government in the practical working of the day-to-day relationships which require co-operation and partnership.

**Political relations**

Political relations between local and central government have not been easy in modern times, since they are often characterised by inherent conflicts of interest and incompatible political objectives. The ambivalence of the relationship was well described by P. G. Richards when he wrote that 'Ministers tend to speak in terms of partnership (with local government) when they want to be tactful and in terms of principal and agent whenever they wish to enforce a particular policy'.[8] Of course, there will always be tension in a relationship which depends upon mutual understanding and co-operation between unequal partners. Yet the relationship is bound to become more difficult in a period of financial constraint when disputes cannot be settled on a basis of differential expansion, and not least because many local authorities are under the political control of the main Opposition party.

However, even in difficult economic circumstances the partnership between local and central government is supposed to involve some sharing of decision-making powers. Yet most people in local government would probably agree with N. P. Hepworth when he observed that 'local government does not share in the decision-making of central Government; it makes representations, but that is not the same thing'.[9] On the other hand, from the point of view of central Government the partnership does seem quite real in that many aspects of central Government policy depend for their successful implementation upon the active co-operation of local government. For example, overall public expenditure restraint is vitally dependent upon local government co-operation at a time when local authorities account for about one-quarter of total public spending. Equally, many of the statutory obligations placed upon local government by Parliament are couched in broad terms of principle which leave the precise methods of implementation very much in the hands of local authorities, not to mention the discretionary powers which depend entirely upon local authority decisions. Furthermore, the local authorities have learned to combine in order to maximise their influence upon central Government. They do this through their representative bodies - that is, the Association of Metropolitan Authorities, the Association of County Councils and the Association of District Councils - and in financial matters through the Consultative Council on Local Government Finance.

While the relationship between local and central government is reasonably clear-cut in constitutional terms, it is rather ambiguous and uncertain in political terms. Neither level of government can really afford to alienate the other and neither can achieve all its objectives without the co-operation of the other. Local government depends heavily upon central Government for financial support, while central Government depends heavily upon local government for the local administration of national services. Thus the two partners are usually obliged to co-operate in spite of their different interests and priorities.

## 17.4 METHODS OF CENTRAL CONTROL

There are four principal methods by which central Government seeks to control local government. Of these financial control is the most important, but we shall consider the others first.

### Legislative control

It is the legislative control in Acts of Parliament which establishes the nature and extent of the subordinate powers conferred upon local government. As J.A.G. Griffith has explained, 'within the terms on which these powers are bestowed, local authorities are autonomous bodies and a Department (of central Government) which proposes to control the way in which or the extent to which local authorities exercise their powers must be able to point to statutory provisions authorising this intervention.'[10] Thus legislative control provides legal safeguards for local government as well as a means of control for central Government.

Such legislative control can take various forms. In many cases the original legislation confers upon Ministers the power to make detailed regulations which are binding upon local government. For example, it is customary for Whitehall to issue Statutory Instruments which set out the building regulations to be observed in the construction of buildings and the planning regulations to be observed in carrying out local developments. In some cases local authorities are given power to make by-laws about public footpaths and other minor matters, but it is always made clear in the original Westminster legislation that these must be confirmed by the relevant Minister. Of course, this legislative control involves two-way influence and communication, since the representative bodies of local government are usually fully consulted in the preparation of Westminster legislation which affects local authorities.

**Policy control**

Another form of central control is provided by the power and influence of Government policy. This can take various forms, depending upon the priorities of the party in office and the legal basis of the relationship between local authorities and the different Departments of central Government. For example, the 1948 Children Act and the 1969 Children and Young Persons Act both stipulated that local authorities should exercise their statutory functions in this area under the guidance of the relevant Ministers, which has meant in effect the policy pursued by the Government of the day. Similarly, the Secretary of State for Education and Science has a supervisory and promotional role in relation to the organisation of schools and the supply of teachers in all the local education authorities of England and Wales. This power derives from the 1944 Education Act, but it has been exercised by successive Governments in accordance with their own educational policies.

Another example of policy control by Ministers and Whitehall Departments can be found in the sphere of housing policy in which successive Conservative Governments have promoted policies of extended home ownership and home improvement, while successive Labour Governments have promoted policies of rent control and public sector house building. In ways such as these the policy of the Government of the day can have a considerable influence upon the behaviour of local authorities. Sometimes it leads to bitter conflict between the two levels of government, but at the end of the day it is central Government which has the whip hand.

**Administrative control**

Administrative control is another form of central control which derives from central Government's responsibility for setting national standards and promoting efficiency in local government. Ever since the nineteenth century it has been accepted that many functions of government in Britain should be national services locally administered. This has always implied the need for administrative control via national standards monitored by central Government civil servants and by powerful, independent Inspectorates. For example, in the case of education there is regular supervision of local education authorities by the officials of HM Inspectorate of Education. In the case of the police, the payment of central Government grants to police authorities is conditional upon satisfactory reports from the officials of HM Inspectorate of Constabulary.

Even wider powers of administrative control are available to the Department of the Environment under Section 5 of the 1972 Local Government Act. This allows the Secretary of State, subject only to an affirmative resolution of the House of Commons, to reduce the amount of rate support grant to a local authority if he is convinced that it has failed to achieve or maintain a reasonable standard in the discharge of any of its statutory functions. To date this particular power has not had to be used. Yet it remains a formidable reserve power available to central Government if and when a local authority were to default upon any of its statutory obligations.

Although the range and power of administrative controls exercised by central Government over local authorities has become increasingly formidable over the years, there has been a countervailing tendency during the Thatcher Government for Whitehall to seek to reduce the number and scope of such controls as a gesture of goodwill to local authorities and a way of assisting them to reduce their administrative costs. The 1979-83 Conservative Government believed that by freeing local authorities from many forms of detailed supervision and administrative control, it would be possible for them to perform their statutory duties in a more cost-effective way. Indeed, there were provisions in the 1980 Local Government Planning and Land Act designed for precisely that purpose.

**Financial control**

The most powerful form of central control is the financial control exercised by central Government. This can be traced back at least to the 1929 Local Government Act in which the earlier system of assigned revenues was abolished and replaced with a system of specific grants, together with a block grant from central Government to individual local authorities. In 1948 this was supplemented by a system of deficiency payments to those local authorities with rateable values below the average. In 1958 the entire array of complicated financial mechanisms was rationalised and the overall Rate Support Grant (RSG) was introduced. This largely replaced the former variety of specific grants with a new general grant to individual local authorities which was calculated on the basis of needs, resources and domestic elements. Further legislation in 1963 permitted individual local authorities to raise an additional rate of up to 1p in the £ for specific local purposes, if they chose to do so. This was increased to 2p in the £ by the 1972 Local Government Act.

Since the early 1970s there have been various half-hearted attempts to find ways of diminishing central Government control of local government finance in order to secure more genuine autonomy for local authorities. However, all such attempts have fallen foul of Treasury determination not to relax its control over any significant portion of public spending or national revenue and the determination of most Governments not to add new local taxes to the overall burden of existing taxation. Thus local authorities have had to rely upon three different and not wholly satisfactory sources of revenue: central Government support via the Rate Support Grant and a few specific grants; local rates on domestic, commercial and industrial premises; and local income from rents, fees and charges for some local government services. All too often local authorities have been caught in a vice between public expectations of constant improvements in the provision of local services and ratepayer hostility to the extra financial burdens which that implies.

The whole question of local government finance was examined by the Layfield Committee in the mid-1970s. This concluded that the main shortcoming in the system was the lack of clear accountability for local government spending.[11] Its principal recommendation was that the financing of local government should be recast on the basis of a prior political choice about the broad direction in which the relationship between local and central government should be developed. Most of the committee favoured a move towards greater local responsibility by supplementing the rates with local income tax raised by the major spending authorities. However, the Labour Government of the day responded to the report by denying that it was necessary to choose clearly between the centralist and localist approaches and so an opportunity for thoroughgoing reform was missed.[12]

In general, local authorities are obliged to raise from local rates on domestic, commercial and industrial premises in their areas the revenue which they need to cover their estimated expenditure on local government services, having taken account of their grants from central Government and their local income from rents, fees and charges. Under the 1980 Local Government Planning and Land Act the Government sought to introduce a better framework for the distribution and control of public funds for local government. To do this it decided to introduce block grants paid to every local authority and it argued that such a change in the system of central Government financial control had three main objectives.

One objective of the change was to ensure that all local authorities of the same kind (for instance, Shire Counties, London Boroughs, etc.) should be able to provide a similar standard of local services if they levied a similar rate in the pound. Another objective of the change was to escape reliance upon past expenditure as a measure of need and to base such measurements upon so-called Grant Related Expenditure Assessments (GREAs) for each local authority which were intended to provide an objective view of the costs of typical standards of local service. A third objective of the change was that while the new system was supposed to discourage local authorities from overspending by progressively reducing the level of central Government grant if a local authority's spending rose significantly above its GREA levels, it would not reduce the freedom of local authorities to determine their own priorities within their financial resources.

Under the 1982 Local Government Finance Act the Thatcher Government went one stage further in its policy of tightening the financial controls upon local authorities. This Act prevented local authorities from raising supplementary rates and precepts during the course of the financial year and subjected their activities to further financial scrutiny by the newly-established Audit Commission. The present Conservative Government has introduced further legislation to curb excessive rate increases by individual local authorities and to provide a general reserve power for the limitation of rate increases by all local authorities.[13] This latest addition to the panoply of central Government financial controls will come into operation in the summer of 1984 and affect the rate-setting of the local authorities concerned for the financial year 1985–6.

Rates, which are a particularly unpopular form of taxation with those who have to pay them, are assessed on the rateable value of the land or buildings concerned (although agricultural land and buildings are exempt). In theory, they represent the rent at which the property could be let (if there were a market for such lettings), less the notional cost of repairs, insurance and other maintenance expenses. Rates are paid every year (normally in two or more instalments) and the abstruse calculations upon which they are based are made about every ten years by the Inland Revenue on the basis of revaluations which take account of inflation and any housing improvements made over the intervening period. Although rates are an unpopular form of taxation, it has never been easy to identify a better way of raising large sums of revenue from local sources without recourse to major changes involving either a shortfall of national revenue or the introduction of new forms of taxation which would compromise other policy objectives.[14]

The financial support of local government by central Government is achieved mainly through the system of central grants to local authorities. These revenue grants take two main forms. Firstly, there are specific grants in aid of particular local purposes, for example 50 per cent of local police expenditure or 90 per cent of mandatory student grants or housing subsidies for poorer tenants. Secondly, there are general grants to the rate funds of individual local authorities in order to increase their overall income, notably in those parts of the country with a poor rateable base. The present system of annual rate support grants was introduced in 1958 and refined in 1966. Until recently financial support of this kind has been constantly adjusted upwards to meet a growing proportion of increasing local authority expenditure. However, that tendency was reversed by the 1979-83 Conservative Government which reduced the average proportion of local authority expenditure borne by central Government from 61 per cent to 52 per cent, and by the present Government which has reduced it still further to about 49 per cent in 1985-6.

The total amount of Rate Support Grant is fixed every year by the Department of the Environment in co-operation with the Treasury and after consultation with the various local authority Associations and the Consultative Council on Local Government Finance. It is supposed to take account of all the relevant factors in local authority finance. It is composed of a needs element assessed for each local authority mainly on the basis of demographic factors, a resources element paid to those local authorities where the rateable base is below the national average, and a domestic element designed to bring some relief to all domestic ratepayers. The most notable results of the system have been a bias in favour of income redistribution from the richer to the poorer parts of the country and considerable power for central Government in its ability to switch or withhold grants from individual local authorities.

The other main form of central government financial control is achieved by the use of Treasury loan sanctions to control all local authority capital expenditure above a certain low threshold. Consent for local authorities to borrow is given in Circulars from the Department of the Environment, some of which provide for automatic loan sanctions for certain key projects and others of which depend upon the local authorities concerned staying within the limits of block-borrowing approval accorded to them each year by Whitehall. In the past local authority borrowing has come from a variety of sources, notably the Public Works Loans Board, the domestic bond market and (for a period in the 1960s) the Euro-currency markets. However, in all cases local authority access to such sources of borrowing has been regulated by the Treasury and the Bank of England.

The 1979-83 Conservative Government introduced a system of capital allocations in an attempt to keep an even tighter rein upon local authority borrowing as part of its overall policy of monetary control. Specifically, the 1980 Local Government Planning and Land Act enabled central Government to control all local authority capital expenditure, whether financed by borrowing or from various revenue sources.

Sensible solutions to the problems of local government finance are hard to find. The sphere of local government is both too diverse and too significant for the problems to be solved satisfactorily in a piecemeal or *ad hoc* manner. With local authorities spending about £32 000m a year in 1983-4 and employing about 2.5m people, their financial impact upon the concerns of central Government is bound to be considerable.

Over the last decade or so relations between local and central government have gone through a difficult phase. Before that local authority spending had grown steadily and usually at a faster rate than the economy as a whole. This was bearable when the British economy was expanding at about 3 per cent a year. However, since the financial crisis in 1976 successive Governments of both major parties have felt it necessary to impose tight constraints upon all forms of public spending. In such difficult economic circumstances the relations between local and central government have become notably strained and the financial problems have not been made any easier by sharp party political differences.

The financial problems of local government have also been made more piquant by the fact that it is legislation proposed by central Government and passed by Parliament which imposes all the statutory duties and most of the financial burdens upon local government. Yet this has often happened when much of the political rhetoric at Westminister (especially from Opposition parties) has apparently been in support of greater local autonomy for local government. When faced with such conflicting interests and tendencies, it is not easy for any Government to solve the problems inherent in its relations with local authorities. To do so, it will probably be necessary to move decisively either in the direction of greater local autonomy for local government or in the direction of greater centralised control for central Government. It appears as if the present Government has made the latter choice, although the longer-term future remains unclear. Whatever happens, it seems certain that the relationship between local and central Government will continue to be strained and difficult as long as it remains on its present hybrid basis.

## 17.5 **FUTURE POSSIBILITIES**

With common sense and goodwill on both sides it should be possible in future to maintain conditions of fruitful co-operation between local and central government. However, there appear to be three basic conditions for this to be achieved. Firstly, it must be accepted by central Government that there are certain national minimum standards for most of the national services provided by local authorities. Secondly, it must be accepted by both local and central government that local authorities are best placed to provide most of the public services which people now expect. Thirdly, it must be accepted by all involved in local and central government that the relationship between the two can only work satisfactorily on a basis of mutual respect and partnership. Even if these three conditions are fulfilled, there will still be some formidable problems for both partners.

**Possibilities for change**

In future there may be some possibilities for change, most of which would have the effect of enhancing the position of local government in Britain. However, only Parliament can make such changes and the present tendency in central Government seems to be in the opposite direction.

Some people have argued that the revenue base of local government should be broadened by introducing new forms of taxation, such as a poll tax or a local sales tax or local income tax. Others have argued that domestic rates should be replaced by assigned revenues from existing national taxation. Others have argued that the costs of education, which are about 50 per cent of all local authority net current expenditure, should be taken over by central Government or that there should be a separate block grant for education. Others have suggested that the revenue from vehicle excise duty or road fuel duty should be made available to local government. However, all the consultations on local government finance have shown that there is no consensus upon a satisfactory alternative to the rates, which is why the present Conservative Government has reluctantly decided to retain the present system.

The present system of local government finance has also been criticised because industrial and commercial ratepayers, who contribute nearly three-fifths of local authority rate income, have no right to vote in local government elections and only a limited influence on local politics. However, suggestions that the 'business vote' should be returned to those who own property in areas where they are not resident (as was the case before 1969) have not found favour with the present Conservative Government. Instead the Government proposes to place a new statutory duty on local authorities to consult representatives of industry and commerce before fixing their rates or precepts every year.

Among the more far-reaching ideas occasionally put forward is the proposal that the electoral system for local elections should be changed from first-past-the-post to one of proportional representation, so that local government should reflect more fully the range of political opinion in the various parts of the country and to diminish the risk of abrupt changes of local policy when one party succeeds another in majority control of a local authority. Another far-reaching idea occasionally mentioned is that the democratic organisation of local authorities should be changed from the present pattern of functional committees to one based upon directly elected chief executives, as is the case in France or the United States. However, such ideas would involve further fundamental reform of local government and therefore have very limited appeal to the major political parties which have already had their fingers burned by previous attempts at ambitious structural reform.

A simpler idea, which has been canvassed for some time, is that the structure of local government should be reduced to a single tier of unitary authorities responsible for both local spending and local revenue raising. It is argued that this would simplify the structure of local government, be more efficient in managerial terms and introduce a more direct form of political accountability. To some extent these objectives will be achieved with the implementation of the present Government's proposed legislation to abolish the Greater London Council and the six other Metropolitan Councils. However, there will still be two tiers of local government in the shire counties and it remains to be seen whether the proposed new structure for the conurbations will be effective.

In general, central Government will probably be wise not to propose new legislation which puts additional statutory duties upon local authorities, unless it can guarantee to provide the extra financial resources to enable local authorities to bear the extra financial burdens. In theory, central Government ensures that any new obligations placed upon local authorities by statute or otherwise are taken into account in the financial arrangements for local government. Yet in practice the position of local government is not fully safeguarded, since local authorities are finding it very difficult to finance their existing functions and responsibilities, let alone to take on new ones.

For their part, those involved in local government will need to modify their attitudes towards the conduct of their relations with central Government. Since Britain is a unitary state, local councillors of all parties will need to remember that although they are accountable to their local electorates, they derive their legal powers from Parliament. This means that their partnership with central Government will not work smoothly unless they take full account of the wider consequences of their actions for the economic welfare of the nation as a whole.

### Local autonomy or centralisation

The relationship between local and central government also has to be considered in the light of broader arguments for greater local autonomy on the one hand and greater centralisation on the other. The arguments in favour of greater local autonomy include the need to diminish the remoteness of government from ordinary people, the desirability of enhancing democratic accountability at local level, the opportunities which could be created for greater public participation, the greater efficiency of smaller units in public administration, and the reduced financial burden upon the national Exchequer. The arguments in favour of greater centralisation include the need for common national standards of public provision, the uniformity of public expectations as to what local government should provide, the attractions for Ministers and civil servants of a more direct and reliable form of control over the localities and the political opportunity which this might provide for abolishing the rates.

With so many tendencies in British society today working in favour of greater national homogeneity and even uniformity, there is obviously a strong case for more local autonomy. As Professors Jones and Stewart have argued, greater autonomy should be encouraged 'not to let loose rampant and uncontrolled localism and the sharpening of geographical inequalities, but to maintain a more balanced array of pressures in public policy making'.[15]

With the increasing politicisation of local government, it seems likely that central Government will be drawn to interfere more and more with the activities of local authorities. This is because the battles of local politics are often the stuff of national politics as well, for example, the imposition of comprehensive education by a Labour Government or the granting of a statutory right for Council tenants to buy their homes by a Conservative Government. It is also because central Government cannot usually afford to allow local authorities to disrupt or undermine national policies, such as the firm control of all forms of public spending by a Conservative Government or the deliberate extension of local authority direct labour departments by a Labour Government. Indeed, in our unitary state it would be naive to suppose that local government could ever be fully insulated from the political battle at national level.

It is possible, however, that greater clarity could be achieved by defining more precisely the boundaries of national and local responsibilities and by distinguishing more clearly between the public spending for which central and local government are respectively accountable. This was one of the objectives of the 1972 Local Government Act and one of the main themes of the 1976 Layfield Report. Yet it has proved difficult to put fully into practice, not only because the Treasury has been notoriously reluctant to relinquish its ultimate control of local authority finance, but also because there is no codified constitution and Supreme Court in this country to regulate such a formal separation of powers and responsibilities.

If the trend towards greater centralisation is really inexorable, it would be wise for national politicians to recognise it and cease paying lip-service to the shibboleth of local autonomy. On the other hand, if national politicians really want to reverse this trend, it will require their acceptance of the freedom for local government to take decisions in its defined spheres of which they may not approve. Of course, this can and does happen now. However, the position of local government would be more secure if there were to be a new constitutional settlement designed, among other things, to order the relationship between local and central government in a more lasting and satisfactory way.

## 17.6 CONCLUSION

It should be clear from this chapter that the position of local government in Britain is neither immutable nor easy to describe. However, it can be assessed in terms of its efficiency, its vitality, its adaptability and its capacity for genuine partnership with central Government. We shall, therefore, conclude by considering each of these aspects in turn.

With regard to the efficiency of local government, it seems clear that the present division of functions is fairly sensible and does not put such a high premium upon the interests of local democracy that the interests of efficiency are unduly compromised. Furthermore, the emphasis upon techniques of corporate management within local authorities and the discipline of tough financial limits set by central Government also seem to have had a positive effect upon the efficiency of local government.

With regard to the vitality of local government, the available evidence is somewhat contradictory. On the one hand, the normal turn-out at local elections is seldom more than about 40-50 per cent of those entitled to vote and at local by-elections it sometimes falls below 30 per cent. This suggests rather scant public interest in the democratic procedures of local government. On the other hand, even a cursory glance at the local press in any part of the country reveals considerable public interest in the actual decisions and policy output of local government. For example, ratepayers are usually very interested in seeing that economies are secured in local authority spending, while beneficiary groups usually favour the expansion of existing services or the creation of new ones. Public interest is also reflected in the volume of correspondence sent to Members of Parliament and Councillors about local authority matters.

With regard to the adaptability of local government, the record over the years has been quite good. However, during the recent period of economic recession when many social needs have increased, the financial resources made available to local authorities by central Government have had to be curtailed. The response of local authorities to this financial squeeze has often depended upon the political priorities of the majority group on the Council concerned. Yet it also appears that local Councillors of all parties resent the financial restrictions imposed by central Government and would like to see changes in the present system of local authority finance which would alleviate their problems.

As for the ability of local government to maintain a genuine partnership with central Government, this has been determined partly by the diminishing extent to which it has retained responsibilities for important areas of public service provision, but mainly by its failure to secure any real measure of financial autonomy. On the former point, local authorities have tended to lose rather than gain functions over the period since the last war. For example, in 1948 they lost control of local hospitals and in 1974 they lost control of personal health services and public water supply. In each case responsibility for the provision of the services was transferred to functional authorities over which local Councillors had little influence and no real control. On the latter point, local authorities have had diminishing financial freedom as the scope and cost of public services has grown and the need for overall public expenditure restraint has been deemed more acute. Until the late 1970s their income from rates and other local sources of revenue covered on average less than two-fifths of their so-called relevant expenditure. Although this balance has shifted and local authorities will cover (in 1985-6) on average 51 per cent of their relevant expenditure from rates and other local revenue sources, it is still hard to argue that they have much financial autonomy. It is, therefore, even harder to demonstrate that they maintain a genuine partnership with central Government.

Even allowing for such problems and shortcomings, local government in Britain has several positive points in its favour. Its diversity contributes to political pluralism. Its institutions offer spheres of political activity to a considerable number of elected Councillors. It stimulates public interest in the local provision of national services. It provides a political and institutional counterweight to Whitehall and Westminster. All in all such attributes should not be underestimated or ignored in what is otherwise a unitary political state and a homogeneous political system.

## SUGGESTED QUESTIONS

1. Describe the structure of local government in the United Kingdom.
2. What are the conditions for a genuine partnership between central and local government?
3. Are the methods of central control consistent with the aspirations for local autonomy?

## NOTES

1. See 'Streamlining the Cities', Cmnd 9063 (London: HMSO, 1983).
2. Report of the committee on the management of local government (London: HMSO, 1967).
3. Report on the remuneration of local councillors, vol. 2 (London: HMSO, 1977).
4. The statutory responsibilities of the Greater London Council are planning, highways and traffic management, waste regulation and disposal, housing, trading standards and related functions, support for the arts, sport and historic buildings, the fire service, education (in inner London), public transport, land drainage and flood protection. It also has statutory powers to make grants to voluntary bodies, to give assistance to industry, to spend up to the product of a 2p rate in the interests of its area and generally to represent the interests of Greater London as a whole.
5. The functions due to be transferred to the Borough and District Councils are planning, highways and traffic management, waste regulation and disposal, housing, trading standards and related functions, support for the arts, sport and historic buildings, civil defence and emergencies, support funding for the Magistrates' Courts and the probation service, coroners, school-crossing patrols, building control, tourism, licensing of places of entertainment, archives and libraries, recreation, parks and Green Belt land, safety of sports grounds, registration of common land and town or village greens, maps etc. in relation to rights of way and gypsy sites.
6. See K. B. Smellie, *History of Local Government* (London: Allen & Unwin, 1968) for a more detailed account.
7. Quoted in 'Local Government Finance', Cmnd 6453 (London: HMSO, 1976) p. 302.
8. P. G. Richards, *The Reformed Local Government System* (London: Allen & Unwin, 1973) p. 166.
9. N. P. Hepworth, *The Finance of Local Government* 4th edn (London: Allen & Unwin, 1978) p. 255.
10. J. A. G. Griffith, *Central Departments & Local Authorities* (London: Allen & Unwin, 1966) p. 49.
11. See 'Local Government Finance', Cmnd 6453 (London: HMSO, 1976).
12. See 'Local Government Finance', Cmnd 6813 (London, HMSO, 1977).
13. See 'Rates', Cmnd 9008 (London: HMSO, 1983).
14. See 'Alternatives to Domestic Rates', Cmnd 8449 (London: HMSO, 1981) for a fuller discussion of these issues.
15. *The Times*, 14 August 1981.

# FURTHER READING

Boaden, N. T., *Urban Policy Making* (Cambridge: Cambridge University Press, 1971).
Byrne, T., *Local Government in Britain* (Harmondsworth: Penguin, 1981).
Cross, M. and Mallen, D., *Local Government and Politics* (London: Longman, 1978).
Elcock, H., *Local Government* (London: Methuen, 1982).
Foster, C. D. *et al.*, *Local Government Finance in a Unitary State* (London: Allen & Unwin, 1980).
Griffith, J. A. G., *Central Departments and Local Authorities* (London: Allen & Unwin, 1966).
Hepworth, N. P., *The Finance of Local Government*, 4th edn (London: Allen & Unwin, 1978).
Redcliffe-Maud, J. and Wood, B., *English Local Government Reformed* (Oxford: Oxford University Press, 1974).
Rhodes, R. A. W., *Research into Central–Local Relations in Britain* (Colchester, Essex University, 1979).
Richards, P. G., *The Local Government System* (London: Allen & Unwin, 1983).
Smellie, K. B., *History of Local Government* (London: Allen & Unwin, 1968).
Stanyer, J., *Understanding Local Government* (London: Fontana, 1976).

CHAPTER 18

# THE LAW AND THE JUDICIARY

There are five main aspects of the judicial system in Britain. There is the sphere of criminal justice which involves the application of the criminal law to cases brought to Court mainly by the police. There is the sphere of civil justice which involves the application of the civil law to cases brought by various plaintiffs, including individuals, corporate bodies and the law officers of the Crown. There is the process of judicial appeal which allows those who are dissatisfied with the verdicts of lower Courts or Tribunals to seek redress or reversal of judgement in the higher Courts of appeal. There is the important sphere of civil rights and duties which determines the complex legal relationship between citizens and the state. There is the sphere of administrative law which involves the quasi-judicial procedures of the various administrative Tribunals and the judicial review of administrative action. We shall consider each of these aspects in turn in this chapter.

## 18.1 CRIMINAL JUSTICE

### Machinery and procedure

The majority of criminal cases are disposed of in Magistrates' Courts and only a minority are tried in the higher Courts. Trial in a Magistrates' Court is summary (that is, without a jury) and takes place before a bench of two or more Justices of the Peace or one legally qualified Stipendiary Magistrate. Most cases are brought by the police who prefer charges against defendants on the basis of legal advice from their lawyers. Magistrates' Courts have original criminal jurisdiction to inquire into all matters triable on indictment and, if they deem the evidence sufficient, to commit the defendants for trial at a Crown Court.

In the minority of cases which go to Crown Courts the procedure is one of trial by jury before a High Court Judge, a Circuit Judge or a Recorder (a practising barrister or solicitor sitting in a judicial capacity). Most of the

Fig 18.1 *The system of Courts exercising criminal jurisdiction*

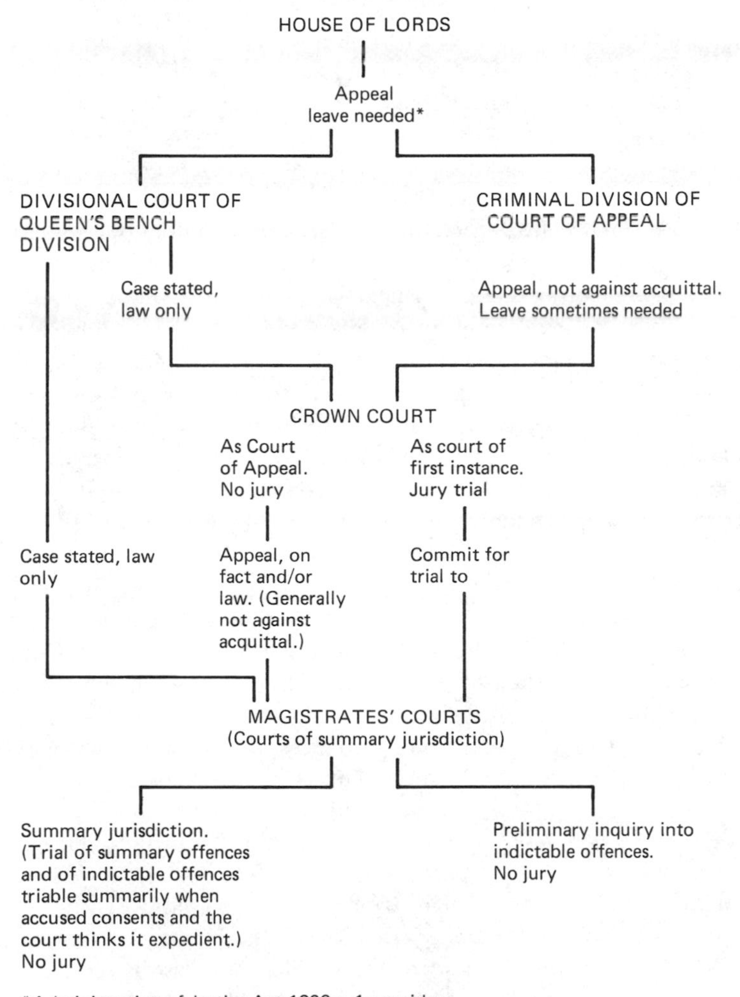


*Administration of Justice Act 1960 s. 1 provides:

(1) Subject to the provisions of this section, an appeal shall lie to the House of Lords, at the instance of the defendant or the prosecutor

(a) from any decision of a Divisional Court of the Queen's Bench Division in a criminal case or matter;

(b) from any decision of the Court of Criminal Appeal on an appeal to that court.

(2) No appeal shall lie under this section except with the leave of the court below or of the House of Lords; and such leave shall not be granted unless it is certified by the court below that a point of law of general public importance is involved in the decision and it appears to that court or to the House of Lords, as the case may be that the point is one which ought to be considered by that House.

Source: R. M. Jackson, *The Machinery of Justice in England*, 7th edition (London: Cambridge University Press, 1977).

more serious criminal cases are committed automatically to the Crown Courts, although even in less serious cases the defendant can opt for trial by jury in a Crown Court rather than summary trial in a Magistrates' Court. In only a few rare cases is the old-fashioned practice still used whereby Magistrates only commit a case to a Crown Court after conducting a preliminary examination of the evidence to see whether such a step is justified.

The most serious cases (murder, rape, armed robbery, etc.) must be tried by a High Court Judge. Other serious cases (manslaughter, serious assault, etc.) are usually tried by a High Court Judge, but sometimes released to a Circuit Judge or a Recorder. Cases which involve lesser indictable offences or those in which the defendants have opted for trial by jury (such as burglary, forgery, dangerous driving, etc.) are usually tried by Circuit Judges or Recorders. In all these cases the most important role of the judge is directing the jury on matters of law. However, the passing of sentence on convicted defendants has become increasingly significant in certain serious cases, since judges have been able to make specific recommendations about the length of prison sentence to be served within the maximum limits laid down in the law passed by Parliament.

**Controversial issues**

There are many controversial issues in the criminal law today. Most of them were carefully considered by the Royal Commission on Criminal Procedure which reported to Parliament in 1981.[1] They include the right of silence for criminal suspects, the exclusion of evidence improperly obtained, the definition of arrestable offences, the extent of police powers to stop and search, the limits on detention in police custody, the use of tape-recordings in the interviewing of criminal suspects and the possibility of transferring the task of criminal prosecution from the police to an independent Prosecutor's Department.

All these issues were debated, if not finally resolved, when the Police and Criminal Evidence Bill was discussed in the House of Commons in 1982–3. Although the Bill lapsed when Parliament was dissolved in May 1983, a Bill along very similar lines has been brought forward in the present Parliament. Ministers have also indicated their intention to move towards the tape-recording of police interviews with criminal suspects and the establishment of an independent Prosecutor's Department.

One of the difficulties in reaching balanced and lasting conclusions in this sphere of the law is that many of the issues raise central questions to do with the relationship between the police and the public, especially in some inner city areas where there are considerable concentrations of coloured people.[2] Another basic problem is caused by the difficulty of striking a fair and effective balance between the interests of the law-abiding majority, which wants the police and the Courts to maintain law and order in a strong and effective way, and the interests of the vociferous minorities which are usually more concerned with the protection of civil liberties and the maintenance of civil rights. Since it is always difficult to strike an appropriate balance between such clearly conflicting interests, the solution is usually sought in attempts to balance increased powers for the police and the Courts with more effective legal safeguards for the law-abiding community.

Those who are strongly committed to the maintenance of law and order have argued for changes in the criminal law and in legal procedures which would enable the police and the Courts to deal more effectively with the current levels of crime and lawlessness. Very few people have argued seriously for a more permissive attitude towards crime or more lenient procedures for dealing with convicted criminals. However, concern has been expressed by liberal-minded minorities about the large number of people sent to prison in Britain compared with other comparable countries, the need for improved procedures to deal with complaints against the police, and certain tendencies for our society to develop in an authoritarian direction wholly at variance with our common law tradition. Such issues will have to be addressed by politicians and other opinion-formers, even if it continues to be easier and more politically tempting to concentrate upon reassuring the law-and-order lobby.

## 18.2 CIVIL JUSTICE

### Machinery and procedure

Most civil cases are heard initially either in County Courts by Circuit Judges or in one of the three civil divisions of the High Court by High Court Judges. However, Magistrates' Courts have original jurisdiction in some cases involving the summary recovery of certain kinds of debt and some domestic proceedings, for example, separation and maintenance, guardianship, adoption, etc.

In the County Courts the jurisdiction is both local and limited. Such Courts deal with actions founded on the law of contract and tort where the claim of the plaintiff does not exceed a small sum (currently £5000); equity cases up to a higher value (currently £30 000) which affect trusts, mortgages and the dissolution of partnerships; most bankruptcy proceedings outside London; and actions concerning land or buildings in which the rateable value does not exceed a small sum (currently £400 a year). They also deal with matters arising from social legislation, such as the adoption of children, the validity of hire purchase agreements and disputes arising from the Rent Acts. Since 1968 all undefended divorce cases (about 90 per cent of the total) have been heard in special Courts designated as Divorce Courts and complaints of racial discrimination are heard in other specially-designated Courts. While barristers and solicitors may appear on behalf of those using these Courts, the judge often has to hear the case on the basis of submissions made by laymen. In none of these cases is there call for a jury.

In the High Court the Queen's Bench Division deals principally with actions founded upon the law of contract and tort.[3] It also deals with actions on bills of exchange, insurance claims, shipping actions and some landlord and tenant actions. Only a small proportion of the actions actually come to Court and fewer than 2 per cent of all cases are fought to a conclusion, since those involved are usually keen to avoid the high legal costs of such cases. Either party may request a trial by jury in cases involving defamation of character, malicious prosecution, false imprisonment, fraud or seduction. However, the final decision as to whether or not a jury shall try a case rests with the judge concerned. In general, the use of juries in this Division has declined to the extent that they are now summoned in only 4 per cent of all cases. Another important function performed by this Division is the supervision of the lower Courts and Tribunals. This is done by issuing prerogative orders, such as prohibition, *mandamus* and *certiorari*, as well as *habeas corpus*.[4] Whereas in former times these rights were available only to the Monarch, today they can be issued by the High Court upon application from an ordinary plaintiff.

The Chancery Division of the High Court, which was established in London in 1873, has effective jurisdiction over the estates of deceased persons, the execution of trusts, the dissolution of partnerships and the redemption or foreclosure of mortgages. In 1921 bankruptcy jurisdiction was added to its responsibilities and breach of contract can be investigated here or in the Queen's Bench Division.

The Family Division of the High Court dates from 1971 when wills and wives were separated from wrecks with which they had been lumped since 1873 when the Probate, Divorce and Admiralty Division was established.[5] Today the Division deals with all domestic and matrimonial cases, guardianship and probate. However, most of its work is concerned with divorce proceedings in an age when one in three of all marriages in this country ends this way.

**Controversial issues**

The main controversial issues in the civil law today are connected with the public image of the law and lawyers and with the costs and delays involved in going to Court. We shall, therefore, look briefly at each of these issues in turn.

It is a widely-held view among laymen that the attitudes of the legal profession and the procedures of the Courts are rather old-fashioned and

Fig 18.2 *The system of Courts exercising civil jurisdiction*

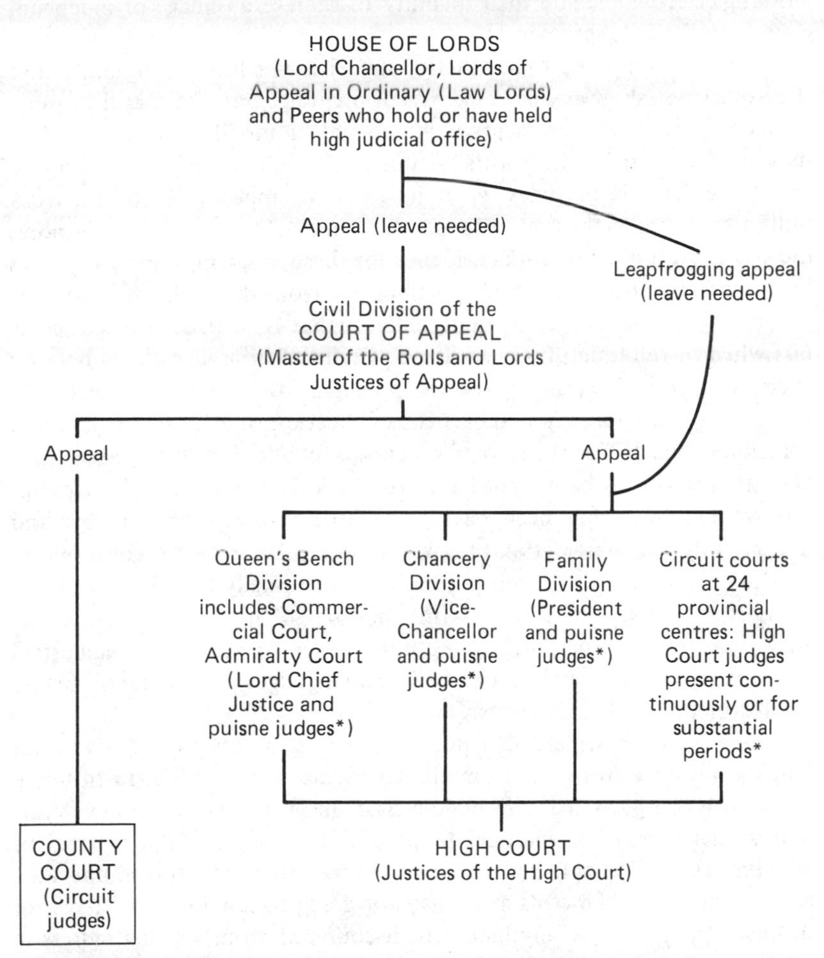


*Judges may, in accordance with Practice Directions, release a particular case to be tried by a Circuit Judge or a Recorder: these remain High Court cases.

Source: R. M. Jackson, *The Machinery of Justice in England*, 7th edition (London: Cambridge University Press, 1977).

distinctly middle class. This is especially felt about those aspects of the law which affect trade unions and local authorities. Indeed, ever since the notorious Taff Vale case in 1901, most leading trade unionists have suspected that the Judiciary is usually biased against trade unions and judicial developments over many years have not done much to dispel that suspicion. As Gavin Drewry has pointed out, 'most of the really telling criticism of lawyers centres upon their failure to win the confidence of working-class people and their inability to achieve an image of independence from the Establishment'.[6]

Judges are supposed to be strictly impartial, which means not only that they must not show any personal bias or prejudice but also that they must exclude from their judgements any political or moral views which they may hold as individuals. Naturally, this is difficult for anyone to achieve and there have been times when judges have appeared to be far from judicially neutral in the eyes of those who come before them. Furthermore, there is at least circumstantial evidence for these misgivings. Firstly, judges have tended to be drawn disproportionately from the ranks of the upper and middle classes and to be quite elderly (that is, with an average age of 60) when in full-time office. As J.A.G. Griffith has argued, 'they have by their education and training and the pursuit of their profession as barristers acquired a strikingly homogeneous collection of attitudes, beliefs and principles which to them represents the public interest.'[7] Secondly, Griffith and others have argued that the judicial conception of the public interest has invariably been based upon the interests of the state and and notably the preservation of law and order, the protection of property and the promotion of certain political views normally associated with the Conservative party. In so far as this may be so, it is not surprising that there are people, especially among minority groups and other embattled sections of the community, who believe that judges are inherently biased against them and their interests.

There is also a widely-held public view that access to the law is not equally available to people from all classes and walks of life. In this connection it is argued that the middle-class image of the law and lawyers deters many poor or inarticulate people from seeking the services of lawyers. To such people legal procedures very often seem too complicated and arcane, while the costs and delays of going to law loom too large for ordinary people to be anything but discouraged from seeking redress in the Courts.

Admittedly, it has been possible to get legal aid in civil proceedings ever since 1926 when the so-called poor persons' procedure was adopted by the Law Society and especially since the 1949 Legal Aid and Advice Act. However, the extent of legal aid available to any litigant has been limited by two tests: (i) whether a solicitor, apart from the consideration of costs, would advise going to Court in a particular case and (ii) whether the applicant falls within the prescribed means-tested limits for legal aid. The effect of these two provisions over the years has been to exclude quite a large number of fairly poor people from the benefits of legal aid, to penalise those who might otherwise want legal representation when appearing before administrative Tribunals and to put at a disadvantage successful litigants who are not legally aided when other parties are legally aided.

Of course, there are other forms of free legal advice available to people – for example, neighbourhood law centres, Citizens' Advice Bureaux and even Members of Parliament – but there still remains a large potential demand for legal aid which probably goes unsatisfied. This situation seems unlikely to change for as long as there is considerable political hostility to the idea of encouraging litigation and to the inevitable extra burden upon public expenditure which such a policy would entail.[8]

Finally, the delays of the judicial system in Britain can be ascribed very largely to the continuation of the adversary procedure in Court and the traditional insistence upon oral evidence in preference to written evidence in most judicial proceedings. These problems have been mitigated to some extent by improvements in the procedure of small claims Courts – for example, the 1973 Administration of Justice Act. Yet further progress in this direction is likely to be curtailed by the limited scope for enlarging the admissibility of written evidence, at any rate in all cases where the evidence is the subject of serious dispute.

## 18.3 **JUDICIAL APPEAL**

### Machinery and procedure

The process of judicial appeal in Britain can be applied to cases of criminal and civil law. Most of the criminal appeals are heard by the criminal division of the Court of Appeal. This is presided over by the Lord Chief Justice or a Lord Justice of Appeal. Queen's Bench judges sit with the Appeal Court judges and there are usually three judges on the bench. When a case raises an issue of general public importance, a further appeal may be made to the House of Lords, but in criminal cases such appeals are rare.

Most of the civil appeals are heard by the Master of the Rolls and the Lord Justices of Appeal, although the Lord Chancellor, the Lord Chief Justice and a few other very senior legal figures may sit *ex officio* in exceptional circumstances. An odd number of judges (usually three) hears the appeals and decisions of the Court are taken by majority.

On important points of law of wider application there is the possibility of further appeal to the House of Lords. Such appeals are made to the Appellate Committee which is the final court of appeal and which can only be overruled by Parliament as a whole passing new legislation. The work of the Appellate Committee is done by the Lord Chancellor, ten Law Lords and a few other very senior legal figures who may sit by virtue of having previously held high judicial office. The Committee is usually made up of five Law Lords and their judgements take the form of motions with each judge expressing his judicial opinion on the matter in question. Until 1966 it was customary for the Committee to reach its decisions entirely on the basis of judicial precedents, but since then it has been prepared occasionally to depart from this principle when it appears right to do so.

Mention should also be made of the Judicial Committee of the Privy Council which was established by statute in 1833. This hears appeals on cases authorised by the Courts in the Isle of Man and the Channel Islands, in Britain's remaining colonial Dependencies and in those member states of the Commonwealth which have chosen to retain the right of direct appeal to it.[9] It also hears appeals from Admiralty Courts, ecclesiastical Courts and the disciplinary committees of the General Medical Council and the Dental Council. The Lord Chancellor is nominally its President, but in practice nearly all the work is done by Lords of Appeal. It hears about twenty appeals each year and is the final arbiter of constitutional issues in the territories and jurisdictions concerned.

The Judicial Committee has been available as a source of advisory opinion for the Crown on matters of public concern or legal difficulty which cannot otherwise be brought conveniently before the Courts, for example, cases relating to disqualification from the Commons or Parliamentary privilege. It had a role under Section 5 of the 1920 Government of Ireland Act in that until Stormont was dissolved in 1972, the Government in London was empowered to refer to it questions relating to the interpretation of the Act, notably issues of legislative competence. More recently, it would also have had a similar role of constitutional arbitration if the devolution legislation of the 1974–9 Labour Government had been brought into effect. In the former case, Section 5 of the 1920 Government of Ireland Act was used only once in 1936. In the latter case, the 1979 Scottish and Welsh Devolution Acts remained inoperative because the referenda held in those parts of the United Kingdom did not demonstrate sufficient public support to trigger the legislation.

### Controversial issues

The process of judicial appeal does not normally give rise to great political controversy, except on those rare occasions when issues of wider political importance are raised in particularly contentious cases.When this happens, judgements in the House of Lords are often a trigger to fresh Government legislation designed either to overturn or to take account of the judicial decisions of the highest Court in the land.

Early examples of this process were provided by the 1906 Trade Disputes Act which overturned the House of Lords judgement in the 1901 Taff Vale case and the 1913 Trade Union Act which overturned the House of Lords judgement in the 1910 Osborne case. Another well known example was the 1965 War Damage Act which overturned the 1965 House of Lords judgement in the case of Burmah Oil. Another notable example in recent times was the 1983 Transport Act which took account of the 1982 House of Lords judgement in the case of Bromley Borough Council *v.* the Greater London Council on the politically contentious issue of passenger transport subsidies in Greater London. In all such cases, when matters of political importance have been involved, one of the major parties has felt obliged to introduce legislation either to overturn or to take account of the legal position as defined by the House of Lords. Such examples demonstrate that in Britain judicial intervention at the highest level on matters of major political importance is by no means always conclusive.

In general, there have been periods of judicial activism and creativity and periods when the behaviour of the judiciary has been characterised by its conservatism and keenness to defend the established legal order. On the whole judicial conservatism has been more in evidence. This is partly a reflection of the inherently conservative background and outlook of the judiciary in Britain to which reference has already been made. However, it also reflects a well-established constitutional attitude held by the judiciary and succinctly expressed by Lord Reid on several occasions. In 1961 in Shaw *v.* the Director of Public Prosecutions Lord Reid observed that 'where Parliament fears to tread, it is not for the Courts to rush in' and in 1972 he maintained that cases which raised political issues should be decided 'on the preponderance of existing authority'.[10]

In these matters much has always depended upon whether the judiciary construes the law literally and narrowly or contextually and broadly. For example, Lord Denning in his many years as Master of the Rolls and Chairman of the Court of Appeal was invariably inclined to interpret the law in a way which was well-disposed towards the underdog in the case, although this did not endear him to the trade unions nor, indeed, to the Law Lords to whom his judgements were often referred on further appeal. Much has also depended on the extent to which the judiciary has thought it proper or prudent to flex its muscles in defiance of the Government of the day. On the whole successive Labour Governments have been more likely than Conservative Governments to find themselves in conflict with the decisions of the judiciary. Certainly the well-known cases of Laker Airways, Tameside Education Authority, Padfield, Congreve, Anisminic and Burmah Oil all seem to bear this out. However, it can also be argued that such examples demonstrate not so much judicial hostility towards Labour Governments but the simple reality that there is always likely to be an inherent conflict between the judiciary, which usually sees its essential task as the preservation of the existing legal order, and all radical parties (whether Liberal or Labour) which have tried to change the established order in a sharply progressive direction.

## 18.4 CITIZENS AND THE STATE

In the modern world the complex relationship between citizens and the state raises political and legal issues of great importance. Citizens expect to enjoy certain inalienable rights, including freedoms of both a positive and a negative kind. There are the freedoms *to* do certain things and the freedoms *from* having certain things done to you. Each category of freedom is equally valuable. Yet in both cases the rights concerned have to be qualified or counterbalanced by certain rights of the state or its agencies to act on behalf of the community as a whole. It is in holding this balance between the rights of citizens and the interests of the state that the judicial system in Britain has had to face and resolve some of the most difficult problems of modern society. Furthermore, civil rights in Britain are to some extent ambiguous, since we do not have a codified constitution or a modern Bill of Rights in which they can be enshrined. We must, therefore, be circumspect when pronouncing upon the various issues which are raised in this sphere of our law.

### Citizenship and free movement

There are the issues which arise from rights of citizenship and free movement of people. Under the 1981 British Nationality Act all British citizens have the same legal rights and status, although this applies only to those with full British citizenship and the position of others resident in this country is limited by the various legal provisions governing the control of immigration. The position is also qualified to some extent by the legal rights and obligations which flow from Britain's membership of the European Community.

Under the 1981 British Nationality Act anyone who is legally a British citizen has the right of abode in this country and hence the right to enter the United Kingdom and to remain here as long as he likes. Such a person cannot legally be deported. However, his right to leave the country can be vitiated if he is without a British passport. In such circumstances it can be difficult to take up legal residence in other countries, at any rate in those outside the European Community which are not, of course, bound by its legal provisions for the free movement of EEC citizens.

### Personal liberty and property

There are the issues which arise from rights of personal liberty and property. For example, although British citizens are free people, in certain circumstances they can lawfully be detained, for example, after arrest and pending trial on a criminal charge or after conviction by a Court on a criminal charge for which the sentence is one of imprisonment, as well as the detention of mental patients or children deemed to be in need of statutory care or control. All these departures from the principle of personal liberty have raised issues of considerable controversy from time to time and have often led to investigations by Royal Commissions or the passage of new legislation. Powers of arrest, which are normally exercised by the police (but legally available to any citizen) are regulated principally by the 1967 Criminal Law Act, although other legislation and a considerable body of case law has a bearing upon these matters.

As for property rights in Britain, these have never been regarded as absolute or sacrosanct. Parliament has legislated on many occasions to limit such rights when they have conflicted with what is deemed to be the public interest, for example, in the spheres of public health, nationalisation or compulsory purchase. As a general rule, there has not been as much political determination to use the force of the law to defend economic or property rights as there has been to defend rights of personal liberty. In this respect British law is in accordance with the European Convention on Human Rights which manifests a similar bias.

Wrongful interference with the rights of personal property and liberty can be countered by various legal remedies in Britain. These include civil action for damages, prosecution for assault, exercise of the right of self-defence, use of the police complaints procedure and even invocation of *habeas corpus*. Yet there are no final or definitive solutions to these problems, since the law governing these aspects of civil rights can be changed from time to time by Act of Parliament, as would have happened if the 1982 Police and Criminal Evidence Bill had become law and as will happen when the reintroduced Bill reaches the Statute Book.[11]

**Freedom of expression**

There are the issues which arise from rights of free expression and their necessary limitations. In this sphere our law has usually relied upon the principle that anything which is not prohibited is permitted. However, the extent to which restrictions have been imposed in civil or criminal law has varied from time to time. For example, the law of defamation protects individuals from slander and libel. Substantial damages may be awarded for injury to a person's reputation and even the threat of such legal action is often sufficient to secure a retraction or to get a newspaper to publish a note of correction. In some cases those accused of defamation can plead absolute privilege (for example, in judicial or Parliamentary proceedings) or qualified privilege (for instance, in fair and accurate reports of such proceedings). The defence of 'fair comment' can also protect expressions of opinion on matters of public interest, even if someone thinks that what has been said is defamatory. In the criminal law there are the offences of sedition, blasphemy, obscenity and criminal libel which theoretically protect society from some of the excesses of free expression. However, in practice such actions are rare and of dubious utility, since it is difficult to get juries to convict on the basis of such ancient laws.

Freedom of expression in the media is also controlled to some extent by the Press Council in the case of newspapers and by the broadcasting authorities (BBC and IBA) in the case of radio and television. In the case of advertising, standards of public taste and decency are monitored by the Advertising Standards Authority. In all these cases such regulatory bodies may not have legal powers, but they do have a powerful restraining influence in their respective spheres. In the circumstances they do quite a useful job as institutional buffers between the media professionals and the general public.

**Meetings, procession and protest**

There are the issues which arise from rights to meet, process and protest freely, subject only to various necessary restraints in the interest of public order. In modern times this has been a particularly difficult balance to strike, since it is bound to involve constant adjustment and compromise between conflicting interests. In principle people are free to associate for political or other purposes. In practice such freedom is not extended to the civil service, the armed services, the police or registered charities. It is also limited by the provisions of the 1936 Public Order Act which do not permit paramilitary organisations or the wearing of political uniforms in a public place.

Public and private meetings for any purpose are constrained not so much by the law as by the need to secure prior permission from the owners of suitable halls or public spaces. It is also the case that public meetings may not lawfully be held on the public highway and that any consequent obstruction is an offence under the 1959 Highways Act. This has special relevance for the right to picket which is supposed to be confined under the 1980 Employment Act to peaceful persuasion in contemplation or furtherance of a trade dispute by people attending at their own place of work or that of so-called 'first customers' and 'first suppliers'.[12] Legal protection against disorderly conduct at a meeting is still provided by the 1908 Public Meeting Act, but in modern conditions this has little practical bearing upon such matters.

In general, the preservation of public order in processions and public meetings depends upon the police who exercise considerable discretion in every case. Among the powers available to Chief Officers of Police under the 1936 Public Order Act are the power to specify particular routes for marches and demonstrations, the power to restrict the display of flags, banners or other emblems, and the power to apply to the relevant Police Authority for a ban lasting not more than three months on all or any category of public processions. The 1979–83 Conservative Government conducted a review of this legislation, but it remains to be seen whether any changes will be made as a result.

Mention should also be made of the more dramatic public order problems caused by riots and serious disorders, such as those which took place in 1981 in Bristol, London, Liverpool and some other inner city areas. The law governing these matters has also been under review and it remains to be seen whether any changes will be made in due course.[13]

**Emergency powers and state security**

There are the issues which arise from the use of emergency powers by the Government and its agencies, together with the related problems of state security. In most serious emergencies the police, fire and ambulance services can cope with the problems which arise. However, there are some occasions when the military have to be called in to assist the civilian power or to deal with particularly serious threats to the community. In recent times the most notable example of this has been provided by the need to keep as many as 14 000 British troops in Northern Ireland in order to help the civil power to preserve peace and public order. Other examples have included the need to counter occasional outbreaks of terrorist violence, especially in London, by calling in the Special Air Service (SAS) and other expert military units to assist the police and the security services. The legal position on all such occasions is that the military have a duty to support the civil power when requested to do so. However, such emergencies usually involve sensitive and difficult issues of public safety which can affect the quality of our society, so they require Ministerial supervison and control at the highest level.

During peace-time a state of emergency may be declared under the authority of the 1920 and 1964 Emergency Powers Acts. These statutes permit the Government of the day to make use of wide-ranging temporary powers designed to ensure the maintenance of essential services, subject to Parliamentary approval of their renewal within seven days. During war-time even more far-reaching powers have been available to the Government of the day in the shape of the 1914 and 1915 Defence of the Realm Acts and the 1939 and 1940 Emergency Powers Acts. These statutes, which have since been repealed, gave the Government of the day almost unlimited power to do anything for the sake of the war effort, including the detention without trial for indefinite periods of suspect or hostile people and the seizure of private property without compensation. Once again the legislation was subject to no more than nominal Parliamentary control within twenty-eight days of the laying of the regulations. In the case of special measures to deal with terrorism, Parliament passed some draconian statutes in 1973 and 1975 to deal with terrorism in Northern Ireland and in 1974 and 1976 to deal with terrorist offences anywhere in the United Kingdom. This legislation confers very extensive powers upon the Government of the day and enables it to take almost any measures deemed necessary to counter such dire threats to national security, including detention without charge for up to seven days and the power to exclude undesirable people from the country.

The interests of state security are also invoked to justify the retention of the 1911 Official Secrets Act, the D Notice system preventing the unauthorised disclosure of official information by journalists (not always with complete success) and the interception of private communications by telephone-tapping and other techniques of surveillance. All these practices continue on the basis of rather tenuous legal authority and subject only to intermittent and indirect control by senior Ministers. However, security matters are also kept under periodic review by the Security Commission, which is a small but respected supervisory body of Privy Councillors chaired by a senior judge which reports regularly to the Prime Minister and occasionally to Parliament.

In these circumstances it is perhaps not surprising that there has been continuing pressure from many libertarian quarters for reform and the replacement of the existing legislation with new legislation (such as a Freedom of Information Act) which would put more emphasis upon the rights of ordinary citizens and less on the needs of national security. The problems of striking the right balance in this sphere have been complicated by the growing use of computers in the public sector, notably by the police and the security services. This has contributed to concern about the need for data protection to control the possible misuse of personal information which is mechanically stored and retrieved.[14]

**International Conventions**

There are the issues which arise from the wide range of civil rights declared in international Conventions and in many cases implemented by our Parliament at Westminster. For example, the principle that all citizens should be equal before the law is a worthy aspiration in Britain as in other countries, although in this country it is not enshrined in a codified constitution. In the last two decades Parliament has passed legislation against racial discrimination in 1965, 1968 and 1976 and against sexual discrimination in 1975. In such cases the attempt has been made to counter and eventually eradicate discrimination from all public behaviour and perhaps, eventually, from private behaviour as well. Most of the initiatives in this direction have been taken by the Commission for Racial Equality and the Equal Opportunities Commission, both of which were established by

Parliament to act as watch-dogs against discrimination in their respective spheres. However, individual citizens who feel aggrieved on racial or sexual grounds can also use the legislation to take cases to Court, if they want to do so.

In general, the protection of civil rights is a matter of wide international concern. This has been so at least since the 1948 UN Declaration of Human Rights and the 1950 European Convention on Human Rights. The latter, which was ratified by the United Kingdom in 1951, provides judicial procedures by which alleged infringements of civil rights may be examined at international level. Thus the action of public authorities in Britain may be challenged, even though they may have acted in accordance with our national law.

The European Convention provides an overt constraint upon the legislative supremacy of Parliament in so far as successive British Governments have not wanted to be found in breach of its provisions. However, the Convention has not been incorporated within the body of our national law on the grounds that civil rights in this country are adequately protected by British law and that such a method of incorporation would be inconsistent with our national tradition of Parliamentary supremacy. It was not until 1966 that the United Kingdom formally recognised the right of individual petition to the European Commission on Human Rights and the compulsory jurisdiction of the European Court of Human Rights in this country. Since that time various proceedings under the Convention have helped to bring about changes in British law and legal practice, for instance, the introduction of immigration appeal Tribunals or the revised rules on prisoners' access to lawyers.

## 18.5 ADMINISTRATIVE LAW

From a political point of view it is administrative law which is probably the most important aspect of the legal system in Britain. H. W. R. Wade has defined this area of the law as 'the body of general principles which govern the exercise of powers and duties by public authorities'.[15] Over the years since the end of the nineteenth century there has been a great expansion of Parliamentary legislation and hence a notable multiplication of administrative bodies created by statute. This has led to growing judicial and quasi-judicial intervention in the field of public administration. Ordinary people have felt the need to appeal to quasi-judicial Tribunals and ultimately to the Courts on many points of administrative law. For its part the judiciary has attempted to compensate for the failure of Parliament adequately to protect ordinary citizens from the shortcomings or injustices which can be perpetrated in the public administration.

**Administrative Tribunals**

In the modern British political system there is a bewildering array of administrative Tribunals which have been created by Acts of Parliament. Some were established as a function of the Welfare State, such as the National Insurance Tribunals which decide disputed claims to benefits under the legislation dealing with national insurance or social security. Some are related to the problems of industrial relations, such as the Industrial Tribunals which adjudicate on claims of industrial injury, unfair dismissal and other employment disputes. Some deal with housing disputes, some with pensions or unemployment, some with immigration cases, some with the National Health Service and some with educational disputes. All exist in order to provide simpler, cheaper, quicker and more accessible forms of justice than are available in the Courts. They are, therefore, an integral part of the British legal system.

The main characteristics of administrative Tribunals are usually clear-cut. They are normally established by Act of Parliament. Their decisions are quasi-judicial in the sense that they find the facts of the case and then apply certain legal rules to it in an impartial manner. They are independent in the sense that their decisions are in no way subject to political or administrative interference. Their membership varies, but they usually consist of an independent, legally qualified Chairman and two lay members representing relevant interests. The members are assisted by clerks who are usually civil servants from the relevant Department. Appeals against their decisions can be made in different ways, since Parliament over the years has created no consistent procedure. Appeals may lie to a superior Tribunal, a Minister, a superior Court or in some cases there may be no appeals provision at all, for example, the National Insurance Commissioners or the National Health Service Tribunal.

The main advantage of administrative Tribunals is that they offer relatively speedy, cheap and accessible procedures which are essential, for example, in the administration of welfare schemes involving large numbers of small claims. Another advantage is that they are well-suited to deal expertly with special categories of cases, for instance, the Income Tax Commissioners or the Medical Appeal Tribunals. On the other hand, the main disadvantage is the institutional proliferation and jurisdictional complexity of these Tribunals. The uncontrolled growth of these bodies over the years has produced over fifty different types of Tribunal, all of which fall within the definition laid down in the 1971 Tribunals and Inquiries Act. They range from those which are very active - for example, Supplementary Benefit or Rent Tribunals - to those which have had no cases at all, such as the Mines and Quarries Tribunals. In such a complex structure there are also the inevitable problems of overlapping and competing jurisdictions and so far little has been done to amalgamate or group Tribunals according to their particular functions.

In these circumstances considerable attention has been paid to the search for adequate and effective ways of controlling and supervising this area of the law. None of the existing methods has proved to be wholly satisfactory, which is why some have looked to Continental practice or overall constitutional reform as the real answer to the problem. We shall, therefore, consider each of the possible solutions in turn.

**Ministerial control**

The traditional view of the problems of administrative law is that the public interest can best be safeguarded by Ministers who are responsible to Parliament. Yet this idea has been recognised as something of a constitutional fiction ever since it was first criticised by Lord Hewart and Professor Robson more than fifty years ago.[16] The criticism then, and even more so today, is that no Minister can possibly be informed about, let alone be held accountable for everything which happens within the enormous number of administrative Tribunals and other quasi-judicial bodies for which he may be nominally responsible.

Even before the Second World War it was recognised that the threat to Parliament really stemmed from the growth of delegated legislation and the threat to the law from the growth of quasi-judicial powers exercised by Whitehall Departments and administrative Tribunals. Yet for many years little was done to tackle these problems, since the challenges of war and reconstruction had to be given higher priority. It was not until after the notorious Crichel Down affair in the early 1950s that some effective action was taken to begin to deal with the problem.[17] A committee chaired by Sir Oliver Franks was established to look again at all these matters and in 1957 it produced a report which was broadly acceptable to the Government of the day. This led directly to the 1958 Tribunals and Inquiries Act which provided for the creation of the Council on Tribunals to oversee the whole sphere of administrative jurisdiction. Subsequently the legislation was consolidated and brought up-to-date in the 1971 Tribunals and Inquiries Act which still sets the ground-rules in this area of the law.

In general, it seems clear that Ministerial control has not been an adequate response to the problems of oversight and review in this area of the law. Indeed, it has amounted essentially to denying the significance of the problem by assuming that the public administration is bound to reflect the public interest, simply because it is headed by Ministers who are responsible to Parliament. Such an idea is obviously defective in contemporary political conditions, since few Ministers ever manage to secure complete control of their Departments and Parliament no longer has effective control over Ministers in most normal circumstances.

**The Ombudsman**

Another approach to this problem has been to create special institutions designed to limit any abuses of administrative power and to deal with such eventualities if and when they occur. In Britain, as in some other countries (such as New Zealand and Scandinavia) this has been achieved by the Parliamentary Commissioner for Administration, popularly known as the Ombudsman. This institution was created by Act of Parliament in 1967 for the express purpose of seeing that the administrative procedures of central Government are correctly followed and that any allegations of administrative injustice or abuse are investigated and, if possible, remedied.

The Ombudsman, who has usually been a former senior civil servant, is appointed by the Crown on the advice of the Lord Chancellor and his constitutional status is similar to that of a High Court judge, that is completely independent of Government. Like a judge, his salary is fixed by statute and charged automatically to the Consolidated Fund and he can only be removed from office by the Crown after addresses by both Houses of Parliament. He appoints his own staff who are usually drawn from the ranks of the civil service. His jurisdiction is confined to the Departments of central Government and the National Health Service, so it excludes the police, the public corporations and local authorities.[18] He can investigate public complaints about the way in which Departments have discharged their administrative functions, although his jurisdiction does not extend to international relations, Court proceedings or the contractual and commercial transactions of central Government. There are also other statutory limitations upon the scope of his jurisdiction. For example, he has no right to investigate cases where the complainant has a right of recourse to an administrative Tribunal or a remedy in the Courts, nor complaints raised more than one year after the date when the complainant first had notice of the matter.

Public complaints to the Ombudsman are normally referred via a Member of Parliament, although some are now made directly to him. Once the complaint has been received, it is for the Ombudsman to decide whether or not it falls within his jurisdiction. In fact, fewer than half the complaints submitted fall within his jurisdiction and are therefore investigated. Of those which do, elements of maladministration have been discovered in about one third of the cases. All official documents, except Cabinet papers, have to be produced for inspection at his request and he has the same powers as a High Court judge to compel any witness to give evidence. When an investigation is complete, the Ombudsman normally sends his report to the MP concerned who then conveys it to the complainant. The Ombudsman has no executive powers, but his reports often suggest appropriate remedies upon which the Departments concerned normally take action. These may include outright financial compensation, tax remission, administrative review of earlier decisions or revised procedures to prevent any repetition of the errors which have been identified. The Ombudsman has always been supervised and supported in his work by a Select Committee of the House of Commons which examines his reports and may take evidence from the Departments involved in his investigations. This helps to ensure that his recommendations are carried out. Such methods of oversight and control may not be perfect, but they do provide the public with a form of redress which is widely appreciated.

**Judicial review**

Another way of dealing with any injustices or abuses which are perpetrated by the public administration is that of judicial review. In this respect the basic leverage for the judiciary is provided by the doctrine of *ultra vires* which holds that acts of the public administration are unlawful if they go beyond interpretations of the statutory position which reasonable people could reasonably accept. It is this doctrine which enables the High Court to set aside administrative decisions which, although perhaps within the literal scope of the statutues, are plainly unreasonable. In most cases, of course, the issues involved are complicated and controversial, since the nub of the problem is usually the degree of discretionary power which can properly be exercised by the public body concerned. The judiciary therefore has the difficult responsibility of interpreting the meaning of statutes on the basis of what reasonable people would regard as a reasonable interpretation. This can be approached in a narrow and literal sense or a broad and contextual sense and much will depend upon which path is chosen by the judges concerned.

When a complaint against the public administration is brought before the High Court, several legal remedies are available to the plaintiffs. There are the traditional prerogative remedies which were originally vested in the Monarch, but which are now available to ordinary citizens. These are *certiorari* to quash an administrative decision already made, *prohibition* to prevent a public authority from considering a matter which it has no statutory right to consider and *mandamus* to compel a public body to perform a public duty. Then there are the two non-prerogative remedies which are usually more useful nowadays. These are an *injunction* to prohibit a public body from doing something which would be illegal and a *declaration* which is simply a statement by the Court clarifying the legal position, so that the powers and duties of a public body can be more precisely defined.[19]

Judicial review is impartial in the sense that it is in no way concerned with the position of the complainant or the power of the public body about which the complaint may be made. Yet there are weaknesses in such procedures. For example, the Court can only intervene if a plaintiff starts legal proceedings. It can only deal with the case before it. It usually lacks the detailed expertise of the public administration which it seeks to control. It cannot oversee the ways in which its remedial orders are carried out. It proceeds so slowly and expensively that many would-be plaintiffs are deterred from going to law in the first place.

In conducting the process of judicial review, the judges tend to be guided essentially by the principles of natural justice. These are (i) the right of the complainant to be heard before the relevant decision is taken and (ii) the absence of prejudice on the part of the public body charged with the duty of adjudication. However, these principles are not presumed to apply to Ministerial decisions when the relevant legislation permits a degree of administrative discretion or to legislative functions, such as the establishment of clear rules for general administrative application. This emphasises the delicate balance which has to be struck between the interests of the plaintiff and those of the general public. The balance has shifted back and forth over the years, but on the whole the Courts have been guided 'more by policy than by precedent, more by what they think is fair and reasonable than by rigid rules'.[20] Judicial review is, therefore, a more than usually political form of justice.

However, since about the mid-1960s the judiciary in Britain has taken more account of the principles of natural justice and has been prepared to play a more active and interventionist role in political matters.[21] This has been especially evident in cases bearing upon individual rights, such as personal property, personal liberty, freedom of movement, possession of office or access to employment. It could also be argued that the tide of judicial opinion has turned against unpopular groups of which the rest of society has often had a fairly low opinion, such as trade unions or students. Whatever may be the eventual consequences of these movements in public opinion, the judiciary has begun to show a real willingness to use the process of judicial review to deal with the abuses and injustices which can occur in the public administration.

**Continental solutions**

There are some who argue that none of the foregoing methods provides sufficiently effective ways of controlling the public administration. Such people maintain that the only effective counter to administrative abuse would be the establishment in Britain of an administrative division of the High Court as in France or a general administrative appeals Tribunal as in Sweden. This approach has been advocated by those members of the judiciary who would like to see the process of judicial review extended into all parts of the public administration. Yet it would almost certainly be a non-starter in Britain in view of the widespread suspicion in this country of the idea of giving the judiciary a more prominent political role than that which they already enjoy. Certainly most of those on the Left of British politics would oppose such a deliberate extension of powers and competence for the judiciary and many on the Right would be dubious about the desirability of translating French or Swedish judicial practices to this country. Thus none of the Continental solutions seems likely to be adopted in this country, not least because Parliament would certainly feel threatened by the importation of such foreign practices.

**Constitutional reform**

Finally, there are some eminent legal figures, such as Lord Scarman and Lord Hailsham, who have argued the case for far-reaching constitutional reform entailing a new Bill of Rights and the introduction of a codified constitution which would be interpreted and protected by a powerful Supreme Court.[22] Those who favour this approach to dealing with the problems of administrative law have to contend with the traditional British view that our civil rights and political liberties are most secure if founded upon the custom and practice of the common law. Of course, they argue in their turn that the traditional view is now obsolete and ineffective, mainly because it takes insufficient account of the scope and complexity of public administration and Governmental activity in modern political conditions. The conclusion which such advocates of constitutional reform have drawn is that there is now a need for a new Bill of Rights containing a formal statement of contemporary civil rights and public duties.

However, there are several difficulties with such an approach and a number of conditions would have to be met before it could be put into practice. There would need to be a codified constitution which ordinary citizens could invoke in any dispute with public authorities. There would need to be a Supreme Court entitled to interpret and protect such a constitution. There would need to be a willingness on the part of the judiciary to play an explicitly political role and public acceptance of a foreign conception of the rule of law. Above all, Members of Parliament would have to be prepared to see Parliament itself assume a role which implied an end to its traditional constitutional supremacy. It is only necessary to enumerate these conditions to make clear just how difficult it would be to bring about such far-reaching constitutional changes in Britain.

Among those who favour such changes, Nevil Johnson has argued that 'the challenge is to construct a different relationship between law and politics and in so doing to give law . . . a new and wider part in the regulation of the affairs of society'.[23] While such a challenge may seem exhilarating and attractive to some lawyers and academics, it is likely to find little favour with most practising politicians, since they usually dislike the idea of political issues being settled by decisions of the Courts. In this country they prefer to rely upon the present constitutional arrangements which have served them well for so long. Thus until this radical idea gains much more political support in the political parties and in Parliament, it is unlikely to offer a realistic way of controlling the public administration in Britain.

## 18.6 **CONCLUSION**

It remains to be seen whether the judiciary in Britain will develop into a much more creative element of the political system or whether it will remain fundamentally conservative in its outlook and practice. There are clearly major implications for the traditional doctrines of Parliamentary supremacy and Ministerial responsibility if the judiciary does adopt a significantly more creative role. Yet it must be said that such a development will depend more upon the Government of the day voluntarily agreeing to be limited by the Courts than upon any decision of the judges to strike heroic political postures. In present circumstances neither condition for change seems likely to be met.

There has never been a truly effective balance of constitutional power between the Executive and the Judiciary in Britain. Such a balance nearly came about in the eighteenth century when central Government was at its weakest, but in modern times the judiciary has usually been careful not to step too far out of line with either the Government of the day or with public opinion. On the whole the judges have tended to be more conservative than Labour Governments, but more progressive than majority public opinion. In the last resort they have been inhibited by the knowledge that 'if they fly too high, Parliament may clip their wings'.[24]

Of course, relations between the judiciary and the other parts of the British political system may change in the future as a consequence of more demanding public attitudes or specific constitutional developments. For example, the public may come to expect more from the Courts by way of judicial protection and redress against the abuses and injustices which can be perpetrated by the modern public administration. Equally, the declared supremacy of European Community law over British law, at least in certain areas enshrined in the 1972 European Communities Act, may hasten the day when the doctrine of Parliamentary supremacy will no longer be the corner-stone of our constitution. Above all, if there were to be a significant measure of electoral reform as a consequence of a political deal done in a future 'hung Parliament', this might lead to wider constitutional reform which could give the law and the judiciary a more important role in our constitutional arrangements. Only time will tell.

## SUGGESTED QUESTIONS

1. Describe the structure and problems of either criminal justice or civil justice in Britain today.
2. What are the main issues in the legal relations between citizens and the state?
3. How appropriate and effective are the arrangements for applying and reviewing administrative law in Britain?

## NOTES

1. See Report of the Royal Commission on Criminal Procedure, Cmnd 8092 (London: HMSO, 1981).
2. For a fuller discussion of these issues see the Scarman Report on the Brixton Disorders, Cmnd 8487 (London: HMSO, 1981).
3. Breaches of duty leading to liability for damages, but non-contractual in the case of tort.
4. *Prohibition* prevents a public authority from considering a matter which it has no statutory right to consider. *Mandamus* enables the High Court to compel a public body to perform a public duty which it is statutorily obliged to perform. *Certiorari* enables the High Court to quash an administrative decision already made by a public body. A writ of *habeas corpus* is supposed to prevent the police from detaining without charge those suspected of non-serious offences for more than twenty-four hours, although in the case of suspected terrorists there is statutory provision for this to be extended to three days within the country and seven days at a port of entry.
5. The reason for this incongruous grouping was simply that all these jurisdictions had a common basis in Roman law.
6. G. Drewry, *Law, Justice and Politics* (London: Longman, 1975) p. 128.
7. J. A. G. Griffith, *The Politics of the Judiciary* (London: Fontana, 1977) p. 193.
8. In 1980–1 about £85m was spent on criminal legal aid, about £35m on civil legal aid and about £20m on legal assistance and advice.
9. Trinidad and Tobago, Singapore, Dominica, Kiribati and the Gambia.
10. Quoted in J. A. G. Griffith *The Politics of the Judiciary*, pp. 183 and 179.
11. The 1982 Police and Criminal Evidence Bill, which lapsed when Parliament was dissolved in May 1983, was a far-reaching attempt by the 1979–83 Conservative Government to extend and clarify the powers of the police, while redefining the balance between the interests of the law-abiding community in seeing offenders brought to justice and the rights of individual citizens suspected of criminal offences.
12. This restricted legal immunity from civil action in the Courts to the employees of the firm in dispute or the employees of a direct supplier or customer of the firm in dispute, thus theoretically limiting the scope for 'blacking' or sympathy strikes.

13. Certain recommendations were made in the 1981 Scarman Report and the future of the 1936 Public Order Act was reviewed by the 1979–83 Conservative Government.
14. The subject of Data Protection was dealt with in the 1978 Lindop Report. This was followed in 1982 by a Data Protection Bill which lapsed when Parliament was dissolved in May 1983. A similar Bill has been introduced in the present Parliament and it became law in 1984.
15. H. W. R. Wade, *Administrative Law*, 4th edn (Oxford: Clarendon Press, 1979) pp. 5–6.
16. See Lord Hewart, *The New Despotism*, 2nd edn (West Point: Greenwood, 1945) and W. Robson, *Justice and Administrative Law*, 3rd edn (London: Stevens, 1951).
17. The Crichel Down Affair involved an area of farm land in Dorset about which misleading replies and false assurances were given by a junior civil servant in the Ministry of Agriculture. Subsequent inquiries established that there had been muddle, bias, inefficiency and bad faith on the part of a few officials, as well as weak organisation in the Department. This led eventually to the departure of the Minister, Sir Thomas Dugdale, who felt honour-bound to resign.
18. There is a separate Local Authority Ombudsman to investigate public complaints about maladministration in local government.
19. An injunction and a declaration are two of the legal remedies generally available to litigants and they are not confined to cases in which citizens seek to challenge public authorities.
20. T. C. Hartley and J. A. G. Griffith, *Government and Law* (London: Weidenfeld & Nicolson, 1975) p. 320.
21. Notably in the Court of Appeal where Lord Denning had a long and active period as Master of the Rolls.
22. See L. J. Scarman, *English Law, the New Dimension* (London: Stevens, 1974) and Q. Hailsham, *The Dilemma of Democracy* (London: Collins, 1978).
23. N. Johnson, *In Search of the Constitution* (London: Methuen, 1980) p. 149.
24. H. W. R. Wade, *Administrative Law*, p. 30.

## FURTHER READING

Drewry, G., *Law, Justice and Politics* (London: Longman, 1975).
Elcock, H. J., *Administrative Justice* (London: Longman, 1969).
Griffith, J. A. G., *The Politics of the Judiciary* (London: Fontana, 1981).
Hartley, T. C. and Griffith, J. A. G., *Government and Law* (London: Weidenfeld & Nicolson, 1975).
Jackson, R. M., *The Machinery of Justice in England*, 6th edn (Cambridge: Cambridge University Press, 1972).
Johnson, N., *In Search of the Constitution* (London: Methuen, 1980).
Marshall, G. and Moodie, G. C., *Some Problems of the Constitution*, 5th edn (London: Hutchinson, 1971).
Scarman, L. J., *English Law, the New Dimension* (London: Stevens, 1974).

Stacey, F., *The British Ombudsman* (Oxford: Oxford University Press, 1971).
Wade, E. C. S. and Phillips, G. G., *Constitutional and Administrative Law*, 9th edn (London: Longman, 1977).
Wade, H. W. R., *Administrative Law*, 4th edn (Oxford: Clarendon Press, 1979).
Wraith, R. E. and Hutcheson, P. G., *Administrative Tribunals* (London: Allen & Unwin, 1973).

# PART VI

# DEMOCRACY IN BRITAIN

CHAPTER 19

# BRITISH POLITICS COMPARED

There is value in seeking to compare the political systems in different Western countries. In order to avoid excessive length or complexity in this chapter, we shall focus upon comparisons between Britain, France, West Germany and the United States. For those who wish to delve deeper into this area of study there are a number of good books available on comparative politics.[1] The purpose of this chapter, however, is simply to draw attention to some of the essential points of similarity or contrast between the four political systems. Within the scope of a brief chapter it is not possible to do more than this.

## 19.1 POLITICAL CULTURE

The political culture of Britain is significantly different from that of each of the other countries with which we are concerned. The unparalleled continuity of political developments in Britain over the centuries provides the first notable contrast with both France and West Germany. In France the Fifth Republic is based on the eleventh new constitution since 1791. In West Germany the Federal Republic is founded on the Basic Law of 1949 which was drawn up in the wake of German defeat and partition at the end of the Second World War. In the United States, although the political system dates from the Declaration of Independence in 1776, the degree of political continuity cannot really match that of this country where we can trace our political arrangements back at least to the Bill of Rights in 1689 and arguably to Magna Carta in 1215.

The degree of cultural cohesion in British society provides another contrast with the United States and arguably with France and West Germany as well. Of course, there are significant class and other divisions in British society. However, such differences are not as great as those which can be found in the United States with its large ethnic minorities and its significant regional variations. In France national cohesion has been a conscious aspiration of virtually every Government since the time of Napoleon. Yet there remain some deep divisions in French society on economic, ideological, ethnic and regional lines. In West Germany the majority of the people seem to be ethnically and ideologically cohesive. Yet due account must be taken of the various political extremists (such as the Baader-Meinhof gang and their followers) who reject the entire basis of contemporary West German society, the various alternative groups (for instance, the Green Movement) whose members are highly critical of many conventional policies in West German politics, and the millions of guest workers from Turkey, Yugoslavia and elsewhere who tend to form their own communities which are linguistically and culturally distinct.

As we noted in Chapter 1, the nature of consensus in British political culture has to be defined rather carefully. Certainly there is still a high degree of procedural consensus about how political problems should be tackled, for example, through Parliamentary channels rather than direct action. Yet there is little sign of policy consensus between the two major parties and much evidence of political polarisation which seems unlikely to be significantly diminished, let alone eliminated.

In West Germany, by contrast, there has been considerable consensus since the late 1950s not only on procedural matters but also on issues of policy. The three leading parties (Christian Democrats, Social Democrats and Free Democrats) have all accepted the basis of the social market economy and only recently has this policy consensus begun to be questioned by the Left wing Social Democrats and the 'alternative' political groups. In France the original Gaullist consensus of the Fifth Republic has become more fragile, especially since President Mitterrand, The Socialist party leader, was elected in 1981. However, there is also considerable continuity of policy, for example, French nationalism in defence and foreign affairs. In the United States, it has often been hard to recognise any durable consensus. Yet with the notable exceptions of the Vietnam War and the Watergate episode, both procedural and policy consensus have remained rather strong. The fact is that the awesome dimensions of American power and responsibility have usually required a high degree of policy consensus notwithstanding the changing priorities and prejudices of successive American Presidents.

As for the element of deference in British society, this seems to have declined sharply as compared with former times. The British people no longer seem to be great respecters of persons and they manifest a healthy scepticism towards those in authority. In this respect they seem to be moving closer to French or American attitudes towards authority, that is, natural mistrust in the former case and rugged independence in the latter case. Certainly they no longer demonstrate the instinctive respect for order and authority which is still evident among the German people on both sides of the inner-German border.

## 19.2 ELECTORAL SYSTEMS

Another significant basis of comparison is provided by the electoral systems of the four different countries. In Britain, the electoral system evolved over the centuries and was frequently reformed to meet the changing needs of different times. The franchise was periodically extended from 1832 to 1969 when the present basis was achieved with votes for all adults over the age of 18 (except lunatics, convicted felons and peers of the realm). However, as we noted in Chapter 3, the essential characteristic of the British electoral system is that it is based upon the plurality principle, that is, the winning candidate needs a majority over each other candidate but not over all of them together.

In the United States, the electoral system is also based upon first-past-the-post. However, there are some significant contrasts with the British system and the most obvious is one of scale. Whereas in Britain 650 MPs are now elected to the House of Commons every four or five years at General Elections and about 26 000 Councillors are elected to 548 local authorities rather more frequently, in the United States there are about 1 million elective offices which require perhaps 130 000 elections a year (although many are held together on the same day). Moreover, in Britain the people vote at General Elections for national political parties and for national party leaders who aspire to become Prime Minister, whereas in the United States the electoral process is more open as a consequence of the widespread practice of holding primaries for elections at state and federal level.

In France and West Germany the electoral systems are very different from ours in Britain, since candidates are elected in more complicated and – some would say – fairer ways. Whereas in Britain with our system of first-past-the-post elections it is frequently possible for candidates to get elected with the support of no more than 35–40 per cent of the votes cast and an even smaller proportion of those entitled to vote, in France there has to be a second ballot if no candidate secures more than 50 per cent of the votes cast in the first ballot. This ensures a greater degree of democratic legitimacy for the victorious candidates, but it also works against the interests of small parties and the more extreme political figures in the major parties. In West Germany, the additional-member system produces an element of proportionality in election results by ensuring that there is representation in the *Bundestag* not only for those candidates who are directly elected (on the basis of first-past-the-post) but also for the additional members who are drawn from party lists in each of the *Länder* in proportion to the votes cast for each of the parties. However, the principle of proportionality is modified by the so-called 5 per cent rule which prevents fringe parties with less than 5 per cent of the popular vote from qualifying for any Parliamentary representation. Over the years since 1949 this rule, coupled for a while with a legal ban on the Kommunistische Partei Deutschlands (KPD) of the extreme Left (the Communists) and the Nationalistische Partei Deutschlands (NPD) of the extreme Right (the neo-Fascists) has proved to be an effective barrier to any extreme elements which might have de-stabilised the Parliamentary system. Yet it was also a low enough hurdle to be surmounted by the Green Movement in the 1983 federal elections.

## 19.3 PATTERNS OF GOVERNMENT

It is when we consider the various patterns of government that we discover some of the most notable similarities and contrasts between Britain and the other three countries. As we have noted already, Britain has a system of Parliamentary government, which means not government *by* Parliament but government *through* Parliament or, more precisely, with the support of a majority in the House of Commons. In this way the British system depends upon the connected conventions of collective responsibility and Parliamentary accountability. It is still collective government based upon Parliamentary support. It is not presidential government in spite of the tendency for the media to portray it in that way.

In West Germany, the system of so-called 'Chancellor democracy' comes fairly close to the British model of government. Although the Federal Chancellor alone is constitutionally responsible to the *Bundestag* for the conduct of the Government, the Federal Ministers have to answer to that body for the conduct of their Departments and they are subjected to a dilute form of British Parliamentary accountability. The provisions of the 1949 Basic Law put the Federal Chancellor on a level clearly superior to his Ministers, whereas British Prime Ministers owe their pre-eminence more to force of personality or political circumstance.

In France, the contrast with Britain is more marked. The Fifth Republic is an explicitly Presidential system of government which separates the Executive from the Legislature (for example, Deputies have to resign their seats when they become Ministers) and which raises the President high above the level of his Prime Minister and Cabinet. The President has the constitutional right to appoint and dismiss the Prime Minister and effective rights over the tenure of other Ministers as well. He has the power to dissolve the *Assemblée Nationale* (theoretically on the advice of the Prime Minister) and to call fresh elections to that body. To some extent his power of dissolution is similar to that of the British Prime Minister, although the latter acts formally under the auspices of the Monarch. The main difference is that in France it is not certain whether the President would feel it necessary to resign if his Parliamentary supporters were defeated in such elections to the *Assemblée Nationale* while he was still lawfully in office, whereas in Britain the Prime Minister normally has to resign (along with the rest of his Government) if his party loses a General Election or is defeated in the House of Commons on an issue of confidence. This was shown by the need for Mr Heath to resign three days after the Conservative defeat at the February 1974 General Election (when it became clear that the Liberal MPs could not or would not support the Conservatives in the Commons) and by the need for Mr Callaghan to resign after Labour's defeat in the House of Commons on a vote of confidence in March 1979.

In the United States, the contrast with Britain is most complete. Whereas in this country executive and legislative power is effectively fused by Ministerial membership of and responsibility to the House of Commons, in the United States the Executive was consciously separated from the Legislature when the founding fathers drew up the American constitution. It is not only that the President is separate from Congress and each from the Supreme Court and judiciary, but also that the Federal Government is entirely distinct from the Governments of the individual states of the Union. In constitutional terms the position of the American President is stronger than that of the British Prime Minister in that the former is hierarchically and formally the chief Executive whereas the latter is formally no more than first among equals within the Cabinet. Yet in practice a British Prime Minister is usually better placed to get his way within his Government and with Parliament than an American President is within his Administration and with Congress. This is because the strength and reliability of the party system in Britain enables party leaders to get their way more often than not, whereas the competing and more heterogeneous power relationships in Washington make it difficult for even the strongest Presidents to get their way most of the time. Nevertheless both political systems are more or less presidential in practice, even though the centralisation of executive authority which this implies is not necessarily matched by a corresponding concentration of real political power.

## 19.4 ROLE OF THE BUREAUCRACY

It is clear that the civil service in Britain is one of the most powerful but least innovative in the Western world. As we noted in Chapter 13, it plays an important part in the policy- and decision-making process, especially when the party in office has been in Government for some time. Yet it is usually cautious and conservative in its procedures and its advice and has a natural bias against new or heretic ideas, unless initiated or sanctioned by Ministers.

The bureaucracy in France offers the most striking contrast with ours in Britain. Since the Second World War the graduates from the *Grandes Ecoles* who fill the higher grades of the French civil service, have provided not only the technical expertise but also much of the innovative thinking in the administration of Government policy. Under the Fifth Republic this has also been reflected in the fact that two Prime Ministers (Couve de Murville under President De Gaulle and Raymond Barre under President Giscard D'Estaing) were drawn from the ranks of the bureaucracy and two of the four Presidents were civil servants at an earlier stage in their careers. Such interpenetration of politics and the bureaucracy is much less common in Britain where the civil service is noted for its strict political neutrality. Indeed, French civil servants often go one stage further by practising what is known as *pantouflage* (literally putting on someone else's slippers) whereby they move in mid-career into positions of power and responsibility in French industry and commerce and very often switch back at a later stage into the world of politics and government. In Britain, on the other hand, such movements usually take place at the end of the civil servants' careers and then on a one-way ticket to the private sector.

The political neutrality which is required of civil servants in Britain is not required of their counterparts in West Germany. Indeed, in the Federal Republic the tendency over recent years has been for the Chancellor and his key Ministers to be supported by senior civil servants who are of the same broad political persuasion as their political masters, if not actually members of one of the parties in the governing coalition. One result of this has been that a high proportion of members of the *Bundestag* are former civil servants and things have been arranged in such a way as to facilitate their transition from the bureaucracy into representative politics. In general, civil servants play a very important role in the federal Government. For example, they provide the State Secretaries of the various Ministries in Bonn and as such they wield considerable power not only in Departmental relations with the *Länder* but also when they represent their Ministers in Cabinet and in the *Bundestag*.

The federal bureaucracy in the United States provides the most marked contrast with the civil service in Britain. This is because its composition is heterogeneous and its higher positions are usually in the gift of the President in office. It has been estimated that every incoming President has between 7000 and 15 000 such jobs to dispense and even then this reflects only part of the spoils system which has operated in Washington ever since the election of President Jackson in 1829. Although the 1883 Pendleton Act later went some way towards reforming the American civil service by introducing competitive exams and security of tenure for many of its employees, the overtly political appointments to the higher ranks of every Administration still set the Washington bureaucracy in sharp contrast to the civil service in London.

At the lower levels of the federal bureaucracy, however, American officials tend to rise through the ranks and to specialise in the affairs of one particular Department. This means that they do not have as much of a corporate spirit as do their counterparts in British or French central Government. Indeed, it is quite normal for the various branches of the Administration in Washington to be at loggerheads and in these circumstances it is often left to the Executive Office of the President to try to draw together the various threads of policy and to weave them into a coherent whole. Of course, this is a problem for central Departments in all national Governments, but it is particularly difficult in Washington where all Presidents have striven to impose their authority throughout their heterogeneous Administrations.

## 19.5 ROLE OF PARLIAMENT

It is in considering the role of Parliament in Britain and the three other countries that we notice the most marked contrasts. Essentially, the British political system is characterised by a powerful Parliament which is effectively controlled by the major parties and accountable to the mass electorate every four or five years at General Elections. As for the House of Commons, it is not so much the institution itself which is powerful, but rather the small number of leading politicians who hold the positions of power and sit on the two front benches.

The greatest contrast with Parliament at Westminster is provided by the *Assemblée Nationale* in Paris. Under the Fifth Republic this has had all the characteristics of a weak Parliament and it has usually been subservient to the President in office. However, it is not inevitable that this should be so and the balance of power between the Legislature and the Executive could be different if the Opposition parties were ever to win an overall majority at the Parliamentary elections which take place every five years between Presidential elections. Such a political and constitutional clash has not yet occurred in the Fifth Republic, but if it ever did, the outcome would not be certain.

The contrast at Parliamentary level is almost as marked between Britain and West Germany, since the *Bundestag* has also demonstrated little ability to control the federal Executive. However, since there has been coalition government of one kind or another in Bonn since 1966, Parliamentary control of the Executive has been exerted principally within the party groups and through inter-party discussions within the governing coalition. Consequently, the Opposition parties have little effective Parliamentary control over the federal Government, although they have sometimes been more effective in the *Bundesrat*, the second chamber in which the various *Länder* are represented and whose approval is constitutionally required in certain cases.

In practice, of course, the contrasts between Parliament at Westminster and its counterparts in Paris and Bonn are not as pronounced as these brief observations would suggest. This is because in Britain the theory of Parliamentary supremacy is usually modified in practice by the Government's dominance of the Legislature as long as it manages to retain the support of a working majority in the Commons. Certainly it would be wrong to confuse the sound and the fury of some forms of Parliamentary opposition – for example, Prime Minister's Question Time – with the substance of effective Parliamentary control, even though some Westminster MPs may still be tempted to do so. As in France and West Germany, it is the politics of anticipated reaction within the governing parties and between Ministers and their Parliamentary supporters which constitutes the most significant contribution to effective Parliamentary control.

This brings us, however, to the sharp contrast which does exist between the independent power of the United States Congress and the rather more nebulous influence of Parliament at Westminster. In the United States Congressional power is seen most clearly in the formidable investigative committees of both the Senate and the House of Representatives which monitor all aspects of federal Government activity. It is also evident in the right of the Senate to 'advise and consent' to international treaties and Presidential nominations for senior posts in the Administration, as well as the right of both Houses to appropriate public funds beyond those requested by the President. Clearly the exercise of such power is in marked contrast to even the most ambitious attempts by the House of Commons to control the expenditure and the activities of the Government of the day. The hard fact is that the so-called 'Mother of Parliaments' does not really wield effective political power, except in the unusual circumstances of a 'hung Parliament' when the Government of the day lacks an overall majority in the Commons and is therefore obliged to make some concessions to the positions of other parties or its own back-benchers.

## 19.6 LEGAL SYSTEMS

Turning to the various legal systems in Britain and the three other countries, it is immediately clear that this country is unusual in not having a codified constitution or a separate structure of administrative Courts. Unlike the position in the other countries where there is a clear separation of powers, the highest Court in Britain, the Appellate Committee of the House of Lords, is subordinate to Parliament as a whole and the most senior judge, the Lord Chancellor, is also a member of the Cabinet. Indeed, the real meaning of Parliamentary supremacy is not that Parliament can dominate and control the Executive, but rather that our independent judiciary and legal system is ultimately subordinate to the decisions of Parliament (effectively the policies of the majority party in the House of Commons).

In France, by contrast, the legal system includes the *Conseil d'Etat* and an elaborate structure of administrative Courts. These Courts deal with all matters of administrative law and are sufficiently powerful to be a barrier to the ambitions of the Executive. Indeed, President De Gaulle introduced the special device of the constitutional referendum as a way of overcoming the power of the *Conseil d'Etat*. This tactic worked for a while, but it eventually let him down in 1969 when the French people voted by a narrow but decisive majority to reject his package of constitutional reforms designed to decentralise the national administration and to increase still further the powers of the Presidency. Thus even under the specially created constitutional conditions of the Fifth Republic, the judiciary and the Courts have retained a position of formidable, independent power.

In West Germany the role of the law is even more fundamental to the political system, so much so that the Federal Republic has been described as a *Rechtsstaat* (that is, a state founded upon the law). This is attributable to the fact that under the Basic Law of 1949 legal considerations have to play a major part in all Government decision-making. It is also reflected in the fact that many civil servants are trained as lawyers in the Prussian tradition. In such conditions the independence and strength of the judiciary is firmly established and the Federal Constitutional Court at Karlsruhe has become one of the most venerated institutions of the Federal Republic. The Court clarifies and interprets the constitution, decides all major disputes between the various parts of Government and arbitrates between Bonn and the *Länder*. Its role is somewhat analogous to that of the Supreme Court in the United States and more powerful than that of the Appellate Committee of the House of Lords in Britain.

The most marked contrast in the legal sphere is between Britain and the United States. Whereas in this country it is Parliament which has the final say in all legal and political matters, in the United States many of the most significant decisions have been made by the Supreme Court – for example, the 1954 decision on school desegregation in Brown *v*. the Topeka Board of Education. There is no legal institution in Britain which is really comparable to the US Supreme Court with its acknowledged capacity for creative and often controversial law-making and its periodic swings from judicial liberalism (as under Chief Justice Earl Warren in the 1950s and 1960s) to judicial conservatism (as under Chief Justice Warren Berger in the 1970s and 1980s). In Britain the Law Lords and the Court of

Appeal may have behaved notoriously from time to time in the eyes of some observers, notably in the politically contentious field of the law governing industrial relations. Yet even the boldest members of the judiciary are usually cautious about encroaching too far into the sphere of positive law-making, since that is widely recognised as the preserve of Parliament and particularly of the House of Commons.

## 19.7 CONCLUSION

The main conclusion of this chapter must be that the British political system is effectively *sui generis* and significantly different from that of other countries. Obviously, there are also some notable similarities with other countries, but it is the contrasts which are most worth recording.

In political terms, probably the most marked contrast is between the British system of Parliamentary government and the French system of Presidential government which under the Fifth Republic permits no more than a subsidiary role for the Senate and the *Assemblée Nationale*. The contrast between Britain and West Germany has more to do with the fact that this country is a unitary state whereas West Germany is a federal Republic in which constitutional power has been deliberately apportioned between Bonn and the *Länder*. In constitutional terms, the greatest contrast is between Britain and the United States, since in the latter case there is clear separation of powers between the Executive, the Legislature and the Judiciary and the distinctive roles of each are determined by the American constitution as defined and interpreted by the Supreme Court.

The main similarities among the four political systems are the growing concentration of political responsibilities upon the heads of Government, the considerable difficulties encountered in discharging these responsibilities to the satisfaction of the voters, and the continuing task of gaining and retaining the consent of the governed at a time when the chances of any Government doing so are fairly small. Although only two of the four political systems are presidential in formal terms, all have moved in the direction of greater presidentialism in practice. This means that there are now fewer alibis for central Governments when things go wrong and greater chances of sharp political changes when the voters are allowed their say.

The British political system stands out from the others covered in this chapter only perhaps in its historical capacity for gaining and retaining public consent for the actions of Government. Obviously, this cannot be an unqualified statement, since such consent is often little more than resentful acquiescence and since sometimes it ceases to exist at all, for example, in parts of Northern Ireland over the last two decades and in some English cities during the civil disorders of 1981. Yet the durability of British political institutions and the stoicism of the British people undoubtedly contribute to a high degree of political stability which has often been the envy of the rest of the world.

All political history shows that public consent can never be taken for granted. The natural laws of politics are not suspended for the British or anyone else. This means that in contemporary circumstances there is no satisfactory alternative to the continuous, untidy and compromising process of democratic politics if old freedoms are to be preserved and new opportunities created. The moral applies to Britain and all other free societies.

## SUGGESTED QUESTIONS

1. What are the main similarities and contrasts between the British political system and that of either France, West Germany or the United States?
2. Is Britain better governed than other comparable countries?

## NOTES

1. For example, see S. E. Finer, *Comparative Government* (Harmondsworth: Penguin, 1974); J. Blondel, *Comparing Political Systems* (London: Weidenfeld & Nicolson, 1973); or G. Smith, *Politics in Western Europe*, 3rd edn (London: Heinemann, 1980).

## FURTHER READING

Avril, P., *Politics in France* (Harmondsworth: Penguin, 1969).
Beloff, M., *The American Federal Government*, 2nd edn (Oxford: Oxford University Press, 1969).
Blondel, J., *Comparing Political Systems* (London: Weidenfeld & Nicolson, 1973).
Denenberg, R. V., *Understanding American Politics* (London: Fontana, 1976).
Edinger, L. J., *Politics in Germany* (Boston: Little Brown, 1968).
Ehrmann, H. W., *Politics in France* (Boston: Little Brown, 1968).
Finer, S. E., *Comparative Government* (Harmondsworth: Penguin, 1974).
Finer, S. E. (ed.) *Five Constitutions* (Harmondsworth: Penguin, 1979).
Hayward, J. E. S. and Berki, R. N. (eds) *State and Society in Contemporary Europe* (Oxford: Martin Robertson, 1979).
Johnson, N., *Government in the Federal Republic of Germany* (London: Pergamon, 1973).
Ridley, F. F. (ed.) *Government and Administration in Western Europe* (Oxford: Martin Robertson, 1979).
Smith, G., *Politics in Western Europe*, 3rd edn (London: Heinemann, 1980).
Sontheimer, K., *The Government and Politics of West Germany* (London: Hutchinson, 1972).

Vile, M. J. C., *Politics in the USA*, revised edn (London: Hutchinson, 1976).
Wright, V., *The Government and Politics of France*, 2nd edn (London: Hutchinson, 1983).

CHAPTER 20

# BRITISH PARLIAMENTARY DEMOCRACY

British Parliamentary democracy has evolved over the centuries. From Simon de Montfort's Parliament in 1265 to the outbreak of the Civil War in 1641 it was based upon the changing relations betweeen the Monarch and the representatives of the various estates of the realm. By the time of the Bill of Rights in 1689 a more explicit constitutional relationship had evolved between the Monarch and his Ministers on the one hand and the Lords and the Commons on the other. It was not until the 1832 Reform Act and the successive extensions of the franchise by subsequent Acts over the period to 1969 that a recognisably modern political system evolved and the relationship between the Government and the people came to assume its current shape. Today both politicians and people live in a Parliamentary democracy which has been formed by centuries of evolutionary development.

## 20.1 THE CONDITIONS OF DEMOCRACY

British Parliamentary democracy has a number of essential characteristics which we shall consider later in this chapter. However, before we can do so, we must understand that there are a number of conditions which have to be met if the system is to function satisfactorily in Britain or in other comparable countries. Joseph Schumpeter described these as 'conditions for the success of the democratic method' and it may be helpful for us to recall his argument.[1]

The first condition was that the politicians active in the political system should be of sufficiently high quality. It would obviously be invidious for the author to comment in any detail upon this point, save to observe that quality is influenced by attitude and that it has been noticeable over the last decade or so that many of our best politicians have been afflicted by a pervasive pessimism about our prospects for national recovery. Clearly high quality is a necessary but not a sufficient condition for successful politicians and cynicism or even defeatism does not improve their chances of success.

The second condition was that the range of political decisions should be limited. This is obviously a salutary point to make in relation to contemporary politics, since the persistence of unrealistic public expectations, often encouraged by unscrupulous politicians at election time, still leads people to suppose that Governments should have a solution to every problem. Unless leading politicians show themselves capable of preaching and practising the virtues of limited government, the problems of democracy are likely to become greater.

The third condition was that there should be a strong and impartial bureaucracy. The importance of this condition is best illustrated by its non-fulfilment, for example, in developing countries where the lack of a suitable administrative infrastructure can be a significant barrier to economic and social development. Ironically, in this country our all too complete fulfilment of this condition may actually be a source of weakness rather than strength in view of the tendencies in Whitehall to adhere to Departmental policies and to oppose radical or heretic ideas.

The fourth condition was that vanquished political minorities (that is the losing political parties) should acquiesce in their electoral defeat and accept the consequences of the voters' verdict. This condition is bound to be fundamental to the satisfactory functioning of any democracy and in this country the rule of the (Parliamentary) majority has invariably been accepted by all parties. Of course, a healthy democracy ought also to include safeguards for the defeated minorities against possible abuse of power by the majority. However, this is bound to be difficult to achieve in Britain as long as our electoral system enables the victorious party (which is normally elected by only a minority of the votes cast) to impose its political will upon the country simply by dint of its overall majority in the House of Commons.

The final condition was that everyone involved in politics, and especially the victorious majority at any time (that is, the winning political party) should show tolerance and magnanimity towards the interests and concerns of all those on the losing side at the previous General Election. This can be regarded as an argument for consensus rather than polarised politics and it is a condition which was broadly fufilled in this country during the twenty-five years or so after the Second World War. However, over the last decade or so there has been growing political polarisation between the two major parties on a number of important issues, such as defence, nationalisation, public spending, etc. If this turns out to be a lasting characteristic of British Parliamentary democracy, it will become more important that leading politicians, when in Government, should act in a spirit of magnanimity towards their temporarily vanquished political opponents. Otherwise they will not be able to expect reciprocal treatment when the roles are reversed and the country will suffer the damaging effects of pendulum politics.

## 20.2 ESSENTIAL CHARACTERISTICS

One essential characteristic of British Parliamentary democracy is that it is representative and so functions in a democratically responsible way. This has some positive consequences for the political system. It endows the Government of the day with legitimacy, although a wise Government will not take its authority for granted. It allows the electorate every four or five years to deliver a verdict on the record of the party in office and the competing attractions of the other main parties. It provides institutional channels of communication between the Government and the governed, although by no means the only channels in a political system in which pressure groups and the media play such an important part. It has the effect of magnifying or filtering the force of public opinion according to the nature of the issue and the requirements of the situation.

Notwithstanding these positive effects, our form of Parliamentary democracy has not secured universal approval. This is partly because all our political institutions have been subject to closer scrutiny and criticism as people have sought explanations for our relative national decline. It is also because some people have been drawn to advocate alternative political arrangements which they claim have been more successful in other countries. We must, therefore, consider the arguments on both sides of this question.

The legitimacy of government in Britain is based upon the fact that the party in office is invariably the victor of the previous General Election and can expect to enjoy the support of an overall majority in the House of Commons on most normal occasions. Of course, it is a qualified legitimacy in that it is valid for no more than five years at a time and is usually based upon no more than the largest single minority of the votes cast at the previous General Election.

This means that we have politics based upon underlying mutual consent between the Government and the people. On the one hand, Ministers accept that there are limits to the action which they can take if they are to remain within the bounds of public understanding and acceptability. On the other hand, the general public is prepared to allow the party in office considerable latitude in the fulfilment of its election mandate. Of course, the limits of legitimate Government action vary from time to time and from one Government to another. Much depends upon the extent to which a given policy runs counter to well-established party or pressure-group opinion. Much depends upon the perceived gravity and urgency of the situation with which the Government has to deal. Much depends upon the opportunities for making progress by stealth without attracting much media attention. Much depends upon the calculated risks of policy reversal in the event of the Opposition parties winning power at an ensuing General Election. In short, such limits cannot be objectively determined in advance, but only deduced from actual experience.

The supremacy of the electorate is based upon the fact that whatever the party in Government may decide to do during its term of office, it is the voters who have the final say at periodic General Elections every four or five years. Yet it is fair to add that such supremacy is qualified in practice by a number of significant factors.

Firstly, the voters are able to exercise no more than intermittent democratic control in view of the relative infrequency of General Elections. The rest of the time they can seek to put pressure upon their elected representatives and remind them of their vulnerability to future rejection if public wishes are not met, but they cannot do much more than that. Secondly, the voters are able to exercise their democratic choice, but only within the limited range of alternatives offered by the main political parties. Thus Conservative voters, who support capital punishment and live in safe Labour constituencies, are unlikely to have their wishes fulfilled. Equally, Labour voters, who support unilateral nuclear disarmament and live in safe Conservative constituencies, are unlikely to have their wishes fulfilled. As for the habitual supporters of third parties, they seem doomed to cast wasted votes at most General Elections. Thirdly, the ignorance and apathy of many voters is another limiting factor, since people who vote without real knowledge of the issues or who do not bother to vote at all, cannot be said to have established their supremacy in the political process in a particularly constructive way.

The importance of the political parties as vital channels of two-way communication between the Government and the people is another essential characteristic of our political system. They are not flawless mechanisms of communication, but they do manage to channel the energies of nearly all political activists within established and lawful political institutions. This is achieved largely because the party political conflict reflects real divisions and genuinely different interests in British society, yet is not usually so vicious or intolerant that it leads defeated minorities to reject the will of the majority.

As long as the political system is working properly, those who have political causes to advance ought to feel able to do so within the framework of one of the established parties. This is one of the reasons why each of the major parties, in particular, has a strong interest in remaining a broad church which can encompass several different interpretations of its political faith. It is also one of the reasons why in 1981 a number of

Labour MPs and one Conservative MP broke away from their parties to establish the new Social Democratic party. If the political parties in Britain were ever to lose such representative qualities, they would run the risk of being by-passed and eventually supplanted by other intermediary bodies better equipped to perform the vital function of political communication between the Government and the people.

Another essential characteristic of British Parliamentary democracy is the way in which the Government of the day usually acts to preserve a broad balance of political power in the community. Such behaviour is designed to ensure that the general interest gets a hearing above the cacophony of special pleading which comes from the many sectional interests. This is not easy for any Government to achieve, since the general interest is invariably weak and diffuse by comparison with the strength and concentration of the various sectional interests, especially those which are in a position to hold the rest of the community to ransom if their particular demands are not met.

In considering this problem, the central issue is how far a typical modern Government can do this while remaining responsive to the diversity of legitimate interests which are represented in any modern society. On the one hand, too great an emphasis upon the protection of the general interest can lay the Government open to the charge that it is not sufficiently mindful of the mosaic of sectional interests which produces such a healthy pluralism in our society. On the other hand, too great a willingness to rely upon understandings and deals with sectional interests can lay Ministers open to the charge that they are downgrading Parliament and moving too far towards the politics of corporatism. Thus a judicious balance has to be struck and if this is achieved, it is a hallmark of real political skill.

## 20.3 OTHER SIGNIFICANT FEATURES

In addition to the essential characteristics just mentioned, British Parliamentary democracy has some other significant features which need to be taken into consideration in making any overall assessment. We shall, therefore, discuss each of these briefly in turn.

### Political polarisation

The current tendency towards political polarisation in Britain derives mainly from the trend in each of the major parties over the last decade or so to adopt more ideological positions in the wake of political defeat at the polls. Thus the Labour party in Opposition began to move discernibly to the Left in the early 1970s and the Conservative party in Opposition began to move discernibly to the Right in the late 1970s. The result is that today there appears to be less consensus and more polarisation between the two major parties than at any time since the immediate post-war period.

Such polarisation is in marked contrast to the more limited political differences which existed during the 1950s and 1960s when each of the major parties broadly accepted the post-war consensus and seemed prepared to abide by the political conventions of the time. It can be argued that since then influential elements in each of the two major parties have become increasingly disenchanted with the limitations of the post-war consensus and increasingly drawn to explore the more radical policies of the Left and the Right. According to this argument, the political polarisation which has taken place is no more than a natural adjustment of the political parties to several years of disappointment with the output of the political system. It is also claimed that the sharpening of the conflict beween the two major parties has had the desirable effect of presenting the voters with clearer political choices than before at each successive General Election.

On the other side of the argument, however, it is maintained that since the two major parties have largely deserted what had traditionally been regarded as the non-ideological middle ground of British politics, there is now an opportunity for new political forces to fill the gap. Certainly this was one of the compelling arguments which led Roy Jenkins and the other members of the so-called 'Gang of Four' to establish the Social Democratic party in 1981 and then to form an electoral Alliance with the Liberals in order to fight the 1983 General Election. The fact that the multiplier effects of the British electoral system worked dramatically against the Alliance parties in 1983 does not necessarily mean that in the long run its founders will have been proved wrong in their analysis of the changes in British politics. After all it took the Labour party about forty years to achieve full major party status in Parliament during the first half of this century and it may take the Alliance parties nearly as long to demonstrate whether or not they can displace one or other of the major parties.

**Institutional inertia**

Institutional inertia is another significant feature of the British political system. Although there have been quite a number of institutional changes made over the last twenty years or so – for example, the reform of local government in the early 1970s and the abortive attempt to introduce devolution for Scotland and Wales in the late 1970s – none has proved to be particularly satisfactory and some have not worked at all. This had led the opponents of institutional change to argue that every such initiative taken does more harm than good and suffers from the law of unintended consequences. They point out that it is a mistake to advocate institutional change as a remedy for political problems which are often attitudinal and even psychological in origin and in this their prejudices seem to accord quite closely with prevailing public opinion.

On the other hand, those who do believe in the value of institutional change now tend to concentrate more and more upon the remedy of proportional representation as the key to unlock many of our political problems. They argue that it is the British electoral system - one of the most basic rules of the political game - which is the most significant obstacle to a fair Parliamentary outcome at General Elections and, indeed, to the adoption of sensible, middle-of-the-road policies by any Government. Yet their argument seems to take insufficient account of the strong vested interest in the existing electoral system which is held by most leading politicians in the two major parties and which has enabled them to share exclusive political power by turns over the four decades since the war. Furthermore, in a nation as instinctively conservative as Britain, the onus of establishing the need for change in any sphere is almost bound to rest upon those who propose it. Thus institutional inertia seems likely to remain a serious limitation upon radical change for some time to come.

**Elective dictatorship**

Lord Hailsham and others have argued that in certain circumstances British Parliamentary democracy can be virtually an 'elective dictatorship'.[2] This is true in the sense that any modern Government with an effective majority in the House of Commons can usually get its way in Parliament, at any rate on all the issues which really matter. Over the last decade or so this has been reflected in the tendency of Labour Governments to impose high rates of direct taxation, to nationalise large sections of British industry and to increase tax-financed welfare benefits. Equally, it has been reflected in the tendency of Conservative Governments to raise the rents of public housing, to legislate about internal trade union affairs and to denationalise large parts of the public sector. Such behaviour by each major party in office has seemed to support this thesis.

On the other hand, it can be argued that an 'elective dictatorship' is an exaggerated description of British Parliamentary democracy which tends to be voiced by those who have lost a General Election and are bemoaning the uses to which their political opponents choose to put the power of Government. The reality is that outside the twin citadels of Whitehall and Westminster there are powerful interest groups with a capacity to defeat or at least to modify the plans of any Government. For example, in 1969 the trade unions were able to use their influence in the Parliamentary Labour party and in the Cabinet to defeat the Labour Government proposals for trade union reform which were embodied in the White Paper entitled *In*

*Place of Strife*. Equally, in 1983 the Stock Exchange was able to persuade the Conservative Government to stop the reference of certain restrictive practices to the Court and to settle for some voluntary undertakings to modify its own behaviour. In general, it is also well understood that Ministers have no more than a limited and conditional tenure of office and that the voters always have the last word, no matter how powerful or even dictatorial a Government may seem to be.

**Limited government**

In contemporary political circumstances it may be more accurate to say that limited government is one of the most significant features of British Parliamentary democracy. This means that whatever Ministers may be able to do in Westminster and Whitehall where they wield considerable power, there are real limits to what they can achieve outside the twin citadels of political and bureaucratic power in London. One obvious reason for this is simply that under British constitutional arrangements no Parliament can bind its successors and therefore there can be no guarantee that decisions taken by one Government will be upheld by the next. Another reason is that there are certain problems in the world today which are not susceptible to quick or easy solutions and which are often exacerbated by administrative inertia, pressure-group resistance or international complications. This means that any modern Government has a great deal less freedom of manoeuvre than many politicians may like to admit.

It seems clear that the gulf between the ambitious objectives of most modern Governments and their modest achievements in office has damaged the reputation of British Parliamentary democracy in the eyes of many in the general public. It has undermined public faith in our main political institutions and increased public cynicism about most of the politicians who play a prominent part in British politics. This has led to many demands for institutional change, notably the introduction of proportional representation and the more frequent use of national referenda. Such prescriptions may not be the answers to our most serious national problems, but they are an understandable public response to our poor national performance over many years.

## 20.4 SOME UNRESOLVED ISSUES

The traditional pattern of political argument between the two major parties since the war has left unresolved some of the most important issues in modern British politics. These include notably the extent to which there is scope for anything more than marginal adjustment in the political system and the extent to which it is possible to maintain public consent for both the process and the outcome of politics in Britain. In both cases the experience of recent years suggests some fairly bleak prospects for the future.

**The scope for change**

There have been few institutional changes of positive or lasting consequence in Britain since the war. When such changes have been made - for example, the reform of local government in the early 1970s - they have often had disappointing results and unintended consequences of a deleterious character. This may have been due to the fact that the changes were not sufficiently radical or comprehensive. On the other hand, it may be that no institutional changes are likely to have much positive effect upon either the process or the outcome of politics in Britain and that the real explanations for our national decline have to be sought elsewhere, for example, in the conservatism of public attitudes and the widespread dislike of the pursuit of economic efficiency at any price.

Of course, there have been significant and frequent changes of policy in Britain since the war. This has led many people to argue that the country would have done better over the years with less doctrinaire Socialism from the Labour party and less free market capitalism from the Conservative party, especially when each is in Opposition. Yet even if it had been possible to do without such political ping-pong between the two major parties, no British Government since the war would have found it easy to deal successfully with our most intractable economic and social problems. Only since about 1976 (when the Labour Government was forced to seek a loan from the IMF) have Ministers come to recognise the case for more limited government and the need for a political approach which takes fuller account of the limits imposed by sectional groups and other organised centres of political and economic power both at home and abroad. Even now there is no universal agreement among British politicians and opinion-formers that successive Governments would have done better if they had been more realistic when setting their political objectives and if they had concentrated upon the limited but essential tasks which only Governments can perform.

**The importance of consent**

Any modern British Government has to give a high priority to the maintenance of public consent, if only because its attenuation or absence can fatally undermine the position of even the most dominant and determined politicians. Of course, in some cases Governments need no more than the tacit acquiescence of the general public in order to carry out their policies. However, for the most part positive public consent is both desirable and necessary for the fulfilment of political objectives and its existence is usually dependent upon a number of pre-conditions. It requires a well-informed and powerful Parliament in which MPs not in the Government have sufficient opportunities to influence the course of policy at formative stages. It requires systematic and genuine consultations between the Government of the day and a wide variety of sectional interest groups. It requires a serious and responsible approach by the media to the great political issues of the day. Yet even if such conditions are met, the maintenance of public consent can still be prejudiced by the harsh decisions and difficult choices which modern Governments have to make.

If any British Government is to deal successfully with the most difficult problems of our time - for example, the bleak prospects for employment, the impact of rapid technological change and the effect of current demographic trends upon the future of the Welfare State - there will be an even greater need for responsible and far-sighted leadership by politicians in all parties. Such leadership is likely to require the elaboration of convincing new definitions of many of our traditional economic and social objectives in ways which could improve our chances of attaining them. For their part the general public will need to realise that many traditional attitudes and assumptions are likely to obstruct rather than assist the new ideas of growth, progress and the quality of life which will form the basis of the new political outlook which is required. Even assuming such an ideological transformation, it will not be easy to avoid further public disappointment and distress unless there is a timely and permanent adjustment of public expectations to more realistic and sustainable levels.

## 20.5 **CONCLUSION**

It should be clear from this book that British Parliamentary democracy is neither easy to describe nor to explain. It is changing all the time, yet in many respects it remains the same. It is therefore imbued with paradoxes and contradictions. While the system allows for strong government, its capacity for legitimising the decisions actually taken is not always so impressive. This may be because some Government decisions are no longer founded upon a sufficiently broad political consensus, as they were for about a quarter of a century after the Second World War. Yet the real explanations probably run deeper and derive from the changes in British society and the decline in our relative national performance.

There are already some signs that a new political consensus may be emerging to replace the received ideas inherited from the 1950s and the 1960s. However, the political system will be able to make the transition 'only if enough people want it to work and are prepared to make the necessary adjustments that the claims of others demand'.[3] This suggests that politicians and public alike will have to strive hard for mutual understanding and accommodation. If this is achieved, it should be possible to maintain enough mutual trust and consent to allow British Parliamentary democracy to continue for a long time to come.

## SUGGESTED QUESTIONS

1. What is the essence of British Parliamentary democracy?
2. Is the British political system successful in attracting the consent of the people?

## NOTES

1. See J. A. Schumpeter, *Capitalism, Socialism & Democracy*, 3rd edn (New York: Harper & Row, 1962) pp. 289–96.
2. See Q. Hailsham, *The Dilemma of Democracy* (London: Collins, 1978) pp. 280–1.
3. S. I. Benn and R. S. Peters, *Social Principles and the Democratic State* (London: Allen & Unwin, 1959) p. 349.

## FURTHER READING

Benn, S. I. and Peters, R. S., *Social Principles and the Democratic State* (London: Allen & Unwin, 1959).

Birch, A. H., *Representative and Responsible Government* (London: Allen & Unwin, 1964).

Brittan, S., *The Economic Consequences of Democracy* (London: Temple Smith, 1977).

Brittan, S. *The Role and Limits of Government* (London: Temple Smith, 1983).

Dahrendorf, R., *Life Chances* (London: Weidenfeld & Nicolson, 1979).

Hailsham, Q., *The Dilemma of Democracy* (London: Collins, 1978).

Hirsch, F., *Social Limits to Growth* (London: Routledge & Kegan Paul, 1977).

Macpherson, C. B., *The Life and Times of Liberal Democracy* (Oxford: Oxford University Press, 1977).

Nozick, R., *Anarchy, Utopia and the State* (Oxford: Blackwell, 1974).

Plamenatz, J., *Democracy and Illusion* (London: Longman, 1973).

Rawls, J., *A Theory of Justice* (Oxford: Oxford University Press, 1973).

Schumpeter, J. A., *Capitalism, Socialism and Democracy*, 3rd edn (New York: Harper & Row, 1962).

# INDEX OF SUBJECTS


accommodation, technique of 202
Act of Settlement (1701) 12
Acts of Union
  with Ireland (1800) 4, 12
  with Scotland (1707) 4, 12
administrative law 307–14
  Administrative Tribunals 308–9
  and constitutional reform 313–14
  Continental systems of 312–13
  judicial review of 311–12
    doctrine of *ultra vires* 311
    legal remedies 311
    natural justice principles 312
    weaknesses in 312
  ministerial control of 309
  Ombudsman 310–11
Administrative Tribunals 308–9
advertising controls 304
Age Concern 83
Agriculture Acts
  1947 83, 87
  1957 87
Aircraft and Shipbuilding Industries Bill 145
Air Ministry 213
Alliance Parties *see* SDP/Liberal Alliance
Appellate Committee 147, 299–300
Appellate Jurisdiction Act (1876) 146
Armstrong Committee 166

back-bench committees (Conservative) 61
back-bench committees (Labour) 64
back-benchers 155–6
Ballot Act (1872) 12
ballot papers 23
Beatty *v.* Gillbanks (1882) 12
Beveridge Report (1942) 6
Bills, stages of 160–2
Bill of Rights (1689) 12, 333
bishops 140
block votes (in the Labour party) 62
BMA *see* British Medical Association
Board of Agriculture and Fisheries 213
Board of Education 213
Boundary Commissions 22
British Medical Association (BMA) 78, 80–1, 88
British Nationality Act (1981) 87, 302
British political culture *see* culture
British politics
  compared with other systems 321–31
    electoral system 323–4
    legal system 328–30
    pattern of government 324–5
    political culture 321–3
    role of bureaucracy 325–7
    role of Parliament 327–8
broadcasting
  cable systems 106–7
  current situation 94–7
  Direct Broadcasting by Satellite 107–8
  financial problems 96
  new technology 106–8
  of Parliament 167
  political problems 96–7
  power of radio 105–6
  power of television 103–5
Bryce Commission (1918) 143
Building Societies Association 78, 88
bureaucracy *see also* Civil Service
  and democracy 334
  role in British politics 325–7
Bushell's Case (1670) 12

'Cabal' 173
Cabinet
  agenda 189
  Central Policy Review Staff (CPRS) 180
  committees 175–9
  composition and functions 174–6
  and decision-making 187–9, 198–9
  Inter-Departmental co-ordination 190–1
  machinery of Cabinet government 174–81
  minutes of 179–80
  origins of 173–4
  and the Prime Minister 183–4, 187–9, 191
  procedure 175
  review of key problems 189–90
  resignation from 188–9
  role of 186–91
  Shadow Cabinet (Labour) 155
  size of 174, 214
  10 Downing Street 180–1
  Whitehall support for 176–80
Cabinet Office 174–5, 179–80
Cabinet Secretary 174, 179
Cable Authority 107
cable systems 106–7
campaign techniques 41
  effect of opinion polls on 118–19
  effect of television on 104

Campaign for Nuclear Disarmament (CND) 79, 84
CBI *see* Confederation of British Industry
central Government *see also* Departments, Ministers
administration of 231–3
control of local government 278–84
Departmental policy 224–5
Departmental structure 214–16
Government functions 216–18
Ministerial responsibility 219–20
Ministerial work-load 223–4
paradox of 216
Parliamentary accountability 221–3
possible co-operation with local government 284–5, 289
problems of 223–5
quality of advice 225
relations with local government 276–8, 284–8
role of Ministers 218–23
structure of 215
work of 214–18
Central Policy Review Staff (CPRS) 180
Chancery Division 297
Child Poverty Action Group 78, 83
Children and Young Persons Act (1969) 275, 279
Chronically Sick and Disabled Persons Act (1972) 274–5
citizens and the state 302–7
civil justice
civil appeals 299–300
controversial issues of 296–9
access to law 298
delays in judicial system 299
image of law, lawyers 296–8
legal aid 298–9
nature of judiciary 298
court system 296–7
machinery and procedure 296–7
civil rights 302–7
citizenship 302
and emergency powers 305–6
free movement 302
freedom of expression 303–4
International Conventions on 306–7
legal remedies 303
and natural justice 312
personal liberty 302–3
property rights 303
public meetings 304
public processions 304–5
state security 306
Civil Service 228–46
blocking power 89
at Cabinet Committees 176–80
composition and functions 228–33
conventions 233–4
definition of 228
ethical standards 234
Fulton Committee and 229, 234
functions 231–3
administration 231–3
advice to Ministers 231-2
bureaucracy management 232–3
policy- and decison-making 232
representation of Ministers 232
future developments 241–6
Ministers as managers 242
Officials as managers 242–4
Government White Paper on (1981) 242–3
judicial control 245–6
judicial scrutiny 241
key aspects 233–8
methods of control 238–41
administrative efficiency 239–41
bureaucratic hierarchy 239
judicial scrutiny 241
Ombudsman 239–41
private sector techniques 239–41
'Rayner scrutinies' 240
*ultra vires* doctrine 241
use of accountants 240–1
and ministerial responsibility 234, 238–9
Northcote–Trevelyan Report 229, 233
numbers 216, 229
personnel 229–31
and Parliamentary accountability 235
priority to Ministers 233
role 217–18
in British politics 325–7
and policy execution 199–202
power of 226
and pressure groups 82–3
strengths and weaknesses 235–8
structural reform of 244–5
Thatcher Government and 243, 244–5
vertical hierarchies in 233-4
Civil Service Department 213
class 4–5
of civil servants 229
of Members of Parliament 154
and politics 46
and voting behaviour 34–5, 37, 43
Clean Air Act (1956) 86
CND *see* Campaign for Nuclear Disarmament
Coalition Government 6
'cohort theory' 115
Communist Party 56
Confederation of British Industry (CBI) 79, 81, 83

consensus 334
  British compared to others 322
  on policy 6
  procedural 6–7
  in public opinion 111–12
Conservation Society 86
Conservative Central Office 59
Conservative Party 73–4
  back-bench committees 61–2
  Business Committee 61–2
  candidate selection 72–3
  Central Council 59–61
  1922 Committee 61
  constituency activities 68–73
    financial matters 69–70
    local and national membership 70–1
    and political power 71
  and electoral system 24
  Executive councils 71
  and House of Lords reform 149–50, 151
  ideological principles 52–3
  image of 41, 116
  and Labour Pary compared 65–6
  Leader of 62
  local government policy 20, 270
  National Advisory Committees 61
  national organization 59–62
  National Union of Conservative
    Associations 59–61
  Party Chairman 59
  Party Conference 59
  and policy consensus 6
  and policy formulation
    in government 197–8
    in Opposition 196–7
  and policy germination 195–6
  political functions 57–9
    primary function 57
    subsidiary functions 57–9
  and postal voting 23
  Prime Ministers of 184, 185
  and public corporations 254, 266
  and Road Haulage Association 86–7
  social composition 71
  support for 29, 32, 33, 38, 39–40, 44–5
    age-based 35–6
    and class 34
    geographical and sociological variation
      in 36–7
    sex-based 35, 44
    from the working class 34, 35, 43
  'Wets and Dries' 52
Conservative Research Department 59
constitution 11–20
  characteristics of 11–13
  conventions and 13, 174
  definition 11
  flexibility of 13
  judicial proceedings and 12
  paradoxes of 17
  scope for change 17–20
    constitutional reform 313–14
    within Labour movement 53–4
    pressures for reform 19-20
    and referenda 17–19
  uncodified 11–12
  views of 14–17
    classic, liberal 14, 15
    empirical 16–17, 18
    governmental 15–16
Consumer Councils 258
Consumers Association 80
conventions 13, 174
corporatism 78, 91n5
councillors 272–3
County Courts 295–6
courts *see also* individual names
  in civil cases 295–7
  Courts of Appeal 299–302
  in criminal cases 292–5
CPRS *see* Central Policy Review staff
Crichel Down Affair (1954) 222, 309,
  316n17
criminal justice 292–5
  controversial issues in 296–9
    law and order 295
    police power 294–5
  court system 293
  criminal appeals 299–300
  machinery and procedure 292–5
Criminal Justice Act (1982) 88
Criminal Law Act (1967) 303
cross-benchers 142
Crown Courts 292–4

'D Notice' system 100–1, 306
*Daily Mirror* 99
DBS *see* Direct Broadcasting by satellite
decision-making *see also* policy-
  making 194–5, 210–11
  in Cabinet and Cabinet
    Committees 187–9, 198–9
  and Civil Service 232
  and conditions of democracy 334
  continuity and discontinuity of 203–6
  deliberate discontinuity of 205–6
  definition of 194
  in Government 198–9
  improvements in 208–10
    and advice to Ministers 209
    and changes in Whitehall 209–10
    and role for Parliament 210
    and support to opposition 208–9
  in local government 277–8

in Opposition 198
and pressure groups 87–8
strengths and weaknesses 206–8
defamation, law of 303–4
democracy *see* Parliamentary democracy
demonstrations 120
at Greenham Common 9, 120
Departments (of central Government) *see also* Ministers
Departmental policy 224–5
Departmental structure 214–16
history of 213–14
Ministerial pattern in 216
Ministerial responsibility in 219–20
reorganization (1970) 214
routine in 217–18
Department of Energy 213
Department of the Environment 86, 213
Department of Trade and Industry 213, 214
Department of Transport 213, 214
devolution referenda 18–19, 119
Direct Broadcasting by Satellite (DBS) 107–8

Ecology Party 56
Education Acts
1944 273
1981 143
EEC *see* European Economic Community
electoral systems *see also* General Elections, political candidates
British compared with others 323–4
criteria of assessment 26–9
current 22
disqualifications 30n2
effectiveness of the legislature 27–8
election Agents 23–4
fairness of results in 28–9
'first-past-the-post' 24–5
mechanisms in 22–4
campaign techniques in 41
effect of opinion polls on 118–19
effect of television on 104
and proportional representation 19, 25–6
public confidence in 29
quality of the MPs 26–7
reform of and SDP/Liberal Alliance 19, 25–6, 29
threshold of success in 28
electorate *see also* voting behaviour
growing power of 14
groups in 32–7
class-based 34–5, 37
floaters and abstainers 33
geographical and sociological variations in 36–7
party loyalists 32–3
sex-and aged-based voting 35–6
participation in politics 45–6
representation in House of Commons 154
supremacy of 336
volatility of 44–5
Emergency Powers Acts 305–6
Employment Act (1980) 304
England
local government in 269–70
unity with Ireland 4
unity with Scotland 4, 12
unity with Wales 4
Erskine May 12, 152n3, 157
European Communities Act (1972) 19, 314
European Convention on Human Rights (1950) 307
European Economic Community
British referendum on membership 18
and pressure groups 84
Treaty of Accession 131
European legislation 222
European secondary legislation 148

Falklands conflict (1982) 131, 158
and Parliamentary accountability 222
Finance Bills 88
'first-past-the-post' 24–5
multiplier effect of 24–25
floating voters 33
France
bureaucracy in 326
electoral system 323
legal system 329
pattern of government 324–5, 330
political culture 321, 322
role of Parliament 327
Freedom of Information 101–2, 306
Friends of the Earth 79
fringe parties 56
front-benchers 154–5
Fulton Committee (1967) 229
Fulton Report (1968) 234, 240, 242

Gallup Survey (June 1983) 35, 40
General Elections 7, 13
1959 103
Feb 1974 28
1979 35, 36, 39, 115, 185–6
1983 22, 28, 34, 35, 36, 38, 40, 41, 44–5
turn-out at 45–6
General and Municipal Workers Union (GMWU) 81
Glasgow Media Group 104, 110n10

GMWU *see* General and Municipal Workers Union
GNP, changes in 8
governmental power 15–16
limitations to 17, 340
and pressure groups 82
Grant Related Expenditure Assessments (GREAs) 282
Greenham Common demonstrations 9, 120
Greenpeace 79, 80

Health Authorities 263–4
reorganization 264
unified structure 264
Health and Safety Executive 79
Health and Safety at Work Act (1974) 79
'Her Majesty's Loyal Opposition' 156
High Courts 292–4, 296
Chancery Division 296
Family Division 296
Queen's Bench Division 296
Highways Act (1959) 304
historical continuity 3–4
Honours Lists 128–30
Houghton Report (1976) 58
House of Commons *see also* Members of Parliament 153–68
composition 153–7
Members of Parliament 154–7
party divisions 153–4
main functions 159–64
legislative process 160–2
Party battle in 160
Parliamentary control in 163
representation and redress 159–60
powers of 157–9
influence 158–9
in theory and practice 157–8
votes of confidence 158
prospects for reform 164–7
broadcasting possibilities 167
budgetary reform 166
mixed procedure 166
procedural reforms 165–6
Select Committee developments 164–5
Select Committees 163, 164–5
Speaker 153
Supremacy of 14
House of Lords 139–51
average attendance 140
composition 140–2
bishops and Law Lords 140
hereditary peers 140–1
life peers 141–2
women peers 141
as final Court of Appeal 299–300
and European secondary legislation 148
party divisions 142
power and functions of 142–8
Bryce Commission (1918) 143
deliberative function 146
functions 143–8
initiation of non-controversial legislation 146
judicial function 146–7
legislative delay 144–5
legislative revisions 145, 162
Parliament Act procedures 143
powers 142–3
scrutiny functions 147–9
proposals for abolition of 19, 135
proposals for reform of 148–50
by Alliance Party 150
by Conservative Party 19, 149–50
by Labour Party 149, 151
previous reforms of 139–40
'hung Parliament' 26, 136
Hunt Report (1982) 107

Independent Broadcasting Authority (IBA) 95
'Inner Cabinet' 188
Inter-Departmental Committees 217–18

Joint Committee on Statutory Instruments 147–8
judicial appeal 299–302
contentious cases 300–1
controversial issues 300–2
judicial activism 301
judicial conservatism 301–2
machinery and procedure 299–300
Judicial Committee of the Privy Council 300
judicial system
and Constitution 12
civil justice 295–9
criminal justice 292–5
judicial appeal 299–302
and relations with political system 314
and review of administrative law 311–12
Justice Report (1978) 101

Keynesian White Paper (1944) 6
Kilbrandon Commission (1973) 26
'Kitchen Cabinet' 180

Labour Party
candidate selection 72–3
Conference 62–4
Conference Arrangements Committee 62
and Conservative Party compared 65–6
constituency activities 68–9

and finance 69
local and national membership 70–1
and EEC membership 18
election arrangements 64–5
and electoral system 24
General Management Committees 71
General Secretary 62
headquarters 62
and House of Lords abolition 19, 135, 151
and House of Lords reform 149
ideological principles 53–5
image of 41, 116
influence of trade unions on 85
Leader 65
National Executive Committee 62, 64, 66, 73, 197
national organization 62–5
Parliamentary Committee 64
Parliamentary Labour Party 64–5, 66
party Chairman 62
and policy consensus 6
and policy formulation 197
and policy germination 196
political functions 58
political inheritance and 38
political power in 71
Prime Ministers of 184.185
and public corporations 253, 254, 255, 266
reform of 20
social composition 71
and socialism 53, 65
support for 29, 32, 33, 38–9, 40, 44–5
age-based 35–6
and class 34–5
geographical and sociological variations in 36–7
middle-class support 43
sex-based 35, 44
Law Lords 140, 147, 299–300
Law Society 78–9, 88
Layfield Report (1976) 281, 287
Legal Aid 298–9
Legal Aid and Advice Act (1949) 298
legal system *see also* judicial system
and administrative law 307–14
Administrative Tribunals 308–9
constitutional reform 313–14
Continental systems of 312–13
judicial review of 311–12
Ministerial control and 309
Ombudsman 310–11
British, compared to others 328–30
and civil rights 302–7
citizenship 302
emergency powers 305–6
free movement 302
freedom of expression 303–4
International Conventions on 306–7
meetings and processions 304–5
personal liberty and property 302–3
public protest 305
state security 306
legislation
delay of in House of Lords 144–5
emergency legislation 162
European 222
European secondary legislation 148
in House of Commons 160–2
initiation of in House of Lords 146
pre-legislative investigation 163
and pressure groups 88
revision of in House of Lords 145, 162
Royal assent to 128
legislature, effectiveness of 27–8
Lib-Lab pact (1977–9) 167–8
Liberal Party *see also* SDP/Liberal Alliance 32, 55
candidate selection 72–3
constituency activities 69
and finance 70
local membership 70
and electoral system 24, 29
Finance and Administration Board 66
and House of Lords reform 150
National Executive Committee 66
national organization 66–7
political functions 57–9
support for 32, 33
and class 34
sex-based 35
Life Peerages Act (1958) 139
Lobby system 102–3
advantages 102–3
definition of 'lobby terms' 102
local government 269–89
Audit Commission 282
and central Government grants 283
committees 272
control by central Government 278–84
administrative control 280
and current legislation 20, 282
financial control 280–4
legislative control 278–9
policy control 279
councillors and officials 272–3
definition of 269
dimensions of local government 284
financial difficulties 284
future possibilities for 284–8
autonomy or centralisation 286–8
co-operation with central Government 284–5, 289

Local government *contin.*
Grant Related Expenditure Assessments (GREAs) 282
Layfield Committee 281
Layfield Report (1976) 287
local authority composition and procedures 272–3
powers and functions of 273–6
discretionary powers 275
division of functions 275–6
statutory duties 274–5
possibilities for change 285–6
qualities of 288–9
rates 282–3
Rate Support Grant (RSG) 281, 283
relations with central Government 276–8
constitutional 276–7
political 277–8
representative bodies of 278
Robinson Report (1977) 272
sources of revenue for 281
structure and composition of 269–73
in England and Wales 269–70
in Northern Ireland 271
in Scotland 270–1
Treasury Loan Sanctions 283–4
Local Government Acts
1888 12
1929 280
1972 269–70, 273, 280, 281, 287
Local Government Finance Act (1982) 282
Local Government (Northern Ireland) Act (1972) 271
Local Government Planning and Land Act (1980) 280, 281, 284

M23 Action Group 80
'magic circle' 126
Magistrates Association 78, 88
Magistrates Courts 292, 294, 296
Magna Carta 11–12
Management of Information System for Ministers 238–9, 247n16
manipulation, technique of 202
Manpower Services Commission 79
media 93–109
broadcasting *see* radio, power of television 103–6
current situation 94–7
new technology in 106–8
power of radio 105–6
power of television 103–5, 108, 113
and public opinion 113–14
structure of 97–8
the press 93–4, 99–103
current situation 93–4
freedom of information 101–2
influence and bias of 99–100
role of the Lobby 102–3
secrecy and censorship 100–1
Members of Parliament *see also* House of Commons, politicians
back-benchers 155–6
characteristics of 154
class characteristics of 26–7
composition of 153–4
education 26–7
front-benchers 154–5
in Opposition 27–8
pay and conditions 156–7
quality of 26–7
as 'virtual representatives' 154, 169n4
Metropolitan Authorities 275–6
Ministerial responsibility 13, 219–20
and the Civil Service 234–5, 238–9
collective 220
individual 219–20
and public corporations 257
Ministers
accountability to Parliament 221–3
and Crichel Down Affair 222
and European legislation 222
and Falklands conflict 222
and Statutory Instruments 221–2
advice from Civil Service 231
advice for new Ministers 199–200
appointment and dismissal of by Prime Minister 182
control of administrative law 309
Departmental policy 224–5
differences in 200
examples of influential Ministers 218-19
as managers 242
non-Departmental 215
pattern of within Departments 216
power of 225–6
priority over civil servants 233–4
quality of advice to 225
relations with public corporations 253–6
representation of by civil servants 232
resignation of 188–9
responsibility of 219–20
role of 218–23
routine of 217
Senior Ministers in Cabinet 175
wider advice for 209
work-load 223–4
Ministers of the Crown Act (1937) 174
Monarchy 125–7
financial position 134–5
possible future problems 135–6
powers and functions 125–33
assent to legislation 128
and colonial consitutions 131

choice of Prime Minister 125–6
conclusion of treaties 131
creation of peers 128–9
creation of public corporations 131–2
declaration of war 131
dissolution of Parliament 127–8
formal functions 131–2
granting of honours 129–30
head of the Commonwealth 132
mercy and pardon 130
public appointments 130
symbolic functions 132
unpublicised functions 132–3
and the Prime Minister 125–6, 132–3
projection of 134
and the public 133–4
public attitudes 133–4
Monopolies and Mergers Commission 258
Municipal Corporations Act (1835) 276

National Coal Board (NCB) 88
National Economic Development Council (NEDDY) 83, 262
National Farmers Union (NFU) 78–9, 83, 87
National Federation of the Self-Employed 78
National Front 56
National Government 18, 126
National Society for Clean Air 86
National Union of Conservative Associations 59
Central Council 59–61
Executive Committee 61
General Purposes Committee 61
National Union of Mineworkers (NUM) 80–1, 88
National Union of Teachers (NUT) 88
nationalism 5–6, 10n3, 32–3
Nationalist Parties *see also* Plaid Cymru and Scottish National Party 55–6
NEDDY *see* National Economic Development Council
negative voting 40
new technology, impact of 106–8
nomination papers 23
non-voters 33
Northcote–Trevelyan Report (1854) 229, 233
Northern Ireland
local government structure 271
Northern Ireland Assembly 271
political parties in 56–7, 75n9
unity with England 4
voting in 33
Northern Ireland Act (1982) 271
NUM *see* National Union of Mineworkers
NUT *see* National Union of Teachers

O'Connell Case (1844) 146
Official Secrets Act (1911) 100, 101, 306
Ombudsman 241, 310–11
procedure 310–11
status and jurisdiction 310
opinion polls 118–19
on Monarchy 133–4
Opposition
composition 155
decision-making in 198
and discontinuity of policy 205–6
'Her Majesty's Loyal Opposition' 156
increased support for 208–9
and policy formulation 196–7
of Conservative Opposition 196–7
of Labour Opposition 197
and policy germination 195–6
Outer Circle Policy Unit 101

Parliament Acts
1911 12, 15–16, 139, 143, 144
1949 139, 143
Parliament Bill (1947) 143, 144
Parliament Number 2 Bill 139–40, 149
Parliamentary accountability 221–3
and Civil Service 235
and control of public corporations 257–8
and Crichel Down Affair 222
and European legislation 222
and Falklands conflict 222
and Statutory Instruments 221–2
Parliamentary democracy 333–43
characteristics of 335–7
balance of political power 337
elective dictatorship 339–40
importance of political parties 336–7
institutional inertia 338–9
legitimacy of government 335
limited government 340
new political consensus 342–3
political polarisation 337–8
politics of mutual consent 335–6
representative quality 335
supremacy of electorate 336
conditions of 333–5
unresolved issues 340–2
importance of consent 341–2
scope for change 341
Parliamentary draftsmen 201
Parliamentary Labour Party (PLP) 64–5, 66
Parliamentary Private Secretaries (PPSs) 154–5

Party loyalists 32–3
patronage 182–3
Peerage Act (1963) 139, 140, 151n1
peerages
  creation of by Monarch 128–9
  hereditary 129, 140–1
  life 129, 141–2
personal liberty 302–3
Plaid Cymru 5–6, 32–3
  ideology of 55
Pliatzky Report 259
PLP *see* Parliamentary Labour Party
police
  relationship with public 295–6
Police Act (1964) 262
Police and Criminal Evidence Bill 294, 303
policy-making *see also* decision-making 194–5, 210–11
  and Civil Service 232, 234
  continuity and descontinuity of 203–6
  decision-making 198–9
  definition of policy 194
  improvements in 208–10
    greater role for Parliament 210
    increased support for Opposition 208–9
    structural changes in Whitehall 209–10
    wider advice for Ministers 209
  stages in the process 195–203
    key aspects 203–8
  policy execution 199–202
    advice to new Ministers 199–200
    channels of communication 200–1
    consultations in Whitehall 201
    executive decisions 201
    Ministerial differences 200
  policy formulation 196–8
    in Government 197–8
    in Opposition 196–7
  policy fulfilment 202–3
    technique of accommodation 202
    technique of manipulation 202
    technique of political shock treatment 203
    technique of public opinion mobilisation 202–3
  policy germination 195–6
    in the Conservative party 195–6
    in the Labour party 196
  and pressure groups 85–9
  strengths and weaknesses 206–8
Policy Units 180–1
political campaigns *see* campaigns
political candidates
  campaign expenditure 23
  disqualification 23
  procedure for 23–4
  selection of 72–3
political culture 3–9, 321–3
  characteristics 3–7, 321–3
  consensus, two kinds 6–7
  cultural cohesion 4–6
  definition 3
  historical continuity 3–4
  moderation of Governments 7–8
  possible changes in 9
  public detachment from politics 8–9
'political impossibility' 117
political minorities 334
political parties *see also* individual parties
  party battle in House of Commons 160
  constituency activities 68–73
    candidate selection 72–3
    financial matters 69–70
    local membership 70–1
    major party contrasts 65–6
    political power 71
  definition 51
  divisions in House of Commons 153–4
  fringe parties 56
  ideological principles 51–7
    Alliance parties 55
    Conservative party 52–3
    Fringe parties 56
    Labour party 53–5
    Nationalist parties 55–6
    Northern Ireland parties 56–7
  image of 40–1
    and influence on public opinion 116
  importance in democracy 336–7
  national organisation 59–68
    Conservative party 59–62
    Labour party 62–5
    Liberal party 66–7
    Social Democratic party 68–9
  political functions 57–9
    primary 57
    subsidiary 57–9
  political polarisation of 337–8
  representation of in House of Lords 142
political issues of 115–16
political power, balance of 337
politicians *see also* Members of Parliament
  effects of public opinion on 116–17
  qualities of in democracy 333–4
politics
  British politics compared 321–31
  and broadcasting 108–9
  as entertainment 103
  influence of 115
  and media 108–9
  and press 93–4, 99–100
PPS *see* Parliamentary Private Secretaries

press
  concentration of ownership 94
  current situation 93–4
  and freedom of information 101–2
  influence of 99–103
  political bias of 99–100
  and role of the Lobby 102–3
  and secrecy and censorship 100–1
pressure groups 77–91
  advantages of 89
  cause groups 79–80
  and Civil Service contacts 82–83
  and decision-making 87–8
  definitions of 77
  disadvantages of 90
  financial power of 84
  functions 77–80
  interest groups 78–9
  involvement in politics 85–90
  and legislation 87
  loyalty to 81–2
  membership of 80–1
  organization and power of 80–5
  and policy execution 88–9
  and policy formulation 87
  and policy fulfilment 88–90
  and policy germination 85–7
  political leverage 82
  and public opinion 117–18
  publicity value 83–4
  voting power 84–5
Prime Minister
  and Cabinet 191
  and Cabinet decision-making 198–9
  Conservative and Labour compared 184
  and Monarchy 125–6, 132–3
  origins of office of 173–4
  power of 181–6
    dominance of Cabinet 187–9
    crisis management 186
    in Government 183-4
    interpretations of 181–2
    and ministerial appointments and dismissals 182
    national power 186
    in Parliament 184
    party political power 185–6
    of patronage 182–3
    Policy Units 180–1
    and right to recommend dissolution 185–6
  sources of advice for 180–1
  10 Downing Street 180–1
Private Bills 147
Privy Councillors 156
property rights 303
proportional representation 19, 25–6
  additional member principle 26
  and single transferable vote 25–6
Provisional Sinn Fein 6, 33
  ideology of 56
public *see also* electorate
  detachment from politics 8–9
  ignorance of politics 113
  and the Monarchy 133–4
Public Accounts Committee 239
public corporations
  characteristics 252–3
  forms of public ownership 252
  methods of control of 256–8
    Consumer Councils 258
    debates in Parliament 258
    Efficiency Audits 258
    ministerial responsibility 257
    Monopolies and Mergers Commission 258
    other mechanisms 258
    parliamentary accountability 257–8
    Royal Commissions 258
    scrutiny by Members of Parliament 257–8
  municipal ownership 252
  NEDO Report (1976) 256
  problems of 253–6
    arm's length relationship 254–5
    diversity 254
    myths and realities 264–5
    and relations with Ministers 254–5, 255–6
    and statutory duties of 255
    theory and practice 253–4
  scope of 252
    future guidelines 265–6
  1961 White Paper on 255
  1967 White Paper on 255
  1978 White Paper on 266
Public Meeting Act (1908) 304
public opinion 111–21
  composition of 111–14
  consensus and controversy 111–12
  definitions of 111
  effects of 116–20
    and opinion polls 118–19
    on politicians 116–17
    and pressure groups 117–18
    and public demonstrations 120
    and referenda 119–20
  formation of 114–16
  informed opinion 113
  inheritance and experience 114–15
  issues and images 115–16
  mass opinion 113–14
  mobilisation of 202–3
Public Order Act (1936) 304–5

public sector *see also* public
corporations 251–66
advisory committees 262–3
composition of 251
defined 251
Departmental Committees 261–2
fringe bodies 259–61
advantages and disadvantages 260–1
characteristics of 259–60
defined 259
QUANGOs 259
scope of 259
future guidelines 265–6
future prospects 264–6
Health Authorities 263–4
methods of control 256–8
NEDO report (1976) 256
Royal Commissions 261–2
significance of 266
Water Authorities 263
1961 White Paper on 255
1967 White Paper on 255
1978 White Paper on 266
Public Works Loans Board 283

QUANGOs (quasi autonomous non-governmental organizations) 259
Queen's Bench 296–7

radio
and broadcasting of Parliament 105, 167
financial problems 96
local radio 96, 98, 105–6
national radio 95–6
power of 105–6
political problems 96–7
structure of 97–8
Rate Support Grant (RSG) 281, 283
rates 282–3
'Rayner scrutinies' 240
Redistribution of Seats Act (1944) 12
Redistribution of Seats Number 2 Bill 144–5
referenda 17–19, 119–20
advent of 119–20
and capital punishment 19
on devolution 18–19, 119
on EEC entry 18, 119
special cases 119
Reform Acts
1832 12, 139, 173, 333
1867 173
Representation of the People Act (1969) 12
Road Haulage Association (RHA) 86–7
Robinson Report (1977) 272
Royal Charters 131–2
Royal Commissions 261–2
Royal Commission on Criminal Procedure (1981) 294
Royal prerogative 13, 125, 130, 131
RSG *see* Rate Support Grant

Scotland
and devolution 18–19
local government structure 270
nationalism in 32–3
political parties *see also* SNP 56
unity with England 4, 12
Scottish National Party (SNP) 6
ideology 56
votes for 32–3
SDP (Social Democratic Party)
Assembly 68
constituency activities 69
candidate selection 72, 73
finance 70
local membership 70
political power 71
Council for Social Democracy 68
and House of Lords reform 150
organization 68, 69
political functions 57–9
SDP/Liberal Alliance 32, 74, 338
campaign techniques 42
and electoral reform 19, 25, 29
and electoral system 24
and House of Lords reform 150, 151
ideological principles 55
image of 40
and policy consensus 6
support for 33, 38, 40, 44–5
age-based 35–6
and class 34
geographical and sociological variations in 36–7
sex-based 35
SDLP (Social Democratic and Labour Party) 33
Select Committees 163, 166
development of 164–5
sex differences and voting behaviour 35, 44
Shadow Cabinet 155
Shelter 78, 83
SNP *see* Scottish National Party
Social Democratic Party *see* SDP
Social Democratic and Labour Party *see* SDLP
Social Security Act (1975) 262
social unrest (1981) 9
Socialism and Labour Party 53, 65
Socialist Workers' Party 56

Society of Conservative Lawyers 87
Sommersett's Case (1772) 12
Southern Rhodesia Act (1965) 148
Speaker 153
Speaker's Conference (1917) 25
Standing Committees 161
Statutory Instruments 147–8, 201, 262
  and accountability 221–2
  Joint Committee on 148
*Sun The*, 97
syndicalism 76, 91n6

television 94–5
  B.B.C. 94, 96–7, 106, 107
  Cable Authority 107
  cable television 106–7
  Direct Broadcasting by Satellite 107–8
  effects on campaigning 104
  effects on electorate 103–4
  as entertainment 103
  financing of 96
  I.B.A. 94–5, 106, 107
  ideology of news 104–5
  influence of 103, 108
  neutrality 104
  power of 103–5, 108
  programme content and bias 96–7, 104–5
  structure 97
*The Times* 99
Tomlin Commission (1931) 228, 247n1
Town and Country Planning Association 87
trade unions
  influence on Labour Party 85
  at Labour Party Conference 62–4
Trade Union Congress (TUC) 79, 81, 83
Treasury Select Committee 243
Treaty of Accession (1972) 131
Tribunals and Inquiries Act (1971) 308
TUC *see* Trade Union Congress

*ultra vires* doctrine 241, 311
United Nations Declaration of Human Rights (1948) 307
United States 330
  electoral system 323
  federal bureaucracy 326–7
  legal system 329
  pattern of government 325
  political culture 321, 322
  role of Congress 328

Victoria, Queen 29
'virtual representation' 154, 169n4
voting behaviour *see also* electorate 32–47
  class-based 34–5, 37, 46
  electoral groups 32–7
  floaters and abstainers 33
  party loyalists 32–3
  future uncertainties for 42–6
    alienation of electorate 45–6
    electoral volatility 44–5
    middle-class Labour voters 43
    participation rates 45–6
    policy-based voting 42–3
    sex differences in voting 44
    working-class Conservatives 43
  geographical and sociological variations in 36–7
  influences on 37–42
    Government record 39
    image and technique 40–1
    policy-based 39–40
    political inheritance 38
    self-interest 38–9
    sentimental 40
    summary 41–2
    sex- and age-based 35–6
  voting procedures 22–3
    postal 23

Wales
  and devolution 18–19
  local government in 269–70
  nationalism in 32–3
  nationalist party *see also* Plaid Cymru 55
  union with England 4
Water Authorities 263
West Germany 330
  bureaucracy in 326
  electoral system 26, 323–4
  legal system 329
  pattern of government 324
  political culture 321, 322
  role of Parliament in 327–8
'Wets and Dries 52–3
Whitehall *see also* Civil Service
  conventions of 233–4
  structural changes in 209–10
  variations in 228–30
Wing Airport Resistance Group 80
Workers' Revolutionary Party 56
working-class
  support for Labour Party 34, 35
  support for Conservative Party 34, 35, 43

'zero sum' politics 9
Zimbabwe Independence Act (1980) 131

# INDEX OF AUTHORS AND POLITICIANS


Alford, R. 48
Almond, G.A. 10n1
Amery, L.S. 15, 21n4, n5, 149, 153, 168n2
Anne, Queen 127, 128
Armstrong, R. 243
Armstrong, W. 169n15
Ashford, D.E. 212
Asquith, Herbert 182, 192n4
Attlee, Clement 180, 185, 192n5, 204

Bacon, R. 268
Bagehot, W. 12, 14, 21n1, n2, n3, 125, 132, 137n5, 138, 139, 152, 159, 169n7
Baker, K. 106, 110n12
Ball, A.R. 76
Barker, A. 268
Barker, Paul 8
Beaumont, P.B. 268
Beer, S. 52, 53, 75n4, n6, 76, 92
Beloff, M 331
Benemy, F.W.G. 138
Benn, A. 53, 64, 66, 67, 75n13, 76, 100, 109n2, 130, 137n4, 151n1, 236, 247n11
Benn, S.I. 343
Benson, Lord 261, 268n15
Bentham, Jeremy 111
Berki, R.N. 331
Bevan, Aneurin 188
Bevin, Ernest 219
Birch, A.H. 10n3, n5, 21, 47n8, 121n1, 227, 343
Birt, J. 109n7
Blackstone, W. 12, 20n1
Blake, Robert 191, 192
Blondel, J. 10, 46, 47n18, 48n76, 92, 169n3, 212, 331
Blumler, J.G. 103,110n9
Boaden, N.T. 291
Bogdanor, V. 21n8, 30n4, 31
Bourn, J. 248
Bowen, Geoffrey 259, 268n11
Bridges, Lord 229, 247n2
Brittan, Samuel 99, 343
Bromhead, P.A. 21, 31, 151, 152, 170, 227
Brown, George 188
Brown, R.G.S. 227, 248
Bruce-Gardyne, J. 212, 227
Burke, Edmund 51, 75n1, 169n4
Butler, D.E. 10, 21n8, 31, 38, 47n9, 48, 114, 121n6, 122, 137n12
Butler, R.A. 192, 212
Butt, R. 170
Byrne, T. 291

Callaghan, James 18, 149, 158, 167, 181, 185, 204, 325
Carpenter, L.P. 152n8
Carrington, Lord 141, 149, 219
Cartwright, T.J. 268
Chamberlain, Joseph 52
Chamberlain, Neville 126, 158
Chapman, R.A. 248
Charles II 128, 173
Chatham, Lord 173
Cherwell, Lord 180
Churchill, Winston 126, 149, 158, 180, 188
Clemens, J. 122
Cook, C. 48
Crew, Ivor 34, 39, 40, 47n1, n12, 48, 115, 122
Crick, B 152, 163, 169n10, 170
Cross, M. 291
Crossman, R.H.S. 14, 149, 164, 192, 212
Crowther-Hunt, N. 227, 247n5, 248
Curran, J. 110

Dahrendorf, R. 10, 343
Davies, John 219
Day, Alan 227
Dell, E. 268
Denenberg, R.V. 331
Denning, Lord 301
Dicey, A.V. 4, 21n2, 111, 121n2, 127
Disraeli, B. 51, 173
Donoghue, B. 181
Drewry, G. 248n18, 297, 315n6, 316
Drucker, H.M. 76

Eccleshall, R. 75n3
Eckstein, H. 92

Eden, Anthony 126, 181, 188, 192n3, 204
Edinger, L.J. 331
Edward the Confessor 213
Ehrmann, H.W. 331
Elcock, H. 291
Elcock, H.J. 316
Elizabeth II 125
Eltis, W. 268

Fallon, M. 137n4
Field, F. 92
Finer, S.E. 10, 21, 31, 76, 77, 92, 331
Foot, Michael 40, 65, 122n10, 140
Foster, C.D. 268, 291
Franks, Oliver 309
Freud, Clement 101

Garrett, J. 248
George II 125, 128, 213
George IV 128
George V 126, 127, 128
George VI 126
Gibbs, Humphrey 129
Gilmour, Ian 16, 21n7, 52, 75n5, 76, 110, 141, 151
Gladstone, W. 173, 181
Gordon-Walker, P. 192
Griffith, J.A.G. 278, 290n10, 291, 298, 315n7, 316
Grove, J.W. 268

Hailsham, Lord 16, 19, 21n6, 313, 316n22, 339, 343
Haldane, Lord 214
Hamilton, Willie 135
Harrop, M. 110, 122
Hartley, T.C. 316
Hatch, J. 268
Hayward, J.E.S. 331
Healey, Denis 204, 246
Heath, Edward 6, 52, 117, 126, 180, 185, 204, 214, 325
Heclo, H. 248n27
Hepworth, N.P. 277, 290n9, 291
Heseltine, Michael 238
Hewart, Lord 309, 316n16
Himmelweit, H.T. 40, 47n15, 48, 121n7
Hirsch, F. 343
Hodder-Williams, R. 122
Holland, P. 137n4
Holton, B. 91n6
Home, Lord 126, 141, 150
Hoskyns, John 181, 211n5, n6, 236, 247n12
Howells, D. 247n8
Hunt, Lord 211n6
Hutcheson, P.G. 317

Jackson, R.M. 316
Jay, P. 109n7
Jenkins, Clive 81
Jenkins, Peter 99
Jenkins, Roy 338
Jennings, W.I. 152, 153, 168n1, 170, 193, 216, 227
Johnson, Nevil 20, 21n9, 122, 313, 316, 331
Jones, George 191, 287
Jordan, A.G. 82, 91n8, 92, 212
Joseph, Keith 74
Judge, D. 170

Kaufman, G. 227
Kavanagh. D. 10n1
Keeling, D. 248
Kellner, P. 227, 247n5, 248
Key, V.O. 111, 113, 121n3
King, A. 192, 9, 193
King, R. 92
Kinnock, Neil 65
Kogan, M. 92

Lakeman, E 31
Lawson, N. 212, 227
Leonard, R.L. 31
Levitt, R. 268
Lloyd George, D. 140, 180
Longford, E. 31n8

Macdonald, Ramsay 126
Macfarlane, L.J. 122
McKenzie, R.T. 47n3, 48, 57, 75n10, 76, 78
Mackenzie, W.J.M. 26, 30n5, 31, 77
Mackintosh, J.P. 31, 187, 191, 192n6, 193, 212, 227
McLean, I. 31, 48
Macleod, Iain 126
Macmillan, Harold 126, 137n3, 141, 180, 182, 204
Macpherson, C.B. 343
McQuail, D. 103, 109n8, 110n9
Mallen, D. 291
Margach, J. 109n5
Marsh, D. 92
Marshall, E. 170
Marshall, G. 21, 138, 227, 316
Martin, K. 138
Marwick, A. 10
Menhennet, D. 152
Middlemas, R.K. 91n5
Milford, Lord 142
Miller, W.L. 48, 76
Minkin, L. 75n12
Mitchell, A. 167, 170

Montfort, Simon de 333
Moodie, G.C. 21, 77, 91n2, 122, 138, 227, 316
Morgan, J.P. 149, 156
Morley, Lord 181
Morrison, H. 15, 21n4, 138, 152, 170, 193, 226, 227, 255
Mother Theresa 129
Mount, F. 181
Murray-Brown, J. 138

Noble, T. 10
North, Lord 173
Norton, P. 21, 170
Nozick, R. 343
Nugent, N. 92

Owen, David 68

Palmer, J. 152
Palmerston, Lord 225
Parris, H. 227, 248
Parsons, Anthony 180
Peel, Robert 111
Pelling, H. 91n9
Penniman, H.R. 31, 48, 121n8, 122n11
Peters, R.S. 343
Petrie, C. 138
Phillips, G.G. 138, 152, 317
Pitt, William 173
Plamenatz, J. 343
Pliatzky, L. 268n13
Powell, Enoch 126, 140
Pryke, R. 268
Pulzer, P. 31
Punnett, R.M. 10n4

Ramsden, J. 48
Ranney, A. 21n8, 122
Redcliffe-Maud, J. 291
Redwoood, J. 268
Reid, Lord 301
Rhodes, G. 268
Rhodes, R.A.W. 291
Richards, P.G. 277, 290n8, 291
Richardson, J.J. 82, 91n8, 92, 212
Ridley, F.F. 331
Robertson, D. 48
Robson, W.A. 268, 309
Rodgers, W. 211n3, 212, 248
Rose, R. 10, 76, 91n1, 92, 110, 111, 119, 121n4, 122, 138, 193, 211n1, 212
Rothschild, Lord 180, 261, 268n15
Rush, M. 122, 170
Russell-Smith, E. 248
Ryle, M. 169n11, 170

Salisbury, Lord 174
Salisbury, Marquess of 126, 149
Sandys, Duncan 219
Särlvik, B. 39, 40, 47n1, n12, 48, 122
Scargill, Arthur 81, 91n7
Scarman, Lord 19, 313, 316n22
Schumpeter, J. 333, 343
Seaton, J. 110
Sedgemore, B. 247n10, 248
Self, P. 248
Seymour-Ure, C. 110
Shackleton, Lord 141, 149
Silver, A. 47n2, 48
Sloman, A. 247n14, 248n26
Smellie, K.B. 290n6, 291
Smith, A. 103, 109n6, 110
Smith, B. 212, 248
Smith, G. 331
Sontheimer, K. 331
Spence, J.D. 122
Stacey, F. 317
Stanyer, J. 248, 291
Steel, D.R. 227, 248
Stewart, J. 287
Stokes, D. 10, 38, 47n9, 48, 114, 121n6, 122
Studdert-Kennedy, G. 77, 91n2, 92, 122
Suleiman, E. 193

Tatchell, Peter 75n14
Taylor, E. 170
Teer, F. 122
Thatcher, M. 41, 44, 53, 74, 117, 121–2, 141, 150, 180, 181, 182, 264
Thomas, George 129, 141
Thompson, A.W.J. 268
Thorneycroft, Peter 188
Thornhill, W. 268
Thorpe, Jeremy 126
Tivey, L. 268
Trenaman, J. 103, 109n8

Verba, S. 10n1
Vile, M.J.C. 332

Wade, E.C.S. 138, 152, 317
Wade, H.W.R. 307, 316n15, n24, 317
Walkland, S.A. 165, 169n11, 170
Walpole, Robert 173
Walters. Alan 180
Whale, J. 110
Whitelaw, William 129, 141, 219
Wildavsky, A. 248n27
William IV 128
Williams, Francis 180
Williams, Marcia 180
Williams, Shirley 68, 76, 207

Wilson, Harold 6, 18, 126, 149, 180, 181, 192n1, 193, 204
Wood, B. 291
Wootton, G. 92
Worcester, R.M. 110, 122
Worsthorne, Peregrine 99
Wraith, R.E. 317
Wright, V. 332
Wyndham, J. 180

Young, H. 135, 247n14, 248n26